BOOKS BY RICHARD LOUV

America II

Childhood's Future

101 Things You Can Do for Our Children's Future

FatherLove

The Web of Life

Fly-Fishing for Sharks: An American Journey

FLY-FISHING FOR SHARKS

An American Journey

~~~~~~~~~~~~~~~~~~

Richard Louv

Simon & Schuster

New York London Toronto Sydney Singapore

SIMON & SCHUSTER
Rockefeller Center
1230 Avenue of the Americas
New York, NY 10020

Designed by Oksana Kushnir

Manufactured in the United States of America

10 9 8 7 6 5 4 3 2 1

Library of Congress Cataloging-in-Publication Data is available.

ISBN 0-684-83698-X

Page 495 constitutes an extension of the copyright page.

*All photos are by the author with the exception of Conway Bowman's picture,
taken by Jon Wurtmann, and the photo of Joan Wulff in 1952, courtesy of Joan Wulff.*

The author is grateful for permission to reprint material from the following sources:

Excerpt from "It's 10 Below, and the Ice Is 3 Feet Thick, So Let's Go Fishing," by Verlyn Klinkenborg, orginally appeared in *Smithsonian* (December 1996), reprinted with permission from the author. Excerpt from "The Monster's Maw," by Burkhard Bilger, reprinted with permission from the author. Excerpt from "The Ruby: Public or Private Rights," by John Randolph, originally appeared in *Fly Fisherman* Vol. 28:6 (September 1997), reprinted with permission from the author. Excerpt from "Hooking Mortality of Trout," by Patrick Trotter, Ph.D., originally appearing in *Fly Fisherman* Vol. 26:3 (March 1995), reprinted with permission from the author. Excerpt from "Land Grabs in Big Sky Country," by John Holt, originally appearing in *Fly Fisherman* Vol. 26:1 (December 1994), reprinted with permission from the author.

continued on page 495

Acknowledgments

This book began one evening in Los Angeles when my agent, Jim Levine, and I met for dinner. Having written five previous books about weighty social issues, I proposed a few potential topics for new books. "More depressing social issues," said Jim. "Yes," said I, "and every time I think about writing about them I get a headache." We looked at our food. Perhaps it was fish. "Have you ever thought about writing a book about fishing?" he asked. "Why?" I wondered. "Because every time you talk about fishing, your affect changes. Fishing makes you happy." Absolutely.

No book is the sole creation of its author. Any credit accrued, therefore, and none of the blame, must be shared with others. First and foremost, credit goes to my wife, Kathy Frederick Louv, whose last fish was caught in September 1981 on the Snake River in Wyoming when she was pregnant with our first son. A few years later, she became a vegetarian and started siding with the fish. Even so, she encouraged me to do this book and her human sympathies and skill helped shape every chapter.

My sons, Jason and Matthew, went along on some of the expeditions. They offered enthusiasm, commentary, and advice on lure and fly selection.

Bob Bender, senior editor at Simon & Schuster, provided steady counsel, sound judgment, sharp scissors, and the best advice that an author can hear: "Have fun. If you do, your reader will, too." Experts who gave early guidance included Al Burt of Florida, Richard Anderson of *California Fly Fisher,* and sociologist Richard Madsen and anthropologist Tanya Luhrmann of the University of California, San Diego. Shanna Dougherty, Christina Maule, Johanna Li, Sean Devlin, and Marilyn Montanez helped keep the writing on schedule—well, almost on schedule

Other friends and relatives reviewed parts of the manuscript or recommended more research (that is, fishing). Among them: Dave Boe, Leigh

Fenly, Mike Louv, Terry Rodgers, Peter Kaye, Anne Pearse Hocker, Michael Kinsman, John Gilmore, Jack Webb, John Bowman, John and Eileen Stroud, Karen Kerchelich, Jon Wurtmann, Nick Raven, Jackie Green, Marie Anderson, Bill Stothers, Jon Funabiki, Larry Hinman, the DMG, and my editors at *The San Diego Union-Tribune*. Jim and Anne Hubble generously offered me a writing hideaway in the mountains. Jim Brown shared a reservoir of knowledge.

Dean Stahl selflessly gave the gift of his talent; he scrutinized every word of copy, listened to each sentence of complaint (about the writing, not the fishing), and shared the joy—he is a fine editor and even better friend.

Bill Frederick sent clips and words of encouragement; even now, nearing the end of memory, he may recall the scent of dawn, the feel of a sudden strike, the sight of a golden rolling, and the light of a fading campfire.

Finally, I wish to acknowledge the anglers who helped create this book. The central characteristic of the cultures of fishing is *generosity*. This became evident early on as I explored the many Internet newsgroups and Web sites devoted to fishing. One site listed anglers in every section of the country who were willing to share information about the fishing in their geographical area. I drafted a letter explaining what I hoped to do and sent it to everyone on the list. Before I logged off that afternoon, I was already receiving e-mail from folks offering to take me out on their waters.

Come fishing, they said.

For Welcome Michael Louv

There's no taking trout with dry breeches.
—Sancho Panza, to Don Quixote

Contents

Introduction: Shop Talk

⟋⟍⟋⟍

ONE WAY OR ANOTHER, we're all anglers.

On a Saturday afternoon before lighting out for the territories, I stopped at Stroud Tackle to see my friends Bill and Eileen Stroud and John Bowman. As usual, I needed the atmosphere more than the gear.

My plan for the next couple of years was to take a new look at my country—through the unique prism of fishing.

Stopping at the tackle store seemed like a good place to start.

Now in its twenty-eighth year, Stroud Tackle is located in a bland stucco building on San Diego's Morena Boulevard. The shop is bracketed by cut-rate furniture outlets, a massage-equipment-and-lotions store, and a building contractor's office. All of this is bathed in freeway noise and jet fumes from nearby Lindbergh Field, and Southern California sun. Walk in from the street, out of that harsh light and sun, let the door swing closed behind you, hear the little bell ring, and you enter another world.

The shop is calming, a refuge from the chaos outside. Flecks of dust glow in thin rays of bright light that splay through the blinds. Your eyes take a moment to adjust. One wall is dedicated to freshwater fish. Across it you see mounted golden trout, rainbow, cutthroats, brown, lake trout, and a replicated 27.4-pound steelhead, sleek and shiny—the state record steelhead caught on a fly, from the Smith River in Northern California.

Everything's a little dusty, as if the fish have been freeze-dried in the arc of their jump, and then shellacked. Bill and Eileen look a little bit like that, too.

The shop's back wall is given over to saltwater fish: halibut, bat ray, marlin, opah, amberjack, sheephead, yellowfin tuna, dolphin, roosterfish, jack mackerel, white sea bass, wahoo, dorado, yellowtail, bonefish, sharks (bonita, tiger, dusky, blue). Until recently, a baby hammerhead shark sat on the counter on a pedestal, but Eileen took him home. She was afraid someone would steal him.

These days, many fishermen consider it more reasonable and correct to photograph their catch, release it, and send the photo off for replication in three-dimensional plastic and paint. But these fish, sixty of them, once moved through green and blue, through kelp and lily pad, through life.

I look around. The mere *stuff* of the store is comforting, all this medicating paraphernalia: hand-tied flies (these days, 90 percent of them tied in Sri Lanka or Colombia or Kenya or some other developing country); Orvis, 3-M, Lamson, and Ross single-action, click and pawl and disk drag reels of Orvis; and Sage, Thomas & Thomas, Scott, Lumis rods, all graphite. Bamboo rods are back in vogue, not because they catch more fish, but because of how they make the angler feel. Special. Elite. Part of a tradition. Bill and Eileen do not carry bamboo rods, because, as Eileen explains, "they're so expensive, one thousand to twenty-five hundred dollars, and the last one I had got stolen here, right out of the store."

Such a theft makes no sense. "Think how you'd feel fishing with a stolen bamboo rod. Kind of defeats the purpose." Or, she says, maybe the thief just sold it. "The latest thing is guys come in here with Scotch tape wrapped around their hands, sticky side out. They run their hands through the fly box, and the flies stick to the tape underneath their hand."

"Next time I see that happen," says John, peering over his glasses, "I'm going up to that guy, close his fingers into a fist, and *shake his hand real hard.*"

"I tell you," Eileen says, "fishing is changing."

The room, only 850 square feet, is packed like, well, a sardine can. Eileen and Bill, both in their seventies, stand behind the counter. Eileen learned to fly-fish as a child, from her father. She does not talk readily of this, but I hope some day to hear her stories. I do know that she is reputed to be a better angler than Bill, and better still than most of the fishers who come into this shop.

Bill, tall, white-haired, a former big-time New York City insurance salesman, stares at you over his glasses and scowls and you're home free. If he scowls at you, it means he likes you.

"What can I do for you today, Richard?"

For the next hour or so, he'll try to talk you out of buying anything. "Oh, you don't need *that*," he'll say. And Eileen, who always hovers next to the cash register as if she's protecting it from him, shoots him a withering look. He doesn't wither easily.

Something about visiting the Strouds, and their volunteer salesman and raconteur, John, is deeply calming to me. Familiar.

I remember the stacks of *Field & Stream* that one old man, Grandpa Barron, who lived next door, would hand me every few months when I was a boy. These magazines were filled with culture and dreams.

Sometimes before dawn, Grandpa Barron and I would walk down the road to the lake, climb in his boat, and glide across the black water. I would watch his hands in the propane lamplight, as they molded the dough bait, and worked the rod and reel with skill. He said little. He did not preach. He did not pry. He was glad to have some company. In silence, we would watch the mist on the water and the widening rings where fish nosed or tailed into the air.

In those years, the act of fishing, the mantra of it, with or without a catch, was a way to keep from drowning, a way to connect to something larger. But, over time, like a lot of people in need of a little renewal, I had drifted away from that sense of connection, had begun to fish more in theory than in reality. Recently, the meaning of fishing, of life, had seemed tenuous. Late at night, as I skimmed across the American veneer, surfed from channel to channel, I found it difficult to think or to feel clearly. As a journalist, too, the latest crisis seemed pretty much like the one before it.

Stroud Tackle brings back that earlier time and offers affirmation.

On this day, I tell the Strouds and John Bowman about my plan, how I'm setting out to explore the cultures of fishing—the people and ecologies of angling in America. Trout anglers, bass fishers; seekers of steelhead, sturgeon, shark, and carp; fly-fishers, ice fishers, bass tournament pros, charter captains, guides, lodge owners, and poachers alike. North, South, East, and West—and of course the Great Midwest. To explore how fishing renews us, and how we can renew fishing by rethinking our roles as stewards.

My modus operandi is simple: identify anglers, legendary and average, men and women, in each of the cultures with something to say about the fishing life and life beyond fishing. They will, I hope, be my Sancho Panzas. With lance (a St. Croix graphite composite rod, bought at Stroud Tackle) in hand, I'll travel to the Meccas of fishing—Orvis, Bass Pro Shop's Outdoor World, bait shops, and coffee shops. I'll investigate the beliefs and industries of each of these cultures: the ethical frameworks, the dialects and the dialectics; the political pools and the perceptual streams.

"So this means you'll have to go fishing," says Bill.

"Guess so."

"Now there's an assignment." He smiles slowly.

Eileen arches an eyebrow. "I say save your time and money. Forget the writing. Just go fishing."

Behind a second counter, John Bowman, with neatly trimmed white beard and aviator glasses, holds forth. A retired teacher, he spends part of his spare time at the shop, helping out with the customers. Many have been coming here for years. He thinks of himself as the Strouds' concierge.

The bell rings, the anglers walk in out of the light and finger the merchandise, dream a little, and eventually move to the counter. The anglers who come through the door are young and old, male and female; they're construction workers and doctors, the unemployed and the over-employed. Some are novices; a few are even better anglers than John or Bill or Eileen. Others are fashion fishers looking for the latest vest. They ask John about the best places to fish in the West, the lakes and streams and pools of Montana and Idaho and California's Eastern Sierra, which John has fished since his son Conway, now thirty, was eight years old. They ask: Where should we stay? What flies should we use on the Owens?

He crosses his arms, elbows on the glass, and advises them to go deep in the fall, with flies that impersonate underwater larvae: "Use a nine-foot leader with a 16 nymph, either a gold-ribbed hare's ear or a pheasant-tail nymph. From the curve of the nymph's hook, tie on twelve inches of 5x monofilament tippet, and tie that to another nymph pattern, size 20 or 22."

None of this code makes much sense to the new fly-fisher, but John, forever a teacher, will spend all the time it takes to explain.

↩ ANGLING IS NOW AMERICA'S favorite outdoor activity. In 1959, according to U.S. Fish & Wildlife Service surveys begun in that year, roughly 20 million fishing licenses were sold in the U.S.; by 1992 the number had jumped to 31 million. In 1998, 44 million Americans fished, according to the National Sporting Goods Association, far exceeding the number of people who participate in tennis or golf. Among men, fishing is far and away the favorite outdoor recreation. But the ranks of women anglers are growing also. Of outdoor activities, fishing now ranks seventh among women.

"Women anglers are not as fashion-conscious as men," John tells me. "Men tend to be into gadgets, but women are usually more interested in the technicalities of fishing; they're really into it. Men are interested in the size of fish they can get, women are more interested in how to fish."

Keep your eye on the women, he advises. "More interesting than the men."

Though in some areas of the country the sales of fishing licenses have fallen slightly in recent years—giving some fishing manufacturers cause for concern—angling's commercial power overall is impressive, to say the least.

The American Sportfishing Association reports that 35.3 million anglers spent $38 billion on fishing trips and gear in 1996, up from $24 billion in 1991. Ad agencies now employ fishing images to sell everything from booze to bank accounts. "Once considered a cane pole and worm crowd, anglers are now courted aggressively by everyone from General Mills to General Motors," *USA Today* reports. Wal-Mart put its name on one national pro tour, Kmart latched on to another. Meanwhile, Pepsi and Coke jockeyed for position, and Fuji Film, Rubbermaid, AC Delco, Wrangler, and Citgo signed on with one pro bass outfit or the other. In 1998, fishing truly reached the commercial big time: General Mills announced that the next sports champion to be honored on the front of the Wheaties box would be a bass fisherman.

Fishing is also getting more organized. The sport has spawned myriad organizations, including TROUT Unlimited, which fights to preserve trout habitat; Bass'n Gal (an organization for women bass fishers), which celebrated its twentieth anniversary in 1996 with nearly thirty-three thousand members, and then closed a year later due to sexism, a story told later in this book; and the 660,000-member Bass Anglers Sportsman Society, which sponsors fishing tournaments, produces a cable television bass fishing show, and publishes *Bassmaster, Southern Outdoors,* and *B.A.S.S. Times*—and plans to open Bass Outdoor America, a $50 million family-oriented theme park in Alabama or Tennessee, complete with a bass boat roller-coaster and a sixty-acre lake with an island the shape of a largemouth bass.

Eileen snorts. "Like to see that."

"Now Eileen, different strokes," says Bill.

Part of the reason for this growth is the movie, *A River Runs Through It,* released in 1992 and based on the Norman Maclean novella about family and trout-fishing in Montana. Also contributing are big-money bass tournament circuits and advertising. But a deeper current moves below the surface: nature hunger. The baby boom generation may be the last one to share an intimate, familial attachment to the land and water. Today, development erases suburbia's last islands and peninsulas of open land and wild water.

But judgments are often premature and mysteries abound. Fishing, as

John Bowman says, "is always about more than fishing." Today's fishing is about the tension between commercialism and romanticism, between the growing popularity of angling and limited waters, between past and future, between innocence and knowledge. The waters we fish, and how we fish, reflect larger political, ethical, even spiritual issues. How shall we reconnect to nature? How should we treat fellow creatures of other species? How do we hold fast to what is old, timeless, and slow? If the cultures of fishing begin to communicate and work together—something they have not done in the past—could anglers become the most powerful and effective environmental lobby?

I claim no expertise at angling. But I do hope to learn a thing or two about how to catch a fish. I'll explore the cultures of fishing, see a fair bit of my country, and travel its currents. The way I figure it, if you want to know America, go fishing.

I'm eager to get started, but before I leave the shop, I buy a couple of flies from Eileen—well, more than a couple. Hard to get out of there without loading up, despite Bill's efforts.

"You can tell a lot about people by fishing with 'em. Places, too," says John. Cheerfully defying California law, he lights up his pipe. "Keep in mind that fishing to some people becomes an obsession because it's what Sam is doing, it's what everybody else is doing. It's like when people began wearing bell-bottom trousers—they wore them because somebody else had them. Keep your eye on the difference between fashion and fishing."

He points the stem of the pipe at me. "Here's my advice. Get out of the country." I laugh. He explains: "A couple hundred miles south of here is a place that will show you what fishing was like before it got . . . complicated."

He rummages around behind the counter and finds a pencil and a piece of paper and writes down a name and a Baja California, Mexico, phone number. "I'll tell you one thing I like about fishing is it gets me to places where there aren't many people. It's probably the camaraderie, too. Although I know that's a contradiction. Some people think it's a damned religion." He pauses. "I'll be quite frank: It's almost a religion with me. I do believe in a Supreme Being, but I'd rather go fly-fishing than go to Mass. Hell, if I go out onto a stream and I don't catch any fish, I still feel that way. I see a couple of nice birds or a fish jump or a deer or a moose or whatever the hell, or another fly-fisherman. I love to watch people fish; I love to watch fly-fishermen. Especially my son, he's a hell of a caster."

He scribbles a second phone number and slides the piece of paper across the glass. "You go see Conway. He'll tell you something about fishing."

Eileen wryly interjects, "That Conway, he's been coming in here since he was little. We always took him fishing. He filled up the bay and the lakes with rocks. He was a little brat." She smiles, drops some flies in a little plastic container. "He *loved* to eat squid. I used to flinch when I watched him eat 'em. He'd eat tentacles, head, eyes, and everything." She shudders.

John laughs, a short bark from the corner of his mouth, as I head out. "See ya," he says, from behind the counter.

The door opens, the bell rings.

Headwaters

~~~~~~~~~~~~~~~~~~~~~~~~~~~~~

Master Pedro now came back, and in a cart followed the show and the ape—a big one, without a tail and with buttocks as bare as felt, but not vicious-looking. As soon as Don Quixote saw him, he asked him, "Can you tell me, sir fortune-teller, what fish do we catch, and how will it be with us? See, here are my two reels," and he bade Sancho give them to Master Pedro; but he answered for the ape and said, "Señor, this animal does not give any answer or information touching things that are to come; of things past he knows something, and more or less of things present."

—Don Quixote

It Changes Everything

~~⌒~~

When you're fly-fishing for sharks, the line between lunacy and sanity is pretty thin. Twelve miles off the San Diego coast, former grunge rocker Conway Bowman stopped the eighteen-foot aluminum boat with the upswept bow. The sea lifted us. We were just beyond the bank where the Pacific Ocean's floor plummets from fifty fathoms to three hundred, where an upwell brings food to the surface.

Sharks like it here. Conway likes it here.

At thirty, he's a handsome guy, lean and hard and tan, with a three-day stubble and closely cut hair. He wore a fleece jacket, khaki shorts, tennis shoes, Orvis sunglasses, and a wide straw hat. He was excited and intent, couldn't wait to get out there, but he forced himself to stay within the bay speed limit. The motor growled. We passed a lolling cigarette boat.

"More gauges than a spaceship," he said, squinting at it.

Several kayakers were leaning into the offshore wind and heading out to sea. Some kayakers paddle five miles out with their fishing gear to catch giant sea bass. Sometimes they're joined by even hardier breeds, belly boaters—anglers suspended in fancy inner tubes—and surfboard anglers. Like the kayakers, the surfboard anglers paddle out in their wet suits, rod held in their teeth, a fanny pack around their waist to hold lures and snippers. These anglers favor kelp forests or the floating kelp beds that break away in storms or are chewed loose from their rock anchors by sea urchins; the beds attract yellowtail, dorado, rockfish, and opaleye. Suspended, feet dangling, the belly-boat and surfboard fishers move above the kelp forest, watch it twine down into darkness. They sit out there all day and sometimes at night, listening to the hissing and popping of life in the kelp.

Here's how extreme it gets. On July 7, 1998, Scot Cherry, a 6 feet 4 inches tall surfboard angler, caught a 140-pound thresher shark while fishing a mile and a half off La Jolla. It was nearly as long as Cherry's 13-foot longboard. During the forty-five-minute fight, the shark towed Cherry for five miles at about 10 knots—fast enough to create a wake behind the board. Cherry's ambition is to surf behind a shark.

Compared to these anglers, Conway seems . . . conservative.

Over the noise of the engine and the pounding of the hull, Conway described his earliest memories, which were of fishing.

> I remember my father, this big man walking into the kitchen with albacore as long as his leg. I'd watch the way he cleaned the fish with authority. I'd sit on the floor and just look at him.
>
> We'd go fishing every weekend. He'd get me up when it was still dark. The mornings always smelled like pipe tobacco. I remember his Ford Falcon, and his hat, and his red checkered Filson jacket, and his boots. I still have those boots. He didn't use them anymore, so I just took them. Up until a few years ago, I used to wear them when I fished. They're in my closet now.
>
> I must have been about three years old. It was a very cold February day. My father and I were out fishing on Lake Jennings, and I remember he had on this big white coat with a big woolen collar. He was sitting there baiting my hook and he threw it out and we were using cheese bait. I got hit. He set the hook, and handed the rod back to me, and I'm reeling and reeling. It was a large trout. I was really excited and so was he. He went down and took it off the hook and put it on a stringer and put it in the water, turned around, and I went into the water after the fish. Just to play with it, you know.
>
> This was the middle of February, it was probably thirty-two degrees out. I remember him getting into the water and just *taking* me, you know, and running me up to the car and putting me in the car and taking me home. With the fish of course.

Conway pushed the throttle and lifted the Bayrunner bow over the first swells outside the bay. We were headed out into the high rolling sea now. My fourteen-year-old son Jason was with us. He was wearing dark glasses, a black tee shirt, and a kind of seasick scowl. In recent months, he and I had been having difficulty talking for the first time since he was little. Perhaps a little fly-fishing for sharks would help. Something new for both of us.

Still, I had not realized that the boat would be this . . . small.

We watched delicate, silver fish skim through the tops of the waves next to the boat. A morning chop like this usually gives way to smooth seas once you get farther out. Off on the sea, dark shapes, like quarter moons, floated above the waves, down and up, down and up.

"Porpoise," said Conway, smiling. "They'll come right at us."

"Look at 'em, Jason," I said to my quiet son. "There must be what, fifteen?"

"We can probably hear them," said Conway.

He turned off the engine. We heard nothing. "Sometimes it takes five minutes for the whole school to go through. That was a small school. When pilot whales pass by, you can hear them through the aluminum hull—their high squeal." The arc of the world moved up and then down, and up again. He held a Magellan-Meridian Excel Global Positioning System on which he had programmed the hot spots for sharks, the coordinates of his sightings since January. These were marked by flags on the screen. After a few minutes of drifting silently, listening, he started the engine again and we moved out.

He stood, watching intently. "We're looking for signs of life: bait fish, birds on top of the bait fish, even subtle irregularities in the surface, which could, for instance, signal puddling yellowtail tuna—"

"What do you mean, puddling?"

"They're just kind of up, slurping on the surface. So you're constantly watching for that. Also, you're reading the water. For instance, right in front of us, you see this slick?" Not the oil slick, he said, but a slight change in the texture of the water beyond it, a smoothing. "It's a current break. Fish like current breaks. Usually in a current break, on either side, there's a temperature difference and you always want to fish the warmer side of it. So you're always looking for things like that. These details usually will guide you right to the fish."

He cut the engine again. We were nine miles out. Land was a thin strip of memory. We floated above the inner edge of the Nine Mile Bank, where the depth drops abruptly from fifty fathoms to three hundred; the current far below hits a mountainside and shoots upward, producing an upwelling of water that disgorges biomass—concentrated plant and animal life—from the deep and splays it out along the surface. The biomass attracts smaller fish, and these draw larger predators.

We'll fish here, Conway said, and drift to twelve miles out.

↪ FROM THE FRONT of the slowly pitching boat, he hauled out a crate of commercial "Shark and Fish Chum" and tied it to the back corner of the boat. The top edge was only inches from the water, and when the bow lifted, the stern dipped close to the surface. The box had holes in it, from which bits of fish and fish oil oozed and created a lengthening, widening slick behind us. As the boat drifted, the bluish sheen spread out over the green troughs and moved up and over the edge of the swells and disappeared.

Conway loves to come out here alone in the cool mist and chum the water and wait and then stand on the heaving center console as eight- and ten-foot blue sharks circle. His fly line floating in long fluid loops, he casts to the most aggressive sharks.

Conway makes his living supervising recreation on a nearby city reservoir, but hopes to be one of the first guides on the West Coast to make a living taking anglers out to fly-fish for sharks. This is how fishing cultures get started, by the passion of one angler.

What is it about fishing that attracts you? I asked.

"I don't know, I think it's the tranquillity of it, just being on the water. The water really has something to do with it. Also, the freedom. I fish by myself much of the time. I think it's just me, getting away maybe. I don't know, some people say it's an escape. All the girlfriends I've had—'You're just escaping from reality'—or something like that. But I'm most happy here."

I told him I always think of it as escaping *to* reality.

"Exactly!" he said, grinning. "That's the way I look at it." He pulled out another white bucket filled with chunks of mackerel and sliced them into smaller pieces. On most trips, he catches his own mackerel, but today he was in a hurry, and used the commercial bait. "I think it's the freedom, the sense of accomplishment. Fishing makes you feel worthy, it makes me feel worthy."

Why worthy?

"You've done something, you've actually . . . I don't know how to describe it."

The slick stretched out behind us, widening. "Sometimes in the chunk slick, when there's a lot of birds, it means there's going to be a lot of sharks. They usually don't catch the birds but they do go after their feet."

Sharks are attracted to minute currents that come from the reaction of certain metals in contact with one another. The electrical impulses likely mimic the spark of life that means food in the shark's world. So Conway places a zinc plate on the bottom of the metal boat. "It causes some kind of energy that really gets them going," he said. The smallest sharks come in first, followed by the larger sharks, which often arrive a couple hours into the fishing. He wanted to slow the boat's drift, so he tossed out a driftback—a kind of water-dragging parachute.

The slick deepened in color.

"People have a preconceived notion that sharks are vicious. Well, not really. Not most of them. Not the blue sharks. Fishing for blues is actually very much like catfishing, which I like to do, too. You sit, you do a lot of pondering. But then you *see* them coming, which is different from catfishing."

As we waited, he rigged the rods. He uses what he calls chunk flies, simple attractors that imitate (purist fly-fishers will not be impressed) the pieces of fish we were throwing behind us. Usually he sight-casts to the first sharks coming in, before they get to the chum bucket attached to the boat. If they reach the chum bucket they become spoiled by the ease of it. Because the day was overcast, it would be difficult to sight-cast.

A fin cut the water with a distinctive hiss.

"They're early," he said. Usually, the sharks take forty-five minutes or so to show up, but there was something different about this day. Five or six blue sharks, four to five feet long, circled us. One glided up to the boat, stuck its head out of the water, bared its teeth in a hideous smile, and proceeded to gnaw on the top of the chum box. The surface of the water was only a few inches from the top of the boat's stern railing, and the sharks were only a few feet away—this one was less than two feet from my leg.

Conway handed me an oily chum bucket and instructed Jason and me to begin flinging the finger-sized chunks of fish into the sea.

Then he froze. "We have a situation here," he said.

"What do you mean *situation?*" I said.

"We have a mako."

↜ SOMETHING ABOUT THE way he said mako made me want to be home watching a National Geographic special.

As Conway took a 12-weight flyrod from a vertical rod holder, he explained why he considered this a *situation*. The slender, deep-water blue shark can be dim-witted, almost passive—like a catfish that wouldn't mind having you for dinner. But the powerful mako, or mackerel shark, which can grow to over twelve feet and one thousand pounds, slices through the water like a jet fighter at speeds that sometimes exceed sixty miles per hour. When hooked, a mako tends to fly out of the water into a boat, jaws snapping: Jumps of twenty to thirty feet have been recorded. Essentially, the mako is a smaller version of the great white shark, but more aggressive.

Conway practices catch-and-release for ecological as well as safety reasons. "You do not want one of these fish in the boat with you," he said dryly. Thirty-two attacks on humans—and fifteen boat attacks—have been recorded, not a big number, unless you're in the number. He told us of one angler who had met his mako this way. "He had the shark hooked; it ran to sea then turned around and charged back, flew into the boat, and bit the fisherman's thigh. Cut the femoral artery. The guy bled to death in twenty minutes."

Makos, in their way, don't get mad. They get even. A few years ago, a ten-foot mako jumped out of the water and into the boat of a sixty-nine-year-old Fijian fisher. "Immediately, the shark proceeded to eat the fisherman," according to a newspaper report. "His five stunned shipmates tried to kill the shark, but were unable to either stop the attack or remove the shark from both the boat and their friend in time." Another, larger mako attacked a crew of four Fijians. "That crew was unable to remove the shark because of various injuries inflicted upon all of the boat's occupants."

The mako circling us was nearly six feet long. "Are you ready?" said Conway. "This is the ultimate fish on the flyrod. This is the first one I've seen out here. Look at him go! *Look at him go!*"

He handed me the flyrod.

"No, you do the first cast. It's your record." After Conway's stories, I wasn't too sure I wanted to hook the thing anyway.

"Jesus, can I?" he said, laughing.

"Of course! What do you mean, can you? Of course. It's your boat."

Conway's hands were trembling. His face had lost its ruddy color. If he caught this fish, he believed he would be the first fly-fisher to catch a mako off San Diego.

He lifted the rod and flipped a three-inch fly in front of the shark.

The fin hissed past, slicing the slick, the nose of the thing at a slight downward angle. It looked and swam nothing like the blues. It looked . . . mechanical, streamlined like a torpedo. The mako's back was bluish gray with an odd golden-brown reflection on top, gray on the sides, with a flashing white belly.

The fish was not eating, but cruising slowly, watching. If the mako became agitated enough, Conway explained, it would take one of the blue sharks. "If the blue is chewing the chum box or on a fly line, the mako will come up and bite its tail off and then eat him." This mako seemed meditative, focused. It made a wide arc and disappeared. Our hands were bloody from the chum, but none of us would wash them in the seawater.

Jason was standing at the bow of the boat, watching from behind his sunglasses. I was glad he was there, instead of at the stern. But I did not want to show my concern, just as, I am sure, he did not wish to show his. In fact, this felt good. It felt terrific, and probably not as much of a *situation* as Conway was making it out to be.

The shark returned, swerved past the boat, skimming the surface. I stepped back from the side of the boat.

Conway raised the fly above his head and back, and looped the line out over the water. It landed in the slick and moved with the swell. The little blue shark shimmied up to the fly and bumped it with his nose, which was good, said Conway, because it could agitate the mako. This was the moment of truth.

The mako paused just under the surface, ten feet from us. Suspicious, perhaps. Conway pulled the chum fly from the water and cast again, dropped it a few feet ahead of the shark as it made a small turn away from us. The mako slid two feet forward, its dorsal fin out of the water, opened its mouth slightly.

The fly disappeared.

Conway pulled the tip of his rod high in the air. Nothing. The shark had effortlessly bitten through the steel leader and taken the fly with it.

Rather than tie on a new fly, Conway quickly returned the 12-weight flyrod to the holder and picked out a lighter, 9-weight rod with chum fly already rigged. He did not expect the mako to return, but he wanted to be ready. He said the shark's run had been perfect because it was headed away from the boat, at an angle. He told me that if he hooked the mako, I would have to pilot the boat—and chase the shark on fast runs of seventy-five to one hundred yards, and prepare for it to leap clear of the water like a marlin or swordfish. Conway's tackle was too light to bring the fish in directly.

Now the ocean seemed empty. The little blues had disappeared. We were drifting fast, nearly to the twelve-mile point, which may have explained the blues' behavior. The boat lifted on a swell, settled in a trough.

Then suddenly the mako was in front of us, three feet off the stern. It slipped around the corner, now inches from the boat. Conway dropped the fly in front of it. The shark moved forward.

Just before it could take the fly, he pulled up on his rod.

The fly dangled in the air. The mako flashed out of sight. This time for good.

Why had he thrown away his opportunity, his chance to establish a record—to reach his goal?

"Too dangerous," he whispered. His voice was still excited, but with an edge of disappointment. "I couldn't do it. The shark was too close to the boat. It was too dangerous, especially with your son on board." Besides, he added, hooking a fish inches from the boat just wouldn't seem . . . right.

He turned the boat, and, with the engine grinding, we moved back to the nine-mile edge of the drop-off, stopped, and began the drift again. Conway looked up at the overcast, which was thickening, and felt the stiffening wind. If the wind increased, we would return. His boat was too small to handle large swells.

The blues came up to the new chum slick, and Conway handed the 9-weight to my son. Jason flipped the chum fly to a cruising blue, which took it, and Jason hauled it in, a look of sudden lightning in his usually quiet eyes. The shark, a kind of charcoal blue, shot this way and that and rolled frantically. Conway reached down with a thickly gloved hand, grabbed the fifteen-or sixteen-pound blue just behind its head, and twisted it out of the water. Its mouth was open wide, flashing, and Conway took a pair of pliers in his other hand and unhooked the fish.

"Did you like that, Jason?"

"Yeah. It was okay." He was grinning despite himself. So was I.

Conway handed me a rod, and I caught a blue. Conway usually unhooks them quickly in the water but this time, for each of us, he pulled a fish out of the water and held it up, its teeth flashing, and we posed for photographs, all of us smiling, feeling alive.

⇛ HOOKING THE MAKO had changed things. Now the waves had an added snap to them, serrated white ridges along their tops, and the wind was coming up. As we packed the gear, returned the rods to the upright holder, hauled in the chum box, he said he realized that some fly-fishers, the purists at least, look down their noses at fly-fishing for sharks, at flies tied to look like chunks of *flesh*.

"There's so much emphasis on being correct and perfect, on wearing the right clothes and using the right equipment. What I like about fishing for sharks is that it's very basic—maybe the most basic form of fly-fishing you can do, even more basic than pan fishing with a fly-rod, because there's basically only one choice of fly. And maybe it seems more . . . primitive. You're sight-fishing, you're hunting."

And then he told me about one of his fishing dreams. "I've always thought about opening a fly shop, a different kind of fly shop." His eyes drifted off to the towers of the approaching urban skyline. "I'd have good outdoor literature in it. It would be a tackle shop, a bookstore, and a coffee shop also. It might even have its own microbrewery. Beer and coffee

CONWAY BOWMAN

and fishing. Maybe a bagel or two. People would sit around and tell lies about their fishing. Not just go in, buy something, and get the hell out, but stick around, have some coffee, work at a fly-tying bench, tie flies, and tell some lies. Some good stories."

Hey, I said, you could call it "Flybucks."

"Well, it wouldn't just be about bucks. It would be about something that the fishing writer Russell Chatham said: It would be about going somewhere you didn't have to kiss one undeserving ass that you didn't have to."

Conway headed his little boat toward the thin line of smog and shore.

As the boat entered the bay, and he throttled down, he talked about second thoughts: how he wished he had taken the mako. "Silly, but when I first saw the mako, I felt kind of . . . threatened. He made me feel very uneasy when I saw him coming on to the line. The mako cocked his head to one side, looked at the boat, almost like he was saying, 'What are you doing in my area?' He has no enemies, you know, except us. And we have him."

↪ IN THE MONTHS since our trip, Conway has returned often to the up-well. He's pursuing his dream, slowly moving away from his city job and out to sea, into the role of charter captain. He told me recently how he took a friend out fishing, and the friend, seasick, leaned over the edge and personally chummed the water just as a seven-foot mako roared by.

"That was a big fish," said his friend.

Conway decided then and there to buy a bigger boat.

He finally hooked and caught a mako on a flyrod—a six-foot, one-hundred-pound shark. A friend piloted the boat. They chased the fish for an hour. Conway brought the mako in and quickly released it, so the record remained unofficial. And then he sat down, knees shaking.

The Lost World

⌐◝◝◝

A FEW WEEKS after fly-fishing for sharks, my son and I were due to go fishing one hundred years in the past, and we were late.

The Mexican cowboys from the Meling ranch and the fly-fishers from north of the border with their five-hundred-dollar Sage rods had left without us. They were somewhere on horseback winding toward the Rio Santo Domingo, down a foot-wide horse trail with two-hundred-foot drops, the same path Father Junipero Serra took north to plant his string of missions in Alta California in the mid-1700s.

Though the Spanish may have fly-fished in America before the English (more about this blasphemy later), the records do not show that Serra fished this stream personally. Fishing was not the kind of thing that the Spanish wrote about in their journals, suggesting that they considered fishing to be below their station, something for the natives with their little weirs and spears and throw nets. But it's possible to imagine Serra, robes flapping in the hot, dry wind, peering into the waters below at the odd little trout. Serra would not have known or cared about their genetic uniqueness, their linkage to the world's most ancient rainbows: He had bigger fish to fry to the north.

I was here in Baja California with Jason because I wished to catch a unique fish, and to experience what fishing was like before there were so many distinct borders in North America, long before Sage rods, before Orvis, before bass tournaments, before catch and release, closer to the headwaters of the sport. And I could take my teenage son on another adventure with Dad. But Dad was now standing here in the flying dust on a parched knoll in one of the most desolate places on Earth, embarrassed in front of his son . . . who was standing off to the side in his flapping black gothic rock tee shirt, with his face scrunched up in the wind.

I looked at my watch. Five minutes. We were five minutes late. Or maybe ten. And they were gone.

One or two farm trucks bounced over the rock-and-dust road from inland, where in the far distance we could see the peaks of the Sierra de San Pedro Martir range, which rise to ten thousand feet. The stream we were to fish was somewhere to the southwest, deep in a gorge accessible only by horse or mule or foot. The anglers and the cowboys were heading there now. I tried to use the cell phone. My son arched an eyebrow. Fat chance. Who was I going to call anyway?

⌐ HOURS EARLIER, WE had met Dal Potter at Sanbournes restaurant in Ensenada. With his goatee and kind eyes and distinguished manner, he looked like a small version of John Steinbeck. A few years ago, he had moved from San Francisco, where he worked in the building industry, to slower Baja. Potter now arranges fishing expeditions to the Meling ranch, in the foothills of the Sierra de San Pedro Martir, some 153 miles south of the border.

The other fishermen going on this trip sat in the next booth. They were veterinarians from San Diego. They looked a little tense, and were decked out in expensive fishing gear. One of them was wearing thick glasses and a flats hat, the kind usually used in saltwater fly-fishing, with a long visor and neck and ear guard flaps for sun protection that hung down and made him look a bit like Deputy Dawg. Potter showed us pictures of the ranch and described where we were going. Baja, he explained, is a peninsula 760 miles long, 30 to 150 miles wide. Mexico's most important fisheries lie off the sparsely populated coast, but inland the mountains and deserts are, psychologically at least, as far from civilization as anywhere in North America.

"The Meling ranch, where you're headed, is owned by the grandkids of Salve and Alberta Meling," he said, "and the trout-fishing operation is run by Enrique Meling, but you'll be taken down to the river by his sons and brother. Enrique's been ill." Potter coughed into his fist, neatened a pile of photos. Salve was the son of Soren Meling, a sailor who immigrated to Baja from Norway at the turn of the century. As a young man, Salve met and married Alberta Johnson, daughter of Harry Johnson, an immigrant from Denmark and former Texas rancher who had headed west in the late 1800s, attracted by Mexico's offer of free land to settlers willing to settle in rugged Baja. "The Melings struggled for a long time to make it; many of the settlers in this area didn't make it," said Potter. Over the decades, the Melings built up their ranch, claiming huge tracts of central Baja, becoming a power in a territory that had not known much power.

At fourteen, Enrique began a ten-year vaquero apprenticeship, riding the Sierra de San Pedro Martir range at his grandfather Salve's side. His father, now dead, was a cowboy daredevil who teamed with his brother, Andy. Together, they contracted to round up wild steers for ranchers throughout Baja's cattle country.

Today, Enrique is president of the Ejido Bramadero, a communal holding that, including the Meling ranch, is fifty miles wide and seventy miles long and home to only 113 people. The family's cattle herd once numbered in the thousands, but now Enrique and his family only run about two hundred head. Turning away from Mexico's failing cattle industry, the Melings now host paying guests at their ranch and offer limited horseback trips to American anglers in search of wild, rare rainbow trout. Potter is their connection to the North.

The family is careful whom they take into the wilderness of central Baja. "You get sick in there and there's nothing to do but haul you out by mule, and that can take days."

By now, it was time for us to leave Potter behind and head south. Jason and I drove out of the town right behind the group of fly-fishers. We passed between mesas covered with cardboard shacks that seemed frozen in a perpetual slide. Along the road, Indian women carried babies in sling sacks over their shoulders. A school band of uniformed children stood beside the pavement playing their drums and a single trombone for anyone who would listen. Traveling the toll road through the stench of coastal industry, we saw flashes of blue Pacific framed in new white stuccoed vacation casas, built mostly for Americans.

Just beyond Ensenada, the land changed radically. The mesas gave way to scorched desert mountains and green valleys. The road was winding and slow, with speed limits of sixty kilometers (forty miles) per hour, and lined with crumpled boxes of tomatoes; a tractor-trailer truck had gone over a cliff and filled an arroyo below with red pulp. Passing through a village, we hit a crude speed bump that must have been a foot high. The Volkswagen van leaped and fluttered and settled. A few hundred feet down the road a sign advertised the local hospital, which seemed appropriate.

Everything conspired to slow us: the speed limit, the variable quality of the road, the blind curves decorated with small white crosses and plastic flowers honoring dead travelers.

A couple hundred miles south, far beyond any settlements, I stopped the van next to a one-room grocery with the word "Juanitas" hand-painted on the front stucco wall and studied the crude map Potter had handed me. I had lost track of the veterinarians. The dirt-road turnoff to the village of San Telmo was nowhere to be seen. Inside the grocery, refrigerators and shelves were nearly bare. A little girl scurried across a bare plank floor. Juanita, pretty and vague, stared at my map and said in English, "Oh, no, you have to go back to *Comidor.*" So we drove back north, stopped the van in that town, and asked two women if they knew where the road to San Telmo was, and they said, "Oh, no, you have to go *that* way." And pointed south.

Just beyond Juanita's, across a dry wash, we found the road. And discovered then that the fishing party had not waited for us.

⌐ AFTER AN HOUR OF WAITING on the windy knoll, Jason and I got into the van and headed east, where, the map advised, four-wheel-drive vehicles were highly recommended. The van had front-wheel drive at least, and I was determined to find the fishing veterinarians, and to redeem myself in my son's eyes. This was not a particularly smart idea. But most of the fun in life comes from doing things that are not particularly smart.

My goal was to drive east thirty miles, on the axle-breaking roads, to find the Meling ranch, to see if someone could take us down to the stream.

We headed through the long, dusty valley where a river had gouged a wide flood plain. Farms were hidden in groves of palm and cottonwood. We climbed higher on the washboard road, a road of dust and pitted rock and sudden drop-offs. We made our way into the jagged foothills. We crossed a rise and in the valley below we saw the Meling headquarters, surrounded by feathery cottonwoods, a sudden imposition of green. A white sign pointed the way. We wound down to the compound of ranchhouse and outbuildings. A hitching post stood outside a low adobe building, which turned out to be the dining area and kitchen. I knocked at the open door. An old man walked out of the dark kitchen. He was wearing a cowboy hat, pushed back on his head. He had a gray drooping mustache and blue eyes and arroyos for skin. He looked something like Robert Duvall playing Gus McCrae in *Lonesome Dove.*

"I'm Andy Meling," he said. "Who are you?"

I explained our predicament and asked if anyone was available to take us down to where the fly-fishermen had gone. He narrowed his eyes and changed the subject. Wanted to talk, in his perfect southwestern English, of other things, took us back to the kitchen, introduced us to the cook, looked at my son's grunge shirt, looked away, disappeared into a back room, left us standing next to a row of polished wooden tables, appeared suddenly at another door, picked his teeth out there for a while, came back in as if the last thing he had on his mind was us, and why should he have us on his mind? Losing the anglers was my mistake. Why *should* he accommodate us?

Finally he walked up to me, his worn-out roper boots thumping on the scarred wood floor.

"You can stay at my ranchito tonight and tomorrow maybe somebody can take you down," he said.

Maybe. I assumed he meant this ranch, but I was wrong. He told us to follow behind his old Jeep Wagoneer. We headed higher into the mountains, another twenty miles over much rougher road, not a road for a VW van. We saw small pines now, and the air lost its dusty haze. Suddenly, he stopped his truck and jumped out to inspect a large trough carved in the ground, and walked slowly over to the van to tell us about his gold mine. "Just sold it to the Canadians." By now, the light was fading, and I was not particularly interested in the details of his gold mine; for all I knew, Andy was a serial slasher who loved to take strays like us up to the high country and turn them into chum.

"Look, Andy, I'm kind of concerned here," I said, arm on the window, as he stood there admiring his hole in the ground. "Will you really be able to find someone to take us down tomorrow?"

"Mebbe," he said.

Then he picked at his teeth and squinted at the pit some more, as if his squint alone could pull a little gold from the depths. He sighed and walked slowly back to his Wagoneer.

An hour later, he pulled into a little valley of scrub oak, sugarbush, and running springs. I parked the van. We got out and stood under the branches and saw the evening's first stars. He told us he no longer lives at the main Meling ranch. He recently carved out this little "one-man ranchito," as he calls it, his sanctuary. The two-room, dirt-floor cabin sits in the shadows of the Sierra de San Pedro Martir, on the slope of the white granite Picacho del Diablo, *peak of the devil*, which rises 10,154 feet through piñon, pine, and quaking aspen. We could see the peak through the pines, glowing red against violet sky. Cougars and chickarees live up there. And genetically unique trout glide through the high streams—as they do in the Santo Domingo far below.

This is a remarkable, unexpected landscape. In *Fremontia*, a journal of the California Native Plant Society, botanist Thomas A. Oberbauer describes this range as a "true mountain island." The wildlife and plants migrated here during wetter times, and later, as the climate dried, "these mountains must have been cut off from the north." In many ways, he writes, life here is a relic of the Pleistocene, "ethereal . . . primeval . . . an isolated elevational, climatic, and vegetational island." The fauna include the Douglas tree squirrel and the nocturnal "Ardilla voltar" or northern flying squirrel and "an endemic trout (Salmo nelsoni) which is found only in these mountains. Its nearest relatives are more than 150 miles away in San Diego County." The wildlife and plants that inhabit these mountains are relics from a past era. A visit "provides a window to the past." We had arrived.

Andy disappeared into his cabin. Jason and I walked down a path to the precipice overlooking a tangled valley. During the walk back, Andy's foolishly happy Labrador pup came bounding up to Jason, raced in circles around him, and made vertical hops in futile attempts to lick his face. It's a fine thing to watch a fourteen-year-old boy giggle.

We ate skillet stew cooked on Andy's iron stove. We sat in the gathering gloom, the devil's peak above us, around his plank of a table in the two-room cabin with no electricity, only a kerosene lantern and the glow of the wood fire through the cracks in the stove. Andy, who is seventy, introduced us to his two ranch hands, who did not speak English: an aging vaquero with spindly legs, a pencil-thin mustache, and an apron; and Bede, grizzled, squat and stoic, with a long gray mustache and thin, slicked-back hair. Bede sat at the table and watched without much comment, his eyes intelligent but shielded. Andy made a point of telling me that Bede was a Spaniard, "pure in Spanish blood."

After dinner, the two helpers disappeared. Andy produced some tequila, poured me a glass, and we moved outside and sat on rusty folding chairs, watching a manzanita campfire slowly collapse.

"So, is fishing on the river we're going to like fishing a hundred years ago?" I asked.

He thought for a moment. "Older," he said.

He told us about life on both sides of the permeable border. For years, he had worked as a plumber in the United States, an odd complement to his role in these parts as a major landowner, gold miner, and tracker of wild cattle. Down here, memory predates birth. He told us how, in 1911, *insurrectos* rode south from San Diego to turn Baja into a new republic. Forty of these men rode to the ranch, found no one there, killed the milk cows and chickens, and burned the fences. Andy's uncles, as he tells it, formed a volunteer army, rode north by horseback and buggy, and "wiped most of them out at a place called Rio Leon, then followed the last five into a canyon and killed them and that was the end of the revolution." Another kind of American came later: C. E. Utt, a rancher and land developer from Tustin who had a thing for trout.

"Mr. Utt came into this country in late '29," Andy said, pushing a log into the fire with his boot. "He was an orange grower, he'd develop ranches, and sell them; he made a lot of money." During the '40s, Utt, who was in his seventies, hired Andy, then a teenager, to help him transplant *Salmo nelsoni* from the Santo Domingo, the river that runs through the deep canyon far below, at about fifteen hundred feet, to the high meadows at ten thousand feet, by mule. Andy continued:

> I was just a young kid at that time. Mr. Utt asked me to pack him into the mountains so I did. The trout originated in the Santo Domingo, but nobody knows how they got there. They're a kind of rainbow, a very rare kind, their own kind. There is a very small area of the river that they can live in because of the coolness of the water, and it's just high enough. It has deep pools, lots of big, beautiful pools. You can catch those trout there by the hundreds near some falls where you are intending to go tomorrow.
>
> At that time, there was no road, none whatsoever. You could barely make it into the ranch with a vehicle. So we packed in, and we'd be gone for a month, month and a half. We made some special five-gallon tanks with big lids on them and a place where you could pump air into them—a spigot. And we'd go to the pools that had trout—small trout, little things—and we'd catch them. When we had all the cans ready, we'd feed the trout, and we'd pack them on three or four mules, two dozen trout on the back of each mule. Sometimes it would take us two days to get them to one of the streams. We'd spend forty-eight hours straight moving trout. We'd camp overnight, but this was a day-and-night job. Every hour, one of us would get up and pump air into the cans. Every stream up on top that would support trout, we put trout in them. We'd go from stream to stream to stream.
>
> We spent years at this. We put them in La Gruya, Rancho Viejo, we put them in another place called La Santa, and over to San Rafael, and we put them in the Tasajera, all of them, up and down. We stocked all those streams. And in 1947, I went to work for Mr. Utt full time at a ranch down in the San Telmo valley, growing seed for the Haven Seed Company in Santa Ana. So naturally I was together with the old man a lot. He loved this country, he really did. And so we would spend a month, month and a half, packing trout— this is what we did.

Andy passed me the bottle of tequila. Was Utt a fisherman? I asked. "He was a fly-fisherman. He would never fish without a fly, that's it. If he used a bait—no way. I used to follow him around all day long taking

his hooks off the bushes. I lived with the old man continually for five years. I mean, he was a grandfather to me."

"And were you a fly-fisherman?"

"No, hell I wasn't. Maybe if a stream had too many trout I'd take a bunch of salmon eggs—oh, he'd get mad at me." He laughed and passed his hand over his crevassed face, its arroyos deeper in the firelight.

I was astonished. In the '40s, plenty of wild trout streams were available in California. Surely there was no commercial reason for such a quixotic endeavor. Why did Utt do it?

Andy leaned toward the fire, which filled his face with gold and shadows. "Well I guess he thought it was *a good thing to do*," he said, and then was quiet.

In the 1950s, when the old man died, his body was cremated. "We brought his ashes down here and flew over in a plane." And the ashes entered the high streams where the rare little trout still surface in the twilight.

As Jason and I headed for our van under the live oaks, I tried to pin Andy down again about how we were going to get to the river—if we were going to get there. This would be a long trip, I knew, so I offered to pay. "What would be enough?" I asked, and Andy, sucking on a cigarette, then looking at it intently, answered, "It's up to you, whatever you want." I had no idea of the time or distance involved here. I said, "I don't know what's fair. How about fifty dollars."

"Oh, no, that's not enough. Seventy-five dollars."

I agreed.

Andy slept in the trailer next to the cabin and the cook slept out in the open in a bedroll, head resting on a saddle, plaid blankets spread carefully. Bede walked off into the darkness. Jason slept soundly in the pop-up bunk, trusting that the adults knew what they were going to do, and I tossed fretfully all night.

~ IT'S A PRIMAL THING, I guess. Johnny Pumpkinseeds, some biologists call them, get the urge to move fish; so do governments. The British Empire, in a form of ichthyological colonialism, carried trout, particularly German browns, in wooden barrels on schooners to North America, New Zealand, Ceylon, Kashmir, South Africa, and British Central Africa.* People have introduced a wide variety of freshwater sport fish—from bass to sturgeon—into unfamiliar waters. When governments do it, it's called management; when individuals do it, government calls it "bait-bucket biology," at best, and at worst "malicious introduction."

---

*The British imported, too: In the 1880s, rainbow trout were shipped from California. The 1910 *Encyclopaedia Britannica* reported that the rainbow, in the United Kingdom, was "still regarded with some suspicion, as it has a tendency to wander from waters which do not altogether suit it."

Once planted in inappropriate waters, predatory fish can quickly dec-
imate indigenous populations of fish, or other creatures. Fish diseases
can be spread this way. In Montana, biologists have recorded over two
hundred illegal fish introductions in recent years. In the southwest,
largemouth bass have suspiciously invaded desert refuges built for the
protection of the native Owens pupfish; officials suspected locals—
who resented the use of public funds for the protection of nongame
species—of planting the bass.

Then there's the case of the Unapiker.

In October 1997, California Fish and Game officials told the residents
of Portola, a small town in the Sierra Nevada foothills northeast of
Sacramento, that they were evicting the lake's northern pike. Introduced
several years ago by an unknown angler, the predatory fish, if it spreads,
could threaten California's trout, salmon, and striped bass. Said the officials: We'll just drop a little rotenone, a powerful pesticide, into the lake
(a source of drinking water), kill all the fish, and within a month or so,
we'll replant the trout. No way, said the residents of Portola. No wonder.
In the 1930s, the town was dependent on logging, railroad workers, and
brothels. Because of the shrinkage of these industries, the town's population dropped by more than half. Needing a new mainstay, the town
shifted to tourism, including angling. Poison our fish, they said, and you
poison us.

On the day the state poured rotenone into the lake, nearly two hundred armed game wardens, highway patrolmen, and sheriff's deputies
were called in to contain angry protesters, including four who chained
themselves to a buoy. One unknown Californian, whom officials dubbed
the Unapiker, sent anonymous messages threatening to reintroduce pike
into Lake Davis. The officials worry, as one biologist puts it, "that some
local has some pike sitting in a bathtub ready to be introduced at any
time." Months later, the carcinogenic toxin used to poison the fish had
yet to disappear. The state couldn't replant trout. Portola's economy was
endangered. State officials were digging wells to provide local drinking
water. And on April 10, 1998, downstream from Lake Davis at the entrance of Lake Oroville, an angler caught . . . a northern pike.

Sometimes hauling fish up and down mountains is a good thing to do.
Sometimes it's not. But when it comes to people and fish, national, cultural and biological borders just seem to disappear.

So do the borders of time.

⌁ BEDE WOKE US UP AT SIX, knocking on the window in the gray light.
My fancy alarm watch had not gone off. Andy came out of his trailer, hat

pushed back, bleary eyed. We shook hands. I asked again just exactly where Bede was going to take us and how and when. Throughout the afternoon and evening, Andy's plan had shifted several times: It would be an easy trip; it would be impossible; we would be dropped off at the top of the Serra trail and we would have to find our way to the stream and the fly-fishers below, if we could find them, assuming they had not moved their camp. I finally said, firmly, "Look. I'm concerned about safety, about getting lost. My boy's only fourteen. Can Bede go down all the way with us to the camp?"

"Oh, sure, sure, OK," Andy said absently. "He'll show you where the trail is."

Well, that wasn't reassuring, but it was the best I would get. I decided that we would go with the seemingly mute Bede; we would find the Serra trail and if we could not see the fishermen below, I would ask Bede to lead us down. If he refused, we would turn around and return to San Diego.

Bede drove the Wagoneer ahead of us, and we followed him, winding down from the high country of the San Pedro Martir. Far below, we saw clouds thick and white held in the palms of the canyons. The hidden Rio Santo Domingo ran through one of them. We came down into the clouds, moving through the shrouded flatlands where skeletal yuccas seemed to walk across the sand.

He pulled into a ranchita called Zomara. We left the van parked there under willow trees, next to a fence of upright stakes, and transferred our gear and ourselves to the Wagoneer. Several hours of travel remained. Bede drove silently, fast, deeper into the desert, across rock and dirt, higher again into hills that looked like giant ant mounds, some of them scorched by lightning fires. An hour went by. None of us said a word. Another hour went by. I asked him if he had any kids. *Niños? Niñas?* He understood. *"Siete,"* he said, smiling slightly. All grown, the oldest is twenty, or at least that is what I think he said. Children—there was our common language. But that conversation did not progress. More miles went by.

The desolation was disturbing: We would come to a fork in the dirt and rock road, and Bede would turn suddenly, race down a gully and up. He seemed to know exactly where he was going, but I kept thinking: What if by some fluke of bad luck or idiocy we were left behind? What if Bede dropped us off at the river, left, and we failed to find the anglers? Jason and I would be without food, with only a couple small bottles of water; we might have to walk these thirty-two miles back. So at each fork, on an open matchbook, I wrote down "forked right" or "forked left."

Bede looked over at me, from the corners of his eyes, and laughed silently.

"*Es demasiado*," he said, eyes pointing at the matchbook. "*Es demasiado.*"

Indeed, he was right. Too much. Far too many forks in the road to keep track of. Not unlike life itself. I gave up after a while. Crumbs would have worked better.

"Too much." I laughed. So did he. Half of trust is resignation. Now we were friends, of a sort.

He stopped the truck at a stream crossing the rough road, got out, stretched, and walked to the water, squatted down, and brought water from a cupped hand and drank it. He motioned for us to do the same, but concerned about the quality of the water, I declined his offer. He looked at me, smiling for the first time. He took off his faded green plastic ball cap and put it in the water, and then used his hand to run water through his gray hair.

Later, driving down the road, we saw a ranch in the distance. A single adobe house with a couple of outbuildings, and horses grazing nearby, and two green fields. He motioned to the ranch. It was his home, he said, when he can go home. We passed by and began to climb again. It must be an odd thing, I thought, for Bede and Andy and the rest to guide Americans—with our expensive rods and flats caps and polarized sunglasses held to our necks by Dayglo cords—who fish for fun, not food.

Bede wrestled the Wagoneer up a scorched canyon ridge path, throwing his weight into the steering wheel.

"*Numera de millas?*" I asked. He held up six fingers. I was overjoyed. And then we came to a gate. Bede stopped the Wagoneer and stared at the gate, at the chain and padlock on it. He said nothing.

"It's locked."

He still said nothing. He sighed. He got out of the Wagoneer and walked to the gate, shook the chain. The gate was a Meling gate, to keep people out of the valley of the Santo Domingo. The cowboys from the Meling ranch had locked it behind them when they had taken the fly-fishermen to the river. With a cliff on one side and a drop-off on the other, there was no way to drive around it. Jason and I were out of the truck now, staring at the gate.

"Well," I said.

Jason said nothing. Bede took off his old plastic ball cap and scratched his head. I scratched my head. We stared at the lock, hoping it would break. Finally, he looked at me, put his hands around the chain and pantomimed cutting through it. I shook my head. Jason looked back down the road from where we had come. Perhaps, after all this, he would have rather gone home. What a disappointment that would be. But Bede looked at me, and then at Jason, and turned and walked back to the Wagoneer. He rustled around under the seat, and returned to the gate, stuck the handle of a wire cutter into the padlock loop, twisted hard, and broke that sucker open.

Without a word, we got back in the Wagoneer and continued. We traveled several miles, the mountains of Baja stretching out hazy and dry around us.

Then suddenly there they were: a horse and a mule and two cowboys who were throwing small hay bales from a truck. What luck! Seventeen-year-old Daniel Meling, blond, wearing a ball cap and glasses, and another vaquero, a short, rough-looking man with a black drooping mustache and a Western hat, had just come up from the river far below, to haul hay down.

Bede lay on his side under a pepper tree while we waited for them to load the hay. Then they put Jason on the mule and me on the horse and down the hill we went. I turned, thanked Bede as I passed. He smiled slightly, turned his back and walked to the Wagoneer, shoulders round, moving at the same speed he always seemed to move.

Fish Eyes and Lizard Legs

I LOOKED FORWARD and down. The path before us wound far above the gorge. This would not have been a pleasant experience if we had decided to walk down alone, despite Andy Meling's assurances.

We rode for an hour or so. Halfway down, Daniel Meling, who was on foot, realized he had dropped his glasses somewhere behind us, so he turned back up the path, hunched over, eyes glued to the ground.

We went on, and a half hour later came to the bottom of the canyon, to the Rio Santo Domingo, a spreading of finger tributaries, and then a larger current with deep, green pools, willows and cottonwoods dipping into the water, branches trailing in sudden patches of moss. We crossed the stream on the horses and approached the camp where the fishermen were sitting under trees.

As it turned out, everyone was about to go upstream. Their departure had been delayed because some of the horses had disappeared. The five Meling vaqueros were off chasing them. The fishermen and one fisher-woman looked bedraggled and limp, especially considering that this was only the second day of a five-day trip. The veterinarians were sitting un-der the cottonwoods on rickety folding chairs, bent over looking at the dust, paring fingernails, or staring straight ahead. They were decked out in their fly-fishing finery. A couple of them were highly experienced and well-traveled fishers; one of them, though, had never fly-fished. Also in the party was a professional fly-fishing guide and trailer-park owner from Mammoth, California. He was coolly fit, an athletic guy in his for-ties with blondish-white hair. He owned and had brought the latest fly-fishing technology. He looked bored. A couple in their early sixties, from Bakersfield, sat together, slightly separated from the rest: They were, I learned later, thinking about retiring in Baja.

"We waited for you at San Telmo," said Tim, one of the veterinarians, a friendly man with a trimmed white beard.

I smiled. They had not waited that long, I thought.

He explained that the Meling cowboys had been impatient, worried that the light would fade on the dangerous path down to the river. They wanted to get going and would not wait longer than twenty minutes. That seemed to me a reasonable cause for leaving us behind, particularly now that I had seen the path.

Finally the horses were found, and they came rushing white-eyed through the camp. Esteban Meling, the head vaquero, flew past on his cow pony, whipping his lariat through the air. Other cowboys followed. And a couple hours later, after lunch, we headed upstream. In his thirties, Esteban carries more Spanish or Mexican blood than Danish. He is Enrique's brother, and charged with this trip because, I learned later, Enrique was suffering from stomach cancer. Esteban was bright, handsome, and personable; with a mustache, cowboy hat and thick raw leather chaps, he was quietly charismatic. I instantly liked him. We were headed upriver to a waterfall, a place where promoter Dal Potter had said no fishermen from outside Baja had fished before: An unlikely story, I thought, but it was true that the cowboys had, a few weeks earlier, cleared out impassable growth along the river.

The path crossing through the hills, a shortcut between bends in the river, was rougher than the one that had led down. We moved higher at first, the horses struggling along the rocks, the drop-off now a couple hundred feet. The path we were following was two feet wide, sometimes narrower. I watched Jason ahead of me, but knew there was little that I could do if he slipped.

My respect for such sure-footed horses increased with each turn of the path. (Mules are the preferred mode of transportation on such terrain, because their footing is more certain.) Over the years, there had only been a couple of accidents, Esteban told me later. One foolish fisherman had cracked a few ribs when he was thrown from a horse, after running it when the cowboys had told him not to. The major injuries were to the animals. A vaquero had tied a rope too tight around a mule's neck and it had twisted itself around some branches and hanged itself during the night. Another horse had tried to scratch itself with its back hoof and a shoe nail had caught its hide. It fell in the rocks and bled to death overnight.

Rounding a hill, my horse heaved its shoulders high to cross a rock and lost its back footing. Its center of gravity slipped. Its back hooves digging for traction, it started a small slide of rock and clay. It recovered its footing, and scrambled ahead. Both the horse and I were blinking.

We reached stream level again, and the path became more difficult; hard rains had washed out the dirt and left only rocks. So we traversed these rocks, the horses lifting their hooves high in the air, and we moved into the stream itself as the banks became thick with vegetation higher than our heads, even sitting on the horses. I heard a noise and looked down and saw blood trailing in the water. The horse had lost its shoe, and its fetlock had torn on the rocks. I told Esteban, and he stopped beside the stream and quickly reshod the horse. Because the spaces between the boulders were deeper, the horses could easily step in and break their legs. The path was gone. The sun was behind the high canyon walls now. A mile or so on, and Esteban called off the upstream journey. We would not make it to the falls.

We camped along the river. That evening, Jason and I walked upstream with our flyrods. We found a deep pool and a little five-inch trout took my first fly.

I held it spinning in the air and watched its sunburst markings stop and start, stop and start, as it turned, and then dipped it into the water, and eased it off the barbless hook, and it slipped back into the green current.

Dinner was beef wrapped in hand-made tortillas cooked over the campfire, and presented with beer and soft drinks, all hauled down on horseback. The fishermen and the veterinarians and the guide and the couple from Bakersfield stood in the gathering darkness, listening to the hiss of the stream. The stars formed a bright slash above the looming cliffs. Someone commented, in the starlight, that this was the most remote place they had ever been in their lives. One of the veterinarians, who fishes in Alaska, said that even in that distant state you would not feel this far from civilization. "The reason being, just about anywhere in Alaska people have radios." Our guides were carrying no radios, because their signal could not reach beyond the cliff walls.

We stood around the fire for a while; there wasn't a lot of talk because everyone was so tired. People drifted away to their tents and slept deeply under the painted sky, one brush stroke and so many speckled mistakes.

Before falling asleep, I thought of that little jewel spinning in the late afternoon sun.

↩ ANGLERS ARGUE FIERCELY over fish genetics—over which fish is truly native, over the merits of wild fish versus hatchery fish (blamed by many for the spread of whirling disease in the West, which is killing rainbows). But even many of the surviving wild species have been displaced or consciously moved or manipulated. In a sense, trout and bass and

most freshwater sport fish are as much a part of our cultures and as domesticated as cows—as the wild and stray cattle that Andy Meling tracks
in the Sierra de San Pedro Martir. The more domesticated our fisheries
become, the more we hunger for wildness—even unconsciously—and the
harder it is to find. Which is what draws anglers to such places as this.

With the catching and releasing of the little native trout, one of my
goals of this trip was met. Admittedly, it was an irrational objective, to
come all this way to catch and quickly release a fish that was all of five
inches long.

The value of this trout, beyond its beauty, rested in its genes. The
trout of the Rio Santo Domingo, along with a closely related species in
the mountains just to the north, are as close as we can find to the pro-
genitor rainbows that spread thousands of years ago from what would
become northern Baja California and the southernmost county of Alta
California, up the Pacific coast to Alaska, across the Kamchatka peninsula between the Sea of Okhotsk and the Bering Sea, and then spread—
sometimes by the hands of trout worshipers—around the world. At least
according to many fish biologists and Allen Greenwood of San Diego.

At fifty-five, Greenwood makes his living building custom adobe
houses for the wealthy throughout the Southwest. But his obsession (no
less than C. E. Utt's) is trout—the ancient trout of Southern California
and northern Baja. He had educated me about these primitive fish, and
their close relatives—the same species—found in the back country of
my own county.

With his nets and canisters, Greenwood haunts the back country and
Indian reservations (with Indian escorts at his side) of San Diego
County* and northern Baja, searching for what he believes is the genetic
"founder fish," which he insists (and a number of biologists agree) still
lives quietly in some inaccessible pool in some distant, craggy ravine.

During the same month as my trip to Baja, Greenwood took me up
to the mountains east of the city and showed me accessible pools where
small trout panicked and scattered. He scooped one up in his net, put it
in a small aquarium and held it up to the sun; true to its name, it displayed what seemed like hundreds of colors. We both looked at it with
awe.

"See the red tips of its fins? Those are markers connecting it genetically with the trout that came just before the rainbow," he said. "Nothing like these fish. We think they're the oldest form of rainbow trout. We

---

*Known to biologists as an epicenter of diversity and threatened extinction, San Diego County
is populated with more threatened and endangered species than any other county in North
America.

just can't prove it—yet." If he can find a slightly purer genetic strain, it will likely be the ancestor of the first coastal rainbow, "the rarest rainbow trout in the world." This fish would be the genetic Adam or Eve of all rainbow trout everywhere.

It would also provide powerful evidence of the connection between San Diego's and Baja's native rainbow and the nearly extinct Southern California steelhead. Rainbows and steelhead originated along the West Coast of North America between fifty thousand and sixty thousand years ago. Then they followed the retreating glaciers and colonized the rivers to the north, but the original steelhead stayed behind in what is now Southern California. Though seagoing rainbows once ranged as far south as the Rio Santo Domingo in Baja, the southern steelhead has declined for the past fifty years because of damming and development.

Steelhead and rainbow trout are the same species, but not all rainbows venture out to sea and become steelhead. The explanation for this is that rainbow trout take two life forms, some becoming permanent residents that spend their lives in fresh water. Other rainbows lose their reddish stripe, take on a silvery appearance, and travel downstream to enter the ocean as steelhead, returning one to two years later to breed. Why do some rainbows stay on as residents? What biochemical mechanism triggers others to become anadromous? "A plausible theory has emerged," writes journalist Terry Rodgers. "Resident rainbows function as an insurance policy, a genetic seed bank to sustain the species during drought, when portions of a stream can dry up and sever the steelhead's connection with the ocean. When wet conditions re-establish the connection to the ocean, an unknown percentage of resident rainbows are stimulated to go to sea."

"The thinking has always been that if it's (a fish) south of the Tehachapi Mountains, where there's a human population explosion in a desert environment, we can't save them," says Jim Edmondson, director of California Trout Inc. But in 1994, Stanford University researcher Jennifer Nielsen showed via DNA analysis that Southern California's steelhead, from rivers near Santa Barbara, are genetically distinct and a more ancestral population than the same species farther north. "When was the last time you saw a trout next to a yucca bush?" Edmondson asks. These fish are incredibly hardy and unique. Greenwood writes, in a paper respected by biologists statewide, about these genetically ancient fish: "The evidence clearly proves that rainbow trout have been in San Diego County and Baja California as natives, and that rainbow trout have been in Southern California since the end of the Pleistocene."

If Greenwood finds this new subspecies, the discovery could trigger political terror among ranchers, farmers, developers, and bureaucrats who might suddenly be handcuffed by water and habitat restrictions protecting the rainbow of rainbows. Recently, in a small stream on Camp Pendelton, the Marine base north of San Diego, finger-length wild steelhead were found. Steelhead were thought to have been extinct this far south, but there they were, and Greenwood and many others are on the case, with their nets and aquaria.

☞ I WOKE EARLY and walked in the gloom to the water. The guide from Mammoth was out already, fishing in solitude across the river.

I found my way to a higher pool. The fish scattered, spilled pearls rolling across a green floor. I went to the head of the pool and cast across to riffles and caught an eight-inch trout that shot out of water as I set the barbless hook. I shook it off the hook without touching it. The trout fought hard for its size and gave me all the pleasure I needed for that morning. I headed back to a good breakfast, thinking about how my fourteen-year-old—because of his height—seemed much older, and of how he had made the tent up the night before: He would, on this trip, become the tent master, and I was proud of him for doing that.

At 10 A.M., the party mounted the horses and rode back to the base camp.

From there, we headed upriver for some midday fishing, unproductive except for one extraordinary pool sheltered under a small, shedding tree. Here, you could wade out into shallow flow, your feet sinking into sandy mud, and cast upstream with caddis flies under the dipping branches, and the water would pop and gurgle with rises and strikes; again, the fish were at most eight or ten inches, but they were aggressive, and there were scores, perhaps hundreds, of them. I laughed out loud, drawing them toward me with long downward swoops on my line, and called Jason over. He stood on the opposite bank and cast into the pool, caught a trout, pulled it in without smiling, as I yelped with pleasure at his catch. He looked at it in the water. "It's dead," he said.

"No it's not, just bleeding."

He looked around, sweating, and said he was too hot to fish. He would head back to the camp and set up the tent. I was irritated at my own irritation. I wanted him to stay. But he was the tent master, I was the fisher. I turned back to the popping pool.

If the fishing urge is genetic, the trait may skip generations or sometimes siblings. I know that my other son, Matthew, six years younger than Jason, has the fishing gene. When he was three, I discovered him fishing in the humidifier. But Jason does not, or at least did not then, quite get fishing, or perhaps he did, more than the rest of us. He related to the fish. Like many children, he cried the first time he caught a fish. Oh, Jason had trembled with excitement at first, but then as the blood rushed from the gills he filled with grief. Most children forget that grief, and the meaning of predatory behavior is placed in a wider context. If we flatter ourselves, perhaps, we think of this wider context as a deeper understanding of nature and our place in it. Or this grief is replaced with greed. Although Jason had enjoyed the excitement of fly-fishing for sharks, the taking of such little trout did not appeal to him—it brought back that old grief. Jason would rather be in his tent with a good book. I reminded myself to be careful not to push him to fish, to respect what separates us.

I caught up with the veterinarians, and we jumped from boulder to boulder, egg-shaped rocks ten and twenty feet across, and fished the deep pools. The fishers, concentrating, were almost deadly serious in their pursuit of a strike. They purposefully avoided the easy places; they had quickly rejected the popping pool and moved higher to where there might be bigger fish. But it was a fruitless search, and after a while, I turned and walked back to camp. Jason was in the tent, reading. The tent master. He had done a good job.

I checked in with him, parked my rod and vest, and walked up under the cottonwoods where Esteban was sitting on a camp stool next to a large iron griddle set over the fire. Hatless, still wearing his chaps, he was tossing the makings of a tortilla back and forth between open palms.

I sat next to him, and in rudimentary English and a little Spanish we talked about the weather, about the river, and finally about fishing. He has been coming to the river since he was sixteen, and summering cows high up in the Sierra de San Pedro Martir, along the streams that Andy and Utt had planted. I asked him if he fished much along the river here or in the streams above. He nodded.

"We catched only what we were going to eat," he said. "I catched maybe three or four at a time. Enough to eat."

"How did you catch them? Did you have pack rods?"

He laughed. No, only branches, or nothing at all. He reached into a small, almost invisible pocket in the top of his thick, stained leather chaps. He pulled out a looped piece of monofilament line and a hook. That was the extent of his tackle. "We used the worms that we can find near some water and we used frogs, lizards." He pronounced it *leezards*. "We cut off the tail. And the legs. We try to cover all of the hook. We just use pieces. And the problem is to catch the first fish only because after you catch the first one, we use the eyes. We squeeze the head. The eyeballs pop out. You can take the eyes and the intestines, very good, very light. You can catch many."

The smaller the fish, the better they taste, he said. "We just clean them up, put in a little salt and some peppers and some flour and we toast them. You eat them with the bones. The big ones are not so good: You have to take out the bones."

I mentioned how serious some of the fly-fishermen were on this trip, about their technique, their gear. His hands were moving quickly, a new tortilla spreading out from the raw dough. His head was down slightly, concentrating. He smiled.

"Some of them will only use dry flies," I added. "They don't approve of bait fishermen. If they heard you were using lizard legs and fish eyes . . ."

"They would get mad," he said, and he smiled a little more. "No, I never tell them."

The fishermen returned after a while, straggling in, and sat down on the folding chairs for lunch, while the cowboys set the tables. The fly-fishers reminisced about trips to Wyoming and Montana and Alaska. Someone said that, in Montana, eighteen- and twenty-two-inch trout are so common that this trip is a little disappointing. They spent the next hour talking about gear, often deferring to the guide from Mammoth, who exuded expertise, with his sullen athleticism. Does all the fancy equipment really make that much of a difference? I asked.

"Sometimes, to catch the bigger fish, the rod matters," said the guide. "A more expensive rod is designed to cast better. When you get to the point when you want to fish a lot of line it really matters. An inexpensive rod is made to be mass-produced and there's no control over how well or how far the rod will cast. A cheap rod doesn't have a lot of the research that goes into it, so it may not load like it should." By "load" he meant the energy that gathers in the rod as it flexes when the line loops behind the angler, energy that will be released on the forward cast. Some of the difference between mid-level and the higher-end rods has more to do with cosmetics than action, he said. "It's like the difference between driving a Mercedes and a Mercedes that's fully loaded."

Most of the intricacies of fly-fishing equipment are beyond me. I asked him why some people use fast-action rods and why some people use slow ones. Was it to get the fly on the water faster? He dismissed this question gruffly and said, "No, it just means that some people like fast action and some people slow action." Clearly I was an ambassador from the unwashed.

But just when I was beginning to dislike the man, the conversation shifted to early fishing experiences. The guide told how when he was a kid, before there were float tubes, he had asked his grandmother to sew a canvas seat into an inner tube. One day, he was out on a lake near his house, floating in the tube, and caught a big catfish. He put it on a stringer. The catfish would swim down to escape, then shoot back up. Every time it shot up, the spike of its dorsal fin would poke at the inner tube. Finally, the fin broke through the rubber, the inner tube collapsed, and he barely made it to shore. He laughed long and hard at himself.

How can you dislike a man who tells such a story? Fishing brings out the best in people. Most of the time.

I found it interesting that the vets, who spent all their working hours keeping animals alive, would, on their vacation time, hook and kill animals.

"We only catch and release," said one of the vets.

"Yeah, we just scare the hell of out of them and let them go," said Tim. "Just like we do with our patients."

As a veterinary surgeon, he spends his workdays doing the intricate work of bone plating and hip replacements on small animals. Fishing, he said, occupies the same part of his brain that has to be both active and technical. "It's technical, but relaxing. By occupying that part of your mind, you can forget work stress—unless you bring your employee manual."

Another vet leaned over and said, "Every vacation he brings his employee manual."

Tim shrugged. "It's the business manual we use, 150 pages. It has the OSHA standards for everything. It even covers whiteout. You know, that you use when typing. In case somebody were to drink it, you'd know what to do."

One of the vets had watched Esteban nail the horse's shoe back on, matter-of-factly, as its blood trailed in the water. "Esteban said, 'No problemo.' And it wasn't any problem, really. Easily fixed." A lot of things in life, he said, are easier fixed than those of us in modern society would suspect. Spare nails and baling wire hold far more of the world together than coaxial cable or microchip circuitry.

The anglers grew restless and began to treat their lines with silicone, and retie their leaders, and prepare for the evening bite. As their work quickened, Tim jokingly began to describe the stages of fishing addiction, and the rest joined in. Stage one: introduction, the first bluegill; stage two is the equipment; stage three is watching fishing shows on television; stage four is total addiction. "Burnout is stage five, but you never reach that," said Tim. "Maybe drowning is stage six."

"Drowning while fishing, not a bad way to go," someone said.

Then the men were off again, moving upstream, leaping again from boulder to boulder, men attempting to be boys yearning to be men. As we moved upstream, I thought of the evolution of Allen Greenwood:

how he now feels such awe for trout and their genetic messages to us that when he fishes, he uses a fly with *no* hook. He casts a fluff of feathers out just to watch the beauty of the trout as they rise.

Later, as dusk fell suddenly in the deep canyon, I slipped off by myself and stripped my clothes and sat naked in the bowl of a white boulder as the water rushed around me. I leaned back to watch the bats swooping down from the cliffs, the saguaro cacti reaching upward and outward. I washed my hair, leaning my head back in the current until only my face was out of the water. No rod, no vest, *no problema.*

Looking up, feeling the water move past my ears, I recalled something Carl Sandburg said: That which is explainable is not poetry. Perhaps that is the way it is with fishing.

꙳ HOW DID FISHING BECOME so enmeshed with who we are, with human culture? Not just fishing for food, but fishing for sport. This thing is a mystery, this strange synaptic connection that transforms fishing from the simple acquisition of food to something wider and beyond logic.

The mystery's roots are simple enough. The earliest anglers caught fish with their bare hands, a technique still employed. "The first Europeans who emigrated to North America learned from the American Indians the fine art of 'guddling,' slowly moving the hand under the body of a resting wild fish until the fish could be seized by the gills and yanked from the water," according to an encyclopedia called *The Lore of Sportfishing.* "There is no reason to believe that *Homo erectus* and other early hominids were not equally skillful at collecting a fish dinner with their hands or primitive fishing tools."

The first rods? Probably sapling branches, used to extend the reach of the line to otherwise inaccessible water. The first hook was most likely not a hook at all but a gorge, "a piece of flint or stone which a fish could swallow with the bait but which it could not eject afterward." Archeological digs of former cave dwellings reveal gorges made of narrow strips of stone or flint flakes, grooved to hold a line. One fishing gorge, estimated to be thirty thousand years old, was discovered beneath twenty-two feet of peat in a French bog in the Somme valley. Paleolithic people carried torches for illumination during night fishing, and this fire likely attracted fish; therefore, light itself might qualify as the first artificial lure. Other early lures were made of ivory and bone, decoys for spear and ice fishing. Around the fourth century B.C., Chinese writings make reference to fishing with a bamboo rod, a silk line, a hook made from a needle, and with cooked rice as bait. Two thousand years before the birth of Christ, an Egyptian hieroglyph depicted figures fishing with a rod and line, as well as with nets. Passages in the Old Testament describe the use of nets and hooks, and fishing as an industry.

But when did the concept of angling congeal as something beyond subsistence? Much of what has been recorded about the history of fishing concerns technology, apparatus, the early models of all that comforting paraphernalia that surrounds us at the tackle store. But what about the *specialness* of fishing—its role in cultural status, and also its spiritual nature?

Certainly, status has been considered part of fishing at least since the Pharisees. The Egyptian hieroglyphs portrayed fishers using short rods and lines and attired in the style of noblemen, indicating that angling had already become a diversion for the wealthy. The earliest references to fishing in Greek and Latin classics have nothing to say about fishing as a form of sport or leisure or as a spiritual experience. However, a passage in the *Odyssey* describes how Scylla seizes the shipmates of Odysseus just as "some fisher on a headland with a long rod" pulls small, gasping fish to the shore. More satisfying is the twenty-first idyll of Theocritus, in which the fisherman Asphalion, who used a rod and fished from a rock, tells of a dream in which he hooked a large golden fish and describes how he "played" it. And Plutarch wrote of a fishing match between Antony and Cleopatra—the first trophy tournament?

Expressions of reverence for fishing exist in early Eastern literature, but fish and fishermen occupied a particularly honorable position in early Christendom. Fishermen were prominent in the Gospels. As a result, the image of the fish became a sacred emblem in paintings and sculpture of the early church; the symbol is due to correspondence between Latin for fish (iccus) and Jesus Christus (ic-thus). On catacomb lamps there are two fish, one swallowing the other. Early Christian art frequently employed the image of the fisherman, often with a line and a hook, and church fathers often alluded to the divine nature of fish and the fisherman. Sites for monasteries in Europe were chosen, in part, for their proximity to good fishing streams. When these were not available, the monks built fishponds—and, fasting, ate fish when meat was forbidden. Spoke St. Augustine: "Jesus is a fish that lives in the midst of waters."

Indeed, the history of Western angling does suggest that monks and nuns were our spiritual ancestors. In her historic volume *The Book of St. Albans,* printed in England in 1486, Dame Juliana Berners, the Lady Prioress of Sopwell Nunnery, advised how to make rod, hook, and line (premium fishing line was braided, then, of the tail-hair of white stallions). This was the first essay on sport fishing. By then, the synapse had clearly snapped. She even promoted conservation:

You must not be too greedy in catching your said game, as in taking too much at one time . . . that could easily be the occasion of destroying your own sport and other men's also. When you have a sufficient mess, you should covet no more at that time. Also you should busy yourself to nourish the game in everything that you can, and to destroy all such things as are devourers of it.

↫ WE FISHED TWO MORE days. On the last night, several of us set up the folding chairs just beyond the ring of campfire light. One of the anglers, Peter, a likable, soft-spoken man, was an amateur astronomer. He claimed his knowledge was modest. As the last bats dipped and turned, we watched the sweep of the beam of Peter's flashlight as he pointed to the stars. He connected the dots to show us the patterns that the ancients had first seen, perhaps after collecting their fish from the weirs or at the end of a single line, baited with eyes. He located several constellations for us and we peered at them through binoculars. He pointed out three stars and told us to follow the line between the stars and then go up one star to the left and there was Andromeda, a tiny, milky cloud scarcely visible.

"That is the only spiral galaxy visible to the naked eye, except of course our own which we are right in the middle of and if you look up and see the Milky Way . . . see, look . . . you can see that we are in an arm of the spiral, looking back into the Milky Way to quite literally the center of our galaxy," he said. Andromeda is named, from Greek mythology, for the daughter of Cepheus and Cassiopeia and wife of Perseus, who rescued her from a sea monster.

We watched a satellite move above us, blinking.

The last time I remembered seeing the night sky this bright was catfishing with my friend Nick Raven on the Pecos River in New Mexico, standing beside a stream just as we were on this night in Baja, seventeen years later.

Several of the anglers joined us. We sat in a semicircle and looked up.

Peter said that this was the first time he had ever gone fly-fishing. He said he had never been much of a fisher. But he was glad that he had come, though not so much for the fish.

One of the fishermen, the one from Bakersfield, said he and his wife had decided, after all, that Baja was no place to retire to. Too primitive. He began to complain about fishing laws in Germany. There, he said, fishing is considered inhumane. "If you catch them in Germany, you have to jerk the fish out of the water immediately; you can't play it because playing a fish is considered torture. It's a law or something. Pretty soon it's going to be that way in America, if the animal-rights people have their way."

There was a long silence. Peter turned off his flashlight and the stars grew brighter. "Odds are," one of the anglers said, "somewhere up there on some planet, evolved fish are probably looking up at the stars and talking about the ethics of humaning. Whether to throw humans back. How to play them."

The other fishermen drifted back to the fire or their tents. Eventually, the fire went out, and Peter, my son, and I were out there alone. We pushed the chairs aside and lay down in the sand and looked up, and I experienced that strange feeling of falling upward that one has when looking so far into the past. "You know," said Peter, whose face we could not see, "a fact of my life that I find difficult to deal with is that when I was younger, growing up in the Midwest, I took the sky for granted." Now he lives in Southern California and never sees the sweep of stars, because of the marine layer and smog.

The odd thing was that these anglers, some of them quite impatient with the slowness of Baja and, to a lesser degree, the small fish, were only vaguely aware of the ancient genetics of the species they were hunting here. But then, most of us are not fully conscious of what we're looking for when we fish. We stumble along the path, along the water, most of us in the dark, looking neither up nor down. Perhaps fishing is not as much about *introspection*, as advertised, as it is about *outer inspection*. Maybe fishing is just a good excuse to look into water or up at stars.

After Peter said good night, Jason and I were out there alone, the cold creeping into us. We couldn't see each other clearly under the stars of Baja, but we could hear perfectly. Suddenly Jason began to do something highly unusual for him, quite out of the ordinary for any teenager. He talked about his experiences at school; a stream of consciousness poured out in the protective darkness.

Finally, we stood up and brushed the sand off and walked back to the tent. Slipping into his sleeping bag, he said, "Dad, did you know that dolphins have more highly evolved brains than humans? More wrinkles on the brain. But nobody knows what they think about."

"No, I didn't know that." I turned out the flashlight and lay there with my hands under my head. He settled down in his bag. We watched the universe through the netting above. A few minutes passed. Jason spoke again.

"And you know, there's this great scene at the end of *The Hitchhiker at the End of the Galaxy*," he said, referring to the novel by Douglas Adams. "At the end of the story, the dolphins escape from earth, and they leave this message for the humans: 'So long, and thanks for all the fish.'"

I smiled in the dark until I slept.

⌁ THE NEXT DAY, the party climbed back on the brave horses and wound its way slowly from the lost world of the Rio Santo Domingo, following the ghost of Serra along the narrow groove of a path he had traveled on his way to California Norte. We followed it up, higher and higher, away from the ancient trout.

By his reluctance to enjoy his father's fishing, Jason had posed the question: Is it right to hurt or kill a fish for pleasure or spiritual connection? I did not have a satisfactory answer. Not yet. From this point on, Jason would have to stay home. School called. But I kept going, to newer waters.

Flyover Waters

. . . The glad earth, the unclouded sky, the fresh breeze, the clear light, each and all showed that the day that came treading on the skirts of morning would be calm and bright.

—Don Quixote

You See That?

THE JET JUMPED PUDDLES, lakes and rivers, arced from the coast to the Midwest, which some folks on the coasts think of as the flyover land. For the most part, the flyover waters are not a place of trout. True, some of the best, unsung trout waters in America are in Arkansas and Southern Missouri. But bass, bluegill, crappie, catfish, and carp are the more traditional residents.

To a degree, there are two main fishing cultures (each with subcultures) in America: One is based on anadromous fish—salmon, steelhead, trout—and another on "spiny rays," as the fishing journals of the Northwest sometimes call bass and crappie and the like.

The divide between these two cultures can be severe.

A well-known steelhead fly-fisher from Washington says he doesn't want to be quoted in any book in which bass tournament fishers also appear, "because they represent everything that fishing is not. It's trophy fishing; it's competition."

Well, the idea that steelhead fly-fishers are purer than bass fishers is a peculiar concept. Of the two kinds of anglers, which one fishes for a threatened species? Which one uses lighter tackle, making it more difficult to reel a fish in quickly, therefore reducing the fish's survivability when released? Which one competes in a straightforward manner—for a trophy, for money—and which one competes by assuming some kind of spiritual, ecological superiority?

"The uppity demeanor of trout fishermen is in direct contrast to the approach of bass fishermen, who make considerable pretense of illiteracy, regardless of their educational background," according to outdoor writer Charles F. Waterman. "A trout fisherman describes his prey as a 'gleaming shard of crimson and silver.' A bass fisherman says he hunts 'hawgs' and hopes he can 'gouge some of them big ole sows.' There must be something in between."

Must be, indeed.

Not every anadromous fly-fisher thinks all bass anglers are rubes. And not every bass angler thinks that trout worshipers are all snobs. The fact is, the two cultures are starting to blend, which is good news, unless you believe in piscatorial purity.

These days, I prefer fly-fishing, but I'm a product of the Midwest, the land of bass and crappie and catfish and carp and the smell of gasoline fumes on morning water—a scent that activates the endorphins. When it comes to fishing, we're all pretty much a product of where we came from.

I looked down at the quilt of eastern Kansas, the shining, brown ribbons stitching it all together. The plane began its descent.

⌐ TO MANY FOLKS, particularly in the Midwest, Harold Ensley is as recognizable as David Brinkley. And he's just as much of a television pioneer. I grew up in Kansas City watching *The Sportsman's Friend*, Ensley's fishing show. Along with three other men—Charlie Davis, in Los Angeles, Gadabout Gaddis in Boston and Mort Neff in Detroit—he invented the fishing show genre in the first years of the 1950s. He made it all up in a period when people at least tipped their hat to the idea of unshakable integrity.

Now, here I was, riding with one of my childhood heroes.

"Did you see the name of that town? Tightwad, Missouri. They got a Tightwad Bank there," he said, as he drove his trademark red Ford station wagon toward Truman Reservoir. I tried, for the first time, to ask him what he thinks of today's sportfishing television industry, one of the modern engines of the cultures of fishing. Particularly bass fishing. He changed the subject.

"Right down the road there's a town called Racket," he said.

Cars slowed and people stared at Harold. They honked and waved and smiled.

Those of us who grew up in that windswept geographical core of America, felt as if we existed on a balancing point. To the east, one sensed condensed green, wooded density, people, and power; to the west, the long expanses of myth. Missouri, a slave state, was Southern; Kansas, a free state, was plainly righteous.

As far as one could imagine, there was water. The plains seemed a sea—and, in fact, once were. Midwestern children turned over slabs of limestone; ringneck snakes, fragrant and shiny, slid among the fossils and imprints of invertebrate ocean-bottom arthropods, Cambrian trilobites with flat, oval bodies covered by horny shells, and the bones of tiny, ancient fish. They were everywhere, just below the waves of wild oats and Kentucky bluegrass. To the west, near Wichita and Hutchinson, a friend recalls, children would walk behind their fathers' plows, watching the overturned earth for petrified sharks' teeth as inland-water gulls followed in the sky above. She says, "My father's world was half sky. In a sense, he *was* at sea."

And to the south and southeast, in Missouri, Arkansas, Oklahoma, the vast impounds were suddenly everywhere, courtesy of the Army Corps of Engineers. Table Rock, Bull Shoals, Taneycomo, and the older Grand Lake and the Lake of the Ozarks. Culturally and economically, the dams changed this part of the Midwest forever, and Harold Ensley made sense of it. He and the other TV pioneers virtually created big lake largemouth fishing. Their TV fishing shows created the commercial market, which led to big-money bass tournaments and the industrialization of freshwater sportfishing.

Today, he's somewhere in his eighties (he does not disclose his age) and for forty-seven years, his show has never left the air. True, his airtime has dropped from weekly prime time to thirteen episodes a year, but he's still syndicated on sixty-three stations from Maine to California and in two provinces of Canada. He's determined to be the last man to leave the water.

⌐ I'D CALLED ENSLEY from California, told him how much he had meant to me as a kid, and asked him if I could go fishing with him and write about it. Sure, he'd said, why not? When I had pulled up at his little tract home in Overland Park, Kansas, just after dawn in the sprawling suburb west of Kansas City, I had been surprised by his size. I remembered him, of course, as being much taller on television. But I recognized him immediately even though I hadn't seen his image for thirty years.

He wore baggy chinos with lots of side pockets and a kind of a three-tone shirt, and aviator glasses. His blue eyes were focused and intelligent. He had a wisp of reddish hair on top of his head, and ruddy cheeks, and his jaw was still square and large, his smile full of strength and impishness.

"You're late," he had said, with a slight edge.

But right now, he was in a terrific mood, driving down the highway toward Truman Reservoir with all these fans waving and hooting at his station wagon.

"Let me tell you how it all started," he said.

I was on radio at first, in the '40s, out of Joplin, on a little thousand-watt station, WMBH. I broadcast Little League baseball games, by telephone, from a cornfield. How the radio fishing show came about, is, there was a new milk plant down on the Oklahoma border, and it's still there. Half of it was in Oklahoma and half of it in Missouri. I guess they did that for tax purposes. My boss sent me down there to sell a promotional package to the milk plant and the other merchants down in Seneca, right at the edge of Grand Lake in Oklahoma. Well, the fellow that ran the milk plant was a good friend of mine, and he also ran a filling station—Wiley McGee was his name. I went in to Wiley and I said, "Wiley, give me a ten-dollar bill." Now if you can imagine this, the spots, probably thirty-second spots, were ten dollars. Wiley hardly ever cleaned up, wore a pair of bib overalls, sold a little bit of fishing tackle and minnows and craw-fish. But he liked to fish. I just went in there and he was busy and I said, "Wiley, right quick, give me a ten-dollar bill." He just reached into his billfold and gave me a ten-dollar bill and went on waiting on a customer. So I made out a receipt and he said, "What'd I buy?" And I said, "Well, you just bought yourself a radio ad." He said, "It isn't worth it." I said, "I know that! But I got your money." And I laughed and he laughed. And he said, "What I want is a fishing show." I said, "OK, I'll get you one."

But then, Harold thought, what's a fishing show? Well, said Wiley, "Everybody says to me, 'When the fishing gets good, call me.' And I don't have anybody to call to find out. The newspapers down here don't do anything, so I've got to have somebody to call." So Harold returned to Joplin and talked his boss into letting him do a radio fishing show. "I told him, I'll get people to report to me from all of these lakes around the country and I'll put it on the air."

We'd do that radio show every Saturday morning, and Wiley would pay for it. We dug out an old theme song, Smiley Burnett's "Well I Might Have Gone Fishing." Beautiful song. Ten years later, I had Smiley Burnett on my TV show in Kansas City and he sang it. I was going to have him on for five minutes. And he said, "How about another song? Here's one I sang on the Gene Autry show, 'Catfish Take a Look at My Worm.' I kept him on for thirty minutes.

Anyway, I'd had that radio show out of Joplin two weeks and the Chamber of Commerce called me and said, "Hey, we hear you on the radio. We've got a little money to spend. Would you do a show for the Chamber of Commerce in Noel? Noel, Missouri, that's where people all send their Christmas cards to have them sent out from. Pretty little town down on the Elk River, quite a resort town back in those days. So I did a show for them. Then I moved to Kansas City in '49. And there wasn't a station in town that would hire me. Except for a new station, in Independence, Missouri, KCMO.

I drove down to Warsaw, where we're going today, tried to talk the Chamber of Commerce into paying for the telephone calls to collect the fishing reports because I was doing the show for nothing. They didn't bite. But there was a fellow who had a resort down there—he's dead now—I went to him, Scotty was his name. Pretty little resort, I'll never forget it, hoot owls and cold night air and the little cabin on the Pomme d'Terre River; it's part of the lake now. The resort operator liked my idea for a fishing show. I told him: "There's only one thing I ask. You pay for the call and you tell me the truth. If I find out you're lying to me, I'll cut you off."

We passed the Blue River and fields pinned to the earth by bales of hay. At almost regular intervals, we crossed little brown creeks. Here, I thought, was an authentic voice of Main Street America, from a time when the world was more local than global, so familiar and yet now so strange. Nothing fancy; just the world in a three-dollar spot, ten dollars tops. This is the culture from which most fishing in America springs. For better or for worse, this was Harry Truman's America, and the America that Ronald Reagan conjured up in specific words and in the pauses between his words. Politicians who have tapped this place in the national heart have prospered, at least for a while. Whether that America still exists is an open question; perhaps in cultural islands, it does. Handshake to handshake, Harold built up his contacts in Missouri, northeastern Oklahoma, northwest Arkansas, and Kansas: boat docks, resorts, bait shops. He collected no salary in the beginning; made his money only from commissions. He would drive all night to get to a lake, fish Saturday or Sunday, and come back on Monday and give his fishing reports on the air. He found sponsors: Sears, and two years later, Ford. And he found his audience. Down at the Playcomo Ford plant, the workers would get off their shift at 4 P.M. "Nobody even thought about drive time making any difference back then. But a lot of the Ford workers would go out and sit in their cars, you know, if they had a car, and sit there together and say: 'Well, Harold says Lake of the Ozarks is where the fish are biting; let's go to Lake of the Ozarks.' And the thing just snowballed."

Such a different time it was, a time before people had "lifestyles," a time before virtual reality or theme parks, a time when personal recreation was more pickup than organized; a time when, in the wake of the Depression and World War II, folks probably felt thankful just to be alive, and a simple thing like watching a bobber, well, that was true pleasure. I thought of all those auto workers sitting in their cars at the end of the shift listening to Harold. Fishing, though less sophisticated than it is now, must have had more cultural importance then, if only because there was less to do and fewer distractions, and the sheer *quietness* of fishing must have soothed many of these men, not far removed from the fury of Normandy and Guadalcanal. Harold immediately recognized the potential of television. Or his wife did. "It was '51 or '52. She said 'Why don't you do a television show?'"

He drove to Sears and watched the showroom television and thought about what a TV fishing show would look like. In 1953, he made his move, convincing KCMO, one of the two new stations (which was filling empty airtime with local weddings), to let him fill some airtime with fish. The station gave him thirty minutes at 9:00 P.M., in what later became known as prime time, on Monday nights.

He decided to combine live TV with on-location fishing films—essentially showing home movies of his angling adventures. He bought a little Revere magazine-load sixteen-millimeter movie camera with good Angienoux lenses for five-hundred dollars. He was, and still is, his own cameraman (and to this day uses 16-millimeter film). When he needed shots of himself, he would hand the camera to his wife or his fishing guest. He adopted a new theme song, which he still uses today: "Gone Fishin'," by the Three Sons, with Texas Jim Robertson singing. The show's out-of-town guests would stay at the Ensley home. "Nobody thought about Kansas City being a place to fish in those days," he said. "Not like Denver, which was considered big-time, because of all the trout fishing." Bass, then, had little cachet. But the better known Harold became, the more the heart of the nation became associated with good fishing, and the more status bass, crappie and even catfish gained.

By the mid-'50s, with two hundred and fifty Ford dealers as sponsors, he was a legend: five radio shows a week, two thirty-minute television shows in prime time, nationwide but mainly in Kansas, Colorado, Oklahoma, Arkansas, and Nebraska. Flyover country.

"I did live TV for twenty-two years, twice a week, and never missed a single show. As I look back, I don't see how physically it was possible, mixing the live with the film. I'd go to Alaska and I'd have to be back by the next Monday night. Twice I got in fifteen minutes before having to go on the air. I was still doing a radio show then. Sometimes I'd do my radio show from phone booths. But for TV, I had to come home. I'd be

HAROLD ENSLEY

out in Utah, drive thirteen hundred miles in twenty-six hours, go directly to the station, shave, and get on the air."

He liked live TV just fine. Especially the live animals. "A guy called me from out in Kansas and he said, 'I got a big catfish and everybody said I ought to call you.' I said, 'How big is it?' He said, 'Seventy-two pounds.' I said, 'What condition is it in?' He said, 'I've got him in a horse tank.' I said, 'Bring him in and we'll put him on live.' He put that tank in his Ford pickup truck and drove right in on the set. He lifted that fish up live and he splattered water all over the cameras and everything else."

Harold smiled at the memory, wrist on the steering wheel, cap pushed back. I told him I remembered my father laughing about the time Harold had a dog on the show, and it bit him. I asked him if he remembered that.

"Yeah! I got a scar right here!" He turned his wrist over and stuck it out toward me. "Tore a good shirt from me, right on live television. I tried to turn his head, it was a Saint Bernard."

Somebody else's dog?

"Yes. And I petted him, played with him all the time until he got on the air." Harold laughed.

"I thought all these years maybe my father had . . ."

"Oh, no. True. I had a coon hunter from Sedalia brought a coon on, ate crawdad tails. Didn't do much. And he said, 'Heck, I've got a young coon dog out in the car.' I said, 'Go get him.' That dog smelled that coon and just cut loose—you never heard such a racket in your life. Chased that coon up a boom mike and you couldn't hear anything, pandemonium— and I'm trying to get my director to get a picture of the coon and all he's got is the greasy coveralls of this guy's butt. Live television was exciting!"

What interested me most about the birth of the television fishing show was the issue of ethics. How did Harold establish his own ethical guidelines, and how do they relate to television today? In 1953, this was fresh territory.

"I didn't know how anybody made a fishing show, and I didn't worry about how anyone else did it. I knew that if you were to tell the truth and show things for what they are—that was the only way I knew how to do it. It's not a big Hollywood production, and I wasn't trying to make it a big deal for anybody. Because the fishing itself is exciting enough."

One decision he made early on was not to take cigarette or liquor ads, a remarkable decision considering the traditional link between smoking, chewing, drinking, and fishing.

> When I first realized I was going to be on TV, that night I went home and I said, "I just agreed on a contract with Mr. Hartenbower at KCMO." And my wife said, "Did you tell him you wouldn't take a cigarette or liquor sponsor?" I said, "No, I forgot to." She said, "You better call that man." I called him at home—I didn't know him—I just had that meeting with him. I said, "Mr. Hartenbower, I hate to bother you at home but I forgot to tell you that I don't smoke and I don't drink and I don't have any right to go into a man's living room and suggest that his kids smoke or drink." He said, "Well, that's where all the big money is!" And I said, "I know and I want to be on television real bad, but I want you to know that I'll not accept it." And he said, "Well Ensley, if you think you can make it without them, I think I can too."

An issue more specific to the eventual evolution of the fishing show was the pre-catching of on-air fish.

> Universal Pictures shot an hour show down in Florida, where they selected seven national water-sports champions: the water-ski

champion, scuba-diving champion, the national saltwater fisherman, and I was national freshwater fisherman. They asked me,
"Where did you learn to fish?" I said, "I haven't learned yet, I'm still
trying." I had a typical New York director. He said, "I hear you got a
television fishing show." I said, "Yes." He said, "What time is it on?"
I said opposite *Peter Gunn*, which was the number-one show in
those days. He said, "How many viewers you got, two?" I said, "No,
I've got three. My little girl and my wife watch it."

The director told me to pre-catch the fish to be used during the
filming. And I said, "I won't do that. I don't do that with anybody, I
don't let anybody do it on my show. I've fished with Henry Fonda,
I've fished with Clint Walker, I've fished with the *Gunsmoke* crew,
the *Beverly Hillbillies* crew, and a lot of big stars and I've never let
them in any way do that." But he said, "I got news for you, you're
not going to be on this newsreel." I said, "I've got news for you. I
could care less. I don't need to be on your show."

Things got pretty tense. But we started down the river anyway.
One of these glass-bottomed boats with all these tourists came by,
and my guide pointed at me and said, "There's the world's champion fisherman, any minute now he'll pull out an eight-pound
bass." Well, I couldn't catch a fish. Here comes this big barge with
the Universal crew with a big thirty-five-millimeter camera. They
yell out, "How's Ensley doing?" Guide yelled back, "Ensley's doing
all right, the fish aren't cooperating!" And they let the barge run
into the bank, making all kinds of racket. It was a mess. Everybody
mad.

I thought, "I'll just lay it right back in that pocket," just a little
V-shaped thing. I threw the bait and the water just exploded, an old
bass had it. Wasn't a big one, weighed four and a quarter pounds.
Producer was yelling at the cameraman: "Get a picture of Ensley!
Get a picture of the fish!" When the fish jumped he wouldn't have
the camera on the fish, but on me. And when he had the camera
pointed at the water, the fish wouldn't jump at all.

I asked Harold if he had *ever* faked a shot—taken a fish out of the live
well and hooked it on for the camera's sake. He looked at me. "I just
won't do it. I never have. And like I say, I've done shows with Henry
Fonda and a lot of big stars and I've never let them do that. I decided just
out of honesty not to, but I'll tell you what, you can't fool fishermen.
These guys that are hooking fish on their line and stuff like that, people
know."

"What do you mean 'hooking fish on the line?'" I asked.

"Well, I'm not going to say any more."

"All right. So are fishing shows still honest, as far as you can tell?"

"I'm not going to say. I'm not accusing anybody of anything."

↩ WHATEVER HAROLD AND THE OTHER fishing-show pioneers started out to create, the current reality is . . . different. Channel surf today, by broadcast, cable, or satellite dish, and here's what you'll likely see. Smooth, sharp, high-tech fishing shows with MTV pacing in which the content is indistinguishable from the commercials. *The BASS Masters*, *In-Fisherman*, *Saltwater Sportsman*. Saturday morning ESPN hunting-and-fishing packages, mostly focused on bass, and linked to the big-money bass tournament culture. Subscribe to satellite dish services or cable, and you can watch whole networks dedicated to fishing and hunting, including The Outdoor Channel and The Outdoor Life Channel, each with twenty-four-hour outdoor programming.

"Who says fishing isn't a spectator sport?" writes Brent Frazee, outdoors editor of the *Kansas City Star.* "Not the thousands of couch potatoes who wake up early each Saturday morning and immediately reach for their television remotes. They live vicariously—at least in the winter—through the casts of television's newest stars, guys who work out of a fishing boat." Jimmy Houston, for example, "a guy with blond, shaggy hair who looks more like one of the Beach Boys than a fisherman." Houston's signature salute is to kiss every largemouth he catches, a full-on buss on the fish lips. The nonconsensual act has caught on among tournament bass anglers. The shows have a southern accent. *"Son! Little bedda fish,"* hollers Roland Martin, every time he lands a bass. Bill Dance draws the kind of fan adoration usually reserved for big-league sports stars or rock stars. Between the cable networks TNN and ESPN, Saturday morning alone has eight half-hour fishing shows. "Add the syndicated shows aired on other networks and Harold Ensley's show on Channel 5," writes Frazee, "and you have enough casting and catching to turn even the most avid fisherman into a zombie." James R. Babb, writing in *Gray's Sporting Journal*, offers this description of Fish-TV:

> Like angling in general, Fish-TV splits into two camps: hardware fishing (mostly for bass) and fly-fishing. The hardware shows rely more on how-to techniques than do fly-fishing shows, which in reaching for atmosphere usually come up with cotton candy. Perhaps this is why the average bass fisherman is better at what he does than is the average fly-fisherman. But most hardware shows take an industrial, Audel's diesel-manual approach to instruction, coldly

conveying ruthlessly efficient ways to fill the stringer as quickly as possible.

The ethical challenges and complications of industrial-strength fishing television illustrate just how far TV fishing has evolved—or, some would say, devolved—from the essentials. To create one half-hour show, it's not unusual for Roland Martin to fish and film for four days, using a "chase boat" to shadow him. Another star, Al Linder, describes hauling a crew thirty-five miles on an old trapper's trail to find a good fishing creek with twenty-pound northerns, and, to prevent camera batteries from freezing, using hand saws to cut branches for a fire on the ice. On that trip, two of the crew of five ended up with frostbite. The suffering pays off. ESPN's top outdoor shows regularly receive the kind of viewer ratings usually earned by an NFL game. Fishing shows earn about thirty million dollars a year for TNN.

Fish-TV is not without critics.

"Actually, no one should have time for these poorly camouflaged 'infomercials,'" writes John Husar, outdoors editor for *The Chicago Tribune*. "Don't believe what you see in most of these things! They are shows, not documentaries. Entertainment, not religious truth. They, for the most part, are paid spots with bought time, like beauty aids and religious programming. Their method is to hustle, hustle, hustle products or certain commercial connections. How many TV fishing shows have you ever seen that promoted live bait? Now ask how many sponsoring tackle manufacturers make and sell live bait." And where are the women? For a while, Dawn Wells, who played Mary Ann on the sitcom *Gilligan's Island*, starred in a little-known fishing and outdoors show. Other women anglers have attempted to move into television, but sponsors for such shows are scarce, despite the increasing commercial power of women in fishing. Critics also object to the staged catching of fish, the fact that some of the stars own private ponds stocked with lunkers used on the shows. Frazee writes, "Go to practically any lake, and you'll find an old-timer who will tell you about the time a TV star came there and tried to borrow fish from others when the going got tough."

Meanwhile, a new generation of TV fishing hosts, perhaps a better one, is emerging. Doug Hannon, ESPN's "The Bass Professor," films "fascinating underwater scenes of game fish," as Babb points out, "beautifully photographed, more like PBS nature documentaries than typical how-to fish videos." Fish Fishburne, thirty, host of the often hilarious syndicated show, *Go Fish*, says he wants "to bring people who don't fish into the show and (have them) say, 'Hey, that looks like it could be really fun.'"

Fishburne joined the professional fishing circuit at eighteen. Rather than relying on the usual sponsorships from big tackle and boat manufacturers, he turned to his grandmother (he calls her Team Grandma), who advanced him money to buy a bass rig and to pay tournament entry fees. On his show, he's as frenetic as Robin Williams. He dances on his boat, screams, laughs hysterically, catches fish on multiple rods, spreads cheese on his body for sunscreen, and, to make his catches seem bigger, holds a magnifying glass to them. He had his name legally changed from Claude to Fish. Some of his shows border on surreal performance art. On one program, dedicated to what he called "ladder fishing," Fishburne sat on a folding ladder in the middle of a pond; his father sat on another ladder a few feet away. And both men caught fish.

"There is a misconception about fishing. It has always been perceived as a good-ol'-boy, redneck, chewing-tobacco, beer-drinking sport. We are trying to change that image. We are also trying to incorporate family values into the show, so it's not just perceived as an individual sport. Mom, Dad, and the kids can go and have a good time," says Fishburne.

What an irreverent concept. Fishing should be fun—not zen (necessarily), not competition (necessarily). Fun. As I watch most of the other fishing shows, however, I'm struck by how far they've drifted from that essential innocence—and the personal intimacy of Harold Ensley's time. But haven't we all?

⤷ ONE HUNDRED AND TEN miles from Harold's home, we approached the dam at Truman Reservoir, a sixty-thousand-acre impound about the same size as the Lake of the Ozarks, the first lake in this cluster of inland seas.

"It's pretty windy up here," said Harold. He looked a little worried. "I've seen the time when there would be five hundred fishermen right along the bank here on both sides, and 120 boats. I would say they took two hundred thousand crappie out of here last spring. Isn't that beautiful along there? The Corps of Engineers is responsible for the greatness of fishing in the Midwest. Most of the outdoor writers fought it, environmentalists fought it, and it cost the taxpayers millions of dollars. But it was a great thing."

Harold started pushing for catch-and-release, for bass, years before it was popular. "I saw the writing on the wall. If we didn't return the fish then we wouldn't have any fish." He now argues for barbless hooks—for all anglers, not only fly-fishers, who already lean in that direction. "Single barbless hooks. Treble hooks kill too many fish. And the people that make those hooks aren't going to like me for saying that."

I asked him about his earliest years fishing.

We lived north of Dodge City. I was born on a cattle ranch. My dad didn't fish, my mom didn't fish. We had a little creek right through our ranch. We had a working ranch, bunkhouse, riders, the whole bit. I learned to ride before I learned how to walk. I caught little bullheads. Once in a while maybe I'd luck into a chub. Then when I got a little older and could walk a little farther, my brother and I found some spring-fed ponds, a creek really, but there were spring-fed holes that were maybe eight, ten feet deep. We'd get up early in the morning and milk cows and then help dad get the horses ready and he'd go out in the field working. My brother and I, we'd walk barefooted about two miles up to this place, catch grasshoppers for bait. Oh, we caught some nice bullheads. I've never been anywhere where I haven't caught fish. Nobody showed me anything either, in most cases. Learned by trial and error. I started out with a willow pole, any kind of string I could get, and I made my own hooks. Copper wire that held the ingredients tag on a bag of the seed cake that my dad fed to the cattle. I couldn't put a barb on it, so if I got a big fish I'd have to drag him up the bank. If it was a little fish I tossed him over my head.

"So you started out with a barbless hook," I said.
"That's right."
"You're coming full circle."
"I hadn't thought about that. That was a long time ago."
He pulled away from the dam, the gravel crunching under the tires. "I'm sure that God gave me some natural ability both on the end of a fishing pole and in front of the camera. I think the good fishermen are born with a natural talent, like baseball players or musicians—I know that to be a fact. I can just tell by the people I deal with."
He drove to the marina and we sat in the car looking out beyond the dock to the choppy water.
"It's going to be touch and go. The doctors don't want me out on rough water," he said. His back was hurting. He glared at the water.
"If we go out there today, we're going crappie fishing," he said. He turned to me. "If you'd insisted on goin' bass fishing today, I wouldn't have taken you."
"Why's that, Harold?" I asked.
Well, he said, he finds bass fishing a little boring these days.
"Why do you like crappie fishing?" I asked him.
"'Cause I find crappie *intriguing!*" he exclaimed, leaning toward me,

his eyebrows shooting up. The way he said it made crappie seem like angling's Holy Grail.*

We got out of his station wagon, pulled out his rods and gear, and walked down to the dock, to a tackle shop under the eaves.

Inside, the walls were coated with Polaroid shots of hefted dreams— channel cats, bass, crappie, even a hyperbolic bluegill or two—most of them held out toward the camera for proper visual inflation. The shelves and racks were filled with PowerBait Power Shiners and "neonz" Powerworms and Buddha Baits Popfires and Heddon Zara Spooks and spoons and snakes and Shad Raps and little Rattle Traps and a rainbow of jigs.

The owner of the marina shop, Marty Zych, was standing behind the counter. The bait shop came to life when Harold entered, and Harold knew it. Ball caps floated behind the racks and came our way.

"I want to tell you about this guy," exclaimed Harold to Marty, pointing at me. "He asked me, 'What's your favorite fish?' And I said, 'Crappie.'"

"He probably thought you were going to say bass or walleye or something," said Marty, conspiratorially.

"So is crappie your favorite fish, too?" I asked Marty.

"Oh, God, yeah, that's all I do. Tommy, hell, he used to work the circuit," said Marty, pointing to one of the approaching ball caps. "And Murphy over here guided. They're all tournament bass fishers, or they used to be. Murphy, when was the last time you bass fished?"

"Two years ago with Ricky."

"I've got two friends, big bass tournament fishers, and neither one of them pick up a bass rod anymore," said Harold, leaning on the counter. "And you know, I saw this press release for some new book and it said there are more bass fishermen in the United States than all the other sport fishermen combined. And that's a *lie*. They didn't ask you, did they, Marty? They didn't ask me."

"That sounds like one of them political polls," said one of the ball caps.

"Go down south, go down there for a month and see how many guys are bass fishing and how many down in Green Bay, Mississippi," said another cap. They were moving in closer. "Look how many people are crappie fishing in the summer and spring."

---

*Ken Schultz offers linguistic advice. "Crappie are like that Chinese dog called a Shih Tzu. Most people don't say the name of that dog in a way that comes out very flattering. Ditto for the poor crappie, which, if it was pronounced by more folks as if it had the letter 'o' instead of 'a,' as in 'crop,' we would all be better off." Ken Schultz, *The Ultimate Book of Freshwater Fishing* (Indianapolis: Master Press, 1997), p. 20.

"I told him I'd guess fifteen to twenty thousand on the weekend here, just crappie fishing," said Harold.

So maybe this crappie thing is a bit of a rebellion against industrial-strength sportfishing, or an alternative to all this talk of catch-and-release. No problem taking out a bucket of crappie, they're so oversexed and prolific.

I said to the men, "I'm having trouble getting a complete answer from Harold about why crappie—what's the mystique of crappie? At first he said crappie are smarter than trout, then he retracted that."

One of the caps, not sure if was Tommy or Murphy, nodded slowly. "I tell you what, big crappie are pretty cunning."

"I caught a two-pounder Tuesday, that's a good fish," said Murphy or Tommy.

"Why *crappie?* What's the mystique?" I repeated. "They're cunning?"

"Hottest months of the year you could catch two hundred fish a day," one of the men said. Maybe they all said it at once; hard to tell. "You can't do that with any other fish. The best part is, the hotter it gets out here the better the crappie fishing is."

I gave up on the crappie mystique. Marty and Tommy and Murphy spent the next twenty minutes talking about how bad the fishing was to-day, how the lake had turned over, pulling all the muck up from below, how the wind had blown them all off the lake. No way anyone's going to catch anything today, they said.

"Well now I'm going to find out if you're the real Harold Ensley, or an imposter," I said.

Harold grinned, lifted his chin. The caps snorted. A snort of admiration. And he and I headed out of the bait shop.

↩ WE GOT DOWN to the dock area, where his bass boat is stored, and pulled off the tarp. He assigned me to unlock the holds and when I turned around he was on the dock, scurrying around like an agitated crab. He had his rod out and rigged already! He was moving quickly from slip to slip, dropping a little plastic jig into the water, staring in-tently—and grinning, oblivious. I watched him with awe. We hadn't even gone out in the boat yet, and he couldn't wait. He just *had* to get his line in the water.

I knew that feeling. It doesn't matter how tired I am, when I get near a lake, I just want to get on that water. The only difference was that Harold stopped and talked to everybody; he just loved talking. Unlike many anglers, he likes people as much as he likes fish. He's out to catch both.

And damned if he wasn't already getting bites.

"Crappie," he said, his teeth flashing.

After a few minutes he handed me the rod and walked, with some difficulty, back up the ramp. "Forgot the life jackets. You try."

I waited until he was gone and stepped over to where he had been having his bites. Two minutes later I jerked a silver and black speckled crappie out of the water. I laughed out loud. All these years later, I caught Harold Ensley's fish!

We scooted out on the water. His boat was moderately powerful, seventy horsepower, as I recall. Harold likes his gear, but he doesn't get all smarmy over it. An electronic fish finder is important in today's fishing, he says, especially in the big lakes, but you can outsmart yourself with it, locating catfish when you really want bass—or bass when you're after crappie. A hydrofoil stabilizer, though, that's a must. "Greatest thing in the boating industry that came out in my lifetime!" he yelled over the engine. "Got one on this boat."

His windbreaker was flapping in the wind; he rounded a point and I looked out over the broad water, at the virgin shore, a tangle of tall oaks, mostly without leaves. It was a warm day, despite the wind. He pulled up in a small cove, killed the engine, and hooked us to one of the dead tree branches sticking out of the water. He called it a "stob," a term I had never heard.

He wasted no time. In an instant, his jig was dropping out of sight down along the stob. And he was hunched over, staring intently at the water. I followed his lead, with a "Harold Ensley" rod, carried by Wal-Mart, which he had prerigged.

"So what's this jig called?"

"Puddle Jumper. I didn't invent this; I invented the Reaper."

"Have you ever gotten bored with fishing?" I asked.

"Never. Well, if I was just retired, do nothing but fish, I'd get tired of it."

"Is that right?"

"Yes, but I've got a purpose. I'm testing lures, I'm always testing ways to catch fish."

A bass boat and two fishermen, big guys with ball caps and overflowing bellies, floated nearby. Perhaps they saw "Harold Ensley" written on the side of Harold's boat. They floated closer. And I saw one guy turn to the other and mouth almost silently, "It's Harold Ensley himself."

Harold bantered with them for a while, across the water, about the fishing and the weather. But the two men in the boat never let on that they knew it was Harold. That would somehow not fit the code of the water.

After a while, they pulled away, and Harold went back to focusing on his line, his fingers holding the rod like a fine violin, feeling its tone and timbre. And then he began to elaborate on his nondenominational philosophy of fishing:

> Any fisherman that looks down on another fisherman—we'll say he's a trout fisherman and he looks down on a carp fisherman—to me he's missed the boat. If a guy likes to carp fish, Lord bless him, that's what I want him to do. It doesn't take any more skill to be a good fly fisherman than it does to be a good spin-fisherman. I know that to be a fact, I've done both. But a lot of people, they think, "Well, if he don't catch trout or if he don't fly-fish . . . he just don't know what it's all about."
>
> I was down here one time and a guy called over, a young fella, one of the typical pro bass guys, and he said, "How many keepers you catch?" He didn't recognize me; I was all bundled up and he was too. In fact, I didn't even look up. I said, "Keepers? What are you talking about?" He said, "You know, fifteen-inch bass." I said, "I'm not bass fishing, I'm crappie fishing." He said, "Oh, you're one of those crappie fishermen!" with disdain. And I didn't look up. I just said, "Well, let me tell you something, young fella. It takes more skill to be a good crappie fisherman than it does to be a bass fisherman." And he said, "Well, you've probably never caught any bass in your life."
>
> Out of self-defense, I proceeded to tell him about some of the Hall of Fame bass I've caught, and he went away.

I asked Harold if, after all these years, he thinks there are stages of maturity of an angler, over a lifespan.

"Well, I don't know what you mean by maturity."

"Well, you know the stage where you have to catch everything in sight, or the stage . . ."

"That wouldn't be maturity. That would be *stupid*. I don't want a guy out here counting fish on me."

He stopped talking for a while, and peered at his line, down past the surface. As I watched him, I thought of little Harold with his bent-wire hooks, searching muddy waters for bullheads and chubs. Now, after years on the water, after pioneering the TV fishing show, after all these decades—even now as an old man in his eighties—the magic of fishing has not left him. He leaned over the edge of the boat, smiling slightly, watching the line. Something tugged it.

"You see that?" he said. "You *see* that?"

He was grinning like a fourteen-year-old.

⌒ HAROLD HAD PUT US on some fish. We caught a good number of crappie. After a while I forgot I was supposed to be interviewing him, forgot the distance of age and time between us. Then he turned to me and said I had the touch; he could tell. I swelled up—and right then a crappie hit my jig and I missed the strike. Harold just smiled.

Later, we drove north as the light faded, stopped at a buffet, where he loaded his plate with fried catfish, then we got back in his red Ford station wagon and headed home. We passed a little graveyard, with a tiny, white clapboard church next to it. A single American flag was planted in the middle of the graveyard. And I thought: It's such a beautiful country.

"Right down that road down there is one of the best crappie fishermen I ever met," said Harold. "His daughter had a baby three months ago and she shot herself last week. Left a little three-month-old baby."

We traveled a ways in silence.

"Future is going to be great," he said after a while. "I see these kids who are so nice, so well-mannered, just sweet youngsters interested in fishing. With the Corps of Engineer projects we've got more water than we ever had. People are going to have to take less, share more. But I think the future of America and the future of fishing is great. We've got the best crappie we've ever had in history. The girls are more beautiful, the boys are not." He smiled. "There's probably a little less concentration today on integrity and honesty. But there've been bad people since the beginning of time and there'll be bad people until the Lord closes the door." He said he's glad he's lived so long; he's fished for creek chubs and he's fished with the Apollo astronauts. What more could a Kansas boy want?

By the time he pulled into his driveway, it was after midnight. We unloaded his gear, and he invited me in. "Pardon the bachelor pad," he said. The house was humble, with spare furnishings. The kitchen table was piled with papers. On that table was a big scrapbook filled with pictures from his life and career, including a magazine story from 1960, with photos of Harold Ensley and Harry Truman. The two men looked identical, as if they had been separated at birth. The clipping was signed by Harry Truman, who wrote, "Good luck, Harold, and you better get a guard."

His 1952 Bell & Howell projector still sits on his kitchen counter. He still threads developed film through its sprockets, points the projector toward his kitchen refrigerator, and reviews the films he still shoots for his TV show.

Almost offhandedly he told me how, in 1993, a few weeks after his wife had died, he had sat in the kitchen alone, in the dark, watching the first film they had shot together. Harold had not seen that film in more than four decades, but that night, he watched it hour after hour, rewinding and repeating, watching the same fish leap across the smooth surface of the refrigerator.

I left his house loaded down with bags of plastic baits, which he sent with me for my kids. He'd call me, he said. He had some more stories he wanted to tell me. He stood outside the open garage door as I backed down the driveway. I stuck my head out of the window.

"You're the real Harold Ensley," I said.

He smiled, turned, and walked back inside the house.

Mall Fishing

SOMETIMES A SIMPLE destination is reached by traveling the road of excess. The road now led to one of the Meccas of the new, industrialized, high-tech world of fishing: Bass Pro's Outdoor World.

In the morning, I had picked up a college friend in Kansas City, in a rented Toyota, and headed south, toward Springfield, Missouri. Jewell Scott and I attended journalism school together at the University of Kansas, dated a few times, and became lifetime friends. Jewell is a big wheel in Kansas City, Missouri, director of the Civic Council. As we drove toward the Ozarks, the number of farmhouses, churches and signs advertising country-western acts increased in frequency.

I had invited Jewell along to catch up on old and new times, but I found her perspective on fishing, and later Outdoor World, helpful. A reality check from a native who had stayed native. As a baby-boomer approaching fifty years of age, Jewell is part of that last generation of Americans connected to land and water by the familial strand of farming.

"When we were children, we went to stay with our grandparents on the farm," she was saying. "Our grandfather would get us up at four in the morning and we would go to the pond and we would fish for crappie and bass. The idea was to catch your breakfast. And so we would, by 5:30 or so, have enough for a meal, and we would take it into the farmhouse. Then my grandmother would fry up the fish in cornmeal and we would have that and fried eggs. A typical farm breakfast had to last you, of course, until noon, and through all the chores. But they fished to eat. It wasn't sport.

"It was just a fact of life, that was the way it was," she said. "You have to remember my grandmother came west in the late 1800s with her circuit-riding minister father. My grandfather's family had lived on that farm forever. Everything they ate they raised themselves, whether it was the cattle or the chickens or the eggs or the fish in the pond. There was a rule, though, if you caught a fish that wasn't ready to eat, you put it back in. My grandfather was very strict about that, that you didn't fish a pond to death, you had to conserve it and you had to make sure that you were constantly restocking it and ensuring its continuity."

Jewell, who is single, is as strong and feminist a person as any woman I know. But as we drove, she surprised me. "What you hear in many women's circles is, the way to meet rich men is to get into fly-fishing because you have to be rich to really get into fly-fishing and so that's the place to go, that's the new frontier, that's the new bar," she said.

"What? Is that right? In the *Midwest?*"

"Right in Kansas City. Not a lot of women will tell you that, but when you sit around with a group of women and they're talking about how to meet men, one of the things that often comes up is, 'Well, we could go fly-fishing.' In Kansas City, there are groups of women taking fly-fishing lessons and actually flying out to the Rockies to fish. Whether they meet men, I don't know . . ."

She shrugged.

"Everybody has to have an outlet. It may be sexist, but, you know, that's the way life is. Men go to certain places to meet women, women go to certain places to meet men. That's as old as time."

We passed the signs pointing to the town of Humansville, and then left it behind. We saw a growing number of churches, brick or clapboard, doors shut, insular, as we moved deeper into the real Bible Belt. And more farmhouses, the statelier, Southern kind, and a huge billboard advertising Glen Campbell's show and another for a Japanese fiddler who plays bluegrass. Both appear at Branson, Missouri, ahead, the Vegas of country music and culture.

I wondered if there was something about the sensibility of the men women might meet through fly-fishing—Jewell had not mentioned bass-fishing (though I was to meet women later, the women of Bass'n Gal, who were drawn to that culture, but not to meet men).

"Fly-fishing has a certain romanticism about it. There probably is something about men who fly-fish," she said. "They can be fanatics, which may not be a real positive because they don't have much time for the women. Or it may mean that they're back-to-nature guys, caring and thoughtful and all of those kinds of things. Maybe it's a cultural issue. You know, the good 'ol boys who bass fish . . . and also, people think of fly-fishing as going to exotic places. You hear the stories of people going to faraway places, South American retreats and Canadian retreats."

The next town was Branson, a small community with not much over four thousand residents. Branson has over thirty country music theaters that draw millions of tourists annually. But nothing in Branson, as an individual draw, compares to Bass Pro's Outdoor World.

"Good lord," said Jewell, leaning forward to better see the fishing mall as we passed the worst kind of strip development and came toward one of several large entryways shaped something like . . . crosses. Right in front of us, several pick-ups were converged along with a small Japanese car. Horns honked and fingers flew.

"Not exactly a relaxed setting," said Jewell.

The faux-log buildings of Outdoor World sprawl across vast parking lots; the complex is essentially a giant suburban mall dedicated to fishing, and to a lesser extent hunting. Everywhere, flags fly. American flags, Bass Pro flags. Sparkling, metal-flaked bass boats bracket the entrances like military honor guards. Giant tractor-trailers, one after another after another, pull up to unload new merchandise. Next to them is a motorcoach-only parking area, where charter buses exhale tourists—the motorcoach people, as they're called here—from all over the Midwest. Several were pulling up right now; I could see rows of eager faces behind smoked glass. There's the Outdoor World bank, an ATM center. Across the street is the Outdoor World RV center, more flags whipping in the wind, and across another expanse of parked cars is an Outdoor World Wildlife Creations taxidermy. Midday on Sunday it was almost impossible to find a place to park. I cruised the aisles for a while.

"Iowa, Ohio, Arkansas, Oklahoma, Texas," said Jewell.

"What?"

"License plates." Minnesota, Alabama, Kansas, New Mexico, South Dakota, Arkansas, Wisconsin, Florida, Illinois, Mississippi. And more. This was just down one row of cars.

We finally found a parking spot and walked inside: One route led to the retail outlet, the other to a fish and wildlife museum. Above the milling crowd was a sign that said, "Welcome to Outdoor World's great sporting goods store." We walked past stuffed but welcoming elk, opossums, raccoons. Another sign announced, "More outdoors for your money." This place was so big you needed a map, and in fact a rack of maps was available.

"What, no compasses?" said Jewell.

We trekked deeper, hiked through thickets of jostling elbows, past a stuffed black bear pointing onward with lifted paw, and stopped briefly at an indoor trout pond. Stuffed geese hung on monofilament line over the water. Kids lined a limestone wall around it, looking down into the water at the speckles of pennies, quarters, nickels, and dimes—and at rainbow trout and a solitary bass hugging the bottom. A boy of about eight reached in and picked up a turtle and took it out and looked at it. He put it on a log.

We walked on. Ahead was a wall-sized aquarium with bass, pike, a big blue catfish, a four-foot gar with vicious-looking teeth, and what I thought at first must be some kind of deep-sea fish, but it was a forty- or fifty-pound carp. Forget political correctness—from one wall hung the stuffed heads of African deer, a hippo, a rhino, and big-horned sheep. And as we came out into the center of the mall, I looked up and caught my breath. From three stories above us, a waterfall shot out over fake limestone, past a huge moose head, burst forward and then down, down, down into a pool twenty or thirty feet deep.

"Look at the size of that! Look at that!" I said to Jewell.

We stood there smiling, first at the waterfall and then down at the green and emerald depths of the clear pool: lunker bass and channel catfish cruised below. And crappie, too—that higher life form.

We walked upstairs along the edge of the waterfall. On a ledge above the water, there was a Missouri snake exhibit leading into a McDonald's. Pilot blacksnakes, copperheads, eastern garters, red-sided garters, Great Plains ratsnakes, western mud snake, eastern hognose, prairie kingsnake, eastern coachwhip, northern watersnake, midland watersnake, western ribbon snake, western fox snake. The McDonald's had seats all along the edge so you could look down into the pool. And above all this, high up on an overhanging branch of fall foliage, was a facsimile of a bald eagle.

We stood on the ledge, leaned on a railing, and watched it all: 175,000 square feet of retail therapy. This is terrific marketing, I thought. Watching those fish certainly makes you want to rush out into the aisles to buy Fishin' Buddy III fish finders, Bone-Dry Titanium Neoprene Waders, or a Deluxe Butt-Seat that's "concave shaped for comfort." Or at least a new rod and reel and a Bayou Boogie to crank through that pool. We stood there and surveyed the great lake of rods and glass cases and arcing bass replicas and churning ball caps and families with carts loaded with small children and new still-in-the-plastic gear, surrounded by grinning wild teeth and upheld paws.

"I admit it. I've got the fever," I said.

Jewell giggled. "I do too." She covered her mouth with her hand.

⤺ IF HAROLD ENSLEY is the recent past, this could be the future of fishing, and for many, it's the present. Harold Ensley represents a more personal era, or at least a smaller one, when fishing was a self-manufactured sport; this is high-energy packaging, brilliant merchandising, nature as theme park.

One term retailers are using for this approach is "reality merchandising." Another is "shoppertainment." Whichever, it's revolutionizing the way Americans spend whatever leisure time they have left. Anne Moore, a reporter for *Crain's Chicago Business*, writes: "While some retailers, such as software merchandiser Egghead Inc., are leaving the street and moving onto the Internet, an increasing number of Chicago-area merchants are outfitting stores and showrooms so shoppers can touch, feel, try—and even shoot—before buying. In these extravagant emporiums, ambiance is everything." Moore quotes J'Amy Owens, president of Retail Group Inc., a Seattle consultancy. "There's a new humanism coming to retailing; these businesses deliver something more than goods. It's the cost of doing business now. Retailers have to do more than entertain."

Another way to look at it is that reality, and nature, are slowly slipping into the almost purely virtual, and reality shopping is just a rest stop on the Information Superhighway. Or at least Interstate 44.

↬ BASS PRO'S OUTDOOR World is the world's largest sporting goods store, according to Nonna Woods of the Missouri Division of Tourism, and the number-one tourist attraction in Missouri. It beats Branson, the Gateway Arch, and the St. Louis Cardinals as a tourist magnet. It has massive freshwater and saltwater aquariums, a daily fish-feeding by a diver, the four-story waterfall, an indoor log cabin with a water wheel, and even has its own barbershop. It sells more than thirty thousand items, from $9.95 Crappie caps to $23,995 packages of Tracker boats, motors, and trailers—and, of course, retail therapy. More fishing malls are planned. Michigan economic development and tourism officials predict people will travel from several states and at least one Canadian province to see the 135,000-square-foot Outdoor World being built there. Cabela's, Bass Pro's competitor, headquartered in Nebraska, is planning a similar complex. Maybe even bigger.

We sat down at the McDonald's for a while with Gary Jones, a group sales manager. Balding, forty-five, lanky, with gold-rimmed glasses and an easy smile, he talked about how working here had become his passion, since leaving teaching. He grew up in St. Louis, came to Springfield to attend college in '69, then taught school. I asked him why he left college teaching to work at Bass Pro.

"I love the students. I just became disillusioned with all the politics. So I took the summer off. I was in here one day, talking to a friend who works here. He told me it was the greatest place in the world to work. So I started in '84.

"And it is the greatest place. For the people who come here, it really is like a journey to Mecca. It's destination shopping. A lot of people take their vacations and come here; everything is geared around a trip to Bass Pro."

And not a hook touches the water?

"Nope. But that's okay. I always look at it like this: If I'm working up front with a cashier, I always remember that people are spending money to have fun. When you go to the grocery store and the cashier hits the total and it's one hundred and ten dollars, you don't usually say, 'Oh, goodie, this is really great!' But here, you do. The cashier says it'll be three hundred dollars and the customer will say, 'Oh, I got by cheap this time!' They enjoy spending money because it's going to give them enjoyment in return. I think that's what's neat about the industry that we're in.

"We're expanding soon," he said. "We'll have three hundred thousand square feet then, and that strip mall you saw driving in here, well, we'll be replacing that."

Undoubtedly, Outdoor World is beneficial to the region's economy, but I wondered how many Mom and Pop bait and tackle stores Bass Pro had put out of business, not only in Springfield, but across the country, because of its aggressive mail-order business. Ironically, the milieu of these bait shops—ones like Strouds'—along with the actual waters of fishing, is exactly what Outdoor World has attempted to copy.

"I don't know how many of those shops existed in this town before Outdoor World," said Jones. "This company found a niche and it just expanded." Just like when Wal-Mart moves in, I thought: Goodbye to the small Main Street businesses, whose spirit Wal-Mart attempts to emulate. "I mean, there's still a bait shop down by the lake and our customers use it when they've forgotten to buy something here."

Do you fish more or less than when you first came here?

"I fish less."

Why is that?

"Time. I have six acres at home so if I'm not here then I'm cutting grass or cutting trees. But I try to get out during the spring, maybe a couple of times."

Looking down from the balcony at all the faces, I told them they seemed different from the faces one customarily sees in a mall.

"Yes, yes, yes, they're here to have fun. I've been here for twelve years and it is just . . . I've always described it as 'It's been quite a ride.' It's been an A-ride in Disneyworld because it's just a happy place."

I asked him why Outdoor World has a barbershop.

"It's part of being a one-stop destination. The barbershop services a lot of fishermen, a lot of vacationers who like to zip up and get a haircut real quick."

The motorcoach people.

"Yes, we have motorcoaches. Part of being a destination."

Mainly retirees?

"That is correct. They have a fun time in here, they really do. They really enjoy it and we enjoy them. They're always in here looking for something unique for the grandson, that little souvenir to take back. I had a woman in this morning, and she said, 'I've got an hour and I have fourteen grandsons and they all like to fish. I need something for them. They almost all walleye fish. How about a lure?' So I took her to the Land of the Walleye."

"You have a place called that?" said Jewell, raising her eyebrow.

"Yes we do," he said proudly. "Three entire aisles of nothing but wall-eye gear."

He looked around. The crowd seemed to be swelling suddenly, moving in waves in a single direction. "This is usually the time of the exodus. We really get hit hard from around three to five, people starting to head home, back to Kansas City." I was dying to ask a final question.

"Have you ever let anybody fish for the fish in the pools here?"

"No, no we haven't. There's no fishing: We have signs."

"Has anybody ever tried?"

"No, no. Well, I'm not sure, I don't know what the cleaning crew does at night."

"Imagine, poaching at Outdoor World," said Jewell, and Jones laughed, but not too hard.

Just then, Jones was pulled away by his walkie-talkie to what he called a "customer opportunity."

↩ AS JEWELL AND I headed off on our own again, I began to understand that Bass Pro is something of a church, in the southern-midwestern branch of the religion of fishing. The Southern Bassist Convention. Our Lady of Abu Garcia. If the spectacle of the place was a bit much, a bit removed from the actual experience of fishing, well then so it often is with brick-and-mortar spiritual temples.

Along one wall, near the McDonald's entrance, was a display of relics: old photographs from the '40s or '50s, including one of Dwight Eisenhower next to a fisherman holding a long stringer of bass. Such stringers used to be the central totem of fishing. You never see stringers anymore

in the catalogs and fishing magazines, not since catch-and-release became the custom. Near the photos was a case holding antique fishing
paraphernalia: reels and plugs, Barracuda Split-Shot Sinkers from long
ago. A Jointed Pikie Minnow from the Creek Chub Bait Company.
Pflueger Reels. An Outdoor America catalog, from February 1928. And
a framed letter from Jim M. Owen, describing preparation for a float trip
down one of those now-dammed rivers.

Down one aisle, we passed two over-six-foot good 'ol boys wearing
white tee shirts, camouflage pants, camouflage-pattern ball caps. They
looked like they had been out on the lake for just about forever, but
there they were buying New Age nature sound tapes. And then I met
Armend Perres, a stout fellow wearing aviator glasses, jeans, a ball cap
festooned with metal and plastic pins commemorating the long-distance
trucking business. A ponytail flowed down his back, and he had a full
beard with a stripe of gray down the middle. He was carrying a shopping
basket filled with lures and line and other gear, and he was holding a new
fishing rod in his other hand, upright. We heard his testimony.

"I'm from New Hampshire, a little town called Swanzey. Actually,
there are a lot of parallels between the Ozarks here and where I'm from.
It's largely rural, which is like this is. The hunting, the fishing, pretty
much the same deal. I've got a tractor-trailer and I've got a delivery here
Monday anyways, so we've got the whole day. I don't got anyplace to go
until 1:30 tomorrow."

He grinned happily. He held up the basket to show me the goods.
"Scoop your buds. That's what you do here. You get the new stuff before
your buds can get it delivered from the catalog."

I told him I'd wondered about all those tractor-trailers out there. In
addition to the ones unloading sporting goods, there had been a whole
row of rigs parked together.

"Some of the guys are like me," he said. "I stop here when I'm coming
through, providing I've got enough time, because I'm with a whole
bunch of other people that fish. So it's like, 'Wow!' This is one of my
places to hang out, you know? It is just like an oasis for me."

So is this the ultimate truck stop?

Well, I vary between this place and another one in Nebraska
called Cabela's. This is like, "Hey, let's hang out! Look at all this cool
fish stuff!" You know? Stuff I really don't need but it's like, 'Wow,
I've got one of these *now*!' A lot of guys do this. Like to decompress.
I park the truck and it'll be there when I get back, I don't worry
about it, I park it out there, I come in here, I do my thing in here.
It's the next best thing to actually going fishing.

ARMEND PERRES

    I drive forty-eight states. I carry a fishing rod around in my truck. I know of at least a half a dozen other people that carry fishing rods in their trucks just out of my company. There's times when I get a chance to fish. I've got a couple places where I've got friends and they'll go, "Hey. when you're in town, call me." Or I'll just stop some place. Lot of times I've got to go deliver something, but I can't deliver until maybe the following day and I'll pull in maybe nine o'clock in the morning and there might be a small stream or a small pond. I'll go find a bait shop and the bait shop'll sell me a license.

The tough part is finding a place to park the truck. I've got fishing licenses right now in five states. I've got a sixty-five-foot-long vehicle, a fifty-three-foot trailer plus a big tractor. But most of the time I'm under schedule, I'm under the hammer. I got to get going, I've got three hundred miles to go and six hours to do it. Doesn't really give me a whole lot of extra time. I might get to actually go fishing once a month. I train new drivers, so I got extra responsibilities. People go, "How do you stand being away from home?" This is it. [Motioning with his hand around the fishing mall.] This is how I stand it.

Oh, and there's one other way he copes with the stress. I asked him if he ever drives over a bridge and looks down at a stream or a river or passes the arm of a lake and he just can't stand not stopping—and pulls that big rig over and grabs his rod and jumps out and goes fishing.

"I troll," he said, laughing. He mimed leaning back in a truck seat, his eyes closed in reverie, hands settled on his belly and fingers interlaced as if he were holding a fishing rod. "My trainees are driving and I'm trolling. My trainee'll look over at me and say, 'What're you doing?' And I'll just smile and say, 'I'm trolling.'

"Here's how you do it. You just pretend you've got a rod stuck out the window. Catch a big ol' catfish or bass. The other guys say, like, 'This guy's going around the bend!' And I say, 'No, I'm fishing, man, I'm on vacation in my mind. If I can't do it, I might as well imagine it.'"

It was hard to tell how old he was. "I'm forty-four. I've been doing this, well I got my license in '76, so I'm going on twenty years, off and on. I've got a mechanical engineering degree, but I hate working in the office. Basically, with a lot of engineering, you wind up in an office, you wind up bored. My degree's so old anyway that I'd have to go back to school. I like the truck." And truck trolling.

⤙ JEWELL AND I wandered on. We paused, with some degree of reverence and confusion, in front of the ultimate Outdoor World relic: the "World-Famous Ethel."

She was displayed like a dead pope, or Lenin in the tomb. She floated, suspended in time, in the air of a glass case. A plaque revealed that Ethel lived from 1975 to 1994.

> Ethel was known throughout the world as the largest large-mouth bass in captivity. She was caught November 26, 1986, in Lake Fork, Texas, by Mark Stevenson from Plano, Texas. At that time she was a Texas state record at 17 pounds, 10.6 ounces and was 11 and a half years old. Ethel came to the Bass Pro shop Outdoor World on May 5, 1987, where she grew to over 20 pounds, was 32 inches in girth and 28 inches in length. She was a star of the daily fish feeding show and was featured in millions of bass pro catalogs. She passed away at age 19, more than twice her normal life expectancy, due to natural causes.

⤷ WE WERE NEARING closing time. But several Outdoor World powers-that-be had suggested I talk to Terry Tanner before I left. Tanner, they said, fishes with George Bush. Tanner, they added, was one of the most knowledgeable people in the country on the cultural spread of fly-fishing into the domain of the bass, and was steeped in the cultural lore of the Ozarks.

Tall, handsome, part Cherokee (and unlike half the population of these parts, who claim to be part Cherokee, looks it), Tanner is Bass Pro's "lead sales associate" at the Outdoor World White River fly shop, and in charge of fly-fishing catalog sales. Fly-fishing is Bass Pro's fastest-growing market. Jewell and I spent an hour with him. She said later that he seemed to have emerged whole from the land of this region. I asked him about his background.

His father's family owned the first general store in Jefferson City. His mother's side is Cherokee and her great-grandmother traveled the Trail of Tears to Oklahoma and managed to break away in Monett, Missouri. In 1945, his family moved from Jefferson City to the small town of Ava, Missouri, which later was the county seat of Douglas County. But when Tanner was growing up, Ava still had board sidewalks, gravel streets. In those days, he learned the language of the hills, of the isolated descendants of Irish and English homesteaders, with its idioms: *spar* for sparrow; *nar* for narrow; *crick* for creek; *wasper* for wasp.

"You'll stumble onto some waspers. That's the way they talked, and some still do. You can imagine an English teacher's problem trying to teach these kids how to talk, if they could get them to school. I remember in the first grade, some of the mothers were so protective of those kids, bringing them into the schools, they would stand outside the windows to watch and see what's going on, what they were doing in there. They brought in food for them, 'I brought my son a bottle of this sody water here.'"

Tanner's father worked for the state highway department, but many of the people of the Ozarks moved away, unable to make a living from the land; many went to California to work as migrant laborers, leaving their homesteads behind. "When the state came in to try to find a place to run the highways, there were no property owners, they didn't even have ownership! So the state just assumed it." The same was true when the Army Corps of Engineers built the dams of the great lakes: The water flooded thousands of ghost farms. "Back in those days, down through here, land sold from $2.50 to $5.00 an acre. Anybody with any kind of foresight or imagination should've bought it all because it's worth so much now to the retirees moving down. I often remember talking to Dad, saying, 'Dad, why didn't we buy a couple thousand dollars worth of that land down there?' He said, 'Son, because I didn't have a couple thousand back then.'"

Much of the fishing of his childhood environment was, indeed, primitive. Tanner is sure some people still set fish traps, as locals did when he was a boy, though it's illegal. "Some people did it because they needed something to eat. They made the traps out of slats. The trap could be anywhere from very small, maybe three, four, or five feet long, all the way up to fifteen feet, on some of the bigger rivers. Called them fish baskets."

The most interesting types of fishing that he recalls from this earlier culture are sucker-grabbing and noodling.

> Sucker-grabbing was quite a thing. Suckers are essentially huge minnows, a bottom-feeding fish similar to carp. This kind of fishing, during the spring sucker run, involved a rod and a reel, the old bait-casting reels, and they would tie on a huge treble hook. They'd usually cut the bottom point off so that the hook would ride upward in the water. They would tie a piece of white rag up about two and a half feet in front of it. Cast it out and a bunch of suckers come up, and the men would watch and when one would pass where his nose was just coming to the white mark, the men would know that that was the place to set the hook. Suckers' instinct is to go like *this* [nose up], so the fisherman would pull up and hook the sucker in the back of its body. You can still get down in these hills and find people who grab suckers. Fish up to eight pounds or so. The sucker fishermen even climbed up trees so they could see better, or if it was a place where there was a tree or canopy over the creek, they

set up an old stepladder and got up on top and fish from up there. That was before Polaroid sunglasses. Of course, even nowadays they'll have those on, too, and climb the trees. They still do it. The town of Nixa, Missouri, believe it or not, has a sucker festival, and it's a three-day event.

Monster catfish were and still are caught by hand—or "noodled." Noodling is the odd and old practice of spring wading in muddy river or creek waters, feeling under the banks for the holes where big catfish lodge themselves, feeling for their bellies and stroking them to relax them, then feeling for their gills and yanking them out of the holes, their spikes slashing. Sometimes men wrestle eighty- and one-hundred-pound catfish this way, and they have the finger stumps to prove it: Snapping turtles also live in those holes. "When I was a kid, that was done quite frequently. It was kind of dangerous, but the guys who did it, and some men still do it, are amazing. I've heard of guys getting their hand and then their arm through the gill, and it's quite a wrestling match. It's something that I would never care about doing."

In a wonderful description of this peculiar way of fishing, Burkhard Bilger writes:

> The origins of noodling are difficult to imagine, much less prove. In North America archeologists have found fishhooks made of bone, weirs of wood and stone, and perforated shells for sinking nets. But noodling leaves no traces; it is as ephemeral as some of the boasts it inspires. Native Americans, by all historical accounts, had a peculiar genius for killing fish. Hernando De Soto's men, trudging through swamps in search of El Dorado, saw lines of Indians splashing in pools, scaring up fish and whacking their heads 'with blows of cudgels.' The ethnographer John Swanton collected accounts of southeastern Indians lassoing sturgeon by the tail and drugging fish with buckeye and devil's shoestring. Others mention Indians attracting fish with torches, harpooning them with lengths of cane, and shooting them with arrows. In 1775 a trader-historian named James Adair first described 'a surprising method of fishing under the edges of rocks' among southern Indians: 'They pull off their red breeches, or their long slip of Stroud cloth, and wrapping it round their arm, so as to reach to the lower part of the palm of their right hand, they dive under the rock where the cat-fish lie to shelter themselves from the scorching beams of the sun, and to watch for prey: as soon as those fierce aquatic animals see that tempting bait, they immediately seize it with the greatest violence, in order to swallow it.

Then is the time for the diver to improve the favourable opportunity: he accordingly opens his hand, seizes the voracious fish by his tender parts, hath a sharp struggle with it against the crevices of the rock, and at last brings it safe ashore."

So, said Tanner, the fishing cultures of the Ozarks had moved from sucker-grabbing and noodling to the technological marvels of tournament bass fishing. And now it was turning over again, in a way. There was, he said, something personal and up front about hovering in a tree and dangling a line down to a sucker, or going hand-to-spike with a hundred-pound flathead catfish. Primitive perhaps. Older. But then, so is fly-fishing. Despite its evolved intricacies, fly-fishing just seems . . . closer . . . to the fish, full of ancient intimacies. That's how Tanner sees it.

One thing that people don't realize about the Midwest, he added, is that "in any direction from the Springfield area, you can go north, south, east or west within about an hour and a half and be in trout waters." Indeed, that's true: Missouri and Arkansas boast little-known but fine rainbow and brown troutwaters, including tail-water fisheries below the dams on the White River, the Norfork River, the Little Red River. Cold water from the depths flows out behind the dams, and the big trout thrive. "They get huge," said Tanner. "One floated up dead the other day, a thirty-eight-pound fish. A couple of years ago, a guide friend of mine caught one on a flyrod, using a salmon fly, weighed nineteen pounds, eight ounces.

"The Ozarks is one of the few areas where we still have relatively clean air, relatively clean water. People, a lot of them retirees, are coming back. I've met people just in California and I talk about night fishing and they say, 'What do you mean, night fishing? You go out after dark? We don't go out after dark where we live.' They go out after dark here."

⌁ HEADING BACK TO Kansas City, Jewell and I admired this gracious land. We traveled under low clouds, watched the narrowing brim of golden light beneath their rim, the setting sun coming through now and then. And the rolling hills and the open fields between the woods, and the farm ponds perfectly still and gold, and the convenience stops that have been here for years, with their predictable racks of fishing lures and canisters of blood bait, stink bait, cheese bait, some made locally.

"I can't help but think about what a far cry Outdoor World was from sitting on the bank of my grandfather's pond with a bamboo pole and a hook and a worm, fishing for breakfast," said Jewell.

We could see the bales of hay, the threads of limestone, the old farmhouses, too small for their white, Southern colonnades. Jewell said it's strange to think that in some of these houses, owners of slaves once lived. Lightning dropped from a sky full of slanted light and lit the waters ahead.

"You know what the most amazing image at Outdoor World was for me?" said Jewell.

"What?"

"When the bus people, the seniors with their name tags, poured in, and some of them sat in the boats on the showroom floor. Their hair was so white. They were all staring straight ahead. They weren't talking. You could almost imagine them with their lines in the water, trying to be quiet so they wouldn't scare the fish. It was very important to them, to be there. Right there."

She asked me where my next stop would be.

"I'm going to join a bass tournament."

She smiled and looked out the window. We approached a bridge crossing. The sign identified the river as the Osage River. It was wide, brown, and languid, with little sucking roils. I did some truck trolling, but I kept my eyes open. On our right, a rainbow arched into a distant field, and large drops of rain began to bang the windshield.

The Contender

〜ᔛ〜

A᠌ᴛ 3:30 ᴏɴ ᴀ ᴄᴏʟᴅ and rainy May morning, Joe Godar was watching, out of the corner of his eye, "The Hawaiian Tropic," a cable-television parade of big-breasted sportsmodels, as he packed food into an Igloo ice chest.

Godar turned away from the screen and hauled the Igloo down a short flight of stairs to his garage and loaded it into a hatched compartment in his Skeeter, a spotless eighteen-and-a-half-foot black metal-flaked bass boat with a 150-horsepower Merc outboard. He had the look of a man thinking about a distant battle: calm, steady, but not as yet uninterested in "The Hawaiian Tropic."

In the family room his sidekick stirred. Don Wilkymacky, thirty, heaved himself up from under a sheet on the couch waving the remote control. "No *more of this,*" said Wilkymacky, a dark-haired, two-day-bearded photocopier salesman, who had driven the night before from Evansville, Indiana. He lurched across the room in his Jockey shorts and threw on his jeans and shirt, sucked on a cup of coffee that Joe had left on the table for him. Half a cup later, he found the remote control and turned "The Hawaiian Tropic" back on. Well, he said, maybe two for the road.

Godar, thirty-four, a real-estate salesman who lives in Cleves, Ohio, a suburb of Cincinnati, had picked me up the night before at the Greater Cincinnati Airport in Kentucky and we had crossed the great, muddy Ohio River (where Joe had won his first bass tournament). At Anderson Ferry, we crossed by slow ferry from Kentucky. Up and down this stretch of river are historical markers, including ones that designate the Underground Railroad that moved fugitive slaves from Kentucky into Ohio and on to Canada. The farther east you go in America the more history anglers know about their waters, especially their rivers. But Joe's mind was already on fishing. Up the bank of the river we saw a distant figure struggling with a pole. Something splashed a few feet out in the current.

"There it is!" said Joe.

"It's a big one, look at it."

"It's a catfish, see the way it's moving around."

The ferry reached ground, and Joe drove his red Ford Explorer into the free state of Ohio, talking all the while about Zip the Ripper. "Friend of my father's. His nickname is Zip and he's in his mid-sixties. He'll go out and find fish when nobody else can. Most frugal man I know. Had the same boat for thirty-five years until he sank it in Kentucky Lake on a rough day; he finally just beat it to death. He lives off fish. We call him Zip the Ripper because if he sees you with a fish, he'll just take it from you and it's off to the cleaning board. The fish doesn't have a chance."

I slept that night on a basement couch in Joe's immaculate suburban house. He and his wife are quintessential suburban Americans: They went to college, work hard, save a little money, have a few dreams and a mortgage. They own two car phones. Their house contains several radios, a computer and modem, a thirty-two-inch TV in the living room, a rear-projection home entertainment center in the basement rec room, and a third TV in their bedroom. They receive close to a hundred cable channels. They're thinking about getting a satellite dish. A semipro tournament bass angler, Joe harbors the ambition to become a full professional.

He grew up fishing near his family's cabin on Rocky Fork Creek, which winds through the bluffs of southwestern Ohio. Daniel Boone is said to have evaded Indian pursuers by hiding in caves above Rocky Fork. Five miles downstream, the creek connects with Paint Creek, which eventually makes its way to the Ohio River.

That evening, Joe had shown me photos of the fishing cabin in the woods that his family has owned for a century. One grainy black-and-white photograph was of his grandfather in the 1930s or '40s, holding up a string of catfish—the old man's mouth a straight and serious line. Joe also produced photos of himself, handsome and eager, in his semipro uniform: a startlingly red shirt and white ball cap, with patches advertising Skeeter, Lunker Lure, Triple Rattleback Jig, and Flerlage Marine. Also: a flier announcing "Joe Godar, 1994 Red Man Winner on the Ohio River." One win and Joe was already giving fishing seminars. "STOP AND TALK TO JOE! HIS BOAT WILL BE ON DISPLAY FOR ALL TO SEE! Worm Fishing on the Ohio River!"

And now, before dawn, Joe said it was time to go. Wilkymacky clicked off the TV. Time to head north, to the Lake Erie kickoff of the Buckeye Division Red Man Tournament Trail.

꙳ As JOE HAD explained, the typical bass tournament can be small and local, or a large regional or national event. You pay an entry fee that can range from a few dollars to thousands of dollars. Some tournaments, primarily the ones held by local clubs, are buddy tournaments—you and a friend can team up. But the big-money tournaments are match events. The organizers pair you randomly with another angler: One angler who has brought his own boat is matched to an angler without a boat. You launch at sunrise and fish, usually, for eight hours. Your goal is usually to catch five keepers (twelve inches or longer) and bring them back alive. During a tournament you can cull your fish, meaning that if you catch more than five fish, you keep the bigger ones and let the smaller ones go. At the end of the tournament, the anglers bring their fish in, and the angler with the most weight wins. Often, a contender takes first place by only ounces. A prize is also given for the largest individual fish and other categories.

Many anglers compete only occasionally, entering local tournaments. But professional bass anglers follow a circuit, fishing a series of tournaments that can range over many states. Through the season, they accumulate points and pounds to qualify for national events.

However strange this culture may appear to some people, it deserves respect as a surprisingly democratic sport. Anyone can take a chance, even without a boat.

For example, in Texas, for a $100 fee, you can join the KILT FM 100 Bass Tournament, a wild affair that allows "you to fish out of anything that floats"—bass boats, johnboats, pontoon boats. Granted, this contest is structured in an unusual way—it's the angling equivalent of the Oklahoma Gold Rush—but it illustrates how open the culture is to newcomers. As the *Florida Times-Union* reports, the tournament pays ten thousand dollars each hour for the biggest fish; theoretically, an angler could win eighty thousand dollars a day by catching the biggest bass each hour. In 1996, the contest drew more than five thousand anglers—an astonishing number of competitors. Imagine a golf tournament attracting that many duffers.

As with other tournament sports, money is a lure. In four competition days of a Bassmaster Megabucks tournament (conducted by the world's oldest and largest fishing organization, the Bass Anglers Sportsman Society), anglers compete for a half million dollars in prizes—with $70,000 to $100,000 going to the first-place winner. The winner can also collect as much as $1 million in subsequent product endorsements and other residuals. The Red Man All-American awards $100,000 to its winner. Wal-Mart's Forrest Wood Open (named for Arkansas boat builder Forrest L. Wood of Ranger Boats) offers the largest cash prize in fishing history—a $1 million purse, with $200,000 to the top pro and $40,000 to the top amateur. All this for *fish*.

The fuel for the dream is the sponsor, who buys a piece of each of these men and women, who, in exchange for free gear or often paltry subsidies, decal their boats or stitch colorful patches to their shirts and caps to broadcast the virtues of Ranger Boats, Evinrude Outboards, Chevrolet Trucks, Delco Voyager Batteries, Lowrance and Eagle Electronics, Wrangler Rugged Wear, MotorGuide Trolling Motors, Flowmaster Exhaust Systems, Plano lures and tackle—and all the rest.

Bass-fishing is becoming a major spectator sport. Tens of thousands of fans attend weigh-ins at the major, end-of-the-season tournaments. Twenty-eight thousand spectators watched the final-day weigh-in at the 1996 B.A.S.S. Masters Classic, in Greensboro, North Carolina. The audiences don't end there: The pro bass angler's most ambitious dream, which Joe Godar admits to, is to someday have one's own TV fishing show. But the burgeoning fishing seminar business—the stars are top- and middle-level pros—is the next-best thing to life on the tube. Brent Frazee, outdoors editor for the *Kansas City Star*, describes tournament bass fishing as one of the few sports where people can get close to their heroes. "The popularity of the fishing seminars is somewhat a new phenomenon. Less than 20 years ago, a few local experts would get up on the stage at a sports show and maybe attract a small group of curious fishermen. But today the experts are national names—made famous by the BASS tournament circuit and television—and the crowds are huge."

Competition bass-fishing shows no sign of losing its growth curve, even internationally. Angler Toshinari Namiki, from Japan, fished 1997's B.A.S.S. Masters Classic.* "Tournament fishing is promotionally in its infancy. You could say we are where NASCAR [the auto racing circuit] was several years ago," Erwin Jacobs, owner of Ranger Boats and chairman of the Wal-Mart FLW Tour, told the *Arkansas Democrat-Gazette* in 1997.

---

*Like baseball, bass-fishing and bass tournaments have jumped the Pacific. In November 1995, the Japan Bass Classic fishing tournament drew twenty thousand people—and a professor at the Tokyo University of Agriculture offers this recipe for the newly popular black bass: Put a whole bass through a mixer, ferment it with the same kind of malt used to produce katsuobushi (dried bonito flakes), deodorize." The recipe is not likely to catch on in Atlanta. Miyuki Nakajima, "Anglers, Fish Industry Tangle over Bass." *Mainichi Daily News*, November 27, 1996, p. 20.

Jacobs was known as "Irv the Liquidator" on Wall Street in the late 1970s when, in his past life, according to *USA Today*, he "sent chills through corporate board rooms at takeover targets such as Walt Disney and Kaiser Steel." Jacobs believes he has the formula to bring even more prominence and spectators to what is already the nation's largest participation sport: a television deal with cable networks that exposes pro anglers—and their sponsors—to an audience of 60 million anglers nationwide. "In five years you can expect to look at your TV and see a woman up there in the top five. You're going to see a high-profile pro-am with big celebrities and a name charity," he told the *Democrat-Gazette*. "Fishing is non-discriminatory. Anyone any age can do it. And we're going to do this in record time. This thing has a life of its own."

Competition anglers do not become champions easily or cheaply. They spend grueling months working the circuit, living in motels, driving their $70,000 to $100,000 rigs (four-wheel-drive vehicle and boat) in zigzagging patterns around the United States, lake to lake, river to river, watching the weather, building their scores, hoping against hope for that one sweet hawg to rise from beneath a lily pad or submerged log—that fattened, spawning, grub-inhaling million-dollar dream of a fish. It's out there. It must be.

Tournament bass-fishing is among the most American of sports—maybe the most American, because it was created purely in America, with no detectable influence from beyond our borders. And it *is* a sport (not a lottery): It takes luck, yes, but skill too—a knowledge perhaps as intricate as that required in fly-fishing: a mental cataloging of hundreds of plastic worm patterns in green pumpkin, watermelon, June bug, and sour grape; of jigs with soft plastic trailers, spinnerbaits, diving imitations of shad, crippled-minnow stick lures, and soft plastic jerk baits; of outboard maintenance; of the lunar tables. And if an angler hopes to advance up the ranks, to become semipro or pro, he must own or develop a set of collaborative social skills not required in most other kinds of angling.

This is a larger, more intricate culture than mainstream America imagines. If it receives any attention from the intelligentsia, it is as the butt of jokes. Yet within the very heart of the country, this floating community rides on waves the color of money.

↩ JOE SAID GOODBYE to his wife. In the driveway, caught in the blinding headlights of the red Ford Explorer, she clutched her bathrobe together and told him to be safe. She had a look of . . . tolerance . . . in her eyes. Mist was beginning to fall. He pulled the trailer and the long black

Skeeter out of the driveway and down the silent suburban street past the bland split-levels with the porch lights on, and up a vacant exit to Interstate 75. We were silent. Joe sipped his coffee. Don was slow to fully wake; he was jackknifed in the back seat, crammed in there with the tackle boxes, his feet up on a duffel bag. I was sitting in the front seat as Joe drove.

Don angled himself so he could stick his head between the two bucket seats.

"Isn't this kind of crazy?" I asked.

"You know, if you stand back and look at any sport, it can be silly," said Joe, as he accelerated up the nearly empty highway. "But if you have that passion for it and you like it . . . I look at my neighbors, getting up in the morning and standing on the golf course in the fog and rain. I like to play golf but I would never get out of bed for it. Maybe on a special day I might, but for fishing—I don't think twice about it. Weather doesn't bother me. I'll come back from fishing all day and my wife will say, 'So, how did you do?' 'Well, just a few little ones, nothing too big.' 'Why do you keep doing that?' 'I don't know, it's just what I want to do!' You don't even think about it, it's just second nature."

Sipping coffee as he steered, Joe delivered a quiet soliloquy:

> I've always wanted to do something. I was a good baseball player, I'm a pretty good businessman—I own a health club with my wife, in addition to selling real estate. But I never stuck with anything— like baseball; I didn't put my nose to the grindstone and say, "I'm going to be a professional baseball player."
>
> I just thought, "Well, that's so hard, I can't do it." Today I sit there watching a game, and I think, "I'm better than him, I could do that." But he's out there and I'm not, and the only thing that took him there was the will to do it.
>
> As I got older, I thought, "My shot at professional sports is gone; that was just a dream that came and went." But here's the thing: I didn't want to die and not have *tried* something, not have taken it as far as I could take it.
>
> Then one day something happened. I had fished the little club tournaments and buddy tournaments for years. The next level was the Ohio River Red Man tournament. The guys I fished with didn't want to do it. They said, "Oh, you can't fish the Red Man, you can't fish against the pros." But I realized that those pros are coming to fish the river that we fish every weekend. What's the difference if I'm in my boat fishing eight hours for a buddy tournament or I'm in my boat for eight hours fishing a Red Man tournament? It's the

same water, the same fish, I do the same thing. So I signed up for the next Red Man.

During the tournament, I was in awe, intimidated. All these boats shooting up the river like some kind of navy, and the impressive trucks, and all these guys with patches on their shirts saying what companies sponsored them. That first Red Man, I only caught one or two fish. My mom and dad showed up for it; my wife came down with my little daughter. Don came down. They were all at the weigh-in at the end, and all I had was a little measly few fish.

And then came the second Red Man Ohio River tournament. I signed up again. It's a draw tournament: You draw a boat partner by chance, and I drew a pro named Ralph Gordon. I was the nonboater in that one. I was nervous. I didn't know anybody there from Adam. But as soon as Ralph saw I was putting fish in the boat he started helping me out. He said, "What do you want me to do and I'll do it for you." He had fished for years before I even thought of fishing, but he saw what I was doing, and he all but quit fishing just to help me. He positioned the boat several times so I could make the casts that I wanted and those casts produced fish. Instead of trying to fish the spots that I was catching fish on, Ralph let me fish those spots alone until I was ready to move on.

He told me that I wouldn't appreciate the kind of day I was having until years later and he was right. I wish I could relive that day over and over. He was a complete gentleman and professional. I remained a casual friend with him over the years. He always chuckled when he saw me. I found out at the first tournament this year that he had had a heart attack and died in late winter.

I did not believe what was happening that day on the Ohio. It was one of those days when you're telling yourself it's happening but it just doesn't feel real. My mind and my body were in two different spots.

During the chaos of pulling the boats out—it takes hours—I was sitting in Ralph's truck getting ready to pull his boat up the ramp and he's in the boat and everybody's running up to him, "Ralph, Ralph, how did you do?" Everybody knew him. And he said, "I didn't do nothing. *He's* going to win it, he's got five good ones." I'm just sitting there smiling and they're saying, "Really? How did you do it, buddy?" And I'm saying, "I don't know! I think I got some good fish." And this little kid walks by and he goes, "Hey mister, do you know who's winning this thing?" And I said, "People say I am!" And he says, "Really?" It felt weird telling the kid that.

At the weigh-in, I'm standing there waiting and they start off

naming the winners, and to this day I can hear the announcer, Sonny
Reynolds, on the loudspeaker saying: "First Place, on the Ohio
River, fifty points, three thousand dollars goes to . . . " I think there
was a vacuum in my body for five seconds. Just sitting there like a
zombie: "Joe Godar! Let's give a big round of applause!"

You get this feeling in your stomach: You know that this *isn't* impossible to do. Some of the fishermen are magicians out there,
putting fish in the boat. But everyone gets their day—and then it's
your day and you're one of them. When I won that tournament I
felt it was a kind of *blessing*. It was almost as if someone had said,
"You like this, you can do this. Go on, son."

I had no business winning that tournament. You remember that,
Don. I really didn't. I'd be the first one to admit it.

Like a pope, Joe raised his hand in the air and made a blessing sign.
"You have no business winning any of them," said Don from the backseat. The two friends laughed as the rain sliced across the road ahead.

"I missed the camaraderie and competition of sports, too," Joe continued. He missed the sense of community. "You don't get a lot of that
in . . . real life."

So, in the past, Joe *could have been a contender*. Now a great deter-
mination has welled up in him, almost a religious conviction, that bass-
fishing is his calling—that this, *this* will be his way.

He drove in gray dawn rain and ominous wind. Lake Erie, in this
weather, would not be kind. Still, I was looking forward to the contest. I
had never seen a bass tournament (except at a distance, with some unpleasantness, when tournament fishers in their power boats would go
shooting past, leaving the rest of us three-horsepower-rental-boat peas-
ants in their wake), but I was beginning to get the fever. Joe would show
me the ropes: I was to *join* this one, fish in it.

Hell, maybe I could be a contender.

꒰ WE WERE HEADING NORTH, just as tournament bass-fishing, rooted in
the rural South and lower Midwest, has moved. In the South, the poor-
est region of the nation, men (and some women) in the past were more
likely to hunt and fish to put food on the table. Then, dams, built to revive the economies of the South and lower Midwest, became the wombs
of the new culture. Unlike "the urban, industrialized North, the South
had a ready audience—or market, if you will—primed to be sold on the
joys of big time bass fishing," Norman Geoffrey writes in *Sports Afield*.

The evolving language and technology of this culture fit the new aquatic environment. "The trees, the brush, the farmhouses, rockpiles—all underwater now—provided excellent cover and habitat for bass. 'Structure,' fishermen were soon calling it. A new breed of bass fishermen learned how to read the bottoms of these lakes by studying old topo maps drawn before the ground was flooded." Anglers learned how to use depth finders and lowered thermometers to understand the structure and its environs. Bass-fishing, as Geoffrey aptly puts it, "was becoming 'high tech' before anyone had ever used the phrase."

As the South awoke economically, the entrepreneurs arrived on the scene, "people with an eye for the main chance and the nerve to go for it. . . . They were going to ride the largemouth bass to glory." The promoter of promoters was Ray Scott, an Alabama insurance salesman who, while lying in bed in a motel room one night in the '60s, had a revelation. He envisioned a formalized, ritualized bass tournament with rules and regulations and stars and big money just like a golf tournament. If it worked, he would create a circuit for a new breed of pros—bass pros—to ride.

At the time that must have seemed a laughable hallucination. Student rebellion and urban riots were inflaming the country; throwing a bass plug for money surely seemed out of time and place. Or did it? The television show *Hee Haw*, a hayseed knockoff of *Laugh In*, was among the most popular programs, and country-western music, about to be redubbed country music, was to go powerfully mainstream. At that point, though the intelligentsia would be pained to admit it, the New South, the Sun Belt, and the great rural Midwest were more of what the future would be, politically and culturally, than the burning universities.

Scott created the Bass Anglers Sportsman Society, and, in 1971, announced that he would fly the pros (professional only because Scott knighted them such) from Atlanta for the first B.A.S.S. tournament, with a top prize of $10,000. It would be held at an undisclosed location—a masterful tease to the press. The location, appropriately, was Las Vegas. One hundred and fifty spectators watched the weigh-in at Lake Mead. Fishing would never be the same. In his trademark buckskin vest and white cowboy hat, Scott "did for bass fishermen what Elvis did for rock-and-roll," according to Henry Reynolds, former outdoors editor for the *Memphis Commercial Appeal*. "He provided the forum for anglers to showcase their talents and elevated the sport of bass fishing to respectability," wrote Gary Laden in the *Atlanta Journal and Constitution*. Scott did it with a vengeance. "The bass is the most revered superstar of the South," he once said. "The states of the Stars and Bars can only be brightened by the yawn of a big largemouth bass." To Scott, fishing wasn't about relaxation, it was about boat-to-boat combat, economic conquest, war.

Now came fast boats, celebrity anglers, depth finders with liquid crystal displays, underwater cameras, and Global Positioning System units used to mark honey holes. Lure companies even employed the latest bio-tech research to design scent impregnated lures. All of this spread from the South and lower Midwest. Imagine Stonewall Jackson's troops and Quantrill's raiders charging north in flotillas of shining, metal-flaked Nitro Center Dual Console hawg busters, enlisting border state volunteers like Joe and Don along the way, and you get the picture.

But only part of the idea.

↪ JOE'S EPIPHANY on the water, as he had described it, was analogous either to the habitual gambler's first win or to a brush with our nation's better angels.

Joe had sent me a copy of *Tournament Angler News,* a national tabloid. He had written a short article, of which he was rightly proud, called "Fishing Used Water." Joe had advised anglers facing a day on waters that had been pounded by other fishermen to "stick with your strengths and with what you think will work in that situation and keep your lure in the water. Sooner or later, the fish will start to feed or they will hit a bait out of curiosity and if your bait is in front of them, well, you just might win that tournament." He sounded like a Rotarian. And he added his own homily: *"Confidence is the best lure you can use."*

The sun was up now, but you could barely tell. We skimmed past the Taco Bells and the gray farms, some of them deserted, past clusters of trees, shivering in the wind, perhaps some of them the Ohio buckeye, for which this Red Man Tournament was named. The state's official tree once grew here in large numbers, but no more.

Ohio takes its name from an Iroquois word meaning great or beautiful river (referring to the Ohio River), and a system of nineteenth-century canals established the early patterns of commerce. I looked out over the wet farmlands and thought of the Underground Railroad that had moved so many slaves north. When the Civil War broke out, more than thirty thousand Ohio residents volunteered to fight in the Union Army, more than twice the federal quota for the state. This is the state, too, of Cleveland race riots in the '60s and Kent State University, where, in 1970, National Guardsmen fired into a crowd of students protesting the U.S. bombing and invasion of Cambodia, killing four and injuring nine. Such a long time ago that seems now, a moment fading into history like the old farmhouses hidden by sheets of rain—or those towns and creeks to the south, lost in waters raised by the Army Corps of Engineers.

"When you were kids, did either of you find fishing an escape from something else?" I asked.

"Yeah," said Don. He leaned forward from the backseat. "I remember days being in school daydreaming. Projecting myself on the water, dreaming about the lures. My mom would go to the grocery store and I'd run to the local department store to basically fondle the lures. Horrible."

He shifted around in the backseat. "I still do it."

"So do I," said Joe. "You're mesmerized."

The medicinal paraphernalia of fishing.

"This is how addicting this stuff is," said Don. "You show me a lure and I'll tell you the name of it. I can probably tell you the size and the weight of it. I can tell you the manufacturer, I can tell you how many colors it comes in."

Don and Joe have a larger, more expensive habit now. Boats! "Have you seen the new Blazer bass boat?" Don asked Joe. "It looks similar to a Bullet but better paint. It's hot."

"The really nice boats are the Tritons."

"Triton's made speedboats for a long time. Triton's got one of the hottest speedboats on the market."

So what's the deal with boats?

"It's half ego and half function," said Don. "You want to fuel your ego by having the nicest rig out there."

He crooned from the backseat. "Oh *mannnn* . . . the colors, the lines, the ride, the engine, the horsepower, the trolling motor, the depth finders, the hydrofoil, the counter-rotating prop. The gel coat and the sparkle. Some of these boats have power steering. The whole rig. You've got guys who have a $20,000 house and a $40,000 boat. I know guys personally like that: On one of my first bass tournaments, I pulled an ol' boy with an '84 Hydrosport with a 200 Suzuki and that thing was bad to the bone. This guy had a house that cost him $10,000 and I think he fully mortgaged his house, mortgaged his truck, his wife, and he kept buying new motors, so I think he had to turn in one of his kids."

Still, function counts more than looks, Joe stressed. "The biggest thing people misunderstand about pro bass fishermen is that they see these boats and they think we're nothing but glorified race-car drivers on the water. Once you get into fishing at that level, you probably care less about the boat than anything else. You bang it up. You're just using it as a tool to get from one spot to the next. We're concerned about how fast our boats go, but not for the reasons people think. I want to go ninety miles an hour not for the thrill but because if I don't, there's going to be all these guys beating me out to the good spots on the lake. This Skeeter behind us will go about sixty, sixty-five miles per hour. Some of the bigger boats will go eighty, ninety miles per hour. And reliability is important. You start getting a boat that's three and four years old; you don't want to get stuck out there. So most of the pros trade their boats in frequently. They don't get too attached to them."

"Yeah, but it's not bad to have that bigger, badder, bestest expensive boat," said Don. "See, there are no limitations, as fast as you can go is as fast as you can go. If the water is like glass in the morning, that is such a stimulating thing. You pull out of a cove or a tributary into the main branch when it's like glass and you know you're just going to tear it up. There's no limitations."

No limitations, indeed. Certainly speed limits aren't much of an issue on most of the lakes. Neither is horsepower. Some of the biggest, baddest boats are equipped with a mechanism that injects nitrous oxide into the engine. Equipped with this system, and specialized props, a few bass boats can go 115 and faster, running one hundred miles without regassing.

"That's *extreme*," said Don. "So sometimes it's kind of scary to think about it. You got a ding-dong in a bass boat, with a nitrous-oxide system strapped to it, going ninety, a hundred miles an hour . . . and there's no boat training out there. You don't have to exhibit skills to be going this fast on the water. You just have to be able to buy the boat. The worst thing is in the fog. You'll hear engines out there when you're just idling. Then you know somebody is out there burning it up and they can't see any better than you can."

Speed counts, but so does distance.

"You want to know that if you're going to go fish a tournament, that if you have to run sixty or a hundred miles because you know there's fish in a certain spot, you have the ability to do it," said Joe. "With these bigger boats you can start strapping down sixty gallons of gas. Some of the magazines are beginning to rate how many miles you can get out of a tank of gas, how far you can go."

When you go to the boat and tackle shows, what do you get the most excited about?

"Walking in the door," Joe said.

"The hot sportsmodels," Don said, laughing. "The scantily clad babes. Large silicone breasts."

Like the ones we were watching this morning?

"I was not watching those gals! I know how Joe is and I thought he would be offended if I didn't let him see those babes."

Speaking of gear, neither Joe nor Don is interested in fly-fishing, or golf for that matter, which they consider too . . . materialistic. And too trendy. "It's getting snootier," said Don. "All those rich dudes out there smoking cigars with their $250 flyrods."

That's only a *moderately* priced flyrod, I said.

"OK, a $2,000 flyrod, hand-built by an Indian from Guatemala or something. From the special bark of a waca-waca tree. Cracks me up. I was at my sister's wedding and there's this rich girl there and she's talking about tying her own flies. It's just like, 'Oh, God!' "

Hey, I said, a bass boat costs a lot more than a $500 rod.

Don snorted. "But at least you've got wheels on this thing, you can't put wheels on your flyrod."

"Hey, Don," said Joe. "People make fun of people buying a $2,000 set of golf clubs. I've probably got $2,000 worth of lures in two or three boxes."

"Well, $2,000 worth of golf clubs is $10,000 worth of frustration." Anyway, Don added, fishing doesn't have to be so expensive. "One of my favorite things to do in the world is to go *wet-legging*. Put a pair of shorts on, get a rope, tie a little tackle box around my waist, put my chewing tobacco in my hat with my fishing license, go get in the creek and go out and fish and not come back until the sun starts coming down. Looking for smallmouth at the end of a little set of rapids, that's what heaven would be like to me."

Thinking of this, Don pulled a tin of Skoal out of his pocket, tore off a piece of the fibrous goo, and stuck it in the back slot of his cheek. "Your after-breakfast chew," I said. "You're juiced now."

You never know about people. It's tempting, when you're driving through suburban America, to think that all those boxes contain the same story, the same background. Wilkymacky and Godar, despite their "Hawaiian Tropic" talk, were devoted to their wives and families, and in many ways quite straitlaced. Don said he'd been a bit of a wild man in his youth, "but I cleaned up, cleaned up my language." Indeed, as the trip progressed, and he loosened up even more, Don started using the word "effing." Not fucking. Effing. But their apparent cultural conservatism took second place to their belief in laissez-faire capitalism.

Don said there are three kinds of people in the bass-fishing world: the ones who have sponsors and are wearing their sponsors' advertising patches and emblems on their shirts. "A lot of the pros do that. Then you've got your Joe of the world, who has a couple sponsors and he has certain particular lures that he fishes, so he publicizes those lures by what he wears on his shirt. And then you got me. I wear whatever I can put on my body. I don't have any effing sponsors."

Joe marketed himself to sponsors because he sees bass-fishing as his future full-time business. One lure maker, Lunker Lures, answered his letter, sent him patches, which he fastened to his shirt for his second Red Man tournament.

"After the tournament that I caught the five bass at, I was at the weigh-in where they do the interviews—find out what lures you use, take pictures—I just happened to have on my tournament shirt with my patches—you don't know when something like that will happen. You just take small steps." He sent copies of the photographs and press accounts to Lunker Lures, and said, " 'Here am I. I wore your tournament shirt and I won that.' That's how you get noticed by these people, how you get contracts with sponsors."

A typical bass pro might have ten sponsors who, in addition to supplying him with equipment, pay him $5,000 a year for wearing the advertisements and showing up at boat and tackle shows to promote the company's products.

"That's your basic fifty thousand dollars a year to get you on the road," said Joe. "It's like what you see with auto racers on the NASCAR circuit. A tournament winner gets interviewed, and say he's sponsored by Strike King Spinner baits, so he'll say, 'Well, you know I've got that new Strike King double-blade willow leaf spinnerbait, that's what I caught it on.' If you pay attention you'll see he's got a Strike King hat on, Strike King patches on." The ultimate sponsorship comes when a pro gets his own TV fishing show, to "be a bass-fishing spokesmodel," as Joe puts it. Don dreams of having his own boat store, but Joe—telegenic, well-spoken, ambitious—wants to be a star.

Confidence, I thought, is the best lure you can use.

"Hey, you know Joe and I already have show-business experience, through our former business affiliation," said Don, offhandedly. "We used to be male dancers."

Pardon me?

"Yes, we were," said Joe.

"He was the Buttless Cowboy and I was the Long Ranger," said Don.

"I dragged him into it," said Joe.

They worked their way through the University of Cincinnati that way. "We would dance Thursday, Friday, Saturday night, do closing shows on Wednesday and Saturday nights and do private parties," explained Don. "Somewhere between three and twelve shows on a weekend, going all the way through Sunday afternoon or Sunday night. In a week, we'd come home with two or three thousand dollars cash in our pockets. One girl came up to me one time and I'll never forget it. She said, 'You look like an ex-boyfriend of mine, I was wondering if you'd kiss me.

JOE GODAR

I'll pay you.' I said, 'Whatever.' So she sticks this money in my G-string. I didn't pay attention, I figured it was a buck or something—she was cute, I was going to kiss her anyway. And she stuffs a hundred-dollar bill in my G-string. It was great, free drinks, all the girls in the world."

That was when Joe and Don started fishing together. And the rest, Don said, is history.

"I couldn't believe the money in dancing," said Joe. "A young kid twenty-one, twenty-two years old making that kind of money while going to school. It was unbelievable. After six months of dancing for tips at parties, I thought: there's a business here. Several of us started booking clubs and bachelorette parties. We started traveling. Did it for about ten years in Ohio, Michigan, Missouri, Tennessee. We called ourselves the LA Dream Team."

Had any of you ever been to Los Angeles?

"No." He laughed. "It was purely marketing. We were in shape; we were blond."

"It's all marketing," said Don. "It's all marketing."

With this marketing talent, you could go from being the Buttless Cowboy to being the Buttless Bass Pro, I suggested.

"I don't know how the sponsors would take that," said Joe.

"The concept and the idea is the same," said Don. Lures and G-strings. "Same concept."

⌐ TIME PASSED. We fell quiet, listening to the rain and hiss of the tires. As the Explorer neared Lake Erie, I mentioned that all of this seemed a long way from the little Rocky Fork of Joe's boyhood and heart.

"You're right," said Joe. "Tournament fishing is entirely different from going out to our log cabin for the weekend with my father, wading in a stream, and fishing for smallmouth. I'll be gone for three weeks to fish the tournaments and then come home, and I immediately want to go out to our cabin to relax. The cabin and that river are part of me. Did I tell you my wife and I named our second girl, Sutton, after the town that our family cabin is in? Her full name is Sutton Bainbridge Godar. She was conceived there."

On Rocky Fork Creek, he fishes and moves slowly. Sometimes, as he wades in thick rubber waders, he forgets he is carrying a rod; he studies the new log jams and the curves of the river. He knows every turn, every pool, personally.

Not that tournament fishing is without a sense of connection to nature. Joe described the Tournament Trance: "I know when I'm in it. It comes with time on the water. It's the ability to know and 'see' underwater—see your lure bouncing along. You know what it feels like when it's hitting the bottom of the lake. When you have that feeling—it could be a little tick or it could be a slight movement, it could be just a little shimmy in the line, as the fish sucks the bait in, tastes it, and then begins to spit it out—instantly without even thinking you just set the hook with a real quick sweep and you pull a fish out. If you fish with guys who fish that way, in a slow manner, you'll see them just—they're in a trance.

That's probably the farthest out you'll see somebody. Time goes by real quick. You look down, never up, and an hour and a half goes by. The focus is on getting fish, *nothing* else.

"I have a definite taste and dream for both of these kinds of fishing," he said as we entered Sandusky, the town hosting the Red Man tournament. "I need both worlds."

The Contest

～❧～

WE DROVE THROUGH Sandusky, bunched up against the water of Lake Erie—which, I saw with a shock, was frothing with high, ominous, pea-colored waves clear to the horizon—and into a town called Milan, on Sandusky Bay, and checked into the Super 8 Motel. After unpacking, we drove over to a buffet restaurant and met Joe's and Don's networking partners.

This is where the tournament world gets particularly interesting.

We had arrived two days early to prefish the lake, to find the under-water structure, the hot spots, to test lures and plastic baits, to gauge the lay of the water. Competition is the point, but the culture is surprisingly cooperative. If an angler is well networked, he shares his pretournament information with his buddies—anglers with whom he will be directly competing during the tournament. Such information is invaluable; if you have it, you can rig your rods with what works, and shoot your boat directly to the hotspots on the tournament day. Joe calls tournament fishing an "information sport."

He had arranged to meet at Shoney's Restaurant with professional bass angler Bill Buncie of Depew, New York, a suburb of Buffalo, and with Jim Thompson, of Attica, New York. Buncie, fifty-two, is a tall, wil-lowy, dark-eyed man—immaculately dressed in his Red Man shirt and cap, festooned with many more patches than Joe's. Before he became a bass pro, Buncie was the hazardous-waste-site supervisor at Love Canal, a town east of Niagara Falls, New York, and site of an abandoned toxic chemical waste dump. The waste contributed to a high incidence of birth defects and illnesses in the neighborhood. Buncie was in charge of cleaning up the water. Thompson lives across the road from Attica Correctional Facility at Attica, scene of one of the nation's bloodiest peace-time encounters since the Indian massacres of the late nineteenth century.

"Attica's got a good reservoir right next to the prison," said Thompson, a big, gentle, slow-talking man with thick glasses. He pushed the glasses back up his nose as he talked.

We were sitting at a booth, all the men with their caps still on. (This is a new custom in America: Ball caps are usually not removed while their owners are eating, and certainly not if the man is a fisherman). Joe met and bonded with Bill Buncie at another Ohio tournament; he drew Buncie as his boat partner, and was impressed with his humor and his persistence. When Buncie grabbed a bass, the fish "put a hook through his thumb, and that big fish was jumping in the back of the boat and it just ripped his thumb right open," Joe recalls. But Buncie kept fishing with his hand wrapped, and won the $3,500 top prize. Since then, when Joe and Bill (and Bill's frequent fishing partner, Jim Thompson) fish the same tournament, they meet to trade information, before prefishing the waters, and afterward.

Part of the purpose is self-defense. The famous pros, especially if they've had television time, can call up the local anglers hours before a tournament and grill them about the water conditions, what the fish are biting on, the hot spots. Said Joe, "The big-name pro will find guys that win the local tournaments and he'll call them up and tell them, 'I'll take you out on my boat, maybe put you on my show, if you show me where the fish are.'"

Buncie picked at his plate of food. "I don't feel that their fishing skills are any better than mine, but they have connections on a body of water. One tournament, down at Ross Burnett Lake, there was a good area with a very shallow creek, maybe eighteen inches of water, and it emptied into a back bayou, a back area of cypress trees that was known to have bass—a local had told this celebrity pro, and his buddies, about that spot. But with the bigger bass boats, the pro couldn't get up there." So, before the tournament, the celebrity convinced the local angler to swap boats for the day: his $25,000 rig in exchange for the local's $8,000 flat-bottom aluminum boat. "It paid off." In defense, the lesser-known anglers, semipro and pro, form loose alliances, like the one at this table.

"The first tournament I went to," Thompson recalled, "I saw all these guys going to one guy's room; they worked as a team. It's tough when there are eight guys and they're all dividing the water and getting a good view on what's happening on that lake. Try to fish against that."

"Eight heads versus one," said Buncie. "You just can't cover water like this, or any water, by yourself." Few sports are this dependent on insider or shared information. "There aren't that many sports that are so dependent on information, period," he added.

If this is an information sport, I wondered if anglers ever spread disinformation. "Oh, yeah," said Thompson, pushing his glasses up his nose. Circuit etiquette and the rules of alliance are not written down anywhere. Enforcement is purely social—but with bite. Woe to the angler who is a member of an alliance but withholds information or provides disinformation.

"I wouldn't use his name but we had a fellow, he's in our bass club, and he wanted to share information," said Buncie. "We were fishing a tournament on the Potomac River. He had a map marked by a local guide. He told us he forgot where the map was. But the guy who drove with him told us the map was in his truck and that fellow knew it. He used the map himself and didn't share it with us, even though we were supposed to be working as a team on the river. He used the information and just didn't bother to cut us in. So right now he's on our bad list. He calls and asks, 'Bill, you fished this water before, will you help me out?' And I say, 'No.' He knows why, I told him. I said, 'Remember that map deal?' It's going to take me a lot of years to forget it."

Reputation matters more than luck in this culture. Beyond luck and skill, everything in this world depends, as Buncie said, "on getting to be known as a decent guy, period." While it's true that anyone can join a circuit, that doesn't mean they'll be invited into the circle of information. "If you say tomorrow, 'I'm going to quit writing and become a pro fisherman,' you join the association and you sign up for the tournaments and you fish. And you can be a professional fisherman," said Buncie.

Even if I've never won a tournament?

"Right. But usually you don't last long on the circuit because your experience is low. You're going to take it on the chin; you won't win any money and you're going to be spending a lot of money. Usually the other guys can tell that your knowledge is not there. You won't get the respect. You won't get into the circle."

Or more specifically, you won't graduate from the outer circle (if you've managed to make it out of isolation, as Joe has done) to the inner circle.

I asked Buncie if he was in the inner circle. "I'm on the edge. I've fished about two years with the top professionals. Most of them recognize me now and we speak. Jimmy Houston, Denny Brauer. They've seen my face enough and they know I'm there. Sometimes I'll draw one as a partner. That helps. Like Jimmy. You get to talk to them for eight hours in the boat, if they feel like talking. Jimmy kind of interviewed me, asked me where I'd fished, what I'd fished. He got an idea of what I could do. They can tell when you're fishing with them how good your skills are, too. They tend to test you out."

Cheating on the circuits does happen, but probably not often. Small local bass tournaments are especially vulnerable. For example, in a notorious 1997 case, four Waco, Texas, fishermen were charged with fraud after the Hewitt Bass Club Tournament on Lake Waco. Such fishing fraud is a Class A misdemeanor under the Texas Parks and Wildlife code, carrying fines of $500 to $2,000 per fisherman and jail terms up to one year. Had the prize money exceeded $10,000, felony charges could have been filed. Wardens had been tipped off that bass were stashed in a wire basket in Lake Waco; the wardens found the cache of live bass and inserted invisible pit tags, which can be read with an electronic scanner, into the fish. The game wardens used a scanning device at the weigh-in, and nabbed the culprits.

The use of lie-detector tests in major fishing tournaments has a chilling effect on attempts at cheating. Tournaments also make it hard to cheat by moving to the draw format rather than the buddy format. Some local tournaments allow close friends to fish together, but the big tournaments do not. You draw a name the night before and must fish with this angler. No angler can leave the boat during the tournament, which usually lasts eight hours, and no one can fish alone. If your partner-for-the-day gets sick and must return to land, the tournament operators will assign an observer to go back out on the water with you.

The most important preventive measures come from the anglers themselves through vigilance and social pressure. Most infractions aren't as dramatic as stashed baskets of fish, but are more related to boat conduct and interpretation of the rules.

"One guy in a small tournament I fished was fishing with one rod in hand and over his shoulder he heard a fish break on the surface," said Joe. "He set that pole down, picked up another pole, cast over there, caught that fish, put it in the boat, but still had his lure out in the water, from his other rod. And that's illegal. You cannot be fishing two poles at a time in a tournament. Technically that was what he was doing because he didn't finish his retrieval on one rod before he cast his other rod. He ended up winning that tournament and at the end of the tournament he was in the parking lot joking about how he caught that fish and without knowing it, he was standing right next to the tournament director. He was disqualified and he lost that tournament, though he had not consciously cheated."

In the draw system, anglers can enter in three ways: as a boater, a nonboater, and a guaranteed boater. If an angler with a boat brings a nonboater (as Joe had brought Don—and me), he's a guaranteed boater. "If you and I are registered as boaters, and we draw each other as partners, we discuss whose boat to take—maybe my boat's bigger than yours," Joe explained. "Or we flip a coin." Once on the water, the rules of conduct are partly codified and partly unwritten etiquette. Some partners are talkative, others are not, but certain protocols are worked out early.

Joe elaborated:

> You try to establish real quick what the netting policy will be. You ask your partner: How do you net the fish? Do you want me to net your fish? What do you want me to do when you get a fish on? A quick back and forth to establish that. I always tell the guy, "This is a team effort for eight hours, I don't think I'm competing against you. You and me have to act as a team." Because if you start fighting over something it just ruins the whole day mentally and you're through. But there are guys that I've drawn and we hit it off great and the day goes good and everything clicks. Boom, boom, boom. We fish the same style, we fish the same water, we joke. It's a good day. But then you get some guys on your boat that your personalities just conflict, you're butting heads, and that drives me nuts. They're in your ear, as soon as you put your trolling motor down: "Joe, let's go over here." "I just started, let me fish here for five minutes." "Oh, I think we got to be over here!" It breaks you down and you start worrying about the guy in the back of the boat instead of worrying about how you want to fish. I don't like that. But it's the luck of the draw. Legally, the two participants in the boat are supposed to split all decisions fifty-fifty, regardless who owns the boat. In practice, normally what happens is the boater is more experienced and draws a nonboater person with less experience. If you, say, draw a person who's a guide on that lake, and he says, "I know where these fish are," it's common sense to say, "OK. This is your water; let's go with your fish." It usually works out and there's rarely any trouble.

Still, trouble can happen. Back-boating, for example. That, said Buncie, is when the boater, who's usually up front controlling the trolling motor, doesn't give the nonboater a good shot at a fish. "You're fishing the back of the boat and he swings the boat to where he gets a cast at where the fish are, and you don't get a chance at it. If your partner back-boats you and keeps you from catching fish in any way, anything he catches doesn't count in the tournament. You can actually have your partner disqualified for not being a sportsman."

That would seem exceedingly hard to prove: one angler's word against another's.

"If you do that to somebody, you better be sure you're right," said Buncie. "You have to have a good reputation—especially if you go and accuse a celebrity pro. The people who run these tournaments have to know you for a while and know that you're a decent person. This is not a hasty decision: If they don't know you they talk to fishermen who do. If people find out later you've unjustly accused someone, you won't be fishing tournaments. It comes out sooner or later. Word goes out and you might as well hang it up."

Some anglers like Buncie go beyond the understood code and impose their own rules.

"Nobody smokes in my boat. I paid too much money for the thing. And no chew. Unless they swallow."

"You don't let them chew?" cried Don.

"They ain't spitting that stuff over the side of my boat!"

"Oh, man, you communist!"

Buncie, like most tournament anglers, detests fishermen who speed near "civilians," as he calls them. "Most of the guys, they're out there to have a good time and they're sportsmen. But all it takes is one jerk. If he runs into a civilian fisherman, that's bad for everybody in the tournament. They come blasting down the water, sixty or seventy miles an hour, blowing close to some family, causing a big wake. I've seen guys do that to families with kids in the boat."

The table was littered with coffee cups, dessert plates, and beer bottles by now, but Buncie had one more story to tell, a harrowing tale about the fishing partner from hell.

It was a couple years ago. We were fishing the Red Man tournament. I happened to draw a young guy from New Jersey. He was only twenty years old and he was a real know-it-all; he was normally a B.A.S.S. angler. We both had boats, we had to flip, and I lost the toss. I had fished a lot on that water because I had been down there a week prefishing. We're running way up into D.C., which is about thirty miles upriver. He's got a Gambler, which is a fast boat. We run upriver at about eighty miles an hour, he's cutting across all these sandbars, and the tide was in at the time.

You can run that fast if you stay in the deep channel. But where he was running there were logs, sandbars, rocks, and steel stakes. He was cutting too close to shore. He had a helmet with a face shield on, and I reached over, knocked on his helmet a few times, and said, "Move out into the channel and stay with the markers." Well, he told me what I could do. And I thought, "This guy is going to be a really good guy to fish with."

We fished for a few hours and I'd catch a fish, he'd get mad, throw his rod down, kick the trolling motor and we'd leave. Every time I'd catch a fish we'd leave the area. He kept telling me all the time how stupid and ignorant Red Man fishermen were, that only B.A.S.S. guys were good fishermen. I have a hot temper and I try to control it, but I was getting fed up. Finally it gets to be about 1:30, and I said, "We're on my time now; we're going back to the launch." He gets in the boat, we start heading back downriver, and he crosses over that shallow side again. This time the tide is out and there were six bass boats lined up in a row fishing that rock pile and stakes. We were heading right toward them. I banged him on the shoulder and he gives me this [the finger]. I'm leaning over yelling at him, "You can't cross here!" He just pushes me away, he's bearing down on these guys, and the guys on the boat are waving their arms. He's running right at them.

So finally I reached over and I pulled the kill switch. He jumped up, he threw his helmet down, he called me a bunch of four-letter words, and he was going to punch me out. I stood up and said, "Look, you're a lot younger than I am and you might get the first punch but I guarantee you you're going over the side of this boat. I've had enough of your crap." "Eff-you, eff-this," he says, "this is my boat." He starts up again, jacks up the speed, and starts to run through the shallows. It's a single console boat so I put my foot up on the console and I braced myself and the guys are yelling at us, as we're bearing down on them, we're doing about sixty an hour and the guys start moving their boats to get out of the way.

All of a sudden the boat goes straight up in the air and I thought we were falling backward. We came back down fast and I left the seat, went right to the front of the boat, I hooked the front seat with my shoulder and still went over the edge of the boat and bent that seat right over with my shoulder. My feet went off the boat into the water, I had a hold of the front seat for dear life, and I bent that front post.

Then I was mad and I wanted to kill him but I'd hurt my shoulder; I was in such pain I couldn't do anything. I just wanted to kill him. I was shaking, I was so mad. And he stands up and throws his helmet down and was going to jump in the other guy's bass boat and get him, because the other guy yelled what a stupid ass he was. And I'm standing there and I hear water running and I say, "You ass, you punched a hole in the bottom of the boat." He said, "Shut up and sit down." I said, "Give me my fish, I'm going in the other guy's boat. I'm going back." But he starts the engine up real fast, and I sat down. But there was a hole in the boat. Not only a hole but half of the lower unit was missing. He'd broke one of the blades. And that motor shook and vibrated and he throttled it and took off and just threw me down in the seat. The boat was shaking and the water was starting to come up through the drains in the floor. The motor blew; she cooked right there. We finished the rest on the trolling motor. At the dock, I got up to get my fish, but before I could, he turned around, opened the live well, and threw my fish overboard. So it took me out of the tournament and the regionals, and nearly killed me. He said, "I don't give a crap about you or the boat or nothing." And he left.

I went to the Red Man officials and filed a legal protest and he's banned from fishing from any Red Man tournament, and I heard later that he got banned from B.A.S.S. because he pulled some other stunts. He actually beat up his partner. He's the worst guy I've ever run into. The guys that know me say, "You didn't kill him?" I guess in my old age I'm calming down. I wasn't in any shape to do anything to anybody anyway.

↬ MANY PEOPLE, PERHAPS most, think of fishing as a solitary occupation, and for many anglers it is. But not on the tournament circuit, and in fact, not for anglers in many other fishing communities. *Community.* The word doesn't seem easily associated with fishing, but community is something that many anglers are searching for. Scott Berg, author of *Lindbergh*, describes Charles Lindbergh as an emotionally isolated young man, who was drawn to aviation partly, he says, because "aviation created a brotherhood of casual acquaintances—people constantly coming and going—in which he felt comfortable." That description rings true of the bass tournament culture, particularly for those who have made a profession of it. Joe Godar talked with great feeling about Ralph Gordon, the man who opened the door to that world for him, and helped him win his first tournament, but he describes him as a "casual friend."

For some men and the few women who travel the circuit, the floating community can become more of a home than home; their closest relationships can be the ones they have on the road. Watching them, I wondered if some of them have, or had, troubled home lives and fishing had become an escape from that, and now is the ultimate escape—to the floating community of casual friends.

"At the point when I started taking tournaments seriously, Shannon

and I were just getting married," said Joe. "We didn't have good commu-
nication, and we did have some problems. After that first year, we sat
down and we had a good conversation. I told her, 'I don't do anything
else that takes me away from family. All I want to do is fish. I want these
weekends, these times to fish—and is this all right?' Once she came to
grips with knowing what I wanted, and I learned to tell her well in advance of a tournament, it's been good."

Are there such things as bass widows? I asked Joe.

"Yes, definitely."

I reminded Joe of the bumper sticker: "My wife says if I go fishing one
more time she'll leave. Boy, I'm going to miss her." "Yeah," he laughed, a
little sheepishly.

And it's going to get harder. To be a professional bass angler, Joe will
have to be away from home, on and off, about 30 percent of the year, he
estimates. "You figure 365 days, you're probably traveling 120 days. Some
guys pitch tents in the park. Or they sleep in their truck. Some guys take
their families, and the family stays in a camper or motor home or a hotel." Is Joe considering taking his family on the circuit? "I don't know, it
just depends on the investment. You've just got to sit down and do your
numbers. You've got to have a travel vehicle, whether it's a truck or a camper, and you've got to weigh the expense of what you're buying against
hotel expense or a motor home." Such a setup isn't going to happen for
Joe anytime soon; for one thing, his wife—strong and independent-
minded—has a life of her own, one that actually does not involve fishing.

As Joe talked about the conflict between the world of pro fishing and
family life, a cloud passed over his face. I had the feeling that he had
been so blinded by the sun of his American dream that he had not fully
smoothed that wrinkle over. Silent as the other men plotted, he pushed
his cap back on his head and sat there in the restaurant booth, staring.

↪ THE NEXT DAY, the day before the actual tournament, we prefished
Lake Erie. Having slept with Buncie's story of the partner from hell, I
was feeling a touch of ambivalence about the Red Man tournament, and
perhaps some anticipatory seasickness considering the size of those storm
waves. We had to wait for a break in the storm during the morning, but
by afternoon the waves looked—passable. In any case, Joe and Don
couldn't wait anymore. They were almost quivering with fish itch.

Joe backed his trailer down a ramp at Sandusky Bay; we threw on life
jackets and headed through the relatively smooth bay to the wall of
waves rolling at its mouth. We were heavily medicated with Dramamine,

but when we hit those waves I wasn't sure the drug would take. As he approached the first big swell, Joe gunned the 150-horse Merc and the bow shot up and then the nose came down slightly, pointing like an arrow toward the horizon. We were slicing along the tops of five- and six-foot swells, and the engine groaned up the sides of them, caught its breath as we flew across the trough—and seemed as if it *stopped* when the fiberglass hull hit the curve of the next swell. Each time the Skeeter's hull hammered down, a sickening shudder went through the boat, up my spine, straight to my cortex. After a few waves, my back hurt, my teeth felt loose, and seasickness was my least concern.

As Thompson had described the night before, riding such waves—especially anything over six feet—is tricky:

> If you're getting too much air under the boat between waves, your propeller will hit air instead of water, and you'll stall in the air. . . . Power up so you don't slide backward down the swell and stuff your motor . . . keep control of the wave, when you come off the top, just slide forward and down . . . timing is crucial because waves are not symmetrical; you can spike right into a wave . . . the force of that wave coming over your boat usually cleans off your depth finder or your windshield; the force is comparable to somebody hauling off and punching you in the chest. . . . Get the nose up, throttle up, get the bilge pumps on to get that water out—because if the bow stays down, the next wave's going to cover you and shove you down, take you out of the boat. . . . You've also got to be smart enough to know when to get off the water; you come in early and you're disqualified. But you're alive.

All this for fishing. As far as I could tell, we were still alive when Joe found a spot he liked, a half mile or so from shore. We tried fishing in what Joe referred to as the Vermillion area, and then Ruggles Beach, "great areas for spawning fish this time of year."

In most bass tournaments, the object of desire is the largemouth black bass, but we would be fishing for smallmouth black bass. The smallmouth has a shorter upper jaw than the largemouth bass, is differently colored (in Lake Erie, the smallmouth are a yellowish orange), and has a slightly different shape—somewhat blimpish. The smallmouth is a smaller fish than the largemouth. As of this writing, the U.S. record for largemouth is twenty-two pounds, four ounces, caught in 1932 on Montgomery Lake, Georgia; the record for smallmouth is 11 pounds, 15 ounces, caught in 1955 at Dale Hollow Lake, Kentucky. Pound for pound, smallmouth bass are harder fighters. Smallmouth fans can be more fanatical in their devotion than largemouth anglers—even more convinced of the superiority of their fish than anglers who fly-fish for trout.

In an instant, Joe and Don had unfastened the Velcro that held the rods tight to the high, flat deck of the boat. The lake was relatively quiet out there, especially after the roar of the engine. Joe leaned over the side of the boat with a thermometer and read the temperature. He explained that we would be using white tube baits—simple plastic baits that slipped over a heavily weighted hook. The tube baits imitate bait fish. "We'll also be fishing brown tubes that imitate crawfish and green plastic grubs on the bottom, in eighteen to twenty-one feet of water, temperature between forty-eight and fifty-one degrees. This is where the smallmouth have moved up to spawn; they like structure, the small groups of rocks—which is what I was looking for on the graph." Joe handed me a rod with a baitcasting reel and I flipped out a white grub. The boat slid gently up and over the swells. We drifted. Suddenly Joe's rod shot up, bent, and he reeled fast. Don grabbed a long-handled net and scooped a three-pound smallmouth from the water.

It was a beautiful fish, rounded and fat and shining that peculiar orange color. Joe grinned. We were on the fish. Over the next four hours, we caught several each, but Don quit fishing after the second hour. I looked around and saw him flat on the deck, arms stretched out, green as the stormy waters of Erie.

Ruggles Beach was less productive, and Don suffered through without complaint. Convinced that he had found a good spot for the next day, Joe headed back to the dock.

The next day, the storm returned and wiped out the prefishing. But at Shoney's, Joe and Don and Buncie and Jim Thompson pushed their coffee cups aside, took out pencil and pens, and spread writing paper and a topo map over the table. They reported their prefishing results. "The thing is they're sluggish now because the water is cold," said Thompson, pushing his glasses up. This tournament is usually won at a stretch of water called the White Mansion area; that's where most of the anglers will bunch up. "Knowing that, it's hard not to go there," said Thompson. Nonetheless, based on his prefishing experience, Buncie recommended a particular shoreline, called Kelly's, with shoals in shallow water. "I think they're coming in from the deep water right now, the forty-foot water," said Buncie. "Usually they come from down east of the lake, the Cleveland area, and migrate up. Being the water's deeper out in the middle of the lake there may be a chance of finding bigger fish on the shoals." Joe told the other men about Vermillion, and they wrote that down, studied the lake map. "What's your plan, Don?" someone asked.

"Make sure I don't draw someone with a fifteen-foot boat, so I can survive," he said. Thompson was unsatisfied with the pooled information; he said his plan would wait until the drawing of partners. Perhaps he would draw one of the locals who had been prefishing the lake for two weeks prior; if so, he would share with these men what he learned from the local. What struck me was their desire for pinpoint accuracy. "That's because someone who has that knowledge can get there fast; they'll have charted a lot of places out, down to the foot, using a GPS unit. You can be fifteen feet away and won't get a bite," said Thompson. They went back to the map, caps pushed back on their heads, hunkered over it like generals planning a shoreline invasion, murmuring and marking.

An hour later, boats in tow, they drove to the check-in, held in the hall of a nondescript industrial park in Sandusky. I edged into the room packed with several hundred anglers. The room was smoky and stuffy, and the men, some with their wives and kids, stared straight ahead as the tournament organizers prepared the microphone. The men ranged from chunky to emaciated. A third to a half of them had facial hair of some kind. Eyes were tired but intent; many sat stiffly upright. They were rural men, most of them, or at least that was what their looks suggested. They seemed deeply serious. Suddenly it seemed as if I was looking at a Mathew Brady photograph, an image from the Civil War, but instead of blue or gray, they were red: Red Man caps with Ranger boat windbreakers. Instead of the Union Jack, I saw a Red Man Tournament Trail banner. If some angler castes are from the privileged ranks of deferment, this caste was the one that went to war. These were the sacrificial soldiers. A high proportion of them were Vietnam veterans, I suspected. I could not remove the impression from my mind. This was the America that had fought and died so miserably on hallowed ground, come back to haunt the opening of the Buckeye Division, in the year nineteen hundred and ninety-seven.

Tournament organizer Sonny Reynolds, a slight, muscular man with a craggy face and long black hair falling from his Red Man cap, jumped up on a chair in front and held a microphone to his mouth. "Welcome, guys!" He studied his clipboard, and began to offer instructions for the following day. "OK, I need two boats. Anybody here that has a boat with them and can't use their boat, I need two boats. We got one here? Does he have his hand up? I can't see."

The wind shook a back door; the weather was miserable. "It oughta be a beautiful, balmy day tomorrow, eighty-five, calm winds," said Sonny: The men laughed. "All the mothers and mothers-to-be in the room, I'd like to wish you all a happy Mother's Day tomorrow. Ma'am, it takes a strong woman to put up with a fisherman. Especially on Mother's Day. Ladies, we do appreciate you putting up with us, that's the truth."

Now came the commercials—and the rules—in a language all their own.

You all know our Red Man tournament sponsors for the 1997 season? Red Man chewing tobacco . . . CITGO premium gasoline, Abu Garcia rods and reels, Energizer batteries. How many of you are running new Ficht engines? I'll tell you, if you want to save two thousand dollars a year in gas and oil get you a Ficht fuel-injected engine because it'll save you a bunch of money. Is Tom from Old Milwaukee here? We've got a treat for you this year. Armour meats, the beanie-weenie people. Get your jalapeño sausages as you come through registration. We'll know you all ate them for breakfast when there's a blue haze out over the water. Ranger boats, keeps everybody afloat. Keystone spinner baits, a new corporate sponsor this year, and they make a great spinner bait. How many of you use painted blades on your spinner baits? The paint will not come off of them. Period. Tom Stewart, where's Tom at? We will have a service team at the ramp in the morning if anybody has any early morning problems; Tom Stewart will be there. If all of you don't know where Tom is, he's at Lake Shore Sports Center. Tom and Pat Stewart, right over there, keeps you going and they are in Clyde, Ohio. They are the Evinrude-Johnson service team here for this tournament. I'm your tournament director and I'll be back next year [the crowd applauded and cheered.] I was gone last year and it's great to be back. I do want to say that to you all. Sharon registered you all in, our assistant team is Larry and Jen. It's all for one and all on the Red Man tournament trail. If you have any problems, come and see me. If you have any questions about our rules, come and see me; I'll talk to anybody, any time about anything. That's the one thing I can guarantee you. The other thing I can guarantee you is that we do enforce our rules. To the letter. So if you have any problems with that come and see me and I'll be glad to talk to you about that. I appreciate you being here, come and fish the rest of the tournaments with us and you might make the top thirty and end up in a Red Man regional—have a shot at that hundred thousand dollars at the Red Man All-American.

One of the assistant organizers brought up a barrel with the anglers' confirmation slips in it. Sonny reached in.

"Tony Maxwell, come on up here, I've got something for you. Tony, I got a Stren hat for you, I've got a seven-hundred-fifty-yard spool of Stren Easy Cast line. You going to catch a lot of fish tomorrow? Well, if you don't, here's a crying hat for you." He handed him the line and a Stren cap. The men laughed. "We got three hundred eighty fishermen tomorrow; go ahead and give yourselves a hand."

And they did. One hundred and ninety-one boats would be in the water the next day; thirty-eight of the 380 would win money. The first-place prize, over $4,000; with over thirty cash prizes in descending amounts, and $1,000 for the biggest bass of the day. Sonny reeled off the rules.

> I won't go through the whole list. Any time the engines are running tomorrow, that includes boat check in the morning, have your life jacket on, zipped up, secure. All boats used in the tournament must be equipped with an ignition kill switch and properly aerated for a recirculated live-well space capable of holding two limits of fish. How many boats are we going to have tomorrow? You know, the year before last we set a Red Man Tournament Trail record, we had two hundred seventy-two limits and weighed in 3,952 pounds of fish. We going to break that tomorrow? I think so. Partners, you must discuss the schedule of boat operation prior to takeoff. I'm going to touch on something here real quick. I want to remind the boaters that the nonboaters are entitled to their half a day in the front of the boat if they so desire. . . . It's only fair that nonboaters help to compensate the boater, for taking you fishing tomorrow. We suggest that you help with his expenses. . . . You'll be fishing a five-fish limit, twelve inches long; measured mouth closed on a flat board. . . . Boats 1 through 63, you'll take off at 6:00 A.M., your check-in time will be 2:00 P.M. Boats 64 through 127, you'll take off at 6:15 A.M., your check-in time will be 2:15. Third flight, boats 128 through 191, you'll take off at 6:30 A.M. and your check-in time will be 2:30.

Susie Bentley, an authoritative, no-nonsense woman, spoke from a microphone below Sonny. "Sonny runs the tournament and I run the boat ramp," she said. "If you work with my people tomorrow, we'll work with you. First-flight guys going out tomorrow, get in there early."

Her voice is loud, commanding in comparison to Sonny's firm crooning. One guy in the crowd pushed out his belly and said, loudly, "I left home for *that*?"

Joe leaned over to me and whispered, "A lot of those guys in there aren't interested in becoming spokesmodels."

Then Sonny began to call out the randomly paired boaters and nonboaters; men pushed their way to the front to meet their mates, shook hands, and turned together to finish the paperwork and pick up the sponsors' freebees at the front—Ranger hats and packets of Red Man chewing tobacco. I had already paid my entry fee of $75. Joe pulled a knowledgeable local, Don was matched with an older man, short, seemingly confused, with a minimal boat (Don suddenly looked queasy). I lost track of Buncie and Thompson, but then Sonny called my name. "Louv! Miller!" and I moved forward. Ken Miller found me, and we shook hands a bit awkwardly. He was tall, friendly, with a slow smile, oversized ball cap pushed back on his head and over the tops of his ears. He reminded me of the actor Tim Robbins.

Out in the parking lot, we talked briefly. I told him I was new at this, so he was welcome to have my 50 percent of the decisions tomorrow. Well, that's OK, he said, I'm here mainly to try out my new boat. He ambled around a corner and pointed to it. That's not a boat, I thought, that's a *rocket*. White and maroon and sleek, and much longer than Joe's Skeeter, it seemed to stretch across the lot as if had already released its booster. On its flank was the word *Champion*.

"Um, Ken, how many horsepower is that?" I said.

Ken smiled proudly. "Two hundred. Never opened up." This would be its maiden voyage. He was, he told me later, thirty-six, and he had lived in Toledo all his life. He works as the foreman in a packing plant and had been doing weekend tournaments, locally, for a few years. He was married, the father of two kids—including a boy whom he had thought about bringing here this trip, "but the wind was up so bad there was no way."

The next morning, at 4:00 in the Super 8 Motel parking lot, Ken pulled up with the Champion behind him. Joe and Don were packing Joe's boat, and Joe handed me two rods and a Day-Glo orange rain suit. "You'll need this," he said, eyeing the Champion. The temperature that morning was hovering just above freezing. I slipped the rainsuit over the thick extra clothes I was already wearing. Stuffed out, limbs stiff, I felt like an astronaut in a space suit, and struggled up into the cab of Ken's truck. He was quiet as he drove.

At Sandusky Bay, he joined a line of other four-wheel vehicles towing bass boats, sat until 5:00 A.M., and then slowly began to move toward the bay, plumes of exhaust wavering between taillights and headlights. Finally I saw the water, and the sight was awesome, even beautiful. Out on the water, bass boats were slowly moving out, assembling in a loose formation stretched across the bay. They looked like the floating fireflies at Disneyland's Pirates of the Caribbean, with their running lights moving out slowly, the hunkered fishermen sipping last-minute coffee, some of them slipping on helmets. Above the flotilla was a thin, lit cloud of exhaust and steam. From inside the cab, the flotilla seemed perfectly silent. I rolled down the window and heard it then: the vibrating rumble coming across the water.

"That's a freighter coming in. I thought the land was moving!" Ken said. "That's a big freighter. Those are interesting to get hit by."

I made small talk as we waited for our turn at the ramp.

"What kind of mileage do you get on your boat?"

"About two or three miles to the gallon. We got almost sixty gallons so we can go a long way. I think we can go about 120 miles on what gas we've got. We ain't going that far."

"Let me know what my half is."

"There is no set figure, usually the guy gives twenty, twenty-five dollars. If we win, you'll pay nothing." He laughed. "Let's put it that way."

The rumble was growing louder out on the water. A man came by and knocked on Ken's window, stuck out his hand with a card in it. "Boat-towing service, case we get in trouble out there," said Ken. He always brings a spare prop. "The one thing about it, no matter what you do, when you go to do this, something is going to break on this boat. This is a brand-new boat, every one of these boats putting in today, something's going to break. It may be minor, it may not be nothing, but something will break, I will have to work on this boat when I get home before the next tournament. Same with car racing."

Car racing?

"Yeah I did that for a number of years."

Car racing?

"Hey, this lady's a trip, wait until we get up there." Susie Bentley was standing outside a booth that each truck stopped at, and she checked them off, and took their fees if they had not already paid. She looked at Ken's blue truck, then she looked back at the boat and she said, "Nice rig but it don't even match!" Ken's neck seemed to pull into his jacket. She waved us on. He wheeled around and backed the Champion fast down the ramp into the black water. He jumped out, unhitched the boat, and I drove the truck up to the parking lot and parked it. A few minutes later, the engine humming, we were slipping across the bay, looking at our flight group, marked by a numbered plaque, weaving our way through the fireflies. The protected bay was still as glass, but the wind began to pick up. Lake Erie, we had learned, was not yet calm. Not at all. In fact, though most of the storm had passed, the swells would be as high or higher today.

I took the box of Dramamine from my pocket and popped another tablet in my mouth.

"So Ken, hey, tell me. How does this compare to racing cars?"

"This is a lot more enjoyable because it lasts longer."

Tournament bass-fishing must be cheaper, I said. "Not the initial investment. I've got $60,000 in this rig right here, $30,000 for the truck and $30,000 for the boat. With car racing you can get away with about $20,000 initial investment. But car racing gets more expensive later. For one thing, you can't get insurance on a race car. Lot of similarities, lot of dissimilarities. Fishermen are a cleaner crowd, no doubt."

We watched the spectacle of the 380 boats revving their engines, moving toward Sonny Reynolds, who stood in a lead boat holding a bullhorn barking commands. "Flight one . . . *flight one.*" His voice snapped across the water, and the first wave of boats, like a squadron of bombers, leaped into the air and with a deafening roar and a cloud of fumes shot toward the mouth of the bay, disappearing behind their own flaring plumes.

The air was filled with the smell of gasoline and exhaust. This wasn't fishing, this was a military operation.

Ken reached down under his steering wheel and pulled out a helmet and handed it to me. He took out another and pulled it down over his head, and snapped the visor down. "Flight two . . . *flight two.*" We moved up, the engine louder, getting ready. I braced myself. I leaned toward Ken and raised my voice above the noise: "Obviously racing cars is more dangerous."

His helmet turned toward me slightly, eyes on Sonny. We were edging to the front. "About the same, probably because the safety factors for the cars now, the rules are so strict because so many people got killed earlier. If you get in an accident they've got the equipment built so strong now that generally you can walk away from it." He patted the Champion's steering wheel, his breath floating out into the cold air. "You get in an accident in one of *these*, you're dead. You hit the water at seventy-five miles an hour, I don't care what you're wearing, it'll kill you."

"Flight three . . . *flight three.*" The Champion leaped up onto the water as if it were doing a pushup on fingers and toes, and it launched into the rising sun, gulls shooting up and out. My helmet snapped back and I hung on for dear life. This wasn't the way Joe had driven, slowly out to the swells, gradually accelerating; this was a breakneck race. Ken's gloved hands shimmied back and forth with the steering wheel. We reached, as he told me later, sixty-five miles per hour before we hit the swells. Sixty-five in a car and sixty-five in a boat are different things, particularly when the air is near freezing and the driver beside you is determined to beat every other boat in the world out to the best fishing spots. He *flew* past the other boats. I vaguely noted Joe's Skeeter as we blipped past it.

Twenty boats, thirty boats, Ken passed them all, and then he hit the first swell and the boat felt as if it was flying through the air, not over the wave but *above it*. With a longer boat, he was able to skim the tops of these swells without dipping down often, but in especially large troughs, this did not work, and he came down hard—but expertly, so that he did not stuff his engine or slice us into the next swell. A mile out and there wasn't a boat in sight. If awards were given for this part of the tournament—and a race it *is*—Ken Miller would have won, gloves down.

The fishing, of course, was anticlimactic. And rare. Miller was not a man to stay in one place long (unless Toledo counts). He raced from spot to spot, jerked his rod at the water, stared at it, became impatient, and fired the engine again. His goal, he said, was to catch the largest fish of the day, rather than achieving the largest five-fish weigh-in. He would go to where he thought the big fish were—which was a half hour this way, twenty minutes that way, an hour another way. He couldn't let the boat float still. We moved, and moved, and moved again. We spent more time flying around Lake Erie, I think, than fishing. For some tournament anglers, I suspect, this is the point. I asked Ken if he preferred fishing for competition or . . . normal . . . fishing. "I guess it's just the competition." He struggled for words. "I don't know how to put it. I'm going brain dead here, I've only had three hours of sleep. It's the adrenaline, get that adrenaline going." But it's not just the speed, it's the spectacle. "Wait until you see the weigh-in, you'll see what I mean. You'll say, 'Where the hell did these fish come from?' I hope we get them because I need them. Somebody gets them, I just hope it's us."

We caught a few smallmouth. Ken latched into what appeared to be a spiky six- to eight-pound walleye, which he shook off his hook in disgust.

We came back early, to beat the crowd.

↴ BY THREE IN THE AFTERNOON, most of the fishermen were in from the lake. I sat on the grassy bank and watched the troops come home. Joe was out there in his Skeeter, cleaning it down with a small mop. He saw me watching and reached into the live well and pulled out a nice big bass, and waved his hat in the air and grinned happily. A big steel-sided van pulled up next to the reviewing stand; "Tackle Shop On Wheels" was printed on the side of it. Sonny was up on a stand, with a Red Man banner snapping in the wind behind him, holding plastic bags of bass in the air and a microphone to his mouth. The weigh-in had begun.

"*From New Marksville, West Virginia, five-fish limit, eleven pounds, ten ounces.*"

This part of the ritual takes hours, and boats are still stacked up waiting to get in. Ken and I released our fish when it was clear that our
weight would not come close to placing. The men pulled their fish from
their boats' live wells and dropped them into official Red Man plastic
bags half-filled with water. Hundreds of anglers stood in a long line, each
of them holding a bag of fish—chunky smallmouth, their flanks curved
and pressed against the plastic—and as they passed a trough, they dropped
the plastic bags in, holding on to the tops. An electric aerator roiled the
water; this gave the fish a reviving goose. At the stand, one of Sonny's as-
sistants grabbed each bag in succession and hefted it up to the scale in
front of him.

*"Richard Levitz from Columbus, Ohio, five-fish limit, eleven pounds even,
eleven pounds zero ounces. It'll get interestin', it'll get interestin'. . . . Come on
up. Joe Baylor from Westerville, Ohio, five-fish limit, ten pounds, seven ounces."*

After the fish were weighed, a woman grabbed each bag, turned its
mouth, and slipped the fish into a second tank of briskly aerated water.
The tank was out of sight, behind the stand, a few feet from the water's
edge. I watched a grizzled, craggy man with a crumpled ball cap slip his
arms into the water to stroke the fish. He stroked them, stroked them
gently, bringing them back to life. His hands under the bellies, holding
them in the water, stroking their white bellies, massaging them, moving
them forward to pull water and oxygen through their gills. It was one of
the most strangely nurturing sights I have ever seen. A second woman,
grandmotherly with white hair, waited for each fish to recover, and then
plucked it out of the water and slipped it into the opening of a white
plastic pipe. The fish slid through the pipe, twenty feet or so, and into
the bay. Two boys crouched and bobbed on the shore at the bottom of
the tube and watched the fish come out of the tube and into the bay.
Three dead bass floated in the water at the end of the tube, which
swelled with live smallmouth beginning their getaways. No one knows
how many bass die unseen after they're released this way.

Bill Buncie had done well. He said one fish had broken his rod. He
was confident it would be the largest fish of the day, but that was not to
be. Don scowled as he rested under a tree. When Joe had dropped him
off at 4:00 A.M., Don's partner didn't even have the prop mounted yet.
He was a slow man, far too slow for Don's itchy ambition. But now, Joe
was up on the stage, beaming, with a bag of bass, five keepers with a total of twelve pounds. (He had found his honey pot, and caught twenty-
five of them—all around two pounds; it's a common occurrence on the
lake, to find a school of fish all the same size.) He placed in the top third
of the tournament contestants, and Bill Buncie and Jim Thompson placed
right behind him.

Sonny held Joe's bag up in the air, and Joe raised his arm and the crowd applauded and whistled. Joe looked like a professional up there— a potential bassin' spokesmodel and future star. A . . . *contender!*

∽ HOW DIFFERENT THE tournament world was from what I had expected it to be. I had assumed it would be powered by greed and competition (competition and salesmanship were certainly part of the energy of the thing), but I was surprised at how connected people felt to each other, how cooperative they were.

One might argue that the fishing tournament world is no different from the circuits of golf, or tennis, or rock concerts—just another form of the restless, commercial American dream, all that roaming in search of the brass ring, the main chance. But the fishing circuit contains an added element: It takes place in nature. A man-made reservoir may not be the most literal and pure expression of nature; gasoline-sucking power boats might not have been the vehicle of choice for Natty Bumppo; Thoreau, encountering a fully equipped Roland Martin, would have wept. But the men who follow the circuit also move with the cycles of nature; even behind the wheels of their rigs, they're figuring weather, spawning periods, water temperature, the stage of the moon.

Not many of us live that way these days.

Also, relative to other sports, the bass tournament world is open and democratic. But it's not diverse. Studies by the U.S. Fish and Wildlife Service show that bass anglers are predominantly male, one-third are ages twenty-five to thirty-four, and about half have college degrees and good incomes. You'll see few blacks, Hispanics, or Southeast Asians hauling metal-flake bass boats.

Some sponsors, such as PRADCO (Plastics Research and Development Co.) of Fort Smith, Arkansas, have tried to increase the number of blacks and Hispanics promoting the company's lures and line on the tournament circuits. For instance, PRADCO paid Michael Echols's $600 entry fee and travel expenses at four B.A.S.S. Eastern Invitational tournaments in the 1997–98 pro fishing season. A maintenance supervisor at an Athens, Georgia, apartment complex, Echols, who first fished competitively with the Master's Bassers, a Christian fishing club, grew up dreaming of being the first African-American to win a major bass tournament. A PRADCO spokesman told *The Atlanta Journal-Constitution* that if he prospered, "It would be like what Tiger Woods meant to golf after he won the Masters."

In the Red Man tournament on Lake Erie, I saw no women anglers, though I might have missed them. I did see one African-American angler, with a bag of fish at the weigh-in. Despite good intentions and pleasant words here and there, the tournament world has fostered subtle discouragement of minorities and the blatant exclusion of women. So some blacks have created their own local clubs, and women have created a major subculture—their own natural resource community—within the tournament world.

Barbara "Sugar" Ferris made sure of that.

Sex and the Bass'n Gals

∽✎∽

SUGAR FERRIS WAS DRIVING her rented Cadillac toward Canton, some-where in East Texas. She was on her way to Lake Fork, one of the finest bass reservoirs in America, (and it's not bad for alligators, either). A cou-ple of weeks earlier, she'd wrecked her big Suburban—"the national car of Texas," she calls the model—and she was in pain from the accident. We were on our way to the Texas Shootout, a small but passionate local women's fishing tournament.

When we arrived, it would become a kind of wake.

Along Interstate 20, the April bluebonnets were blooming. She pulled off the freeway at Canton, drove past a building housing a company named with appropriate Texas bluntness: Truck Stuff. She was looking for a place to eat.

This "old coyote town," as Sugar called it, seems to survive on pro-ceeds from antiques and junk, sold at storefronts and the Canton Auto Swap Meet, which offers to sellers over 2,800 acres on which to spread their eclectic booths. People travel here from all over the country on the first Monday of each month. I had seen antique rows, but never an an-tique town, with all those false-fronted brick buildings housing stores with names like Uncle Junk and Auntiques. This is what becomes of some old Texas towns, like the one in Larry McMurtry's novel *The Last Picture Show.*

Over in West Texas, McMurtry has come home to depressed Archer City, the hometown he left more than forty years ago. He's been buying and gutting the old main street buildings and filling them with books; he hopes to make it a book town, an international tourist destination. I asked Sugar if she had ever considered creating something similar: to revive a dying small town, maybe one near a reservoir, to dedicate it to anglers, their history, and their paraphernalia. Call it Fish Town.

"Never thought of that," she said. "Bass Pro's Outdoor World is probably the closest thing to it. They're building a new one in Grapevine, right outside of Dallas." She turned to me, smiled sweetly. "But that's a lovely idea."

Sugar is a small, rounded, sixty-one-year-old woman with a beautiful smile and an utterly charming, forthright manner. She is one of fishing's living legends, and her fame crosses the cultures. From the shores of Lake Fork to the steelhead streams of Washington State, female anglers credit her, and a handful of other women, including fly-fishing's Joan Wulff, with transforming the cultures of fishing by opening the doors wider to women. Not that women had been entirely excluded: They have a long, proud, and, until recently, untold history in fishing.

Lyla Foggia, in *Reel Women*, the first book to assemble those scattered fragments, describes some of the heroines and historic milestones, including these from the twentieth century:

> Francesca LaMonte of the American Museum of Natural History in New York helped pioneer marine research and produced seven groundbreaking books on fresh and saltwater fish, beginning in the mid-1930s. Helen Robinson was one of a trio of people responsible for devising a technique for teasing a billfish to an artificial fly in the 1960s—a technique that is practiced around the world today. About the same time, Kay Brodney became the first woman to courageously explore the remote jungles of South America in search of freshwater fish so rare that few are aware of their existence even today. International fly-fishing luminary Joan Wulff indelibly altered the way fly-casting is taught, through the school she established with her late husband, Lee Wulff, and her long-running magazine column and books. Marsha Bierman's short-rod standup technique for catching billfish is regarded as the most innovative influence on big-game angling since the sport's official inception in 1898. Most recently, Sugar Ferris. . . .

These women, Foggia writes, "symbolize the innate spirit that too often lies dormant within our souls. They embody those qualities that are within the grasp of each one of us, but that our inner consciousness, like a strict governess, rarely acknowledges as a legitimate exhibition of behavior for women. Through their lives, we are reminded of what we can and might be doing with our own lives—whether or not we ever pick up a fishing rod."

It will always be a puzzle how the myth got started that women do not fish, or at least do not fish in significant numbers comparable to men. Certainly there are ample references . . . to indicate that women have been participating in the sport for hundreds of years. There are also statistics to indicate that women have comprised approximately one-third of all anglers for at least the last 10 years, the only period of time in which quantifiable surveys have been taken. If we have under-estimated their participation, it is perhaps a result of two key factors: as late as the 1960s, many states did not require women to buy a fishing license, and even today, few states ask for an angler's gender on the form that is filled out . . . for either an annual or temporary license.

Sugar Ferris jousted with myths. In 1976, she created Bass'n Gal, the national women's bass-fishing association and tournament circuit; it eventually stretched from Texas to Missouri to New York to Florida. Thousands of women who had been excluded by the male-dominated tournaments or had never fished a tournament (or, in fact, had never fished) entered this new arena. "Sugar Ferris kicked open the door for women anglers, and I walked right through it," says professional angler Kathy Magers of Rockwall. "My life has been forever changed."

At its peak, Bass'n Gal, based in Arlington, Texas, boasted 33,000 members. A few comparisons: the Ladies Professional Golf Association claims 384 players and an additional 1,100 members in its teaching division. "Our players and teachers have to go through a series of qualifications," says the LPGA media coordinator, Laura Neal. "Still, it's amazing that Sugar built a membership that big."

Within the United States Golf Association, which anyone can join, 20 percent of the members—about 160,000—are women. The National Organization for Women, the largest feminist organization in the nation, claims some 250,000 members. Considering that Sugar was recruiting from the narrow world of female bass anglers, primarily in the South, Southeast, and Midwest, it's astonishing that Bass'n Gal's numbers were so high.

Right now, Sugar and I were astonishingly hungry.

She turned the Cadillac into the seedy parking lot at down-home Granny's Kitchen. Granny's is in a two-story clapboard building, perhaps an old farmhouse. Across the road was a fireworks stand *("Buy one get three free")* and a new Taco Bell. A hand-painted sign advertised "Quail, $7.95," and the "Best chicken fried steak in East Texas," and that's saying something in East Texas.

Inside Granny's Kitchen, a radio was playing oldies from the '60s. The walls were covered with icons: photographs of John Wayne, the horns of a Texas Longhorn steer, tumbleweeds dressed up with Christmas-tree lights, farm implements, and a saw painted with a Texas ranch scene.

We sat down and ordered. "You go on. Order that quail." She ordered a hamburger.

As we waited, I asked her about her childhood, how she came to fishing. She said she grew up in Livingston, a small East Texas town seventy miles northeast of Houston, on the fringes of the swampy and wild Big Thicket; the land was covered with humid pine forests and laced with streams.

Like so many people her age, she grew up poor but didn't know it. She was the baby of ten children. She is so distant in age from her oldest brothers and sisters that some of Sugar's nieces and nephews are older than she is.

"We were so self-sufficient that we never really did need anybody else," she said. "My family was so close and loving that when my father's work would change, the whole extended family would move with him. I don't remember, as a child, ever being outside that family." The family's moves, though, were always within a hundred-mile radius of their ranch. Her mother never traveled farther from home than that. Ever. Sugar and her brothers and sisters grew up hunting and fishing; there was no gender difference when it came to that, partly because they needed the food.

Crispy critters wasn't a breakfast cereal then; crispy critters was what we ate. I was raised on food from the wild. My dad was a great outdoorsman and he took great pride in all his daughters being able to help themselves. He died when I was sixteen years old but my mother was the same way. I can never remember us not having a garden; we grew our own food. I used to tell my dad, "I'm hungry," and he'd say, "You've never been hungry in your life."

My grandfather Charlie and his brother came west from Tennessee for the Oklahoma land rush. While they were in that territory, they stole a horse, and my grandfather Charlie took the blame for it because his brother was married with children. His brother stayed and Charlie started traveling, fast. He came through Ouachita, Arkansas, and stopped at a mission. A Ouachita Indian woman had left three of her daughters there, and my grandfather married one of them, stayed there a while, and in 1898, my mother was born. My mother could remember traveling from Arkansas to Texas, when she was eight years old, in an old covered wagon.

I fished a lot with my mother and grandmother. All our pioneer journals are scattered with women who fished and taught their daughters how to fish. It's more than a casual knowledge that we women have with fishing.

My grandmother, who was born around 1865, was a cane-pole angler. Creek bank, river fishing. I remember looking for crickets with her, for bait. In the spring after the catalpa trees would bud, their leaves would be loaded with these little green worms—the leaves would almost turn to worms—and my grandmother would shake the catalpa trees, and we'd gather the fallen worms. And we would rip the bark off to get to the grubs. I can still see her face: pleasant, sweet. She was short like I am. She wore her dark hair back in a little bun, and she always wore a long dress when we fished. She'd hold the worms and grubs in her apron, which she pulled up into a pocket, and she would carry them to the creek.

She died when I was eight. I remember her telling me not to get too close to the water. The way she kept me away from it was she'd say an alligator would get me. Or, she'd say, "the undertoad will get you." I was always afraid of this big toad coming up and grabbing me.

I asked her if she had read *The World According to Garp*, by John Irving. "His character was always afraid of the undertoad." She shook her head.

"Saw the movie, though. I wonder if we're kin. Probably heard it from my grandmother." She smiled. "Try that quail." I did. Tough, dark little bodies. Sugar's hamburger looked like it tasted a lot better. She tore into it with gusto. "On the creeks, we'd catch crappie, perch, a few bass. Some of my fondest memories are of catching those great big old sun perch. Some of them weighed a pound and a half. My grandmother taught me to always look for the eddies on the creek and fish behind the eddies. I remember the coolness under the tall pine trees and the wind coming through the trees. Those wonderful days that we spent. And of course we had stock ponds, and we'd fish in those. Sometimes we'd swim with the fish."

Despite the undertoad.

WE FINISHED OUR LUNCH and headed out on the highway again. One of the best things about traveling in search of fish and the people who fish for them is that you see the land and the water through other eyes.

You see it differently. Instead of trees only, you see trees from a past. Instead of plain water, you see the reflection of a Ouachita woman with her apron full of green worms from the catalpas.

"Look at those evening primroses, aren't those pretty?" said Sugar, pointing to the pink flowers that covered the fields like the finest, thinnest of quilts. "Why, there's some Indian paintbrush and some yellow daisies." We rode smoothly through low scrub oak and mesquite, past spring fields freshly plowed for cotton, soybean, sorghum, hay, maize, peas. Through forests of hickory, cedar, oak, and pecan and then through scattered subdivisions of double-wide trailers. "Tornado magnets," said Sugar, with some affection. "Leaves on those trees are turned over. Means rain."

Beneath her practiced optimism and habitual good cheer, I thought I heard a trace of melancholy.

You know, life is a lot like that old country and western song says: The young folks want to get away and the old folks want to go back, and we spend our lives replacing all the things we leave behind.

When I was growing up you didn't go work in town, because there was no work. We lived 10 or 15 miles out. I had a pea patch, an acre of peas. This is how I made my money for clothes. People could come in and pick the peas for $2 a bushel, or I would pick the peas for them for $3.

At that time, Livingston probably had only 1,500 people. But when I was a girl, I could not wait to leave home and experience the world. And when I did, I left my mother standing on the front porch crying. She was holding onto the front porch because her baby was leaving and I turned around and said, "Momma, I want to tell you something. I've had the happiest childhood that any child could ever wish for. I felt very loved, and I love you and Daddy. I treasure all that, but there are three things in my life that I'm never going to do again. I am never going to shell another pea; I am never going to shuck another ear of corn; and I am never going to iron another piece of cotton."

My mother looked at me, and shook her finger at me, and with tears streaming down her face, said, 'A dog always eats what it turns its nose up at.'

I didn't realize her meaning for many years. Now I can't wait to get to the farmer's market. I stop and buy peas, shell them, put them in the freezer; I shuck the corn; and every piece of clothing I own is cotton and I iron it all. A dog will always eat what it turns its nose up at. Those words have haunted me for years.

As a young woman, Sugar lived in Honolulu, where she worked as a counselor for emotionally disturbed children, and in Houston, from 1967 to 1971, where she worked for an oil company. That year, after a marriage ended, she came home to Livingston as a single mother of an eight-year-old daughter. By this time her elderly mother had sold the ranch. "But all my sisters and brothers still lived in the area; they've never left. I'm the only one who had the adventuresome spirit."

She took a job at a marina at nearby Lake Livingston, "just to have something to do," and three weeks later, a newspaper editor called her. "He had tried to hire the marina owner to do a fishing column, but the owner wouldn't do it. I didn't know how to write, but he said, 'Just be natural, we'll call it *The Incomplete Angler.*' So I started this odyssey, this quest. They had men's bass-fishing tournaments out of this marina. I wanted to see what bass-fishing was all about so I convinced a local guide to take me fishing. I was only out there an hour and I caught two bass on a spinner bait. I guess those two bass just changed the complexion of fishing forever."

She was determined to join a tournament, but the men's circuits and local contests wouldn't allow women to compete. "That was absurd. You don't need great upper-body strength to fish. A string of bass is a lot easier to lift than a three-year-old child." She set out to get to the root of the issue. She called officials of the men's organizations. "All the circuits had what they called a 'sexual privacy' rule. The men who fished in the tournaments were confined to a boat eight hours a day. They couldn't get out of the boat, or go on shore to go to the bathroom. So they'd pee in coffee cans or off the boat, and they didn't want to do that in front of women. Guess they didn't think it would be gentlemanly. And they didn't want a woman doing that in front of them. I teased them, said, 'If you don't know about anatomy by the time you get to be able to ride in a bass boat, there is something seriously wrong with you.'" Sugar kept pressuring the tournament directors, who would ask her: So how would you suggest handling sexual privacy? "I'd just tell that man, 'You go on up front, I'll turn the trolling motor on high, and you just whistle Dixie!'"

Then Sugar learned that wives and girlfriends were often more opposed than the men to women joining bass tournaments. They didn't want their men out there with women pulling down their drawers. *Anything could happen in a bass boat.* "Sometimes women are their own worst enemy."

She recalled how, in the late '70s, a television news reporter interviewed women on the topic. "This one woman had a beehive hairdo piled up on her head, false eyelashes, tiger-striped top, sling-back shoes with real high heels, and she said she did *not* believe that the women should be out there fishing with *her* husband. The reporter asked, "What is it exactly that you object to?" And she put her hands on her hips and backed off and said, 'Hon-ey, when you put ice cream in front of a baby, he's gonna eat it!' I thought that was a hysterical statement."

Sugar considered the sexual-privacy rule and spousal objections silly. "But I guess they didn't feel it was so silly. The men's tournament directors were just not comfortable with women. So I said to myself, 'Golf has women's divisions, so I guess we'll have a division for women in fishing!' And that's what we created."

Starting in 1972, she began to host annual women's tournaments, through the Lake Livingston Marina. Then, during a 1976 Dallas business meeting of the Outdoor Writers Association of America, Sugar Ferris stood up and announced her plan to start the first women's professional fishing circuit.

What, she was asked, would the organization be called?

"Ferris should have seen that question coming, but she didn't," wrote Ray Sasser of *The Dallas Morning News*. With her new husband, Bob, "looking pale and tugging at her shirttail in an attempt to short-circuit the surprise announcement, Ferris flashed on a tackle box that had been personalized for her. In typical fishing industry style, the original brass name plate had been inscribed for OWAA member 'Bassin' Man Sugar Ferris.' Ferris returned the name plate with a typically terse remark about not qualifying as a Bass'n Man. The name plate came back inscribed Bass'n Gal Sugar Ferris, and the name stuck. In retrospect, Ferris would have chosen a different name because of the 'Gal' connotation, and she might have gotten rid of the Bass'n part because it limited the scope of her organization."

"I guess when I started Bass'n Gal, if I'd have called it Better Homes and Bass Boats I would have gotten a lot further than I did," she told me. "We came in around the tail end of the '70s and of course everybody thought it was part of the women's lib movement at the time. I got so tickled because I guess the bass-fishing world thought the next worm we would be dragging across the lake might be a man. I guess they thought we rolled our cigarettes up in our shirtsleeves. But we were just looking for someplace to compete, and someplace to belong. It was really funny. We'd go and set up at boat shows or trade shows and people would come by, men especially, and just be ugly. 'Why don't you stay home and take care of your kids?' I'd say, 'Well, mine are twenty-five and thirty and they've got kids of their own!' "

Clearly, the resistance was more than bladder deep.

Not long after she launched Bass'n Gal, Sugar and her husband were vacationing in Illinois and decided to fish in a tournament there. Sugar charmed her way into the tournament. The story reveals a lot about the resistance, and about Sugar.

I was the only woman, 237 men and me. Well, this guy that I drew the first day he was a log hauler from Missouri, which is OK because my dad hauled logs all his life, worked in the lumber mills, farmed, and ranched. But this log hauler, when they called his and my name as boat partners, he was going around saying, "Who is Sugar Ferris?" They had never said that there was a woman in that tournament. So I tapped him on the shoulder and said, 'I'm Sugar Ferris,' and he got physically ill. He went to the door and threw up. He just couldn't stand the idea of fishing with a woman.

I'll call him Buddy Bubba. I won't use his name because I don't want him thinking I'm making fun of him, because I'm not. When he got physically ill, I thought, "There is something wrong with this guy!" I said to him, "Listen, I don't want to hinder you, let's go to the tournament director and maybe he'll change partners. I don't want to be responsible for anybody being sick because they have to fish with me!" So he said OK, we went to the tournament director, and the director said, "I'm sorry, this is a draw tournament. You cannot choose your own partner. You can either fish with her or disqualify yourself." I thought, "Oh, boy. We're stuck with each other. But everybody has a soft spot somewhere, and maybe God will show me his soft spot."

So the next morning we went down to the dock. I took my rods and reels and everything down there and I said, "Where would you like me to put them?" And he said, "Put them in the back of the boat, put them in the backseat because that's all you're going to do today anyway." I thought, "Oh, boy, am I going to have a fun day. Eight hours with this guy." So anyway I put my rods and reels in and said, "Well"—in an effort to be friendly—"I'm going to go and get some ice. What do you drink? I'll be glad to bring you a cup." He said, "Don't want anything you have or anything you have to offer me." I went and got my Coke, came back, and got in the back of the boat, sat in the backseat like a good little girl. I was feeling pretty dismal, and then this little ol' man and woman came walking down the pier. They had cane poles and a minnow bucket with them. And this guy was very short, and this little woman said, "Oh, are you all going crappie fishing today?" Buddy Bubba stood up, all nineteen foot of him—at least he thought he was—in the front of the boat, puffed out his chest, and said, "We're *bass anglers*, lady!"

And I said to myself, "Thank you God for this sign!" So when we were sitting there waiting to go out I said to this guy, "Buddy, you know the reason I entered this tournament?" And he said, "Don't have any idea." I said, "Well, I'll tell you. I'm just beginning to learn to bass fish. And I can learn so much from you professional bass anglers." Of course I could see his chest swelling more and more and more. And every opportunity I got that day I asked him questions. "How would you bass anglers do this?" I had him eating out of my hand. I took him to where my husband, Bob, and I had prefished and found fish and he caught his limit and boy, he was all swole up. He was just like a big old frog, just swole up. When we came in— he had a limit of bass and I had mine. When we got in line with our bass—this was on an Illinois lake with deep, clear water and not many people had fish—of course Buddy was all swole up and happy about his limit of bass. He told Bob what a great time he had.

I liked Buddy. I admired him and I'll tell you why. When we were fishing that day, I finally got Buddy to talking about himself. He said he had come to love fishing and the competition in the tournaments, but his wife was an extremely religious woman and she did not want him fishing. She wanted him to go to church because she was in church five times a week. They had just had their first baby and she wanted him there with that baby in church. He said, "You know, I love my wife. She goes a little bit overboard on the organized religion. But we've had so many arguments that she finally made a deal with me, that if I would go to church with her at least three times a week—Wednesday night, Sunday morning, and Sunday night—and participate in one church activity, she would never again mention my going fishing, I could go fishing as much as I wanted to. I joined the choir." I told him then, "I admire that—I admire a person who is willing to give up something for someone else, who's willing to compromise."

I still see him every once in a while and I ask, "How's the wife, is she still keeping her end of the bargain?" He'll say, "Yes, she is, and I'm still fishing!"

With much the same mixture of toughness, compassion, and flattery, Sugar charmed the rest of the bass-fishing world—or almost all of it. But in January 1998, Sugar closed Bass'n Gal, after nearly twenty-two years, for reasons she would explain along the way.

"Something else I learned on that tournament. When Buddy and I came back to the weigh-in, I had more fish than my husband, Bob, and the other men wouldn't let it be. They were hooting at the poor man, saying things like, 'Bob Ferris, you couldn't catch your ass with both hands!' Right then, I decided I'd never fish with him in the same tournament again. He protested, but that was my decision. I like competing with men, but I didn't *ever* want to humiliate my husband again."

Ahead, water shined through the trees.

↢ LAKE FORK RESERVOIR is the premier bass lake of Texas, largely because state biologists set size limits on bass that can be taken out of it. Impounded in the fall of 1980, the 27,700-acre lake produces more trophy largemouth bass than most lakes in the country. Consequently, people come to Lake Fork from all over the nation to catch their lifetime trophy bass.

Early in the lake's history, state biologists experimented with crossing Florida strain bass with the native Texas bass, which produced big, tough fish. Such creativity continues. Under something called the Lone Star Lunker program, if an angler catches a particularly big bass, he or she can donate it to the state. A state biologist will drive to the angler, pick up the lunker, take it to a state hatchery, and use it as a brood fish; as part of the deal, the state will make a fiberglass duplicate of the fish for the angler to hang on the wall. The state distributes the fry of these lunkers to lakes or ponds, which over time produce a superior strain of bass—at least for sportfishing.

The investment pays off. According to a survey by the American Sportfishing Association, fishing boosts the Texas economy by more than $6 billion annually. The sport's local popularity was one of the main reasons that Bass Pro's Outdoor World chose a spot next to Grapevine Mills for a future 150,000-square-foot store.

At the time of Bass'n Gal's closing, seven women's fishing clubs in Texas were affiliated with the national organization. These clubs had already planned a joint tournament on Lake Fork, but when the anglers learned of the demise of Bass'n Gal, the occasion became an opportunity for mourning, regrouping, and surprisingly, a good deal of laughter.

When we arrived, a dozen or so of the women anglers here for the tournament were sitting around a long table at Moser's Restaurant at Lake Fork Marina. At other tables, the male anglers hunched over scrambled eggs and bacon, their caps on, of course. They were sunburned. One man looked like a raccoon; he had white circles around his eyes, where his sunglasses had been, the rest of his face scalded by the sun. Mounted bass surrounded the customers. The women were laughing at something that Pamela Dountas, forty-seven, of the Lake Fork Lady Anglers, had just said.

Her hair was slightly spiked, with buzzed sidewalls. Tendrils of hair trailed down over her collar. She wore a red polo shirt, white shorts and tennis shoes. She had a beautiful laugh. I liked her immediately. "I like to hear men scream, so I take them out on rough water," she was saying. "That's the only way I can get them to scream. The sounds of heavy breathing and screaming. Works every time." The women laughed hard and dug into their hamburgers.

In their non-angling time, these women are housewives, nurses, accountants; one is an attorney for American Airlines. I asked them how they felt about Sugar closing down Bass'n Gal.

"We hate it, we're depressed about it," said Karen Woodruff, also of the Lake Fork Lady Anglers. Another woman and fellow club member, Pam Todd, said it broke her heart. "I've only been involved in this for about three years. I got involved after I got divorced. Basically I feel like it changed my life, I suddenly developed a large extended family of fishing friends. It gave me back a life."

"Even as little girls we're in a competitive state with each other" said Dountas. "We're not like the men, who, as little boys with their baseball teams, learned how to be supportive of each other and be buds. Here, we're very supportive of each other; it's nice to go to a tournament and have a bunch of women put their arms around you and encourage you. Most of us have left our husbands and boyfriends behind—"

"Or they've left us behind," someone said.

Dountas continued. "When you're out on the boat with one of your buds, it's like having a good bartender with you; you can talk about any of your problems. The women that I've met through Bass'n Gal are forever friends."

Several of the women nodded. I looked around. The women appeared to be between thirty-five and fifty-five. They all looked as if they had survived a lot of hurt in their lives. "But you were asking about what happened when Sugar went down," said Dountas. When Bass'n Gal went under it was not only like losing my best friend, but almost like losing a mother."

"Can we say closed rather than gone under?" said Sugar, a little embarrassed.

Cheryl Phillips, a tall, fifty-one-year-old mental-health worker from Wills Point, Texas, and the 1997 national Bass'n Gal Woman of the Year, said, "Now there's nothing to do but regroup and try to figure out what comes after Bass'n Gal. Maybe we'll call ourselves the Ex-Bass'n Gals."

"You'll always be a Bass'n Gal," Sugar said softly.

Dountas described herself as a retired minister. She said that Bass'n Gal had become her fellowship. I asked her if she was using that word in a religious sense.

"Yeah, there's a real spiritual connection with a lot of us."

Dountas, as she explained to me later, had been a minister with the Metropolitan Community Church in Dallas and then she attended an Episcopal seminary, but after she completed her training, her Episcopal diocese denied her a ministry because she was, and is, a "practicing lesbian," as she put it. "So I went independent and now I'm just a heathen." She laughed. "I fish every Sunday. Let's see. God or fishing, God or fishing, God or fishing—fishing!"

Woodruff, who lives in a small trailer near the Lake Fork marina, is a short, cherubic blonde with an infectious laugh and wry manner. "Two years ago today, I met my future husband right here at this marina when I was selling ads for Bass'n Gal's magazine," she said. Her husband is a professional guide on the lake.

"Karen and Mark got married on Mark's bass boat out here on the docks," said Todd. "She was out there in her veil." The minister performed the service on the boat. Mark's brother proceeded to throw him in the lake."

Was anybody casting during the wedding? I asked.

"No, but Karen hosted a wedding tournament afterward."

Several women spoke at once. "She had been casting for two years!" "She reeled him in." "He finally bit!" "She set the hook." "Man on!"

"I'll tell you," said Woodruff, with a conspiratorial tone. "Fishing takes on a whole new aspect when you do it in the nude."

The women laughed uproariously and the boys with their ball caps looked around at them slowly.

Not all the women were quite as purposefully colorful. One of them was a tastefully dressed and coiffed member of the Junior League. Somehow it was hard to imagine her flipping jell lizards at spawning hawgs. Though her new husband doesn't fish, she has informed him that bass-angling is essential to her sanity—so get used to it.

"This is not an easy sport," said Pam Todd. "When you go out on tournaments, it's incredibly windy or it's raining or it's cold or it's hot. During night tournaments, we're on the water for twelve hours, stay up all night and fish. This is not something that is in any way cushy. But we crave the feeling, not just the competition, but the anticipation. I have been out there nine hours on the water and not even gotten a *bite*, but I always believe that *something is going to happen*."

"So many men in my life say, 'You can't do that!'" said Cheryl Phillips. "To this day, you hear men on the lake saying, 'Those are two *women* in that boat!' That's a lot of the fun of it, showing them we can do it."

Dountas added, "For a woman to have fun, there's not a lot of definition in that. We're normally the caretakers. When you get into fishing, you learn to take care of yourself—you have to or you're going to get hurt. We do take care of each other, though. We learn to take care of ourselves first and then to think of each other. Not to say we're perfect. At some of the meetings we're bitching and grumping, and you say to yourself, 'That woman needs some *estrogen*.'"

She said a friend had introduced her to Bass'n Gal during the most depressed period of her life. "Fishing is as strong as any antidepressant. I'll always have fishing, that's a constant thing in my life. I may not have a companion, and my truck may not start in the morning, but I'll always have fishing. To me, that's the way I'll bring God back into my life."

Did God leave you?

"Yeah, yeah, he ran away, went to the Baptist church, I think!" The women laughed. "I have a theory about the water. When we're sitting by the water or on the water, just the sound takes us back into the womb. It's a comfort. Spiritually we were all baptized with or in the water. The twelve disciples were fishermen. Look what was fed to the multitudes—fish! Now, I hope they weren't bass, because we don't eat bass. We practice catch-and-release."

"They were crappie," one of the women said.

Dountas grinned. "That must be in the New Testament, that Baptist book of yours."

The conversation shifted with dessert; a waitress set down generous pieces of pie a la mode. The women talked about the expense of the sport, particularly the boats. The talk came fast now.

"Fishing's given us a whole new line to shop," someone said.

"We don't have to go to the mall anymore together, we can go to the tackle shop!"

"And you've never seen anything until you've seen this group of women at a worm bar, thank God they all close at seven or eight at night and not two in the morning. I've seen Lily at a worm bar."

What's a worm bar?

"At a lot of the tackle shops they have a worm bar—like the vegetable counter at the grocery store—filled with every color worm you would want."

Oh, plastic worms?

"Right!"

I thought maybe this was a new kind of sushi. Texas sushi.

"They say it's a good place to pick up a man, but I don't know about that," said Dountas, smiling.

So, I asked, what's different about a typical woman's bass boat from a man's bass boat?

"Ours are prettier, we take better care of ours," one of the women answered. "And we carry cans. I have a very large coffee can in my boat."

"For your very large butt," said Karen.

"Karen needs some estrogen," someone else said.

When fishing with men, some women use portable toilets with pull-around curtains. Sugar said, politely, that one friend of hers pees in the live well. "The boats have double live wells now; she'd use one side and then just flush it out. It's a lot easier than coffee cans sometimes."

So, I asked, now that Starbucks rules, what do you do for coffee cans?

"Folgers still comes in a big can," said Lily Carey.

You recommend Folgers, then.

"Absolutely, great can."

"We ought to get Folgers as one of our sponsors!" said Dountas. "I wouldn't mind driving a boat that looks like a can. I think I'll send them a letter."

"We're already recycling Folgers cans. That'd make a good commercial."

The lunch bunch broke up and laughter trailed them out the door. Several stopped to give Sugar an extra hug. They clearly loved her, and felt that this day marked the end of something, and perhaps the beginning of something else. In any case, it was time for the Bass'n Gals to pre-fish Lake Fork.

They walked toward the water.

⌐ WHY DID SUGAR FERRIS shut down Bass'n Gal? As the *Houston Chronicle* pointed out after the closing, the circuit was never tainted with any of the cheating scandals that hit some of the men's circuits. There were a few controversies. Some competitors complained about favoritism, but ultimately Bass'n Gal's future was determined by money. As fishing tackle, engine, and oil companies merged or were bought out by smaller corporations, they focused their marketing and advertising campaigns on the well-established men's market.

Corporate sexism, and homophobia (or fear of the religious right, which by 1997 was even attacking Disney), also played a role, as Sugar sees it. She witnessed the sexism most vividly in the sponsors' attitude toward Bass'n Gal's slick magazine. Though one outboard-engine manufacturer had sponsored two of Bass'n Gal's top anglers, it continued to send ads that featured only pictures of men. Another advertiser objected to a cover photograph of a woman in a boat built by its competition. Ferris replied: The angler was on the cover because she was that year's circuit champion—not because of the brand of boat she drove.

Some sponsors, like Ranger Boats, a supporter for twenty-one years, stood true. Ranger, she says, "recognized the plight of women anglers." But other manufacturers "were just sponsoring us to be politically correct. We had to constantly prove ourselves. Sponsors were signing long-term contracts with the men's organizations and their tournaments, but only year-to-year contracts with women's organizations—which makes it almost impossible to plan long-term. I'm not sure these people have learned anything about women, or that they have even come to an understanding of equality."

In the long run, the pullback from women's angling makes no sense because the market appears to have plateaued. To increase sales, the sportfishing industry must attract more women and children.*

Indeed, one manufacturer's president, quoted in *Field & Stream*, asserted that the industry needed to involve more women, because the women bring the children along. Yet, this same manufacturer, which had been a Bass'n Gal sponsor for six years, dropped its sponsorship in 1997 after it was acquired by a large corporation. "I called this guy and said, 'I'm so glad to see you make that statement about getting more women involved. We sure would like to have you back on board with Bass'n Gal as a sponsor.' He said, 'Well, you know I would, but we just got to have more bang for our buck.' I told my husband, 'If I hear that phrase one more time I'm going to puke.'"

For years, Bass'n Gal courted Wal-Mart, one of the major sponsors of bass tournaments. "Three out of four shoppers who walk into a Wal-Mart store are women. But we couldn't even get in the door. We tried to get appointments with their people but they were always too busy." The same thing happened with General Mills—a tournament sponsor that, in 1998, placed a male angler on the cover of its Wheaties box. In 1997, seeking support for the 1998 season, Sugar sent out proposals to thirty-five potential sponsors. "From thirty-four of those companies, I never even received the courtesy of a reply. I got one response, and it said no. I did get a call from Sears. The guy asked if I would present a proposal to Sears, because the company was interested in getting into the fishing tournament business and he thought Bass'n Gal would be a good place for them to start. I spent three days on a proposal, shipped it off to him. Two weeks later I'm reading a news release from Sears's PR agency say-

---

*A similar trend is seen in the parallel universe of hunting. Women now compose the fastest-growing group among hunters, "reviving a million-dollar industry that was in danger of stagnating as fewer and fewer men signed up for hunting licenses," according to *The New York Times*. James Barron, "A-Hunting She Will Go; The Fastest-Growing Group Trooping to the Woods Is Women." *New York Times*, November 26, 1997, p. B1.

SUGAR FERRIS

ing it had signed with Red Man Tour. And I never have, to this day, received a reply to anything that I sent them, not a 'Hello, good-bye, kiss my ass,' or anything else. That's the thing that chagrins me."

Some sponsors, however, had more political reasons for pulling the plug. They withdrew when several participants acknowledged that they were lesbians.

"We did surveys of how much gasoline women anglers use. This guy from one gasoline company was real excited when he saw these figures, and went to his bosses to get their approval to sponsor us. Later, he came back and said his company couldn't possibly support Bass'n Gal because it was a family-oriented business and unless I—he didn't use the word ban—excluded lesbians from Bass'n Gal, the company wouldn't support us."

Sugar refused to comply. How, she asked, could she exclude lesbians and still serve women? "A fish doesn't care about the sexual preference on the other end of the line!" And besides, did sponsors ask the male bass organizations to ban homosexuals? Of course not.

Clearly, the industry's economic realities and the political mood of the country had changed. On January 17, 1998, Sugar called it a day.

↬ THE HETEROSEXUAL BASS'N GALS, who make up a majority of the membership, are outraged that female bass anglers would be so stereotyped, that their lesbian sisters had been attacked, or that cultural politics should intrude into the world of fishing at all.

"I'd just like to say something about this homophobic problem," said Lily Carey. "In my opinion, homophobia comes from within the person who has the problem with it. I'm not a lesbian, but I've been asked why I fish with women who are. 'What's going on with you? Are you turning that way?' Well, I'm very, very secure in who I am sexually, so these women are not a threat to me. We don't discuss sex; it's not an issue." To her, prejudice toward lesbians is part of the larger prejudice toward women in sports. "I'm a single parent with three children; I've done my own thing, no help from my ex, bought my own boat. And I'm out on the lake in my new boat, looking good out there, and this guy drives his boat up to me and says, 'Oh, I see your husband let you use his boat today!' "

The other women agreed. Pam Todd: "Most people I've just met, when they find out that I fish think it's very strange for a woman. It carries a stigma, it's a male thing."

So angling women, whatever their sexual preference, find solidarity. Sometimes, opposition strengthens community.

⤳ LATER THAT AFTERNOON, I went out fishing with Pamela Dountas, at her invitation. She backed her trailered Skeeter 150ZX down the ramp, left me with the boat, parked her rig, and we were off. Pam guided the Skeeter slowly beyond the buoys and opened it up. The nose pointed into the air and the boat leaped across the lake, and she let out a high laugh of pure joy—a child's sound of delight. And I laughed, too.

The lake was beautiful that day: scattered clouds, some whitewater—not like Lake Erie, but some real thumpers. She yelled over the sound of the engine that she was glad it was rough. *"Keeps other people off the lake."* We pulled into a swampy cove lined with fallen deadwood and tall oaks and pines, the kind of water in which you could imagine alligators gliding. She was up front, operating the quiet trolling motor with a foot pedal. We were running over logs and stumps hidden just beneath the surface, and the boat's side would lift up and then smoothly descend. This kind of water, particularly out on the open waves, is quite dangerous. Rangers place little floating markers where the most hazardous underwater deadfalls are, but the guides here will tell you not to trust the markers. They drift.

Pamela was busy tying on a five-inch green soft plastic lizard, in a Carolina Rig—hook buried in the plastic, a swivel tied a couple feet above the hook, and a sliding weight above that. She had already rigged my rod.

"So this is the most famous lunker lake in Texas," I said.

"Yeah, if you want a trophy you come here. There's a slot limit here. You can bring in bass from ten to twelve inches, and over 21 inches, but nothing in between. Slot limits are a good thing; nurtures the brood fish."

Women anglers, said Pamela, are uncommonly conscious about such things. It would seem so. In 1977, Bass'n Gal was the first tournament organization in the country to set the low-creel limit of five fish per day, per angler, on its national bass-fishing tour. Five fish are easy to keep alive in a boat's live well, during a day-long tournament. Sugar Ferris pushed for this approach, calling a five-fish limit "one of the kindnesses we owe the fish for allowing us to use them to win a tournament." Within the past five years, most of the other major tournament organizations have moved to the lower creel limit.

In addition, Bass'n Gal was the first national bass-fishing circuit to initiate "paper fish tournaments" on slot-limit lakes. A paper tournament allows anglers to be credited with fish they catch, within the slot limit, by measuring the fish's length, recording it on a score sheet and releasing the fish. The two competing draw partners on the boat must agree on the length. "The Lake Fork Lady Anglers that I fish with, they only do paper tournaments," said Pamela. At the weigh-in, tournament officials translate the fish's length into estimated weight, based on studies by Texas Parks and Wildlife.

"Paper tournaments are particularly important during the spawning season because you're going to pull the bass off the beds. Like now." She tossed her line out, held the rod in one hand, the line in her fingers to feel the delicate pickup.

Here's how the spawning works. "The male digs the bed out with his tail, the females lay the eggs and that's it, she's gone. He fertilizes the eggs and stays there and raises them until they're fingerlings and he defends the nest. The momma, basically, has gone out to lunch, to relax." Unless she decides to come home to eat a few of her kids.*

---

*Dave Whitlock, a premier fly-fishing expert and talented artist, writes that, on occasion, the male may also attack and even eat some of his own fry, "but I believe that this is his method of making them more wary and scattering the school into small groups, which are less vulnerable to predators." He adds, "Thereafter, though, spawning stress causes both sexes to go into a postnatal depression and period of exhaustion. They swim to deeper water. Some females even die during this period." Dave Whitlock, *L.L. Bean: Fly Fishing for Bass Handbook* (New York: Lyons & Burford, 1988), p. 4.

PAMELA DOUNTAS

Oddly, it's customary for bass-anglers to refer to lunkers as female—as she, or her, or sweet thang—regardless of sex. "This is probably because female bass usually weigh more. You're hoping during the spawn that you'll catch one early, full of eggs that are going to add to your weight. I've seen a lot of males caught and if it's a nice-sized bass, the man or woman doing the catching will still call it she, or say, 'Come on, baby!' " She smiled. "I don't mind. I figure anything that's that sweet and that big, it has to be female!"

The trolling motor purred. Pamela sat against a post seat at the bow. We could see visible beds in the shallows, vague circular spots of lighter color, whisked clean by the males. Instinctively, to defend the beds, the males will strike at any intruder—particularly anything resembling an aquatic salamander (known as mud puppies or waterdogs, they crawl along lake or river bottoms), which consider bass eggs a delicacy. As I continued to use a lizard, Pamela switched to a whitish finesse worm—shorter and lighter than the typical plastic worm—and then to a spinner bait, trying to agitate a bass into striking.

"Do you see the fish?"

I squinted. Finally I saw what she saw, a hovering shadow surrounded by smaller moving shapes. "The little small jagged ones are baby fish. Now that's a good fish, you'd like to get that. However, seeing them and catching them are definitely two things. A male, when the bait comes over his head, will bat it with his tail. He can also suck it in his mouth and blow it out before a hook can be set.

I was admiring a big painted turtle sunning itself on a log, when Pamela yanked back and up and set the hook. She yelped—that high sound of delight—and reeled fast, her rod arcing clear to the reel. She pulled it back and over her shoulder, hand spinning, then stopping, let it arc downward again, then pulled up. She did this three or four times. The bass was a big one, perhaps six pounds, all green and silver, white belly flashing through the foam. Water sprayed through the air. I fumbled with my camera to take Pamela's picture. She looked around at me as she reached down to grab the lunker by the lip, thumb on its tongue, in a grasp that usually produces temporary paralysis in a bass.

The bass had a better idea. It snapped its head side to side, violently, and was gone. Pamela dropped to her knees and slapped the deck, grinning.

"I'd have yelled for the net but I was too worried about getting my picture taken." Again, the laugh of delight.

I said, "I didn't think you professional types used nets, I thought you reached down and grabbed them with your hand."

"I was trying to look professional. I would have looked a lot more professional with a fish in my boat."

She stood up, took a deep breath. A nice moment, in any case. "I've seen women on their knees, crying harder over a lost fish than over a man they lost the night before." She checked her line for nicks, then flipped the spinner bait back into the water, skipping it off the top of a log. "That's where my ministry lies now, helping women. 'Don't take that drink, don't be depressed, it's all right. Tomorrow will be a better day. You'll catch one bigger, better, tomorrow.'"

As we worked the cove, she told of fishing once "with a lady from Arkansas. When I caught a fish, I said, 'Jesus, I thank you so much,' and she says, 'Jesus, nothing, *I'm* the one who put you on the fish. You should be thanking me.' So I did, I thanked the Lord and then I thanked her."

I asked her how she started fishing bass tournaments.

"I've fished my whole life. When I was a girl, on the Platte River in Nebraska. Then I didn't fish much for a while. A few years ago, I was having a real depressing episode and a good friend took me to a boat show and signed me up for a Dallas Bass'n Gal tournament. I went to the tournament and my life started to turn around, that day. Basically, fishing saved my life. I don't think Sugar realizes that she's been such an influence on women and young girls. But had she not started Bass'n Gal, had I not found its fellowship, I wouldn't have had anything to live for."

"Were you thinking about suicide?"

"Yeah, I was, definitely."

She deftly moved the boat over a log and into cover.

"Why did God run away, Pamela?"

She laughed. "From me? First of all I was *told* that God ran away from me. I went through Episcopal seminary in Dallas, I served the Holy Eucharist, I believed in it. I hoped that change would come, that the church would view women differently. But then one day I was told by my priest that I could not be ordained as a priest, (a) because I was a woman, and (b) because I was a practicing lesbian. Now, I could be a lesbian and not practice it—but I haven't made up my mind about that yet. My Bible says, 'Many are called and few are chosen,' and up to that point I thought I was one of the chosen."

That was five years ago. A year earlier, her doctors had told her she had incurable rheumatoid arthritis, and chronic hepatitis, which slowly destroys the liver.

"I lost the center core of who I was, the spiritual center core. A lot of people knew who I was, and about me, some people who did not know about me went away just like they told me God went away. Bass'n Gal brought me back to me, first of all, to the knowledge that I could be loved no matter who I was. A lot of my friends had gone away and I choose to just look beyond that. I found friends in this fishing club. And

I found a whole different side to God. A much more tolerant God, with fewer rules. Loves me exactly for who I am, even when I'm nothing. And thank God the fish don't want to know who I slept with the night before."

She works as a counselor now, and fishes as much as she can, sometimes with great pain. At times, she has fished to the end of a tournament day, determined to stay on the water, and immediately after the weigh-in, her friends have driven her to a hospital. "I figure if I am going to die, I am going to do it in my boat. I often say, 'If I can just get up and fish, I will make it another day, another year.' Fishing has given me my health back because I'm outside, in the fresh air, with all these wonderful people. I've had an excellent year. I was only given three years to live and I've already outlived that, so every day to me is a blessing."

Earlier, I had noticed a toy duck fastened to the post of her seat. I asked her about it. "I'm a person who tries to put her ducks in a row, so the Woman of the Year, Cheryl Phillips, gave that to me and told me at least I'd have one duck in a row. That's my lucky duck."

The fish weren't biting; Pamela was scanning the water.

"Sugar quoted me some dubious study, done in New Guinea," I said. "Supposedly proves that Caucasian males between the ages of thirty-five and fifty secrete a pheromone that repels fish."*

"Would you mind keeping your pheromones to yourself? Maybe that's why I don't like fishing with my brother. I thought it was just because he chewed and spit all the time."

She worries about Sugar now. "Reminds me of when I lost the ministry. She has got to be grieving. You can't support something that long in your life, and not suffer when it ends. I tell people to look for the

---

*Sugar Ferris may be referring to another set of studies—of women and salmon fishing. The three most coveted British salmon records have been held by women since the 1920s, according to Mallory Burion, writing in *Shimano Fishing* in 1995. These include the biggest salmon on rod and line, the biggest salmon on a fly, and the biggest spring salmon. One reason may be pheromones, according to Peter Behan, a clinical neurologist at Glasgow University, who has researched the nonfeeding behavior of migrating salmon. He suggests "that either men emit some substance or chemical that repels fish and/or women emit a substance which attracts them," writes Burion. Anecdotal evidence for the male repellent hypothesis comes from a researcher who conducted an experiment at a fish ladder on the Clear Water River in Idaho. "When male volunteers put their hands into the water at the top of the fish ladder, the salmon immediately withdrew and remained at the bottom of the ladder for 15 minutes. When female volunteers immersed their hands in the water, the fish continued to ascend the ladder." This news, if it's true, may not be what women anglers want to hear, because it discounts their skill. While waiting for definitive studies, Burion suggests that male anglers "book exclusively with female guides and wash your hands thoroughly before you go fishing. If you're fishing with me, kindly keep both hands in the boat, and the first guy who asks me to stroke his fly for luck will get a rod tip in the eye." Mallory Burion, "Raising the Profile Women Who Fish." *Shimano Fishing*, North American edition, Vol. 3, 1995, p. 29.

Christ in everybody, look for the goodness in everybody. Sugar's like a female gender of a Christ. She's offered hope to so many women, and she doesn't even recognize it. I hope that I can touch just one person like Sugar Ferris has touched so many of us, just one."

Sugar, indeed, reached out to the dispossessed among women—the domestically dispossessed. Most of the women I talked with at Lake Fork had experienced a divorce or other heartbreak. And she resisted prejudice, even when it came from those who had experienced prejudice themselves. For instance, when a transsexual joined Bass'n Gal, "the opposition came from every direction," said Pamela. "Lesbians said, 'But that transsexual is really a man, he/she's got the arms, the chest; he/she's six-foot something, and can crank a bait better than women.' Their own prejudice came through." But Sugar stood her ground, and the opposition faded. Gradually the transsexual was accepted simply as an angler. "I've fished with her," said Pamela. "Nicest lady. Sometimes she catches fish, sometimes she doesn't; sometimes she wins and sometimes she doesn't. The fish don't discriminate."

Pamela and I fished in silence for a while. We pulled up out of a bed of weeds and she said, "Look at that tail swirl." A bass had taken my bait, and spit it out, and I hadn't even noticed.

We watched the late afternoon sun make lines of white through the tall trees. Two herons slid by, tips of their powerful, slow wings almost touching the water. "This is the best thing about fishing," she said. "It's as if nature does the breathing for you. The Bible says that all things will cry out in the end. I think the trees cry out to us, the rocks cry out, and we need to listen to them."

She stood on the deck, leaning against the tall seat, holding the line in her fingers, smiling in the cooling afternoon air, and said that God has returned to her, of late. "You know, sometimes I'll be watching my line, just breathing, and I'll look up in the branches real quick, just to see if I can catch the angels."

↪ ON THE WAY BACK, hitting whitecaps, scooting across the hard swells, higher since a late afternoon wind came up, Pamela again laughed that high, wonderful girl/woman laugh of pure joy. We glided toward the ramp. She said that every time she comes in from the lake, she has the feeling she used to have as a kid after she got off an amusement park ride: "You're sad that it's over but you have the rush still in your blood." Another bass angler, with his preteen son, pulled his boat in next to us. She was too happy to notice his stern glare.

We hitched up the boat; turning the winch, she said that some of her fellow Bass'n Gals are trying to convince her to do an after-tournament religious service. "I don't know about that. I'd feel pretty funny preaching after being out on the water all day, missing bites and saying 'shit' all day."

She drove us to the pretournament meeting in front of Karen and Mark Woodruff's little Kountry Aire trailer home on the shore of Lake Fork. The women were gathered on the lawn and deck. Sugar was resting in a chair, beaming, wearing fresh makeup. She called out.

"Did you make him scream?"

Pamela put her head back and laughed long and hard, and so did the others.

Some of the women had rescued a baby mockingbird, fallen from its nest, and put it in a bucket. The mother mockingbird would fly to the edge of the bucket, white feathers flashing under its wings, and attend the baby. The women were watching this intently as they waited for the ceremony, the evening draw, to begin.

While waiting, I sought the company of a few men hanging out on the edge, leaning on a trailered and covered bass boat. Three of the men were sheepish and quiet, but Mark Woodruff was having a great old time. Wiry and darkly tanned, thirty-seven years old, Mark was telling "the ultimate blonde story." He had brought it back from the lake that very day:

> I'm fishing and I've got this girl, first time she ever fished. I've got her up in the front of the boat and I'm working on her casting form, throwing Carolina rigs. High winds, so we've got a one-ounce weight on. I look down and her line's swimming off. I hollered at her to set the hook. She turned her reel over, she's looking, and I tell her to set the hook! She's looking, looking, just panicking looking at it. "Set the hook!" She looks at me and said, "Where's the dial?" She thought there was some kind of oven setting or something on it that you turned, I guess, I don't know.

The men guffawed. "My wife told me I better not tell that here," Mark said. And, he added, his wife is blonde.

He lives year-around in the little trailer with Karen. Above their bunk is a photo of a bass. "All our dates were pretty much fishing. We got married in my boat. She informs me it's now our boat—we now have our boat and her boat. Instead of walking down an aisle they put her in another boat and drove her over to me. 'I do' was boat blast-off for the wedding tournament. The reception was at the weigh-in."

I asked Mark what it's like guiding women, compared to men.

I prefer to guide women. They'll listen. You get most men out there and they already think they know a lot about fishing because of the techniques they use on their own lakes. But each lake has its own little quirks. I could take a woman to the dam in forty foot of water and say, "OK, we're going to Carolina rig a jitterbug," and she'll do it. Whereas if I take a man out there, he's going to throw whatever he wants to throw. And you can't convince him otherwise. I can take a woman out who has never held a rod in her hand and in thirty minutes I can have her casting anything I got, flipping anything in the world.

Except this woman today, I said.

"Well, it took a little longer with her but it was a tough, windy day to be trying to teach somebody. She was good, she learned quick. But with male customers, the first thing you have to do is ask them what they're used to fishing. If they haven't fished it, they ain't going to fish it."

Mark took off his hat, wiped his forehead, and laughed. Women aren't more pliable, he said, covering his tracks, just more open to learning.

The women were assembling in front of the Kountry Aire. The mistress of ceremonies stepped forward, wearing a cowboy hat and two holstered cap guns, which she pulled out and shot with flair. She made a few announcements, then she described some of the recent youth projects the Bass'n Gal affiliates had sponsored—one group raised $30,000 for a youth-fishing program for abused and battered children. Bass'n Gal was the first organization in the country to require its affiliated bass clubs to adopt a conservation project and one youth-fishing project every year in order to remain affiliated. She talked about the need for more programs for children, particularly young girls who don't have fathers or fathers who fish. (An interesting statement: Even women anglers often assume that fathers, not mothers, are the primary angling educators.)

The next speaker was one of the few female guides on the lake, and though she slipped away before I could speak with her, she said to the Bass'n Gals, "The papers have been good to me, one of the articles had this headline: 'Woman Invades Man's World.'" Somebody from the audience yelled, "Who says it was theirs in the first place?" The women laughed and cheered. Mark laughed as hard as did the women in the audience. During a lull in the festivities, he leaned toward me and said:

I'm real glad these women are fishing, 'cause they're *fun*. I have a real good time with these women. One time, the Dallas Bass'n Gal invited me to come up to a baby shower for one of the girls.

They said, "There's one hitch. Everybody that goes has to dress up like they're pregnant." So they put me in a blue-jean denim skirt, boobs out to about right here. Blonde wig up there to cover the bald spot. I just told them my mustache was a hormone problem. Naturally, we had to get lost on the way to the house and we got out and my wife wouldn't go ask directions. We pull up to a little 7-Eleven or some kind of stop-and-rob store. She wouldn't get out so I walked in and I knew what kind of reaction I was going to get. So I just acted like I was just normal. I walked in, "Say, man, can you give me some directions?" The dude was on the phone. He was just frozen, he wouldn't move, he wouldn't talk. Finally some lady who was in the store and trying to be cool about it, like nothing was wrong, said, "Oh yeah, I can tell you how to get there," and she gave me the directions. None of the others ever said a word, they just froze.

Yessir. I have a *good* time with these ladies.

⌐ THE NEXT DAY, while the other women fished the tournament, Sylvia Murray, a former Bass'n Gal affiliate club director, took me out in her growling Javelin 400TE with a two-hundred-horse Johnson engine—quite a contrast to her petite, five-foot-one-inch stature. She didn't feel like competing that day, and because of my sex, I was subtly excluded, except as a noncompeting observer. In its own way, Bass'n Gal was as discriminatory as the major tournament circuits once were. Still, I was convinced by now that women's bass-fishing, like women's colleges, offers some balance in an imbalanced world.

The day was overcast, low clouds moving fast; waves were up, so we worked the sheltered coves. As we fished the inlets, Sylvia cast expertly, with feminine grace. She talked eloquently about how fishing provides women with a sense of independence and strength—and about what men and women can give each other. She was wearing a short-sleeve shirt and Lee shorts, belt with a bass etched into it, and fish earrings. She grew up in Odessa, Texas, she said, "where there are no hills and no fish," but "became a fishaholic" one Easter vacation when her family drove to a faraway lake to go crappie fishing.

Being small, I've always had a big self-doubt about my own physical skills and abilities. I've worked at that. After I graduated from high school, I climbed Mount Kilimanjaro. It was harsh and painful, but I did it. I discovered that a lot of what it takes to meet a physical challenge is just mind over matter: If you don't mind, it doesn't matter. Out of fifty, only twenty-three made it, and I was one of them. On top I felt like Zeus, and I watched the sun come up. Fishing is like that. I never thought of myself as being a jock, but with fishing I can catch just as big a fish as the guy who's an Olympic champion. It's not a gender-specific sport, even though a lot of men think it is. I can operate a boat by myself, fish by myself. The knowledge is mine.

It built my self-confidence and opened doors to the world of men. I was a Dallas paving inspector and I had to go out and inspect million-dollar bond projects. I'd go out on these job sites where there was nothing but men—here I was this little, soft-spoken female coming out to tell them if they were doing their job right. Some of them definitely didn't like seeing me come out there. Some tried to intimidate me. But then I discovered that if I walked out on the job site with a jacket that had a bass logo on the back, or started talking to them about fishing or hunting, all of a sudden they would talk to me. And once I could talk to them, then we could discuss the job and be honest with each other. Then, after I bought a bigger boat and got into tournament fishing, those men started asking me what bait I used. It was a wonderful feeling.

I met my husband while fishing—he works for a big tackle company—and he has made me the happiest person in the world. We share the love of fishing. I think fishing can make women more self-confident, even make them better mothers, better spouses, if they could fish with their husbands and families. I also found that race doesn't matter much out here. We all catch fish. My family comes from Mexico; my maiden name is Cisneros; the first part of it, *cisne*, is Spanish for swan, so Cisneros is people of the swan.

She smiled and made a perfect cast; her plastic lizard arced out over the water and landed right on top of a nest guarded by a visible male bass. "Men think a woman who fishes can't be feminine." But out here on the water, she was as graceful as a swan. The water swirled, and she set the hook.

In the afternoon, we picked up Sugar at the ramp and took her out for a while. She was moving slowly and stiffly, and she backlashed her reel a few times. Out of practice. Hurting from her wreck.

Sylvia put us in the middle of a cove, between some dead trees, and she showed me how to drop a salamander . . . right . . . there. . . .

Bang . . . a bass set off with it, came charging up through the opal-colored water. Sylvia shot a long-handled net out and scooped it up.

SYLVIA MURRAY

I stood there holding the bass by the lip, kind of swole up, as Sugar would say.

"*Nice* fish," said Sugar.

"I think it hits three pounds," I said.

"Maybe," said Sylvia.

⤿ ON THE WAY BACK to Dallas with Sugar, I asked her what was going to happen with women's bass fishing after the demise of Bass'n Gal. We were crossing a bridge spanning an arm of Lake Fork, past an island submerged in a blizzard of snowy egrets—or cow egrets, as they're called in Texas. Sugar said she did not know what would happen, but that she supposed things would work out.

In 1997, Willy Cook of Pelham, Alabama, began planning a tournament series for women anglers. And a new organization, the Women's Bass Fishing Association, came into existence. A year later, it had 212 members. That's the way it is sometimes: three steps forward, two steps back.

Despite what Sugar Ferris accomplished for women in what she calls "America's last bastion of male supremacy," she has never received a card, letter, phone call—or even e-mail—from any major feminist leader. But she said she had never really missed that connection until I asked her about it. Perhaps this is because she does not call herself a feminist. But, of course, that is exactly what she is—on her own terms. Here is what might be called the Sugar Manifesto:

> When I was a young girl, I thought sandlot baseball was the most wonderful thing in the world. I'd get on my bicycle in the morning and ride down the road to where the guys were having a game and they'd say, "Aw, you're just a girl, you can't play!" I'd just get on my bicycle and ride off. I'd climb a willow tree on the creek and sit and think about these things. And I did eventually end up finding my way.
>
> People object to change more than they object to anything else, and that has a lot to do with why women are not fully accepted in the last macho strongholds, like bass-fishing. What chagrins me is that the men who run the big companies who don't take women seriously, these are often young men. I would have thought that more of today's young people would have moved forward after twenty or thirty years of the women's movement. It distresses me that I have nephews, two young men—one twenty-six and one twenty-two— who still feel the same way their father did. They have not learned

anything over the years about women, about how to be tolerant, how to accept people as they are. There's still that same old deep-rooted prejudice. But it finally doesn't matter; one way or another we'll find our way.

I guess what I'm trying to express is that, finally, liberation is internal. I felt my own change when I was a girl sitting in that tree, my realization that liberation isn't something that somebody grants to you. It's something you develop for yourself over time. I taught my daughter that. I would like for each young girl to see that. I'd like for my nephews and my grandsons to be more accepting toward women, but I want the girls in my family to know that they don't need the approval of these guys. We don't need permission.

She drove along for a while, not saying anything. We stopped at a "stop-and-rob," as Mark had called convenience stores, and bought some Gatorade and Twinkies, perfect road food. A few miles on down the road, after more silence, she added:

Women do need histories and traditions of their own, not those that have been previously created by men. We need places we can compete on our own terms. That's what Bass'n Gal was. But, you know, we can also change some of these men, and we don't have to humiliate them to do it.

The point of my story about Buddy wasn't that he threw up when he realized he had drawn a woman partner—wasn't his prejudice. The point was that every person has something in their personality that you can work with. You can find the goodness in everyone; you can find something you can admire. Buddy was a great angler and he taught me a lot that day. I just had to bring out the best in him to be able to get to that. In today's society, we sometimes forget that. There's so much rage in people today that we don't take the time to seek out that one thing in a person that will allow someone to rise.

That's exactly what Buddy did that day, he rose above himself when God sent that little old man and woman walking down that pier. We have to keep our eyes open for those moments, and take advantage of them. That's the only real liberation. You know?

Life and fishing move on. Women, many of them former Bass'n Gals, are beginning to compete more aggressively in the major tournament circuits that are now open to them. In March 1998, Wanda Rucker of Cocoa, Florida, became the first woman to win a Red Man tournament.

She finished first at the Red Man Gator Division qualifier, landing five fish totaling sixteen pounds four ounces, to lead a field of 342 anglers. At this writing, BASS Inc., the largest bass-fishing organization, is headed by a woman, Helen Sevier.

Some would say that organizations like Bass'n Gal aren't as needed as they were a few years ago. But Sugar believes they are, and that the fight to claim women's rightful role in fishing (to "refeminize" the sport, as some women anglers have put it) has just begun. Indeed, as I would learn later during my travels, women's fishing organizations are becoming increasingly important—in fact, vital—to the future of fishing, and to America's relationship with nature. This is true not only because of demographics or evolving sensibility but because of the willingness of women to network across fishing cultures.

Sugar Ferris and her fellow Bass'n Gals helped weave the first few strands of that movement. In some circles, that may not seem like much, but in these parts, as Sugar would say, "that's not nothin'."

〜 DANCING RAIN APPROACHED US; the leaves that had turned their backs to the sky had forecast accurately. Sugar smiled as she drove. She said she hopes to write a few fishing and nature books for kids. She plans to spend more time with her grandchildren and gradually move down to her ranch near the town of Comanche, southeast of Fort Worth. "Might even do a little fishing. We've got little ponds with stunted fish in 'em because there's too many of 'em. But mainly I'll just sit out on the porch and drift. We don't have TV or radio down there. I love to watch the deer, and the birds that come to the feeder. Bob has an automatic timer on it and it throws the seed out for them. I have two red oak trees out by the feeder; all the wildflowers in bloom are just heavenly. I have an old blue jay I love, all kinds of birds, tufted titmouse, wrens. When I doze off, I can hear the hummingbirds buzzing around my hair. My daughter says they like me because I feed them." One time she woke up suddenly on that porch, opened her eyes, and saw three dozen wild turkeys sitting on the fence, watching her.

She dropped me off at the Dallas airport, picked up Bob, and headed to that ranch, to the kind of life at which she had once turned up her nose.

Hidden Waters

~~~~~~

The lakes aforesaid send him their waters, and with these, and others that come to him, he makes a grand and imposing entrance.

—Don Quixote

Whitefish Willy and the Northern Lights

꽁꾱

THE COMMUTER PLANE circled over Iron Mountain, Michigan, anchor of
the famous Upper Peninsula: the north woods, wolf country, cold and
wild and about as far from Texas as you can get, short of a trip to Brooklyn. The land below was white and steel gray. There was snow, an expanse of graceful bulges covered with bare trees, circling and spiraling
frozen streams banked with patches of conifers, and great white fields of
untouched snow. I thought of something that Whitefish Willy, one of the
anglers who had answered my earlier e-mail, had told me on the phone.
I had been looking at a map of the Upper Peninsula, at the sparseness of
towns, the apparent wildness, and had remarked that it looked like he
lived in God's country. And he had said, "If God ever came up here, He
might get lost." The plane dropped into a swirling fog of snow, dipped
under a cloud, and the air was as dark as white can be.

Stepping off the plane at Ford Airport was a shock. My eyes hurt from
the brightness, I squinted, and out of the swirling snow appeared the
strangest creature—quite tall, its head and shoulders a single, huge mass
of fur, glowing eyes barely visible. Its torso was thick and its arms stuck
nearly straight out to each side. They were making circular motions.

"Richard?" said the creature.

"Yeah?" I took a half step back.

It stuck out a paw. "Bill Knutsen."

"Knutsen?"

"Whitefish Willy."

He reached up and pulled his head off.

"This is my fishing hat," he said. It was made of fox and raccoon and
additional but unidentified creatures. He replaced the fur hat with what
can best be described as a clown's hat: visored, bright red with white

polka dots, with a high peak that popped up when he took the fur helmet off. Long black hair stuck out from under the hat, and trailed down his neck. Some of it stuck out straight from around his big ears. His face was cherubic: Howdy Doody crossed with Alfalfa.

"Welcome to the North Country," he said.

He grabbed one of my bags and headed for a battered four-wheel-drive Toyota, and we set out for frozen Lake Superior. Willy is something of a legend in the Upper Peninsula, known for his devotion to the lake whitefish (*Coregonus artedi*, he calls it, being one of those rare anglers who refer to fish by their Latin names) and for his independent ways and self-reliance. The homemade trailer clattered and bounced behind us. On it was a sled that he had made from electrical tubing and plumber's piping, and an old snowmobile.

I asked Willy about that fur hat.

"My other nickname is Roadkill Willy. You got to use the resources." He made the hat with a triple layer of raccoon hide and lined it with felt. "I look for dead foxes on the highway, too. I got a prime fox in October there, and I made a surprise hat for my buddy Bobby Meyers, skipper of the *Kala Moiakka*. Sewed it up and gave it to him on Christmas, on a fishing trip. He wears it all the time. He has no pride at all." He laughed. "Me, I prefer whitefish, but Bobby's addicted to trout. He plants ponds on his property with brookies and rainbows. Calls them pond chickens. I raise chickens for food and he raises them things."

We passed a dead deer on the side of the road.

Willy gave it a look, but kept driving.

The deer are so plentiful here that natives who live far from the towns (like Willy, whose farm is twenty-eight miles from any major settlement) fasten deer catchers to the front of their trucks, iron contraptions that work like cowcatchers on the old steam locomotives. "Otherwise you're going to wreck your car. My last truck, I hit seven deer." Tracks peppered the snow, leading down into what Willy called cedar swamp, lowlands covered in the winter with thermal mass, which attracts the deer. The woodlands and waters here are rich in life: fox, ravens, partridge, eagles, snowshoe hare, bobcats. And, of course, fish. Trout, muskies, pike, bass, catfish, and on the big lakes, lake trout, smallmouth bass, coho salmon, sturgeon, and whitefish—which is classified as a Great Lakes herring.

As we crossed the Brule, a good trout stream, he described older times.

> You know, in the old days the families put tents up next to the backwaters during the warm months and spent the weekends fishing. It was the family thing to do.

My father and grandfather, when they had no money for a license or a fishing pole, used to fish with what they called "the government pole." They'd cut a branch and fish for brook trout. If somebody from the government came, they'd throw that branch in the woods. I pretty much learned to fish on my own, when I was a kid up in Ontonagon there, because my father didn't have a lot of time. My first fishing pole was bamboo. My mother bought a shag rug, rolled on a bamboo pole. In the summer, I took that and a hook and kite string and I would get on my bicycle and I'd go down to a hole right by the bridge there and I used to catch chubs and suckers and shiners and trout, too. If you used worms you got all chubs. So I would cut the tail off the chub and use that for bait. The other chubs didn't like to eat chub tail but the trout did. You'd catch trout that way.

A little later in life I used to use my dad's metal bait-casting reel. I couldn't cast with it so I'd wind the line up on the shore and then I'd throw it out like that. My first reel was a Shakespeare: got it at a rummage sale. It was a push-button. You could cast with it.

Ice-fishing was different then, too. People didn't have much money, so they'd take some line and a hook and bait and a twig, and they'd tie a piece of red yarn to the line, and when the cloth went into the hole, they had a bite. You still don't need much equipment for ice-fishing, and you can make most of what you need. That's one of the reasons I like ice-fishing.

Along the road, the snow-covered hills were sparsely dotted in red oak, aspen, and hemlock. In the 1800s, the forests were virgin white pine, said Willy. "The trees were so big, in the middle of the day it would be dark on the forest floor. All the white pine was cut off the Upper Peninsula and shipped to the East Coast; they logged the whole thing, or most of it, with horse and handsaw. Ten years it took them."

Early settlers discovered iron scattered on the surface of this land, which is how Iron Mountain got its name. His grandfather worked in every iron mine in the area. "Cold, damp, and dangerous work. It was all done with mules, and it was hard work, boy. Pasties was the staple. They're a crust of bread, a pocket with meat and potatoes and rutabagas and onions inside. Cornish recipe. A whole meal in a package. Those miners used to keep them under their armpit to keep 'em warm. I'll tell you my grandfather felt sorry for the mules in the mines. They were all blind, because once they went into the mountain they didn't come out. The men would beat them. But some of the men, like my grandfather, would feed them the crusts of their pasties at the end of the day."

The Ford Motor Company operated a plant on the peninsula for decades, using pure iron ore for the casting of engine blocks, and manufactured the wood parts of automobiles, especially for the old "woodies." Willy's father worked for the Ford plant for forty-eight years. And the region is known for its copper, used during World War II for the manufacture of military machinery and copper-clad bullets. But over time, the mines played out; the population declined. Up until the '60s, said Willy, you couldn't buy fast food in Iron Mountain, and the two restaurants in town closed at six o'clock. "If you didn't have your gas tank filled at five o'clock in the evening, you wouldn't be able to get gas the whole weekend. Nobody was open."

Today tourists—a good number of them anglers—and new residents travel across the five-mile-long Big Mackinaw Bridge, which in 1959 replaced a ferry crossing a narrows between Lake Michigan and Lake Huron, linking lower Michigan and the Upper Peninsula. The region remains one of the more sparsely populated parts of the United States, with one of the harshest climates.

I asked Willy if he'd ever left this country.

"Oh yeah. I was drafted in 1968."

In Vietnam, he flew over 350 hours of combat assault sorties as a crew chief door gunner on a Huey, a UH-1H helicopter. Afterward, he returned to the North Country. He did not jump immediately back into daily society. He moved into his family's hunting and fishing camp, a log cabin built in 1938—the kind of camp that many families, rich and poor, keep in this part of the country. He lived there for a year, with woodstove heat, outdoor plumbing, and no running water. He made it through the winter, and there he healed. When he emerged, he worked at a foundry for a while; then he cut wood for a living, did whatever he could for a dollar. Today, he works at a small local factory that, until the late 1980s, made widgets for nuclear power plants but now makes control panels for protecting high-voltage transmission lines.

Why did you come back here? I asked.

> Oh, I loved it up here. I used to be an avid hunter, now I do more fishing than hunting. I've kind of softened up, I guess. The Vietnam experience was enough. I had enough of guns and war. A little more peaceful, fishing, I think. But I still kill; I kill my pigs. And I raise laying chickens, so I got to chop their heads off and I got to shoot the pigs. I get enough killing. I get a turkey, too, and I whack that up. It's instant death; it's not a lingering thing like it is when you've wounded a deer. I feel pretty proud that I can kill a chicken or a pig in a second; it's a humane kill. Better eating, too, you know.

Years ago I used to take a Q-Tip and clean off my gun and care
for it. Since Vietnam, the guns are dirty and sitting in the basement.
I pick one up to shoot my pig or something, that's generally as far
as it gets. Vietnam took the edge off, I think. More than a little.

Two hours later, up on Highway 41, we entered L'Anse, a village at
the head of Lake Superior's Keweenaw Bay. Willy watched the water
drainage along the road, picking up cues about the condition of the lake,
the weather. Out in front of one of the water-beaten cottages, a man,
humped over, moving like a bear, was pouring fireplace ashes from a
wheelbarrow on an icy driveway. Rising out of the water was an odd formation: slabs of ice ten and twenty feet across, carded up over the edge
of the road as if some great hand had thrown down a game of 52 Pickup.
"Jumble ice," said Willy. "Usually happens first ice and last ice. From
freezing and breaking up and freezing again. The wind will blow it and
it starts sliding, and it stacks up over the road. You have to get the front-
end loader to push it off the highway."

Parking the truck next to a high ridge of plowed snow, he looked out
across the frozen lake. "They say boats from the 1800s are down there,
and the rigging and the masts are still there because the water preserves
them. Thirty-nine degrees just about at every level of the lake, year
round, except the upper ten feet. Down three hundred feet or so, supposed to be a whole boatload of Model-Ts. Ford was shipping them
down and the boat sank. A guy could go down there and get them."

He pulled his rig up along a long hump of graded-up snow, leaped out,
zipped up his snowsuit, grabbed his roadkill helmet, slipped it down over
his head, and became, once again, *the creature*. Suddenly, his laid-back
demeanor disappeared. He moved fast. He pulled the snowmobile off
the sled and fastened everything up, threw buckets and satchels on the
sled, then yanked out a canvas snowsuit for me, which smelled of fish
and mildew.

I stepped into it, pulled it up over my body, and zipped it. I put on the
boots he handed me. I rummaged through my travel pack and found a
Russian army cap, the kind made of lamb's wool and gray felt, which I
had bought from a frozen little man in Red Square, who looked barely
more alive than the big waxy doll in Lenin's tomb. I pulled it down on
my head as far as it would go. Willy led me to the back of the sled, instructed me to hold on for dear life. I climbed up on the sled, holding the
back piping.

Mush! I said to myself.

Willy went around front, straddled the snowmobile, a black Cheetah,
and we were *off*.

We hurtled across the corrugated ice at about thirty-five miles an hour. My teeth were chattering. My ears were turning brittle; *I had forgotten to pull down the damned ear flaps.* No way to let go of the bouncing sled to pull them down. The sky was clear and the air biting. In the distance was a thin line of charcoal-colored land and trees, but in one direction—perhaps it was north, I was disoriented—the white just kept going, creating an indistinct line between white ice and white then blue sky with high cirrus clouds. Now we were far from the land, skimming across a moon of ice, Europa with visitors. Little black dots on the horizon became larger. These were the shelters—a few small wooden structures, but more often three-pole teepees, of the ice-fishermen. On a weekend, there can be as many as two hundred shelters on the ice, but today, a Wednesday, there were only forty or so. Willy pulled up to a couple of them, asked how the fishing was (I pulled down my flaps), and then lurched again across the ice. Sasquatch driving a snowmobile.

Finally, looking left and right, using whatever neurological or paranormal alchemy ice anglers employ, he picked a spot and set up camp fast.

"They'll start biting good about 2:30."

BEFORE FISHING with Willy, I thought I knew what to expect from ice-fishing, but I was wrong. I suppose my image of ice-fishing was stereotypical: vast, shanty suburbs of ice shacks where the primary recreation is "ice drinking," as some folks call it.* In truth, there are two kinds of ice-anglers: the alcoholic and the ecstatic. Physically, what came to mind was more along the lines of Minnesota's Mille Lacs ice-fishing culture, not far from Minnesota's Twin Cities, as described by writer Verlyn Klinkenborg: One "high-centered house, teetering on its fulcrum of ice, stands at the end of a cul-de-sac in a neatly organized subdivision of ice-fishing houses, each with the name and address of the owner painted on its side." Some of the houses are elaborately appointed. "There's a persistent rumor around Mille Lacs about the fish house with a hot tub . . . as there is the persistent rumor about fish houses with large-screen TVs and digital satellite dishes. To predict that the comforts of life on the ice will increasingly resemble the comforts of life in suburbia is to predict the merely inevitable." Other ice fishers are a bit more rustic in their approach. Klinkenborg wrote:

---

*While ice-fishing is often associated with drinking, I wonder if the fishing itself is a form of self-medication, a kind of light therapy for individuals in northern climes who suffer from Seasonal Affective Disorder, or SAD.

I visited two anglers who were fishing through the floor of an ancient yellow house trailer with a dropped suspension. There was a flooded fish house flying Old Glory and the POW/MIA flag, with a cellular phone antenna mounted over the door. . . . And everywhere there was a profusion of home-built shacks, each one a rectangular fantasy of plywood and chipboard and scrap paneling. Some neighborhoods were so entirely jerry-built that they looked like a convention of outhouses or a Hooverville from the Great Depression. But that's the appeal of a fish house. There's a peculiarly American pleasure to be had from cobbling together a dwelling out of found wood, making a habitation of almost nothing. (Consider Thoreau, who built his house for $28 and change.) It's a truly national expertise, a remnant of our history as settlers, a virtuosity now preserved largely on frozen lakes.

Like other forms of angling, ice-fishing is becoming more complicated. *Outdoor Life* reports the rapid evolution: "For serious fishermen, there's no more sitting and waiting. They've gone mobile, using electronics and highly portable gear to stalk schools of fish, just like they do in the open-water season." Add to this the information explosion. "Not too long ago, prime fishing locations were a secret shared by only a few veterans of the ice. Now you can find good 'where-to' advice in newspapers, regional magazines, fishing contest results, TV shows, on the Internet." Following the lead of bass-fishing, ice-fishing is going pro, or at least semipro—with $100,000 tournaments and thousands of contestants. Klinkenborg describes one competitive event, for which the Brainerd Jaycees drilled ten thousand holes for six thousand contestants:

> As the clock edged toward starting time, the PA system blared out oldies broadcast by a local radio station. Some of the crowd, the serious contestants, dipped the ice from their holes once again and rechecked what anglers like to call their "terminal tackle." But the rest of the crowd, wearing snowmobile suits and blaze orange hunting coveralls, started dancing to "YMCA" by the Village People. At noon a shotgun blast went off, and the contest began. Anglers dropped their lines into the water, and within moments one fisherman near me stood up and began to run over the drifted snow toward the weigh-in tent. Soon there would be a line of men, women and children waiting to weigh their fish.

Whitefish Willy and his friends practice an almost aesthetic form of ice-fishing, self-reliant, solitary, and in Willy's case at least, nonalcoholic.

In his domain, a melting world, there is no corollary to Bass Pro's Outdoor World. His is not a catalog culture. Self-reliance and frugality are the organizing principles. He makes most of his own gear, or buys it from local manufacturers. Willy's world is Spartan, almost metaphysical, as befits the mystery under the ice, and the creatures below, a mystery that the fancy electronics would not serve well.

His fishing is from an older time. Ice-fishing represents an ancient cultural band that stretches around the northern world. In addition to its northern European links, North American ice-fishing also has roots in Native American and Inuit (what used to be called Eskimo) fishing, and earlier: the common ancestor of Canadian and Greenland Inuit, the Paleo-Eskimos. Their descendants view ice-fishing not only as a source of food, but as a social occasion. The Inuit, too, return to some primal view of themselves, when they ice-fish. They no longer live in igloos—at least not as their main residences—but snow houses are still used as shelters during winter fishing and hunting trips.

The Indian and Inuit influence is reflected in the hand-hewn, painted fish decoys from the Great Lakes region. The decoys, lowered through ice-fishing holes, are still used by anglers like Whitefish Willy, but they were used by spear-fishing Native Americans and Inuit for centuries. In recent years, the decoys have become a hot collectible item, new ones made locally but especially those carved during the Great Depression, when subsistence fishing was more popular. Few carved decoys survive the rugged reality of ice-fishing, which makes them all the more valuable.

Willy makes his own decoys. He carves and paints them and weights them with metal. He uses them when he spear-fishes through the ice. He also makes his own spears, the ten-foot handles of electrical conduit tubing, with spikes from a special spool that he gets at the factory where he works.

He could sell his decoys and spears to collectors and make a nice profit, but he does not.

↵ NOW CAME THE preparation of the ice. He pulled out an auger called a Finnish mora, turned it by hand into the foot-thick ice to cut a hole eight inches across. As he drilled, he explained: "You got three kinds of augers. An ice pick, which is a chisel on the end of a bar, sharpened up. Good for fairly thin ice. If you feel energetic you could probably chop through a couple of feet but it might take you a while. Then there's a hand auger, like this one, a Finnish mora with a removable insert blade. And you also have your gas-powered ice drill, good for thick ice. The gas-powered augers are usually good for cutting an eight- to ten-inch hole in ice thicker than a foot. On the inland lakes—they freeze up earlier because there's no wave action, so the ice can be thirty inches thick—you usually use a power auger." Willy prefers the hand auger "because it always starts."

The blades do, however, need maintenance. Willy sends the blade to a machine shop in Cumberland, Wisconsin, every couple of years to get it sharpened; a surface-grinder puts the proper arc on it, makes it razor-sharp. Sending his blade out is one of the few exceptions to Willy's ethic of self-reliance. The blade is too difficult and dangerous to sharpen at home.

He finished the hole, then reached down with an ice skimmer—a nearly flat ladle with holes in it—and scooped the slush out of the gray-green water. Then he placed a white bait bucket next to it, upside down, for a chair. Then he cut another hole about thirty feet away. He set up his tent over it; a collapsible four-pole tent made of polytarp, a zipper, and four lightweight wood poles—it's essentially a teepee. He makes these tents, which he designed, in his garage. He uses them, and gives others to his friends.

Cutting the hole and setting up the tent took him less then ten minutes.

The easiest way to ice-fish is to use a "tip-up," a truncated fishing rod with a spring-loaded flag that pops up when a fish takes the bait. Willy prefers the simplicity of the ancient way: hand bobbing. "Indians and Eskimos do the same thing we are doing, with the line, and they just lift like that and they catch a variety of fish."

He pointed across the ice. "Those guys over there are using pimples." Pimples?

"Yah. They're pimpling. The Swedish Pimple is a lure—it was originally a Pimpla—made by a Michigan company." He described it as a long cylinder, a piece of metal that represents a vertical feeding minnow. Swedish pimples, he said, are made by the Baydenoc Lure Company in Gladstone, Michigan, fifty miles from Willy's home.

He produced a Finnish geppo, a flat wooden spool about a foot long, with coated, braided wire line wound around it. He dug into a plastic bag and produced a piece of smelt and stuck it on the hook. He let the geppo unwind, and the smelt disappear; the wire line spooled smoothly out by itself. "One wrap around the geppo is two feet, so you can tell how deep you are." The water was exceedingly deep here. "It's just a subtle feeling when you hit bottom." He looped a rubber band around the line at the water level to keep track of the depth. "That'll tell me where the bottom is. The length of line needed to reach the bottom changes with the current. He said he was having trouble finding the bottom; the current was strong, causing the line to arc.

"Also, before you start fishing for lake trout or whitefish, you can make a chum dumper. I got one here. I make mine out of a piece of PVC pipe—drain pipe—with a lead weight and a little rigged trigger mechanism. This is another little gizmo you can't buy; you got to make it. You lower this down to the bottom in probably sixty, seventy feet of water and you fill it with corn or rice or fish food, whatever you're chumming with, and you lift it up about six feet and you jerk a pin out of a hatch door, and it dumps the chum, so that you've got a pocket of food down there to keep the school around it. Then you fish down in the chum."

He showed me how to lift up the line slowly a few inches, and let it drop gradually, again and again, in a steady, slow rhythm. As I practiced, he stood up straight, leaned back with his mitten to his mouth, and howled. The sound was something between a wolf call and a yodel. *"Kala kala kala kala!"* The sound, called out for no reason except for the joy of being out here, seemed to bounce across the lake, and another sound seemed to meet it—not an echo, but another fisherman yodeling, far away, *"Kala kala kala kala!"* He grinned. This, he explained, is the Finnish fish call. "You stamp your feet too sometimes." If one fisherman makes the call, others meet it, and the call moves like a baton across miles of ice.

"*Kala* is the Finnish word for fish. If we catch a fish, we call out *kalamoiika*—which means we're going to have fish soup tonight. My favorite. You cut up potatoes, onions, boil that up with a little bit of cream in there, butter, salt. Then right at the end you chop your fish up and put that in there. That's the best, kalamoiika."

Willy sat on the overturned white bucket, smiling at the hole. The fur of his fishing helmet circled his smile. I wondered if he smiled in his sleep.

This was slow fishing. One writer describes it this way: "Ice-fishing struck me as a bit like fishing for compliments—chilly work and you don't land many." Willy peered at my line as I bobbed it.

"Here, do it this way," he said. He took the line. The subtlety of his technique escaped me. After just a few bobs he snapped his hand up and pulled in the line, throwing it in careful loops on the ice, popped a little lake trout out of the hole, and dropped it on the ice. It was kind of pitiful-looking, almost albino. It quivered, it did not flop. Its eyes were nearly white and its air bladder puffed out from its mouth a bit, due to the change in pressure from the depths to the ice. He left it there, where it froze.

"*Salvelinus namaycus,*" said Willy.

WHITEFISH WILLY

He leaned back, and once more cupped his mittens around his mouth. He yelled, "Kalamoiika!" No answer came from across the ice this time.

↪ BECAUSE THE FISH HE captures rise from such cold, dark depths, their colors are bleached, mainly white or silver. Steelhead and salmon pulled from such depths are difficult to tell apart. In an attempt to explain the fascination of ice-fishing, angling encyclopedist A. J. McClane writes:

> Perhaps its greatest single source of fascination is the drastic change in the relationship between man and water brought about by the dramatic appearance of the ice itself. The waters, which now lie hidden beneath the frozen surface, immediately become a dark, sealed-off mystery and thus pose a tantalizing and compelling challenge to the fisherman. Yet at the same time the latter is suddenly accorded an intriguing advantage; he can walk about boldly on a surface which is normally immune to any approach.

In all probability, ice fishermen are drawn to their sport not as much by the prospect of hauling fish through the ice, as by the instinctively accepted illusion that to do so is closely akin to achieving the impossible. There is a tense expectation in watching a line of baited tilts (mechanical devices that signal a strike), which has no exact counterpart elsewhere in angling—plus the equally unique thrill experienced when a flag suddenly springs erect. Here again, the actual hauling of the fish comes as an anticlimax; the truly satisfying moment occurs when the activated (line) signals actual contact with the alien life of that dark world which lies under the ice.

Now and then the ice anglers will hook into something so large that it cannot be moved. "If it doesn't move, but you can tell it's alive, it's probably sturgeon," said Willy.

These are the redwood of fish; they take seventy-five years to reach the current legal keeper size of fifty inches, and they can live to two hundred years old. In the early 1800s and 1900s, commercial gill net fishermen considered sturgeon a nuisance. When caught, the powerful, leathery fish ruined nets, so the fishermen killed them. On the nearby Sturgeon River, sturgeon would run upstream in the spring, and the fishermen would wade out and kill them with pitchforks. The population was further depleted by the cargo steamers on the Great Lakes that burned sturgeon in their boilers because they were so oily. Today, in Michigan and Wisconsin, grassroots conservation clubs monitor some of the rivers used as spawning grounds by the prehistoric fish; in Wisconsin, one group guards a 30-mile stretch of stream, twenty-four hours a day, to protect spring-spawning lake sturgeon against poaching. "Excellent eating, fried or smoked," said Willy. "The thing is they suck off the bottom and since the lower Great Lakes got polluted and all the pollutants settled to the bottom, they take that into their system. They hold it in there, so they're not recommended for human consumption anymore out of Lake Michigan."

Most Lake Superior ice fishermen prefer pike or bass or trout, but Whitefish Willy, as his nickname suggests, favors the elusive whitefish. "Traditionally, whitefish is not a fish that you angle for because it's so hard to catch," he explained. "In terms of fight, lake trout don't even compare." He likes to "lift" for whitefish.

You put a half-ounce sinker on, about ten inches from that on your line you put a number 10 hook and you put one single salmon egg on the hook. You put that on the bottom, either from the boat or through the ice, and then you lift up slowly and then you feel as you lift. If there's nothing, you let it down again. You lift slowly up and let her down. You keep doing this and then one of those times you'll lift and you'll feel it, it's heavier than it normally is. Whitefish don't strike a lure like a northern or a bass would strike, they just grab onto it. And when you lift, you feel her on there and then you set the hook.

That's the lift method. The other technique that I have good luck with, for whitefish, is the spring bobber method, which would be a fine piece of curly wire with an eyelet on it attached to the end of your pole, extending the pole, and giving it extra sensitivity. A machinist discovered this a few decades ago when he attached a shaving from a lathe, and used it on the end of his pole. You can use the inside of a ballpoint pen, that little spring in there. Fishermen think about things like that.

The ones I catch are from twelve inches to sixteen inches long, but they get up to six pounds or so. That's a good size, excellent table fare. When you get them next to the hole, the larger ones, you can't bring them through the ice because their mouth will tear. You have to use a gaff hook; you stick it down and gaff them to the head to get them up. With their soft, delicate mouths, a lot of times they come off and you watch them in the crystal-blue water going down, swimming back to their home. One of the explorers up here discovered the whitefish and said he could eat them for months in a row without getting tired of their flavor.

He cut another hole for me, a few feet away. We looked at the holes for a while, the deep turquoise eyes. We lifted and lowered our lines. Nothing was biting now. "Fishing is what it is, it's fishing, it's not catching," he said. Not that he minds the catching. In Willy's world, there's no such thing as catch-and-release.

He stacks his catch in his freezer, along with the animals he butchers on his farm. It is part of his self-sufficiency, this life of his that still exists in parts of America, despite the microwave, the genetically squared tomato, the distance of the kill from the palate.

↬ THE HAZARDS OF ice-fishing, or getting to the fishing, in the North Country are considerable. Temporary snow blindness is one problem, he said. "I had it once. Makes you feel claustrophobic. Couldn't open my eyes. The only way I could see is if I went like this." He covered his eyes with both hands and looked through the smallest holes his fingers could make. "I didn't have sunglasses. Since then, I made a pair of sunglasses out of grinding goggles; took lenses out of some gas-welding goggles, and fastened them in there—they had a shade equal to four pair of sunglasses."

Even with normal vision, anglers get lost on the ice. Some anglers bring compasses, in case of a blizzard, or fog, or what's known as snow fog: The wind can blow the snow and ice crystals into a thick soup. "Trying to walk in a straight line, even if it's sunny out, you turn around and look at your tracks and they're gone. You can walk right off the edge of the ice out there, where it stops and the big water starts."

Getting lost on the ice is especially dangerous on a large lake with open sections or ice that tends to shift in large floes. A few weeks before my visit with Willy, on Lake Simcoe, near Barrie, Ontario, anglers were busy fishing when a gap suddenly opened in the ice, spreading quickly until it was more than three hundred feet wide and twenty miles long. Six military helicopters, a hovercraft, and several boats plucked several hundred anglers to safety, but the rescuers suspended operations at nightfall because of blinding snow and fifty-five-mile-an-hour winds. Some two hundred people remained on the ice, huddled in their heated fishing huts, as the temperature plunged to eleven degrees below zero. The next day, rescuers brought another eighty-three to shore—but dozens of them insisted on staying. In a classic understatement, one police officer on the scene, Sergeant Dan Yoisten, observed, "They're determined ice fishers."*

I mentioned this to Whitefish Willy. He smiled and shrugged, and said he could understand the reaction. "They would've lost their five-thousand-dollar snowmobiles. Coast Guard choppers don't take equipment. So they figured it was a big enough block, it'd eventually go back in to shore and they could get off."

Still, Willy takes the elements seriously.

> If your car breaks down out here, you're alone. Not like in the city where a guy is going to come driving by in five minutes, and if you don't have the proper equipment, you can get frostbitten within an hour, just sitting in your car waiting for help. So you got to have the right tools.

*If ice floe racing were a sport, Russians would outdo Americans. In 1998, 640 ice fishermen were rescued in the Gulf of Finland near St. Petersburg after two large ice floes broke loose and began drifting out to sea. Each year, dozens of Russians float away and are lost this way. One Russian told a New York Times reporter: "This is how Russians relax. Who said it's supposed to be comfortable." One cultural difference between Americans and Russians involves bait. Siberian ice fishermen prefer live bait to jigs; some fishermen keep the worms alive pinned in an armpit or warmed by mouth. Michael Specter, "Cold War of Soul." New York Times Service, February 10, 1998, p. A1.

You got to carry a little white gas heater in the car; that's a significant piece of equipment that will save your butt. If your oil turns to tar and your battery is low, you go to try to start your car or snowmobile and you're in trouble. I take that little heater, pump it up, and I put it underneath the oil pan. Leave it under there for about twenty minutes, and that car'll start just like summer. You can take a clogged spark plug out and put it on that heater and burn the oil off of it and get going again. You can use that heater inside your car, if you get stuck. You can melt snow with it, too.

I also carry a propane torch, and tire chains of course, and I've got the ham radio. Rope, snow shovel, and the most valuable tool, a pair of vise grips. You can do everything with vise grips, I don't care what it is. Tremendous strength. You can hold things together, like mufflers or brakes, with vise grips. As a matter of fact, I even carry vise grips in my pocket all the time, a little tiny pair, which has bailed me out of many situations. I carry a knife, a screwdriver, wrenches, and a flashlight, too. All that in my pockets, all the time. Oh, and a pair of reading glasses. That's another thing that's gotten important lately. I was out taking a shortcut through the woods recently and couldn't read the map. So now I carry those glasses with me, too.

One time I had to go up to Marquette, a hundred-mile ride, in a Volkswagen Beetle. My wife and I started out at four in the morning. I didn't notice I had a punctured tire, because the tire was so cold it froze solid before it deflated. It kept rolling.

I've been fishing when it's forty below. Nothing works in that kind of cold, any mechanical thing. Even an extension cord—you go to pick an extension cord up and it doesn't bend. You get your hands cold and they're just like stumps. You can't even put the key in the ignition, impossible. I've heard of guys coming back to their car from fishing and they can't get in their car; they can't get the key in the door. That's why I make my tents so you can put them up and take them down without having to take your mittens off. That's the trick of fishing in cold weather. Once you're inside the tent, out of the wind—even though it's cold out you can heat up and get functioning again.

⌒ AFTER A WHILE, he stood up, wound the line around the geppo, pulled the bait out of the hole, and stared out over the ice at a dark little hut in the distance. He said he thought that was his friend Bill. Recognized the shape of the hut. We set out across the ice and walked up to the hut—a box, canvas stretched over a wood frame, the size of a large doghouse. Nothing fancy about it. The box was silent. Willy bent over and looked through a little slot into the shack.

"Hello, Bill," he said.

"I heard ya coming," said a voice in the box.

"I couldn't touch bottom over there," said Willy.

"Did you use a fish finder?"

"No, no. It's almost 280 over there."

"I just put an additional hundred feet on this line in order to reach bottom. Yesterday I was here and the damn thing was deeper."

"You were here yesterday, too?"

"Yah. I threw back some big ones," said the voice in the box.

I leaned over next to Willy and squinted into the slot. In the dim light—an odd light that came primarily from the hole in the ice—I saw, in sharp, bluish relief, the face of a man in his seventies or eighties. He was wearing a camouflage hat and overalls, watching his bobber in the hole. The light flickered under his features, as if he were holding a dimming flashlight beneath his chin, pointing upward. The old man's face jumped and changed with this light. It is an odd and beautiful thing, Willy told me later, that sunlight can permeate ice and then shine upward through a hole in the ice.

"Any whitefish?" said Willy.

"No," said Bill. "Could you get up to the river? I couldn't get up to the river. Too much damn snow. The lake was all foggy, water on top of the ice, so I just gave up for a while."

He proceeded to complain about the changing fishing conditions at one of his favorite fishing spots, which the old man blamed on the state's Department of Natural Resources—which he called "Do Nothing Right." This was a theme I heard in many places in America. The departments of fish and game—however undeserving of blame most of them are—are held accountable for all manner of environmental change, decreasing fish bites, regulation, the weather, you name it.

"Years ago I used to go out on the ice, put a damn tent over the hole, and fish. We would go out there and . . . shit, you could catch a whole bunch of herring before dark. That hole would be black. Hell, thousands, just *thousands* of them! A whole school went by and you could spear them," said the old man.

"How many years ago was that?" asked Willy.

"Oh, maybe fifty."

"I wasn't even born then, Bill. What happened to all them?"

"Well, in the late '40s, I guess right after the war, the damn lake died off. Some damn thing. No herring, no lake trout anymore. No nothing."

Commercial fishing was responsible for the depletion of herring, once the most plentiful fish in Lake Superior.

"DNR's learning, though," said Willy. "Herring are coming back."

"Oh, they'll never learn," answered the voice in the box. "Son of a bitch, you talk to them sometime! You should see me at those Do Nothing Right meetings. They don't like to see me coming. Son of a bitch. They screw up so goddamn much and they've always got an excuse, no matter what. Everything they put their finger in they screw up. You can't tell them a fuckin' thing—they got a degree, they know everything, you know shit. Ask them!"

The canvas box almost seemed to bounce with agitation on the ice.

"And all you're supposed to do now is catch-and-release! *Anything*. Even crappies and bluegills they want you to catch-and-release. I told that son of a bitch biologist to go back to New York where he come from."

The storm of complaint, as it usually does in the world of fishing, soon blew over. I asked the old man, generally speaking, if the fishing is better here than it used to be, or worse.

"Oh, I don't know. It's always been pretty good," he muttered. "Just not today."

The box quit quivering. I looked in the crack. The old man's face was down; he was concentrating on the hole.

Willy started to tell me what a great fisherman Bill is, but the voice in the box interrupted him—told him to quit jinxing the situation with sentimentality. "You're the reason I'm not catching anything, you're fuckin' me up!" said the box, which shook a little in a new wind.

"Aw, heck, fish are fish," said Willy, smiling. "They don't feed all the time, you know."

When we returned, Willy saw me shivering and suggested I sit in the tent. He had lit a kerosene heater, and I sat there on a bucket staring at the hole, the eerie light shining up through it. I could hear sounds coming from across the ice from miles away. It would take a long time to get into the rhythm of this kind of fishing, I thought. This is definitely an acquired taste. My mind drifted. Interesting, I thought, listening to the wind caress the blue sides of the tent, that I have not heard one radio, not one boom box or television. No music. The men sit out here in utter silence except for the occasional sounds of muttered words, floating across the ice, distorted. The little heater hissed next to my boot; I forgot about the tent.

I stared at the water, the flickering eye. I thought of something Whitefish Willy had told me earlier: how he sits out here sometimes and falls

WHITEFISH WILLY AT HOME

into a kind of trance, staring at the hole, and how sometimes he will be out there in blissful solitude and forget everything—all of his problems, his aches, his pains, his past, his future, and all of the world's problems— and all that he will see is this eye. The tent was stuffy, close; I took off my coat, and stared at the eye, slowly lifting the line that went down through its pupil. Perhaps this is the northern white man's sweat lodge. After a while, anglers see things in the hole—beautiful things, the distant past or perhaps a good future, or dark things; the hole becomes a toilet down which they pour life's disappointments. Either way, alcoholic or ecstatic, they see things in the hole. They see things. And sometimes, Willy had told me, he looks up, pulls back the flap, and the world has changed. He watches the Northern Lights warp the sky, and then across the white and endless ice, he sees deer crossing the bay, or a pack of coyotes, gray-blue against gray-blue, padding between clouds of snow fog. I stared at the eye, and saw this, and drifted, and suddenly the flap flew back and Willy's grinning clown face appeared, framed in roadkill fur, and he said, "Yah! You've been asleep an hour!"

Ice Flying

I STAGGERED OUT into faded afternoon light, a bit nauseated. Maybe the cause was oxygen deprivation, or the heat, or the fumes from the heater. Next to Willy's hole was that one fish; no more. Nonetheless, he was grinning. "They started biting at 2:40. I was off by ten minutes. Not a thing since then."

The sun was dropping fast; he packed up as quickly and efficiently as he had unpacked. He signaled to me to get on the back of the sled (this time my earflaps were down), and we were off. I was holding tight as the snowmobile and the sled whiplashed across a long stretch of corrugated ice, with mounds of snow/ice that made the sled leap into the air. Willy never turned to look at me.

Suddenly the sled hit a series of humps in the ice and . . . we had liftoff. In slow motion, it lifted into the air and began a graceful roll to the right. And then it left me, like the booster stage of a rocket, and I was in orbit.

Well. Now this is special, I thought.

In the bloated brown snowsuit I felt like a flying potato. Superpotato, arms forward, legs behind me, parallel to the ice below.

There went Willy, across the lake, unknowing.

I hit the corrugated ice and slid across it, teeth banging in my mouth, chest and knees bouncing along.

Now Willy was running back to me, bending over, his eyes wide in his roadkill hat.

"You were probably going about twenty," he said, with some admiration. "I never had the sled flip over before. You did a good roll."

He righted the sled and I wobbled over to it and got back on. Later, I discovered that I had cracked or at least bruised a couple of ribs, but right then I was glad I hadn't gone head skating.

After loading up the trailer, he removed his roadkill hat, and he put on his red polka-dot cap.

I complimented him on his hat. He said he had several just like it, in different colors.

"Do you get them that color on purpose—for visibility—or do you just like it?"

"Well my green polka-dot hat was the best fishing hat I ever had."

"Why?"

"I don't know, the green hat caught fish. I wore that one out."

I took my camera from my top pocket to take a photo of Willy and his hat, but the camera would not work. I looked at it closely. The battery was gone. Not dead, gone.

"Yah, what have we learned from this?" he said, in his lilting accent. "That if you rotate a writer at approximately 30 rpm for three seconds, the battery in his camera will fly out of its container."

᪐ TRAVELING THROUGH THE darkening north woods, through the aspen and maple and spruce that had replaced the logged white pines, Willy opened the window and inhaled the cold air. A healthy coyote, with heavy winter fur, slipped across the road in front of us. On rare occasions, wolves make their way down to these forests, and, Willy said, despite the illegality, some of the locals go out of their way to run them down on the road, shoot them, or trap them. The deer people, the hunters, he said, don't want the wolves competing for the deer.

I felt the warmth returning to my body, and my ribs began to throb, but I had that tired after-fishing glow you get when you've had a good day and you're on the way home. For some reason, perhaps it was a long thoughtful gap in the conversation, I asked him if he thinks about Vietnam when he's alone out on the ice.

"Yah, I think about Vietnam. It was a waste of time, is what I think. What we did to the people, what we did to the environment over there, wasn't worth it. I think about how far away it is, two different worlds. One time, I was sitting out on the lake there and all of a sudden here come two jet fighters, low, right over the ice. Just like in Vietnam. It was strange, all right. A lot of guys have trouble with post-traumatic stress and all this. But I slough it off. It's gone. That was bad over there with the war, but fishing is good."

Here, in short, is Whitefish Willy's philosophy of life: There's no absolute right or wrong. We're all part of the food chain, and just about everything can be fixed with a good pair of vise grips.

"People are the same wherever you go. That is, they're all different. Nobody's always right and nobody's always wrong. You can be fairly right or fairly wrong. Choose a path in between: That's what I've found anyway. Religions like Buddhism are in tune with that. And the Indians say, 'I'm a tree, I'm the wind, I'm the water,' and they bless the animals they kill so that they'll return. I like that. We're all part of the web of life. We all take a turn."

Headlights were approaching. "There's a vehicle. It's nice to see a vehicle coming." He looked for shining eyes in the road, for deer crossing. "One thing's sure. Just about everything comes out in the water. The way we treat the earth, everything we do runs down the hills and through the gullies and into the lakes and streams and oceans. It's all there."

⌒ MORE THAN THE FISH, it's the water.

Naturalist E. C. Pielou, of British Columbia, writes in her remarkable book, *Fresh Water*, that a new theory proposes that "loosely packed 'snowballs' of nearly pure snow, the size of small houses, are entering the earth's gravity field from the outer parts of the solar system every few seconds; they have been dubbed small comets, and most of them appear to weigh between 20 and 40 tons. They melt and vaporize when they get near the earth."

Water is not only mysterious at its source, but in its constitution. Water is a "'scientific freak,' denser as a liquid than as a solid—most solids sink in their own liquid, that is, expand when they melt—and is the only chemical compound found as solid, liquid, and gas," writes Thomas Farber in *On Water*. Breaking the rules of physics, "Water is not more dense as temperature falls—ice would sink otherwise—but also, breaking the rules of chemistry, water is both an acid and a base, and so can react chemically with itself or anything else." Water "is formless but never loses its identity, is incompressible but offers no resistance to a change of shape," Farber writes. Because it is the most universal solvent, it is never pure; it carries with it every taste of the earth. It "has no nutritive value, but is the major constituent of all living things."

Water is forever on the move—liquid to ice to vapor and back. "In a word, it is dynamic. In much the same way that every living organism has a life cycle, water has a cycle: it circulates." It transforms, reincarnates. Scientists describe a lake's residence time or renewal time, the average length of time that any particular molecule of water remains in the lake. Residence times vary from a few days in small lakes to several hundred years in large ones, depending on their depth. Lake Superior's is 190 years. In California's Lake Tahoe, the residence time is seven hundred years.

It's the water. "Think of all the fresh water on Earth—liquid water, that is, disregarding polar ice," writes Pielou. "Sixty times as much water as this lies out of sight below the ground. Water is under your feet almost everywhere you go." And deep below our feet, below the streams and lakes we fish, other mysteries abide. In the 1990s, spelunkers, aka cave explorers, encountered stalactites and stalagmites that are not rock, but life. Thin, dripping organisms that secrete acid as strong as battery acid. The shape of little soda straws, with the texture of rubber—or mucus, thus the nickname "snottites"—they cover the ceilings of deep caves in Missouri (near the lakes that my friend Harold Ensley searches for his beloved crappie) and southern Mexico and perhaps throughout the world. Some scientists now believe that such life, living off minerals and without need of air or light, may compose much of the Earth's life. In fact, more life may exist below the surface of our world than above it, fed by waters.

The water created 3 billion years ago is still in existence.

It must be the water. Novelist Tom Robbins posits: "Human beings were invented by water as a device for transporting itself from one place to another." Indeed, water—which some science-philosophers say is so unique that it might be necessary to consider it a metabolizing organism on its own—loses nothing in its transformation from solid to liquid to gas, and back. Says Farber: "The water in our blood will be cloud one day, was glacier eons ago, and will be ice again."

⌒ AN HOUR LATER, we were sitting in Willy's farmhouse kitchen eating a dinner of home-grown pork and vegetables prepared by his wife, Debbie. Outside, geese charged across his snow-covered yard like a foolhardy army. Debbie's laugh filled the farmhouse like the scent of fresh-baked bread. Six feet tall, she's a strong woman with a long braided pigtail and powerful hands. "Some friends call me 'The Big One,'" she said, "and I don't mind at all."

She was born and raised in Iron Mountain. Her parents had just celebrated their fifty-fourth wedding anniversary in the house where Debbie was raised. "We did some traveling when I was a kid but not too far. My dad's parents lived in lower Michigan, in Port Huron, and we would drive there and visit each summer. Got to cross the Big Mac bridge many times. That's as far away as I've ever been from this country right here.

We didn't have much money so my dad never had a decent car to drive. But I was always happy with what I had and never dwelled on what I didn't. When I met Bill, we would go motorcycling together on his Harley. We even took a trip to Minneapolis. That's as far west as I've been. I know this is a great big world but my world is right here."

Willy and Debbie are not at all isolated, at least not intellectually. Internet e-mail helps, via ham radio. Because he's far from any Internet service provider's local phone, Willy connects his ham radio to his computer, types his e-mail, which is digitized, and sends it via radio to other hams in the area. Usually, they talk about fishing. Willy figures the Internet and other electronic connections are going to change the face of fishing; probably already have.

"It's getting more and more people up here in this part of the woods have ham-connected computers now. It's snowballing. You betcha." The fishermen trade notes on catching herring through the ice, on lures, and on using spears.

Willy and Debbie are extraordinarily self-reliant. Have to be. Willy provides the fish; Debbie raises most of the rest of their food. Their two-story farmhouse, built in 1923, previously abandoned, is filled with build-it and fix-it books. The ceilings are covered with intricate baskets. Willy fells trees for Debbie and slices them into strips of wood, and she weaves the baskets. To build a basement beneath the house, Willy constructed a small chainsaw mill to cut the trunks of three thirty-five-foot trees, squaring them for beams. Then he and Debbie placed logs under the house, dug a basement and lined it fifty feet in front of the house, and then "used car jacks and ratchets and soap to slick the rolling of the house onto the new foundation." He and Debbie and her father did this. Alone. They learned as they went.

As a citizen of the disposable mall culture, I'm in awe of Willy and Debbie and their self-sufficiency. It's good to find Americans like this. They reminded me a good life can be built with a little optimism and a good pair of vise grips.

What's it like being married to a fishing fanatic? I asked Debbie, at the dinner table.

"I'm no fanatic!" Willy protested.

Debbie arched an eyebrow. "Our very first date, where did we go?"

"Lion's Lake."

"Ice-fishing, our very first date," said Debbie. She smiled and tapped her plate with her fork.

"Caught two brookies, one a fourteen-incher."

"Let's see, that was what, 1972? And you still remember what you caught and where you caught it."

"Oh yah. There's a big white pine tree there, about twenty feet of water."

Do you remember what Debbie was wearing? I asked.

"No. He doesn't even remember if it was me!" They both laughed. The tone of her voice was loving.

"I don't know if that was you out there! I remember the fish, I remember the hole and the lure. Beautiful brook trout. As best a color as you could ever get out of there."

You haven't said anything about how beautiful she was that day, I said.

"She just retains her beauty."

"He got out of that one!" said Debbie, laughing. "See how he lies? That saying, 'I fish, therefore I lie.' "

"Right."

"Or that other one, 'Early to bed, early to rise . . . ' How does it go?"

" . . . Fish like hell and make up lies. Then there's that one, 'A steady job and a wife have ruined many a good fisherman' ," said Willy.

This was becoming a contest. Debbie leaned over and said, "Or this one: 'Men and fish are alike: They get in trouble when they open their mouth.' "

Debbie fishes with Willy sometimes. She likes it out on the ice. She said she doesn't know how anybody could get bored ice-fishing—not because of the fish, but because of the beauty. Willy hooked his thumb in my direction. "He got bored, there in the tent. It got real quiet for a while in there. I heard a little snoring though. I was waiting for a splash. We put him in the tent and turned the heater on and it was like California dreaming in there."

After dinner, we moved to the living room, the ceiling covered with Debbie's beautiful homemade baskets. In the next room, an enclosed porch, several northern pike and crappies, "*Esox lucius* and *Pomoxis annularis*" he said, are mounted on the wall. The pike were three and four feet long. Sitting in a couch next to me, he picked up what looked like a family picture album, but was full of . . . fish. Stringer after stringer. The fish he caught. Brown trout, steelhead, muskies.

"Most people keep pictures of their in-laws," I said. "You have pictures of all your fish."

"Oh yah, these are my babies, " and Debbie's laugh almost seemed to make the hanging baskets sway.

He was grinning so wide—hadn't stopped smiling since he came lurching out of the snow fog at me at the airport—it suddenly occurred to me: This seems to be the happiest man I've ever met. And just maybe the happiest couple.

Then something odd happened. He led me (limping and craning from my ice flight) upstairs to a spare room and showed me slides of how he and Debbie had remodeled the farmhouse, of more fishing pictures, of flowers. Then came the photos of Vietnam, in the late '60s. Most were taken from Willy's helicopter.

He told a story of how, on the Laotian border, Green Berets were being followed by the Viet Cong; the Green Berets had blown out a landing area in the jungle so that the rescue helicopter could land. Willy's Huey dropped straight into that hole in the jungle and picked up the men—and then a companion chopper flew into a cliff. "Our first responsibility was to secure the downed helicopter and pick up survivors. We wouldn't have room for them with the Green Berets on board, so we told them to get out. Would have pointed our M-16s at them if we'd had to, but they pretty much cooperated. There were only two guys who didn't want to go. One said, 'I got a doctor's appointment.' But eventually they got off and we threw their guns out the door after them—even though the VC were still out there. It was sad but we had to do it." They flew to the crashed helicopter, realized the crew was dead, and returned to pluck the men again from their entrapment. "By now, their clothes were so ragged that you could see right through their pants. It was just one more day."

The next few slides were from high above the vegetation. Willy leaned forward. For the first time since I had met him, the expression on his face was opaque. I couldn't tell if he was smiling.

> That's the Ho Chi Minh Trail down there. That's part of it, that little snake there. There's some defoliated areas. See those trees with no leaves on them? The green that's down there is vegetation, vines, and water. The Vietnamese—some of them were probably Viet Cong—made fish traps. See that V shape down there? They'd go out at night when there were no U.S. troops in the area, and chase the fish into V-shaped traps. That's one way they lived off the land, off the water. That's how *they* went fishing.

The next afternoon, Willy and Debbie drove me to the airport. He detoured past a little piece of ice in the middle of town called Cowboy Lake, to show me a cluster of fishing shacks painted black to absorb the heat. Suddenly he hit the brakes and the car wiggled to a stop. He was pointing, his voice swooping with joy. "That's a robin! We got to go back, I can see it in the trees there. This is not robin country! They eat worms. Do you know how far a worm is through the snow? About three feet, plus you got to hammer through two foot of frost." He said this with admiration, one ice feeder and believer in spring, of another. "If that's a robin I'm calling the *New York Gazette!* You can be a witness. There he is, right there! See that bird there? Unbelievable!"

By the time we got to the airport, a blizzard had moved in. It would drop nearly a foot of snow by the time it ended. Steaming men were de-icing the wings of the commuter plane. I walked toward it, bent in the wind, turned and saw Willy, aka Bill Knutsen, waving, his polka-dot fishing cap and big mitten now barely visible in the flying snow. The airplane took off and everything faded into whiteness, taking on the color of a dream or a nearly lost memory.

Poaching the King's Fish

AFTER SPENDING A FEW MONTHS AT HOME, I headed east once again, to Vermont, this time with my family to visit relatives—and to learn about the roots of the American fly-fishing culture.

Next to me on the plane sat a stocky, long-haired, mustached man wearing a loose blue paisley shirt, Bermuda shorts, and sneakers— a refugee from the '70s, or so he seemed. He looked dour. I didn't feel much like talking, so I buried my face in a fishing magazine. Wrong move. "You fish?" he asked, with a broad grin.

His expression had changed instantly.

"Tom Thrailkill's my name," he said. He gave me a fisherman's handshake. That is, friendly. The thing about fishing is that just about everybody has a story, even the guy sitting next to you on the plane. I learned that he was thirty-nine years old and worked for a solar-heating company, among other employers. He said he was taking his girlfriend to Nantucket to fly-fish for bluefish; this would be her first time fishing. One topic led to another, and soon he was regaling me with stories of his glory years. As a poacher.

His poaching career began in 1969, when he was twelve.

"In the summer and after school, my mother would drop me off at the top of Tavern Road in her '64 Bel Air," he said, smiling at the memory. "My friends and I would carry backpacks and fishing rods down the two miles to Loveland Lake. Or, we'd go to Barrett Lake."

I was familiar with Loveland and Barrett, near San Diego. Closed for decades but recently opened, Barrett today is one of the most productive reservoirs in America—with an average daily catch of ten bass per angler.

"After a few years of this, we got a small, aluminum flat-bottom boat," he continued, "and we'd carry it to Loveland or Barrett and throw it down to the water. We called our way of fishing 'hacking at the water, busting water.' We were always using the big topwater lures that make a lot of vibration. It was a very aggressive type of fishing. The more water you covered with that kind of lure, the better your chances were. If I heard someone, I'd stop the trolling motor—but usually, even then, we'd just keep fishing. I'd never stop fishing—and you can ask anybody I ever fished with—even when the sheriff was on my heels or the dogs were there, I never stopped. We were pathetic about it, we were unbelievable."

As the jet passed over New Mexico and the Rockies, he told me of the camaraderie, the joy of the pursuit and of being the pursued—and the strange code of honor that he and his fellow thieves shared so many years ago. "Oh, it was a tight-knit group of us, and we loved the topwater mornings. We used Bushwhackers, Hula Poppers, Shannon Spinners, big old lures that as a kid were just something you could relate to. It was just fantastic knocking these things around. They were covered with teeth marks. Poaching for us was just like going into another world. Unfortunately, it was illegal, but that never stopped me because deep in my heart I knew I wasn't doing anything wrong. And I still don't think I was doing anything wrong. As a kid, this kind of an adventure was intoxicating. The Fish and Game knew us well. One friend of mine, he was on their top-ten list. I never made that."

Tom said he and his young buddies would poach at least two to three times a week, from March to September.

He shared a few more poaching pointers.

If you're committed to poaching, you better have your line wet at all times—even when you're being chased.

The rules are different when you're fishing on land and when you're fishing from a boat. On land you have to blend into the terrain; in a boat, you have to blend in with the water. You paint your boat dark blue or black, and if you have a motor, you paint it the same color. Clothes should be dark and natural, if you're out in the boat. In fact, in the early days, the dam keeper and the sheriff never thought to look at the water, because they figured nobody would be ballsy enough to bring a boat. It just didn't happen.

You take cover everywhere you go. On the eastern edge of Loveland, there was a swamp with old oak trees, willows, cottonwoods, and I'm telling you that we were almost fishing under a canopy. That excited me. We'd put burlap sacks down on the bottom of the boat to muffle the noise. Everything was said in a whisper and if you ever brought anybody that talked in a normal voice—you just didn't. I'm telling you, the good portion of my childhood was growing up talking in a whisper. Every little cove you came around, you'd be hunting for the fish but you'd also be watching to see if you were being hunted.

In the social order of fishing, poachers are the bottom feeders; but it's an old and bloody tradition. In a sense, the wilderness of North America was won by poachers—those explorers and pioneers who, when denied the king's fish, sailed an ocean, claimed a new land and took every fish or fur-bearing creature they could find. Every salmon or beaver taken from a stream in the land of the native people was, in a sense, poached. During its first fourteen years as a national park, Yellowstone was plundered by poachers and thoughtless souvenir takers who damaged the geothermal features. Damage to wildlife was massive; by the turn of the century, poachers and visitors had killed off most of the park's bison and elk.

Today, an average of over 300,000 wildlife poachers are convicted each year, just over half of them for illegal fishing. In some regions of the country, the poaching of fish is overshadowed by the poaching of mammals, especially deer. An Iowa organization that tracks poaching estimates forty-seven percent of reported violations are for deer; compared with ten percent for fish. The reach of poachers is wide: In 1997, authorities busted what they called a "poaching pipeline" specializing in deer, possum, and armadillo that stretched from a backwoods Florida slaughterhouse to Caribbean restaurants in Brooklyn. America's black bears are butchered by poachers and sold to Chinese and Korean markets for their paws (bear-paw soup is sometimes sold off-the-menu at Asian restaurants in New York City for as much as $60 a bowl) and their gallbladders (as medicine). A single gallbladder can bring as much as $10,000, according to Virginia's Department of Game and Inland Fisheries. Ground and sold by the gram, bear gallbladder has a higher street value than cocaine. Though mammals are generally more profitable to poach, some anglers—of a sort—are in it for the money, too.

In 1994, FBI agents, trailing suspected bank robbers, uncovered the biggest caviar-poaching case in the history of the Northwest, and probably the country. Thousands of pounds of caviar were removed from the ancient and threatened sturgeon of the Pacific Northwest. *Seattle Times* reporter Kit Boss described the poacher, Stephen Gale Darnell, as "one of the greatest fish-crime masterminds of all time . . . a handyman from rural Washington who, had he not chosen the path of a poacher, would have been able to spend more time on his inventions, such as a hygienic toilet-seat lifter . . . and a 'fart muffler,' which looks like a hybrid of a plastic rifle bullet, ear plug and cigarette filter."

In Russia, Darnell would be called a *brakanieri*—a "fish pirate." He was found guilty of plundering the Columbia of an estimated twenty-three hundred adult sturgeon, representing as much as twenty percent of the river's adult sturgeon between the mouth and the fourth dam upriver. Ironically, shortly before his arrest, he had written a letter to a local paper criticizing the state for not doing more to rein in commercial fishing. The heading on his letter read: SAVE THE STURGEON! The judge sentenced him to eight months in prison and a $2,500 fine, but said he could keep his rods and reels. Which was a relief. He loves to fish.

Jim Brown, San Diego lakes supervisor, feels a certain amount of affection for some of the poachers on his lakes. As Brown sees it, poaching is a culture with at least three subcultures: those who poach because they want to eat fish (they've fished when and where they wanted for decades, so why should they stop now?); those who poach because the fish are forbidden fruit, the king's fish; and those who poach because they come from societies "in which fish, like all God's creatures, are valued differently, held in a different level of esteem." This category involves a desire for food—and for sustenance, cultural or spiritual, beyond food.

Here's how bizarre it gets. A few years ago, Brown's employees discovered what amounted to a Vietnamese fishing village built on the secluded banks of Lake Hodges, another of America's premier bass lakes. The immigrants were fishing at night, using throw nets. They had built two elaborate fish traps, woven from the roots of the plants along the lake shore. Each trap was the size of a Volkswagen. "They were using these ancient skills right on the site of what was one of the county's major Indian camps, with aboriginal rock art nearby," Brown recalled. "Fishing was a way of life to them; it was part of them, even more than it is a part of me. So we didn't have them arrested. We just chased them away."

Other poachers approach it as an urban thrill sport. Brown tells of the "bass guerrillas"—teenagers and men even into their fifties who dress in full camouflage and ski masks, creep out to golf-course ponds at night and haul in the big bass that live in the ponds. Unlike the utilitarian Vietnamese poachers, the bass guerrillas catch-and-release their fish. "They're like the guys in Sherwood Forest who poached the king's deer. They do it for the sport; they do it because it's the king's fish." That, Brown explained, is the philosophy that undergirds some poaching—but not all of it.

A fourth category of poacher involves a more criminal mind, and often, drugs. Brown says some of the back country and urban fringe methamphetamine manufacturers and distributors constitute what he calls a "secret order of anglers." These poachers, he says, are *real* bottom feeders. Many of them grew up on crystal meth and poached fish; they fish for bass at night, using trout as bait; sometimes they use plastic explosives to bring up the fish; and they're dangerous.

Other poachers are just addled. "They come out right at sunset, fish through the night; they're like cockroaches, almost," one lake supervisor told me. "A lot of guys think they're really mean-spirited, but most aren't. They're long-haired, ride skateboards, listen to Led Zeppelin or punk rock. They range from thirteen years old up to fifty. Some are speed freaks—maybe that's why they're up all night fishing. There's a guy who fishes on my lake, his name is Pinky and he's forty-two years old, and he's never grown up: He rides a BMX bike and has really long hair. He has certain substances working overtime in his system. Pinky's pretty lacking. He's been arrested for hard crimes. But in my encounters with him, he's a really nice person. He's intelligent. I don't know why he poaches. He doesn't eat the fish. Practices catch-and-release. If the police arrest him, he'll be out in two weeks and I'll be chasing him again. I don't want to chase him around the lake every night, so I cut a deal with him. He's got to be out by sunrise."

As America's population increases and regulations on hunting and fishing intensify, so does the pressure and impact of poaching. Enforcement of antipoaching laws is limited by budgets and manpower. A Montana fishing guide explains:

> In catch-and-release and fly-fishing-only zones, it's common to find people fishing at night with cheesecloth bags of fish eggs. We also have a big problem with hoop nets. People use them for catfish but you can catch every type of fish in a hoop net, which can be as long as a truck. You can catch fifteen walleye a day. You can also catch three hundred catfish. The thing with Montana is there just aren't enough game wardens. Look how big the state is. In eastern Montana, one game warden patrols probably fifteen hundred square miles. You're only going to get a small percentage of poachers that way. So the only way poaching can be stopped is just by the ethical ways of people. We just have to say, "Hey, if we want to keep our wildlife around, you can't poach," because the law alone isn't going to stop it.

"No, it isn't," said Tom Thrailkill, when I mentioned what the guide had said.

⌒ As THE FLIGHT ATTENDANTS handed out small, cold boxes of reman-
ufactured food items, Tom warmed to his stories of adventure and mis-
adventure.

"You talk about a poacher's mentality—the mindset starts the minute
you leave the house. You're in the game."

A game played with, say, Clem the dam keeper.

Old Clem would shoot at you but he'd shoot over your head.
Legendary, this guy. He stood about five feet six inches and he was
wiry and he'd jump right down your throat and he drove an old
Ford four-by-four truck. He was a throwback. You'd open the door
of his truck, and the whole bottom of the door panel was full of
chew. That guy, I ain't kidding you, when he'd spit, he wouldn't
make it out the window. He was from Arkansas.

He would take our stuff and hold it hostage. He'd find us and say,
"Whatcha boys catch?" He loved to eat fish, so he'd take ours. And
when he took our boat he'd always ask for a fifth of whiskey before
he would give us the boat back, which I thought was pretty good.
And he was a really nice guy. He always had a story for you, he
really liked kids. I think he had the attitude that, "Hey, I'd rather
have you guys out here doing this than out there doing whatever
else."

One time, we go down to Bitchin' Cove and we're fishing for
sunfish. We wanted to catch as many as we could, that was our goal.
We had a gunny sack with these sunfish and I didn't think anything
was going to happen. There wasn't anybody on the lake in those
days hardly at all. Here comes Clem and the sheriff. I hear over my
shoulder, "Boys! You get up out of there!" We were down on these
rocks fishing. We had a forty-pound gunny sack full of these fish. I
remember this to this day. He pulled us up and he goes, "You guys
are going to jail."

Clem was pretty much all business that day because he had to
walk a long way to get us. He walked probably half a mile, and
he was all crippled anyway—he had a hell of a limp. He and the
sheriff dragged us back up to the road and the sheriff wrote us tickets. And you know what? I never got that ticket in the mail, never
had to go appear in court on it. Nothing ever came of it. I don't
know for sure, but I think that sheriff "lost" that ticket, I really do.
Because my buddy, he didn't have to appear either. I think Clem
convinced the sheriff to lose that ticket. Clem had the biggest old
heart.

The next dam keeper was notorious. His name was Eldin. He

was a bad ass. He would swim across the lake for you. He was about sixty years old but he'd kick the snot out of you if you gave him the chance. One day I'm coming around this point on the lake and I look up and see this guy sitting up on a rock with his back to us, he's got a fishing cap on and he's holding a rod, and I said to my buddy, "Check this guy out." Well, we get up within about forty yards—keeping our lines wet—and I go, "This don't look right." This guy turned around and it was Eldin! He was masquerading as a fisherman. He started reeling off all these citation numbers, section, section, section. He goes, "I got you boys, I know who you are, you sons of bitches."

Eldin was serious about his job. Clem was serious, too—but he had his mind on whiskey and on chewing tobacco. By the time Eldin arrived in the early '80s, the complexion of the whole thing was changing.

We got caught many times. Clem would usually just let us go, but Eldin would turn us in. Even then, we weren't really punished. Because at that time, the judges really weren't too savvy. I went to court one time and the judge goes, "You were fishing? What's wrong with fishing? I did it when I was a boy."

Most of Tom's friends in junior high and high school were into drugs, but not Tom and his fishing buddies. To them, the adventure of fishing was enough of a rush. That, plus the small pleasures, like diving for lures that other anglers had lost. And the moments of strange wonder, like the time he saw a deer swimming across Loveland chased by two wild dogs—and how it escaped.

Over time, Tom and his fellow teen poachers developed an unwritten—even unspoken—code of conduct: "Nobody joins the group unless he's asked in by one of the guys. Don't hurt the land. Never hurt a guy's fence or equipment, don't leave any crap. Use only artificials. In the early days, we'd take home all the fish we could catch, but as time went on we began to catch-and-release ours, or always eat what we took out." Not every member of the group agreed with that attitude. "I'll never forget releasing a five-pounder one day and this friend of mine just about threw me out of the boat. He goes, 'You liberal, naturalist you, you son of a bitch.' And I'm going, 'Get real, Jimmy! Big deal, it's one fish.' We used to go on and on about that."

They also developed a feeling of kinship with the illegal aliens who moved north along the edge of Lake Barrett, only a few miles from the Mexican border.

A lot of guys who used to cross over, they'd look like hell. We'd always give them matches, stuff like that. We'd make sure they got enough food, and we'd give them some of the fish we caught. I would always ask them if they were all right, because some of them would come by and be near death. A friend of mine found a dead migrant. I wasn't there, but it was just a matter of him finding the corpse. He called it in later. That landscape was dangerous.

Some poachers have attempted, and some may have succeeded, catching a record bass one night, transporting it to a nearby lake—stealing a lake record or a bass tournament prize. But Tom wasn't interested. In fact, to this day, he can't imagine joining a bass tournament: The tournaments seem too technological, regimental, too much like the world he wants to escape. Anyway, poaching had its own built-in competition—Tom and his friends were competing with the dam keeper.

Doing what we did when we were young was like Huck Finn stuff, to us. To get into an organized thing was just too normal for us. Speaking for myself and the four guys I fished with, we were all into the freedom of doing what we wanted to do when we wanted to do it. I never had any compulsion to do anything on an organized level. The biggest thing to me was freedom.

I told Tom what Jim Brown had told me about the king's fish. Tom nodded.

I can relate to that, sure. Absolutely, now that you mention it. When I was first poaching, I didn't really know who owned the water and the land and the fish because I was pretty young. But as I evolved, I found out Loveland was owned by the Southern California Water Authority, so I looked at it like—they're a big business; it ain't going to hurt them. Barrett was a city lake, and I knew city lake workers were lazy. They were! A lot of city employees fished quasi-legally back then. In fact, a lot of the up-and-ups from the city—oh yeah, don't ever let anybody tell you different—they fished the closed lakes. I'd be out there working all day to get my fish, busting brush, and here they'd come. And I'll never forget one time, when I was twelve years old, I was down there at Loveland and this guy comes up in a boat—with three guys from the power company—he comes up and charges me, takes my fishing rod. But *he* was fishing. My buddy and I were standing there on the bank; we were crying. It was about a three- to four-mile hike out of there. The guy goes up the lake and then down the lake, fishing. Finally comes back and gives us our stuff back. Now I'm thinking what he *should* have done is put me in his boat and taken me fishing. Come on!

Much of what Tom did or experienced during those years was innocent enough. I can understand the appeal of disappearing into a lost world distinct from the suburban, stucco wastelands. Tom did it, too, for some of the same reasons other people drink or do drugs: to escape. Meanwhile, much of legal fishing today has become a dead ringer for the real world—with permits and regulations with pages of fine print, restrictions on night fishing, and the common use of high-tech gear, those $300 flyrods and $30,000 bass boats.

Still, Thrailkill admits he took poaching too far. By the time he was in his twenties, Tom was flying his buddies in a Cessna to a distant, hidden cove of Barrett, landing on a strip of grass alongside Cottonwood Creek. This was a more serious business. Some days, he caught as many as two hundred bass. He estimates that he poached somewhere around ten thousand fish during his childhood and youth. After a while, poaching fish, at least, lost some of its adrenaline rush. So Tom and his partners went hunting for bigger game. They flew to the offshore islands where they shot elk, until one day they were caught, fined $1,000 each, required to do public service, and threatened with a prison term.* Another acquaintance died while poaching catfish with explosives. Tom decided the risks outweighed the rush. "But one of my poaching buddies, he kept trying to maintain that level of poaching as he got older. He couldn't give it up."

Jim Brown believes that additional social and legal pressure will discourage poaching, but he also believes that there's something about it that invites risk-takers. "Today, in most cases, poaching is considered an infraction or a misdemeanor but historically, people have risked having their hands or arms cut off, or worse. A century or so ago, poachers were killed for taking the king's fish and game." Or, in England, sent to Australia for seven years. "But, whatever the motivation was, they did it," says Brown.

---

*Ironically, environmentalist groups today, including the National Parks Conservation Association, Range Watch, and the Environmental Defense Center, oppose the grazing of elk on Santa Rosa Island, as well as deer, horses, and cattle, by the Vail and Vickers Company, because of the damage the animals do to the natural habitat.

Today, hunters and anglers are increasingly active in the fight against poaching. In 1980 sportsmen in Idaho formed the nonprofit organization Citizens Against Poaching, which operates a toll-free hotline and offers money rewards to citizens who provide information that leads to poaching citations. Then there's the National Anti-Poaching Foundation of Colorado Springs, Colorado, also with a national hotline.

A few years ago, Brown convinced the city of San Diego to open Barrett Reservoir after being closed to the public for decades. While most municipalities around the country have traditionally prevented access to their reservoirs, Brown believes that most reservoirs should be opened to fishing and other recreational sports. Many cities and water authorities are now following his lead.

Brown grew up in the '50s, and spent his summers living and fishing with a dam-keeper's family at another regional reservoir, and he remembers how different it was then. So he restricts the number of anglers allowed to fish Barrett to a hundred per day, three days a week, part of the year. Anglers can only use the twenty-five boats Brown provides—minimalist boats with small engines. This is designed to be fishing right out of the '50s, except for the fact that anglers are required to use barbless hooks and catch-and-release.

When Barrett first opened, anglers from around the state and nation competed for the privilege to fish it, in a monthly lottery. As the day of opening approached, Tom's best poaching buddy was angry—there goes the neighborhood, he said. But Tom entered that first lottery—and won.

In addition to his other jobs, Tom now works part-time for state and private wildlife management agencies. Today, he flies in a helicopter over some of the same offshore islands he once poached, and uses a net gun to capture wild goats. He does the same thing in the deserts of California and Mexico, capturing desert big-horn sheep—to help preserve the species.

This is the way Tom keeps the wild boy in him alive. It's his way of lighting out for the territory.

He fell quiet after a while. I went back to my fishing magazine. And the jet flew east.

Flywaters

~~~~~~~~~~~~~~~

She may guess what I should perform in the wet,
if I do so much in the dry.

—Don Quixote

True Story

❧❧

On the hot July morning I slid down an embankment over the Dog River, holding my St. Croix above my head. An exploding ball of dust and thistles and flying grasshoppers roiled below me, as Peter Cammann thrashed through a wall of weeds twice his height.

"This is just like Vietnam," he said, as he slid on his neoprened butt out of sight. Unlike Whitefish Willy, Peter, at thirty-nine, is too young to have served in that war, but never mind. He was having a great time, and so was I.

A couple of days earlier, I had arrived in Vermont with my wife and sons to visit with my sister-in-law, who lives on a little lake in the woods near Salisbury. Peter Cammann, a fishing guide, had informed me, briskly, that I should prepare for this trip by reading his book, *Fishing Vermont's Streams and Lakes.* "I'm assigning you Chapters 9, 10, 13, and 14 as we are apt to be fishing at one of those locations," he had said in his e-mail. He also gave me precise directions where to meet him, no later than 7:00 A.M., to beat the heat. So I crawled out of bed at 5:30 and drove an hour through the Green Mountains to the Bridge Street Bakery, which is located right next to a covered bridge in Waitsfield.

I was here for the history, to gather a sense of the early influences on American fly-fishing.

The Beaverkill of the Catskills, in neighboring New York, is usually considered the source of American fly-fishing. Vermont has the famous waters of the Battenkill, and the Orvis company, the American Museum of Flyfishing, Diamondback Flyrods, and so on. Perhaps, Vermont is closer to the past, less developed, wilder. Much of the state is geographically dominated by what the geologists call the Vermont Valley.

Paul Schullery, in *Royal Coachman: The Lore and Legends of Fly-*

Fishing, describes the valley as "a long, narrow trough that runs north and south between the Green Mountains (the Green Mountain Massif, if you prefer) to the east and the Taconics (The Taconic kllippe, formally) to the west. Both mountain ranges are almost completely covered with mixed forests, supporting a rich variety of wildlife." Here, shopping mall developers are staking out territory, but the epidemic has yet to spread beyond control. Vermont still has a rough-hewn feeling to it. It's a good place to explore the roots of American fishing, and American fly-fishing in particular.

The roots are tangled. Schullery, one of the sport's preeminent historians, and the first executive director of the American Museum of Flyfishing in Manchester, Vermont, writes that "we fishermen have misunderstood our past by relying solely on books." Fishing writers, most of them writing about fly-fishing, "continue to say stunningly dumb things about how Americans before the early 1800s were too busy conquering the wilderness to fish except for survival rations between Indian wars. What has happened here is that fishing writers rely almost entirely on earlier fishing writers for their information, and they seem to reason something like this: There were no fishing writers publishing before 1800, therefore there must have been no fishing." In fact, historians of colonial America agree that even in the 1600s, sportfishing was one of the most popular and widely enjoyed recreations throughout the colonies. And, Schullery believes, we would all do well to study Native American fishing techniques.

I did. As Peter and I pushed through a patch of wild raspberries, holding our rods high, I mentioned what I had learned about the ancient techniques of the woodland Indians of this region. Among other methods, they liked to catch their fish by poisoning the water with the juice of walnut tree root.*

"But bleach works so much better and it's available at so many more outlets," Peter said, as he disappeared into another thicket.

He loves fly-fishing, but he probably lacks the proper reverence.

---

* Today's fly-fishers would be horrified if anyone tried to use the woodland Indian's ancient fishing techniques. Not much is known about how Native Americans fished on the Battenkill. John Merwin, an esteemed fly-fishing writer, says that this lack of knowledge is mainly "for lack of looking." Much can be surmised, though, from how the woodland Indians fished in the nearby Catskills, on the Beaverkill. They are known to have been less interested in trout than in shad, anadromous fish that traveled hundreds of miles upstream to spawn (and still do today). The Whelenaughwemack people would use river rocks to build a large V-shaped funnel to capture these fish, spears or split sticks to impale or hold them, and brushwood mats as seines to drive fish into shallow areas. The most interesting method used the bark from the root of the walnut tree to poison fish. "The bark was crushed to a pulp to obtain the juices. This ex-

⌐ I CAUGHT UP WITH him on the slate-colored bank of the Dog.

"Look at all the rainbows," he said, pointing to the far edge of the deep pool before us, at whispery shapes in the water. "This pool here is a great habitat, not too many places to hide. The brown trout could be careless, with this little cover. Trout do 80 percent of their feeding below and take the food right off the bottom of the rocks." He was tying a streamer to his leader. "For the last five years, the Dog has been managed as a completely wild trout fishery. Hasn't been stocked for five years. Rainbows, browns, and brook are in here."

In color, the pool was a mixture of greens and browns, and at the far end opaque olive. I looked up into the overhanging maples and elms on the other side and wondered what it was like to have fished here long ago, to have been the first to cast a fly.

The fishing writers tell us this about the spread of fly-fishing: By the 1840s, sport fishermen had discovered the Adirondack region. A few "adventurers were reporting outstanding fishing in the Catskills and the Poconos," writes Schullery, "and others were working their way farther west in Pennsylvania. A few fishermen had discovered (and with unusual discretion, not publicized) the monumental trout of Maine's Rangeley region, and others were starting to fill in the many gaps in the trout-fishing map—Vermont, Virginia, New York, Pennsylvania, wherever trout waters could be found." Then in the 1850s came reports of incredible trout fishing in California and the Northwest. Like many of us, Schullery sometimes imagines himself fishing in that time, and wondering what it must have been like to kill, as one correspondent reported, "570 trout in one day on a Vermont stream, and to do so at the time when there was often no guilt attached to the activity."

Today, despite the impact of acid rain and other insults, Vermont is an example of the resilience of nature. As recently as the middle of the nineteenth century, much of this landscape was deforested and barren, what one historian called a biological wasteland. Fortunately for the land and rivers here, the West opened for business, and loggers and farmers headed for more virginal scapes. Rivers destroyed by logging returned, and the anglers came in greater numbers. Nonetheless, fly-fishing here is challenging.

---

tract was then poured in the riffles at the head of a pool, and when it mixed with the water and was ingested, it drugged and stupefied the shad, causing them to come to the surface, where they were easily collected," according to Beaverkill historian Ed Van Put, writing about the New York stretch of the Beaverkill—or the Whelenaughwemack, as the native people once called it. Other fishing poisons came from the root of a plant called devil's shoestring, turnip root and pokeberry. Edward Van Put, *The Beaverkill: The History of a River and Its People* (New York: Lyons & Burford, 1996), pp. 8–9.

Peter lifted the line off the water, looping it in the air so that it did not drift behind him into the bushes, and roll-cast a streamer across the pool. The fly landed perfectly under an overhanging root.

He's been a professional fly-fishing guide for more than a decade. On the phone, he had sounded hard-bitten, a lanky and toughened New England fly-fishing guide with no time for fools. In person, his face was broad and impish. His waders were torn, and his gear was relatively inexpensive, chipped and worn from use.

As with a lot of opinionated fly-fishermen, his gruffness is only neoprene-deep. So is his irreverence. He owns an 1840 flyrod made of wood—not bamboo—which he picked up at an auction. He's never cast it. Not once. Doesn't have the heart to do it, he says. He loves the lore of fly-fishing, maybe even more than fishing. And despite the popular image of fly-fishers, he's no snob.

The truth is, most fly-fishermen chafe a bit under the self-imposed strictures of the sport. After Peter finished writing his Vermont guide, his publisher sent the galleys to an Orvis consultant for review. "We hoped for a glowing endorsement that we could throw on the back cover. And what he wrote back was, 'This book is rather suspect.'"

"Rather?" I said, fingering through my fly box for a nymph.

"Yeah. 'Rather suspect.' He says, 'Cammann describes a fly here known as the Ausable humpie. And no such fly appears in *Flick's Streamside Guide* of accepted patterns."

"Of accepted patterns?"

"Of accepted patterns. 'And therefore this casts a very, very long shadow on how accurate this book might be.'" Peter took off his ball cap and wiped his forehead in the heat. "And I mean, I've read *Flick's Streamside Guide*. It's one of those things that, you know, you ought to at least look at once in your life. I remember being on the phone with my publisher saying, 'Well I'm certainly glad I didn't tell him about the Royal Bugger.'" He laughed. "Which isn't accepted even by the guy who ties it.

"So there's a certain preciousness to that whole purist mentality and it is quite elitist. And the problem with it is that I think it tends to do two things—which I've resisted like hell in the years that I've worked in this industry—that is to mystify the fly-fishing experience, and more important, discourage participation. It makes the whole process of fly-fishing seem so difficult that nobody can do it. Unless you're bred for it."

Of course, Peter has *some* degree of taste and discretion. For instance, he refuses to fish with mice.

"This old fella I know, he passed away a few years ago, he asked me if I ever fished with bait. I said I do when I fish with my daughter. He said, 'Well boy, I'll tell you those browns, they love mice.' I said, 'You gotta be kidding me!' He says, 'No, no, it works beautifully.' Since then, three or four other guys have told me the same thing. They fish with mice at night."

He didn't sound prejudiced against mouse-fishers, just puzzled by them.

He's even more puzzled by the less fastidious locals who still hunt for big Vermont pike with shotguns. They do make a good story, though. "The pike shooting is really bizarre! I've never done it, I don't understand it. I was always taught that the last place you're supposed to shoot is in the water. They climb up in the trees, look down into the water, and wait for the pike to swim along and fire just underneath the pike. If I understand properly you don't have to hit them. Just the shock of the shot going through the water is enough to stun the fish. I don't get it."

Then they climb down and get the fish?

"I guess."

Or is it shoot-and-release?

"You got me, man! It's way beyond me." He waded up the stream and around the corner. In hopes of catching a brown, I took a cast, with a woolly bugger, at the same overhanging root. I stripped the line in, and just as the fly reached the end of my rod, I heard a . . . kerplunk . . . under the root, and saw rings in the bright water spread. Either something big had just broken the surface—a brown? A beaver?—or a rock had fallen from the cliff above. Peter reappeared, wide-eyed. "Man!" Whatever had caused the disturbance, it was a big brown trout now.

We took a few more casts at the spot. I tangled the woolly bugger in a branch behind me.

"You got a real estate license?" he said. "If you do, you get to keep the bush."

↶ WE MOVED UP the stream, slowly casting. He stood in a pool, held his rod and reel under his arm, and lit a six-inch Macanudo cigar. He was looking down at the clear water along the edge, a cloud of blue smoke drifting upward. Suddenly he nearly jumped out of the water. "Lookit that! Lookit that!" he said. I squinted down around his knees. "Two rainbow fry!" He was seeing things in the water I wasn't seeing. A few minutes later, he pointed to the wake of something moving in the far corner of a deep green pool. He said it wasn't a fish, but he didn't know what it was. "What *is* that?" he exclaimed, as if he had spotted the Loch Ness monster. So far, we hadn't caught a single trout, but my heart was pounding as if we had. This was an exceedingly jumpy guide, I thought. And I liked it.

I changed from the nymph, tied to represent a larva escaping from the muck and rising in the water to find its flight or a rock to climb, to a dry attractor fly that Peter recommended. It was a Royal Wulff, heavily hackled, designed to float high on the water, and imitating nothing particular in nature, designed to agitate the fish. I cast again. A little swirl bumped the fly and I yanked it. This happened three times. "Now why am I losing those bites?" I asked.

He explained: "When the fish sees the fly, it inhales the water surrounding the fly and tastes the water. It doesn't actually bite or chomp on the fly itself and if in that millisecond it tastes the water and the taste is similar to that of a live insect or a fish, it'll swallow the fly whole. On the other hand, if it tastes hackle and hook and the rest, it'll spit it out in a fraction of a second. If you try to set the hook too early, you end up pulling the hook right out of the fish's mouth. If you hit just a shade too late, you're apt to actually hook the fish but it'll be in the outer, fleshier portion of the fish's mouth. The odds of it breaking loose are pretty high. That's probably what was happening. On the other hand, if you hit it just right you'll set the hook while it's still fairly deep and hook the roof of the mouth, or the cartilage around the jaw."

I was impressed with his explanation. Clear, clean, and not patronizing.

He rolled out another three casts, and snapped the rod back when he heard and saw the blip in the water. He puffed his cigar faster, mushroom clouds forming above his hat.

"Fly-fishing is one of the few things fun that I've ever had any aptitude for." He sounded disgusted with himself. "I'm reasonably competent at this. But you can flip back to your level of incompetence again; you can become the inept angler again. We both did it, we both missed three perfectly good strikes."

His face turned sour. He sucked on his cigar.

I asked: When did you learn you were competent, or had this aptitude for angling?

"I don't know, I haven't a clue." Right now, it seemed, he felt like the incompleat angler.

After a minute or two, his ebullience returned. Hey, he doesn't mind getting beaten by a fish, he insisted.

"It's like a shoot-out. You get beat by something that's faster than you; it's OK, that's not so bad. If it's because you completely screw up, that's pretty pathetic. I can see that, of the three strikes I lost just one of them strictly because I wasn't paying attention, at all. That's entirely my fault. The other two, the fish just beat me."

PETER CAMMANN

After a while, we sat down on the bank and unwrapped sandwiches and popped open sodas. I asked him about his background. He said he grew up in Manhattan and spent summers on Long Island. Among his earliest memories were the commercial fishermen there known as the baymen, who seined striped bass, bluefish, weakfish off the east end of Long Island.

"I remember chasing the seining trucks when I was a kid. We used to chase them on our bikes for miles. The baymen would finally stop, put the nets into the surf from a longboat, and you would wait for this huge mass of fish to be brought in. And I remember seeing baymen going into the inlets and collecting the scallops and the eels and all the rest. And that's all over. That doesn't exist anymore. There is still some scalloping going on but it's more farmlike."

We watched the water for a while. He finished his sandwich and carefully rolled the cellophane and paper bag tight and pushed it into a pocket of his vest. He lit another Macanudo. He said his mother taught him to fly-fish twenty-eight years ago in Montana. As a young girl, she had fished there with her parents and brother.

> Six or seven years ago, I went out fishing with my father, my uncle, and my aunt on the Winooski River here in Vermont and my mother came along. She didn't want to fish; she just wanted to sit on the shore and watch. My uncle's a great guy, but he has a terrible habit. If you catch a fish, he comes and fishes right next to you. And he'll push you right off the piece of water you're on, very aggressive. So I'd been pushed off a couple of runs by my uncle and I decided I didn't care anymore and I was going to go back and have a beer with my mother. She asked me if she could borrow my flyrod for a minute. She takes the flyrod—the woman had not held a flyrod in her hand for over twenty years—and started to make these picture-perfect thirty-, forty-foot casts. She does this for no particular reason, not aiming at anything on the water, and after about five minutes she puts the flyrod down. I looked at her and I said, "Why did you do that?" She said, "I just wanted to see if I could still do it." She could be a great fly-angler but it doesn't interest her, which is ironic. Most people struggle like hell to do what she does naturally.

He leaned over, held the cigar up with one hand, and turned over rocks with the other. He pointed at the mud. "Those are mayfly larva," he said. "They'll start to hatch in a month." All I could see was little brown dabs that moved every now and then.

At one time or another, I suspect, every good angler has fantasized about becoming a fishing guide. I continued to cast and asked him what it was like to guide.

"Good guides," he told me, "use their flyrods as nothing more than pointers." He became a guide, he said, so he could spend more time out on the water, but it didn't work out that way.

"When I first started, a guide told me, 'Peter, you're going to reach that awful stage when you're going to hate fishing. And after a dozen years, I've realized he was right. I no longer enjoy guiding. Last year, I didn't fish on my own at all. Hell, I played golf. Then, on the day I closed the guide service, on October 1, I went out and fished the whole day and had a ball." He laughed.

The other issue was economic.

"My associates and I had a great month in May. I personally guided twenty-four days that month and I had a couple of other guides working for me, so you gotta figure we did fifty trips. Each trip pulled in an average of $125, maybe $150 per client. So somewhere between $6,000 and $7,500 came in during that month. Of which—after hiring the guides, paying the monthly insurance premium for these guides, renting equipment because we didn't own all of the gear—we walked away with half of that money, maybe not even half. If you can't get better than a two-to-one return on any investment you make in a business, you're in trouble. That doesn't even include the advertising we did. Big gross, lousy net. So what's the point?"

The best thing about being a guide, and sometimes the worst, is the people.

> Occasionally these people come out to compete with you. To prove something. "You may be the resident expert in this field, but I have all these degrees and I should certainly be able to do this better than you."
>
> Other people turn it right around. I had this one guy, a high-pressure salesman who was wild. We were driving and he was telling me about these awful deals he was trying to put together and how much pressure he was under, how he was really looking forward to this weekend so he wouldn't have to think too much about all that. I'm thinking to myself, "All the guy's doing is talking about work; this is going to be a hellish trip." The minute he got on the water he turned into another person. It took about twenty-five minutes for all of the stress to melt away and then I don't think he said twenty words the rest of the trip. I felt good about that. It was what he needed.
>
> Fishing is the time when you don't think about time.
>
> The last trip I did I ended up with this kid who's about twenty-three years old, does light shows for rock and roll shows. He calls

me up because he's read my book and he says, "I want you to teach
me how to fly-fish. I live out in Minneapolis. I'll see you in a week."
And he drove to Vermont. Got in late the night before the trip. I
showed up at 5:30. He'd been up for an hour. Waiting. I took him
out fishing; he was like a sponge. He picked up so much in two days
that it blew my mind. At the end of the day he was doing everything, absolutely everything, and doing it perfectly. I turned to him
and I said, "You are one of the most satisfying students I've ever
had." He said, "I really appreciate it, but now I've got to head back,
because I only got a week off."

I liked his attitude, which was just, "This sounds like fun, let's go
do it. Let's not think about it, let's go do it." I loved that. That was
my last client. He was the best.

⮑ LIKE MANY ANGLERS, he worries about the trend toward restricting
private waters, a trend more prevalent in the East than the West—but
growing in the West.

I have a four-year-old, and since she was just barely two years old
she has loved to fish. A piece of water where I first taught my daughter how to fish, how to release a fish—where she saw her first brook
trout—is now posted against trespassers. It's a beautiful little beaver
pond and we can't go there anymore. The state recently estimated
that in the Mad River Valley, where I live, 50 percent or more of all
of the river access to the Mad River has been posted. When I moved
into this valley twelve years ago, I daresay only a quarter of the river
was restricted, maybe not even that much. It's a big issue in lake-
front areas, too. In Vermont, you *may not* own a navigable piece of
water. The access can be owned. So if I access a navigable piece of
water from a public access point, or if I have permission from a
landowner to go to the river, and I wade or boat through the water
bordering your land—even if you own both sides of that piece of
river—I have a right to be there as long as I wish to be. As long as
I'm in the water. I've had to argue the fine points of this law with a
few landowners, who come out and announce from the riverbank
that I'm trespassing on their piece of river.

If you control access, though, you control the water. Up here in
Vermont, a beautiful stretch of the Lamoille River is known as the
Ten Bends. A trout club came out and bought up the access on both
sides of the Ten Bends. They called themselves the Ten Bends Club.

Very aristocratic. They won't allow you access to the piece of water unless you're either a member or you know a member—and even then they only want you to fish with fly equipment, catch-and-release. I remember once to my *delight* when I floated down into Ten Bends with a client, we anchored the canoe in the *middle* of this area and we merrily fished anywhere on that water we damn well felt like. And the people on the shoreline screamed at us: "You may not do that on our river!" And we *smiled* and *waved* and I turned to the guy and I said, "Do you have any nightcrawlers?"

⤳ THE STORIES ARE WHAT he loves most about fishing. He had been thinking about this topic for a while and had a few theories about the nature of the fish story. He leaned back on his elbows and elaborated.

First, whether the story is about the fish that was caught, or the one that got away, the primary purpose of a fish story is for the teller to re-live the experience, and the listener to go along for the ride. "I had a guy tell me a story the other day at the gas station about going fishing for striped bass on a river. And he starts pointing at the pavement explaining to me how the fish were stacked up and I know he *saw* the fish."

On the pavement?

"Absolutely. But it wasn't pavement—he saw, and I saw, the *river.* He does this one interesting gesture, and says, 'The fish were three and a half to four feet long,' and he's holding his hands like he was grasping a slightly deflated basketball. And I know what he's doing; he's holding the fish up by the gills and he's looking at the head. For about five minutes, he was back on the river. He relived the whole thing."

Guide stories—as I had learned first on Lake Fork in Texas—are a special subset of fish tales. These stories often have more to do with human foibles or fanaticism than with the fish that got away, more to do with fishing hell than with angling heaven. Peter told about a family of clients, a man, his wife, their two grown daughters, and the eldest daughter's husband.

I met them at around six in the morning. They'd brought two cars and two canoes and I'd brought my truck and a third canoe. We start unloading everything at the reservoir and I asked them if they had any experience with canoes. The two girls both chimed in that they'd been to summer camp fifteen years ago; the parents just looked a little sheepish. But the eldest daughter's husband said he'd been canoeing all over the damned place. Africa, the Rockies, Asia.

An alarm should've gone off in my head, but if it did, I ignored it.

Five clients all day made for a big fee, but self-preservation should've overruled my greed for a few bucks, shouldn't it have? I put the eldest daughter and the Great River Runner in one canoe, the father and his youngest daughter in the second, and I took the mother in my canoe. The Great River Runner immediately starts yelling at his wife and she starts screaming at him. When I turn to see what's the matter, they're paddling, facing each other. . . . The Great River Runner's the one faced wrong way around!

I got them squared away. . . . The mother got into a pretty good fish right off and the three canoes all spread out along the shoreline. Everything was cool until I looked up the way and noticed that one of the canoes had tipped over. I pulled in my line and mentioned to the mother that one of her darling daughters was in the drink. She looked up and saw two figures struggling in the water.

"Oh, my God!" she screamed. We both noticed that one of the two swimmers had scrambled up onto shore while the other one still seemed to be in serious trouble. The mother and I began to pull water, moving our canoe as fast as we could.

"Which one is it?" the mother asked me as we got a little closer.

"Well," I said, "it looks like your son-in-law is the one drowning."

And with that, the mother carefully put down her paddle, picked up her fishing rod and took a cast.

"Fuck him," she sniffed, "I'm going to fish."

Another subset of the fishing story is the fishing log. For more than 150 years New England anglers have been keeping fishing logs and fishing diaries. They kept these things, and still do, and use the information about the conditions of water, weather, and other factors, in order to improve their fishing over time. Said Peter, "For instance, they might write, 'I went to the Lamoille on the fifth of July at four o'clock in the morning and fished until eight o'clock in the morning, saw a gorgeous mayfly hatch, which died off after an hour. I caught six brown trout, none of which was less than eleven inches long, but only two small rainbow trout. The weather was somewhat overcast and the water was sixty-five degrees.'"

Because these logs track the conditions on the stretches of river the anglers frequented, state fish and wildlife departments have collected them all over the United States. They're used as primary evidence of the health, or lack of health, of a fishery. Peter cites a particularly valuable example: Fishing diaries have been used to revive the waters of the Clyde River, that runs through Newport, Vermont, near the Canadian border.

Until 1957, the Clyde was host to one of the state's largest landlocked salmon runs. In 1957, Citizens Utilities, a Connecticut-based public utility company, built a series of hydropower dams along the Clyde—the most notorious of which was called the number 11 dam, which was built about two miles up from the mouth of the river.

"It chewed up a lot of fish in the turbines during the spawning season and made it virtually impossible for the landlocked salmon to move far enough upstream to really have a chance to lay their eggs, fertilize them, and then get back downstream." Part of the dam collapsed in the spring of '94, blown out by a storm. Citizens Utilities had just begun to renew the dam license. "Anglers had been cursing this dam for almost forty years," Peter said. "Trout Unlimited lobbied the state to drop the license. At the hearings, elderly anglers brought their old logs, as did the younger ones—some of them had kept logs, too—and testified about the past and present health of the fishery. Some of the young anglers came in with photographs that their fathers had taken of their catch. And they brought their families' fishing diaries, as well. All of this was used to describe the loss of this fishery over a period of four decades."

As a result, the license was denied, and in 1996 what remained of the dam was removed and habitat was restored, with heavy financial support from Citizens Utilities. This marked the first time in U.S. history that the federal government had not renewed an existing license for a power dam. Peter recalled, "In October of '96, the wild landlocked salmon ran and spawned normally for the first time since 1957 and I went up to the Clyde and caught-and-released between forty and fifty salmon in three hours. They were so thick they were banging against my legs. And the reason it happened is that anglers came in and told a very different type of story."

Such a story, as he sees it, must contain several qualities and elements. "It has to entertain; it has to capture the imagination of the people listening—the policymakers. It must be of absolutely unimpeachable integrity. You may not exaggerate. You must paint the picture as vividly and accurately as if you were capturing it in a photograph. And this is a very fine tradition of the fish story. The natural progression of the fish story is from oral entertainment to oral history to a tool for advocacy."

We pushed through the brush, taking a shortcut upstream to Northfield Falls. Above it, leaning over the current, were the remains of a mill washed out during a massive flood in the '20s. I wondered who had worked there, what their stories had been, and if they had fished the Dog. Peter lit another cigar and hopped from rock to rock, leaving a trail of floating smoke rings. He dropped a weighted woolly bugger between the cracks of the rocks and snapped the rod tip up from time to time. I followed his lead and again missed a few strikes. We fished in silence for a while. The strikes were enough to make the morning slip past quickly. The sun warmed my back as I concentrated, staring into the crevasses.

Peter had to get home to his wife and daughter, so we climbed the embankment near the falls, thrashing our way back up through the brush and tall weeds. Up on the road, he told me he had just accepted a job at a computer company. No more guiding. He said this as if he were trying to sound excited about it.

We walked down the asphalt road, our waders sloshing.

"There's a great story that my father-in-law once told me. He's walking across a bridge and he found a young woman with her feet over the edge of the bridge with her fishing rod out. And he looked down and he noticed that her line stopped about two feet above the surface of the water. And he looked at her and said, 'You know, if you lowered your line a little farther, you'd probably get more fish.' To which she responded, 'Yeah, but I really only do this for the sport.'"

We walked a ways.

"True story," he said.

Relics

∽∾

THAT AFTERNOON, I drove to the American Museum of Flyfishing, in Manchester, Vermont, a two-story gray clapboard building at the corner of Highway 7A and Seminary Avenue, up the street from Orvis central. Gary Tanner was waiting for me. He sported a mustache and beard. His moderately long hair was graying. Somehow I had expected someone more . . . tweedy.

Founded in 1968, the museum was the dream child of *Field & Stream* art director Hermann Kessler, and a group of anglers who wanted to preserve the rich heritage of their culture. In the beginning, it relied almost exclusively on the generosity of the Perkins family of the Orvis company, especially Lee Perkins Sr., who bought Orvis in the mid-'60s. In those days, the museum was housed in a small room in the Orvis store. "As the museum got larger, it established itself as a separate entity from Orvis," Tanner said, "and bought this building and moved here." The museum publishes *The American Fly Fisher*, a quarterly journal.

A willowy, straight-haired fortysomething woman stuck her head into the office. Tanner introduced her.

"This is Randall Perkins."

"Are you married to Perk Perkins?" I asked. Perk Perkins, son of Lee Sr., is the CEO of Orvis.

"Right," she said, smiling slightly.

"That's funny, I always think of Perk as married to you," said Tanner. He turned me over to John Mathewson, the museum's curator, and Perkins, who is the designer of the journal. We headed out of the office, to the gathering of relics.

Mathewson, thirty-four, was tall, blond, bearded, soft-edged, and intense. He did his undergraduate study at Union College in Schenectady,

New York, and graduate work at the University of Vermont. His qualification for doing this kind of work, he said, is that he has a master's degree in history.

"And you're a good fly-fisher, too, right?"

"Actually, when I started here I knew nothing about fly-fishing."

We walked through the lower floor. The museum is primarily concerned with the roots of American fishing history—fly-fishing for sure, but the line is blurred here, between early American fishing and the use of artificial flies. I learned that, as far as can be told, the first American fishing club was organized in Philadelphia in 1732; the New York City government passed the first American law regulating the manner of freshwater fishing in 1734; and the first American angling book—an eleven-page pamphlet—was published in 1743 in Boston.

Mathewson explained that the museum has collected some 3,000 fly-fishing books, more than 1,200 rods, 1,100 reels, between 25,000 and 30,000 flies. In glass cases, you see the remnants of America's parallel history—the one that happened streamside. Through wars, depressions, and assassinations, the fishing continued, like religion, despite the world's excesses.

In the hushed and half-lit rooms, you see the physical history of rod building: rods of two centuries made with stunning craftsmanship by Leonard, Payne, Thomas, Kosmic, Orvis, Murphy, Edwards, and many others. And there, the relics: fly-fishing tackle owned by Daniel Webster, Dwight Eisenhower, Herbert Hoover, Andrew Carnegie, Samuel Morse, Ernest Hemingway.

Hemingway's rod, dark and burnished bamboo, was made in 1936. "He probably picked it up on his way home from the Spanish Civil War. It's a small Faerie rod, one that he would have used on a stream back home," said Mathewson. And over there: rods that belonged to Glenn Miller, Bing Crosby, Babe Ruth. "This one right here is Ruth's. An E. F. Payne rod from New York." And rows of exquisite artificial flies. The masterworks of some of America's best fly-tiers: Theodore Gordon, Ray Bergman, George LaBranche, Edward Hewitt, Roy Steenrod, Joe Brooks, Preston Jennings, Mary Orvis Marbury, and John Atherton, among many others.

The rods, each with its own aesthetic personality, are made of green hardwood, steel, hickory, raw bamboo, split bamboo (with four, five, six, eight, and nine sides), fiberglass, graphite. Their dimensions, make, origin, and other historical details are meticulously recorded in a computer database. The oldest one that can be dated with certainty was made in 1832. Also in the collection are the personal papers of famous anglers.

And lines, containers, tools, magazines, catalogs, artwork, tackle boxes, photographs. My head began to hurt with the detail.

The Egyptians, Mathewson said, probably used a rod for fishing around 1400 B.C. The first written reference to fly-fishing is usually credited to Aelian's *Natural History*, probably written about A.D. 200. Aelian, born in Italy but fluent in Greek, in the third century, after observing the Macedonians fishing, wrote:

> Between Boroea and Thessalonica runs a river called the Astraeus, and in it there are fish with speckled skins; what the natives of the country call them you had better ask the Macedonians. These fish feed upon a fly peculiar to the country, which hovers on the river.
>
> When then the fish observes a fly on the surface, it swims quietly up, afraid to stir the water above, lest it should scare away its prey; then coming up by its shadow, it opens its mouth gently and gulps down the fly, like a wolf carrying off a sheep from the fold or an eagle a goose from the farmyard; having done this it goes below the rippling water.
>
> Now though the fishermen know this, they do not use these flies at all for bait for fish; for if a man's hand touch them, they lose their natural color, their wings wither, and they become unfit food for the fish. For this reason they have nothing to do with them, hating them for their bad character; but they have planned a snare for the fish, and get the better of them by their fisherman's craft.
>
> They fasten red wool around a hook, and fix onto the wool two feathers which grow under a cock's wattles, and which in color are like wax. Their rod is six feet long, and their line is the same length. Then they throw their snare, and the fish, attracted and maddened by the color, comes straight at it, thinking from the pretty sight to gain a dainty mouthful; when, however, it opens its jaws, it is caught by the hook, and enjoys a bitter repast, a captive.

And the reel? The Chinese probably invented it as early as the third century. The Western world, however, lagged behind. Mathewson smiled and said with a slightly conspiratorial tone, "In England during the 1600s, anglers began to use a new invention called the wince or the wheel to add to the rod to which you could store line. It allowed you to cast farther out on the water—and also helped you hide the line quickly, to wind it up fast, in case the authorities came. It was considered a poacher's contraption and most anglers looked down on it for at least

100, 150 years. But by the early 1800s, people had begun to call it a 'reel' and they were starting to use it."

So poachers popularized the reel?

"Yes. Proper people did not use it. They were dapping instead." Dapping was the use of long rods and a kind of floss, a line attached to the end of a pole.

"Has anyone written the history of poaching?" I asked.

"We had a copy but somebody stole it," said Mathewson.

"Is that a joke?"

"Yes," he said laughing. "I don't know of any."

Some of the museum's rarest reels are displayed on the main floor. Among them are the first Kentucky reels, made sometime between 1800 and 1810 by a watchmaker. Its "quadruple multiplier" made casting easier.

⌐ STANDING IN THE midst of this history, I remembered a trip that my older son and I had taken to fish for rare wild trout in Baja. As we rode horses along the Rio Santo Domingo—on the same trail that Father Junipero Serra took north—I had wondered if Serra had fished there, too.

"Hey, listen," I said to Mathewson, "is there any evidence that Father Serra or any early Spanish explorers fished in the Southwest?"

He stroked his chin. "No, not of that. But there is a very old history of fly-fishing in Spain, which developed separately from British fly-fishing. So there was such a thing as Spanish fly-fishing, which was totally separate from English fly-fishing. The Spanish didn't write about it often."

As it turns out, *The American Fly Fisher* published an article in 1984 that described a newly discovered document: "an angling work of extraordinary importance . . . here is something that apparently does not stem from the legendary Dame Juliana Berners (who wrote the first essay on sport fishing) and our British angling heritage." *El Tratadico de la Pesca, Dialogue Between a Hunter and a Fisher,* by the Spaniard Fernando Basurto, was published in 1539, fifty-three years after the publication in England of Dame Juliana's writings on fly-fishing.

Later, I did the math. Columbus sailed for Spain in 1492. In 1497, John Cabot (an Italian whose real name was Giovanni Cabotto) explored the coast of North America for England. The English didn't establish a settlement in America until 1587, at Roanoke Island, off North Carolina—and that one disappeared mysteriously within three years.

Meanwhile, the Spanish stole the march, becoming the earliest substantial European presence in the Americas. Conquistadors landed first on the North American mainland in 1510; in 1513 Juan Ponce de Leon explored Florida looking for gold and the fountain of youth, and Coronado reached New Mexico's trout country a year later—more than seventy years before the English settled in.

All of which is to say that the Spanish may have fly-fished in the Americas, with their own techniques, before the English.

Fly-fishing purists consider England the source of this most civilized sport in America. Gentlemen colonists brought the intricate rituals to the streams of New England, and fly-fishing spread across the continent from there. That's the official story. To suggest otherwise is blasphemy.

For a reality check, I wrote to Andrew N. Herd, a member of the elite London Flyfisher's Club and a noted British expert on the early history of fly-fishing.

"I guess the time frame would fit," he wrote back. "My feeling is that the Spanish didn't suddenly pick up rods in the sixteenth century . . . but against this, Mexico's tradition of fly-fishing is very recent indeed, and although the North American Indians fished with lures (similar to tube flies as it happens) there is no evidence that they fly-fished as we know it—as far as I am aware. The Spanish were too busy plundering the place to do anything else. Or maybe they did bring rods over but found that European methods didn't work . . . It would be a great theory if it could be proved. Very seductive."

Ah, but there's no proof that it's not true. *Viva Basurto!*

↪ THE GREAT MAJORITY of the museum's collection is upstairs where the public is not invited, in several rooms, on row after row, level upon level of metal shelving. Thousands of reels, rods, flies, and fly boxes, are crammed onto these shelves, tagged and dated.

This isn't the only fly-fishing museum or place of preservation. There's the Hardy Museum in Alnick, England, and the Catskills Fly Fishing Center between Livingston Manor and Roscoe, New York. The Federation of Fly Fishers maintains a small collection. And Yale and Harvard universities keep exquisite angling libraries of valuable books dating back to the 1700s.

"The Angler's Club in New York City has an awesome library," said Mathewson. He shook his head. "They've got some things that I wish we had. It's way downtown, on Broad Street down in the financial section. It was bombed by the Puerto Rican Liberation Front in 1974. All the big dogs of Wall Street, the ones who fish, are members of the Angler's Club. It's very exclusive, used to be totally male. The first woman I ever saw there was two years ago."

"But she's not a member," said Randall, who had followed us up the

RANDALL PERKINS WITH A 19TH-CENTURY FLY HOLDER

stairs. Randall visited the Angler's Club only once and found a cardboard sign on one of the men's restrooms, to accommodate women guests.

She picked up a recent acquisition, a beautiful old fly holder made of leather and wood, held together with metal clips. It was very old, perhaps a century, with handwritten notes—a log by some unknown angler, lovingly scrawled at streamside—and old flies pressed between the pages. She turned the pages slowly, gently. Like many who are exposed to fly-fishing, she is drawn most to the artistry—the gracefulness and delicacy and almost otherworldliness of some of fly-fishing's physical expressions. Not the fishing so much as the small details, even the sounds. The names of so many flies do roll off the tongue easily, precisely: the Silver Invicta, Cat's Whisker, Mallard and Claret, Silver Grey, Olive Dun, Gold Ribbed Hare's Ear, Royal Coachman.

It's hard to think of some of these flies as artificial, because they seem qualified for reality by their own existence, independent of what they represent (or in the case of the attractor flies, what they symbolize to fish and fisher). So much of this equipment—the flies, the rods—are the small, perfect expressions of philosopher E. F. Shumacher's admonition that "small is beautiful"—not only the flies themselves but the tools of the fly-tier: bobbin holder, whip finish tool, dubbing needle, hackle pliers, and tiny sharp scissors. And the same goes for the diminutive cases of wood, or even of plastic and aluminum, that hold them, or this old leather fly wallet, folded to hold these particular patterns that truly do not look like anything living, but look instead like something that *should* have lived.

"I love these small things," she said, opening the fly wallet.

No wonder people hoard or protect such beauty. And no wonder so many of the great fly-tiers have been women: There is nothing bullish about fly-tying. Randall seemed lost in the detail of the thing. She looked up after a few moments. She had drifted, I think, on a stream of leather.

↜ WHEN RANDALL PERKINS closed the nineteenth-century fly holder, she asked me if I had met Margot Page.

"No," I said. "Should I?"

"Yes, definitely." She wrote Page's phone number on a copy of the museum's journal. "You should go see her because she's a bridge between the old world of fly-fishing and the new. She's right down the road."

The Fishermom

⌒⌒

VERMONT, AS IT TURNED OUT, was a good place to begin thinking about what might be called *deep fishing*, an uncustomary human relationship with nature.

That afternoon, I called Margot Page and then drove south of Manchester, through the valley that divides the Taconic and the Green mountain ranges, through villages with their quaint, hand-painted signs for ubiquitous antique stores, maple products, cheese, and a store that sells clothes made of hemp. On the clean lawns of Victorian homes, men moved like slow beetles on their riding mowers, and above them the clouds dipped low over high-humped Mount Equinox.

This part of the country is such a contrast with the rest of strip-mall America. Paul Schullery writes that the Battenkill "is changing faster than many of us might like, and it does seem to me that the towns are looking more and more like what people from New Jersey and Boston *think* Vermont should look like rather than what Vermont might normally look like. In fact, one former resident complained that all the newcomers, transplanted from the urban complex known locally as BosNyWash, are obsessed with trying to 'outquaint each other.'" Maybe so, but the aesthetic here, like the familiar pattern of a fine fly, is comforting. Or, given a different mood, disquieting—because it reminds the traveler of so much that has been lost. I drove through East Arlington Village, past its waterfall, post office, and general store/antique center.

Margot Page lives on a slight rise above the village, overlooking the valley, in a 160-year-old clapboard farmhouse, white with green trim, seemingly held to the hill by the deep-rooted maple trees circled around it. The trees are over 130 years old, she told me later.

Page is one of a handful of modern women who have made a name for themselves in the culture of fly-fishing and carry on an old and not often described tradition. Like Sugar Ferris and others in the bass tournament world, these women challenged popular notions about the relationship between women and the sport. Their challenge is larger than fishing, and their influences subtly different, one from the other. Ferris's contribution probably has more to do with women's relationship to organized, competitive sport. Margot and the women of fly-fishing confront a traditionally male culture and have made slightly more progress than women in the more resistant bass tournament culture—at least if one believes the number of ads and commercials that now use women fly-fishers as their centerpieces. Women fly-fishers are extending—subtly, imaginatively—their relationship with nature. At the same time, they're achieving a parallel literature in a culture already rich with the written word.

I knocked on the screen door, and a girl of about nine came to the door, then a woman came up behind her and pushed the door open. Both smiled, the woman with her hands on her daughter's shoulders.

"Shake his hand, Brooke," said Margot Page to her daughter. "And look him in the eyes."

Brooke's handshake was strong and felt practiced. Brooke's name, her mother told me later, was picked because it suggested water.

Margot led me past a cage with two ferrets, just inside the front door, and into her bright, colorful kitchen. She is a good-looking woman, forty-three years old, with a charismatic smile. Her hair is dark blonde and a bit wild, her eyes sharply intelligent. She made me strong coffee for a headache I was nursing, and told me that she had just returned from a fishing trip to Martha's Vineyard.

"We fished for striped bass," she said. "Striped bass fly-fishing is a wild and woolly sport where you don't have any tweediness, it's more *cowboy*. Bigger tackle, bigger environment; your flies are big, it doesn't matter how precisely you cast. When the blitz is on, it's wild and these guys are not beautiful casters, but they can get the thing out there. It is a hot, exploding sport—and it's taking the pressure off of the trout streams."

Margot is the former editor of *The American Fly Fisher*, and the author of *Little Rivers: Tales of a Woman Angler*, a beautiful little book that, along with a handful of other women's fly-fishing books, broke new ground when it was published in 1995. It was, in a way, a declaration of independence. The book was dedicated to her mother, who never liked fishing, and her grandfather, Sparse Grey Hackle (Alfred Waterbury Miller), author of *Fishless Days, Angling Nights*, who was one of America's most famous fly-fishers.

"A fishermom is a mother who fishes," she wrote:

The appellation is the only simple thing about the concept. A fishermom arrives on the stream harried and preoccupied, usually eager to get in the water, but sometimes so much in overdrive that by the time she arrives on the stream any activity at all often seems not worth the effort.

That's because like most fishermoms she has just left her small child with the father who is gearing up for bedtime antics and, if she's lucky, supper, too. Wails, hair flying, and rushing about have preceded her departure and it takes more than the short drive to the river to clear out the debris. It is not until she is cooled by the current around her legs and calmed by the easy rhythm of the stream and the life around it that she begins to fish.

With more women taking up fly-fishing, the number of fishermoms is increasing. While we are not yet legions, we are more than a handful. We are no longer the girlfriend or wife who picks up a rod and wades only for her partner's benefit. We are there because we like to fish and are serious about it. As one fishermom buddy says, "We're not fishing for our husbands anymore, we're fishing for us."

⤳ IN HER GRANDFATHER'S day, such talk of leaving the men and kids behind to stand alone in a river would have been about as blasphemous as suggesting that, well, the Spanish brought fly-fishing to America first.

"Sparse was one of the last icons of the golden age of fly-fishing—from the male heyday of fly-fishing culture centered on New York City," Margot said, as we carried our coffee into her living room, filled with heirloom antiques. "Sparse, as everybody else called him—I called him Deac for Deacon—was the editor of *The Anglers Club Bulletin*, for fifty years, on and off. And he spent a long time on a pilgrimage to find the final resting place of Theodore Gordon, known as the 'father of dry fly-fishing': Turned out Gordon was buried in an old vault in a hidden wall in a cemetery in New York City. Finding him was a big event to that small world."

Sparse, truly one of fly-fishing's icons, took the nom de plume when he wrote energetic articles protesting the pollution of Catskill streams and rivers. He was "not an elitist," says Margot, "but he was a very proud man. A unique combination." As one reviewer wrote, Sparse referred to his writing "with a usual dollop of self-deprecation as 'huntin', shootin', fishin' columns.'" His writing is loving, with moments of pure grace, such as, "a fine flyrod is a magnificent thing, a strain of music made visible."

"In my mind, Sparse was a touchstone for this past world, a world that has died out, a world with pipe-smoking men on the stream, tweeds, and flasks, with men who would meet at the club and tell long stories, men who would exclude women." This exclusivity went (hackle-in-hand) with the private-water approach. In 1991 Joan Wulff, the current matron saint of fly-fishing, wrote:

> "Private-water" clubs offer a limited membership of compatible anglers and well-stocked fishing waters. . . . Open-membership organizations, on the other hand, offer education in the form of clinics, a chance to make friends with other fishermen, and the opportunity to be involved in preserving and protecting the sport through conservation projects. . . . In the Northeast, the private-water clubs started forming in the mid-1800s. No ladies, please, was the general order of the day with a few exceptions. The Southside Sportsman's Club, established in 1866 on the Connetquot River on Long Island, allowed ladies to stay in two annex buildings but did not permit them in the clubhouse itself. Believe it or not, the Beaverkill Trout Club in the Catskills still feels that way, allowing ladies to enter only one of the two buildings. The fishing wife of a male member may fish, but I know of another Catskill club that turned down a friend for membership for the very reason that his wife fished. That was seen as potential trouble!

Margot led me to several old photographs on the wall. One is of Sparse and Margot's mother, at about eleven years of age. He's wearing wool knickers and a fedora, and the kind of thick, round, horn-rimmed glasses that are back in vogue. He's smoking a long, jutting pipe. Margot's mother is wearing a belted leather jacket and beret and knickers, and she is holding a flyrod. Then Margot showed me another photograph, this one with her grandmother Amie, holding a Garrison bamboo flyrod, dressed in waders with creel; her eyes are closed and there is an expression of intense happiness on her face. "Amie was his equal if not his better in fishing. She was a solitary, competent angler who fished with the guides and fished with four women including me over her lifetime, only four women. Amie, whose full name was Louise Brewster Miller, was known as Lady Beaverkill, and she always said, 'I am not a fly-fisherwoman, I am a fly-fisherman.' Back in the '40s and '50s, that was quite a statement."

I asked Margot if she would have resonated so to fishing if not for her heritage.

"It's hard to say. I married into it too. When I was growing up my mother scorned fishing because it was so identified with her father's world, because I think he so owned that world that she couldn't compete. She just thought the angling world was made of slimy fish and men who told long, boring stories. Of which Sparse was one.

"Back then, fishing to me was big, funny, baggy pants and a hat with flies stuck all over it. It was an eccentric hobby but one of pride because Sparse had written this book and he had gotten some publicity, so the family was proud of this odd behavior. My grandmother was also involved in it and they would clamber around on the rocks on the Catskill streams and rivers north of Greenwich, Connecticut, where I was brought up. It was an eccentric and odd sport, and the trout would just turn up on Sunday afternoon, after their trips to the Catskills. The kids didn't like fish; we'd much rather have had hamburgers on Sunday evening, when the fish were barbecued. We'd turn up our noses but our parents were delighted. That's about what it was, I was very far removed from it." As a child, Margot accepted her mother's opinion—that fishing was below her station in life.

Things changed.

In her twenties, Margot went to work for a publishing house founded and run by Nick Lyons, a well-known fishing writer, working in subsidiary rights and publicity. The near-legendary Lyons Press, located in New York City, specializes in angling and outdoor books. She began to meet "these crazy characters" who wrote the books, and the one woman, Joan Wulff, who gave her her first fly-casting lesson in Lyons's loft office, "which was high enough so that I could practice cast, flick back and forth, using a three-foot rod with orange yarn for a line. (This, invented by Wulff's husband Lee, was called a Fly-O.) I would be writing copy and I'd get stuck, so I'd pick up the rod and cast for a little while, sitting at the keyboard, then go back to writing copy."

She also began to learn about the distinguished and seldom-told history of women fly-fishers, beginning with Dame Juliana Berners, followed by a long drought, and then bursting with heroines in nineteenth-century America: New York's Sara Jane McBride introduced scientific entomology to fly-fishing and Pennsylvania's Elizabeth Benjamin was famous for her inventive and realistic flies, made from feathers from roosters, chickens, ducks, pigeons, and bird nests. Mary Orvis Marbury, age twenty, took charge of the Orvis company's commercial fly-production department in 1876, and in 1892 wrote the first definitive reference book on American fly patterns. Then there was Cornelia "Fly Rod" Crosby, who was issued Maine Guide License number one and drew record crowds at sportsmen's shows in New York and Boston in the 1890s. In 1924, Carrie Stevens, a milliner, revolutionized the way streamer flies were tied. Herbert Hoover and Zane Grey were among the fly-fishers who purchased flies from Stevens. Though Margot found this hidden history intriguing, she had yet to go fishing herself.

In 1984, she met her future husband, Tom Rosenbauer, a Lyons author who is now Orvis's vice-president for hunting and fishing catalogs. She moved to Vermont to be with him, and they were married in 1985. She had never fished before that, but now began to learn. "I saw this was a mania of my husband, and had to find a way into it, and eventually discovered that it was in my blood too. I stomped around in his ill-fitting waders and got blisters and tried to do it his way. I'd get caught up in bushes and I made all the mistakes and I felt alone. But over time, gradually, I acquired some skill and began to find for myself what was important about the sport—what the connection was, what I needed from it, how I could do it and be comfortable, on my terms."

When Margot started fishing by herself, she would hear other anglers, all male, whispering on the stream—whispers of surprise and curiosity.

"Is that a woman?" they would say. I didn't think I looked *that* questionable. It was very lonely fishing that way, because in the beginning I had to adapt to my partner's, my husband's, way of fishing, which was maniacal—macho astronaut training, as I would call it. This required going for many hours without food in all kinds of weather. I was still learning and felt that that was the only way to be a legitimate fly-fisher. But as I developed confidence and skill, I began to feel that there was another way to fly-fish, other ways that were legitimate. And that's what I began to write about as I began to develop my voice. When I first started doing pieces it was in the late '80s and it was very frightening to put my small voice out there in the midst of this macho, male tradition. I had to work against the pipe-smoking, tweedy legacy. The legacy of my grandfather. But I know he would have championed what I was doing. He always felt women were far better fly-fishers, not only because of their hand-eye coordination and their dexterity, but also because of their lack of agenda and their willingness to listen. They didn't go in and try to overpower a stream, overpower the tools, or even the prey. If you go into a stream and you're floundering around and beating your chest and not *listening* and not *seeing*, you're going to scare the fish away. You can't impose yourself on an environment. This is a different kind of fishing. It's not only women who fish this way: Many men, as well, approach fishing in this manner. They're the smart ones. They approach the water; they don't fish right away. They watch and listen and stand back and then they try to integrate

themselves into the context of this environment. That is how you
work with fishing, that's how you connect.

In my travels, I heard this refrain often, not only from women, but
from male guides as well: that women tended to approach fishing differently, that they spent more time appraising the water, watching the
edges, feeling the current. So that when they finally cast, the cast was
more precise. And once they began to fish, this view has it, women were
more likely to be aware of what was going on in the water as well as
above it; more cognizant of the plants and animal life on the shore or in
the branches above, more immersed in the totality of it. Over time I
would come to think of this kind of angling as "deep fishing." This wider
interpretation of fishing isn't exclusive to women. The best of male anglers understand it, and fly-fishing literature is rich with the depth of this
kind of angling, which offers more external awareness and a deeper in-
terior experience.

Thomas Gordon must be rolling in his vault. The recent work of female evolutionary scientists has undercut the whole conception of the
man as the hunter and the woman as the tender of the home fire. As yet,
little is known about how early women fished. But, Margot asked, "Is it
only men who have that hunter-gatherer instinct? No. Women may have
set up the weirs at the mouths of rivers near their encampments; perhaps there were tribes where the men all died off or were too crippled
or old and the women had to go out and find the protein. Maybe I would
have been the one doing that. Today, I release my fish. I don't particularly like to eat fish. But fishing still satisfies my need to feel . . . how can
I put this? *I've caught it. I have mastered it. I have used my tools as a human being to catch something that's wild and alien.*"

Beyond the hunt, beyond the thrill of pursuit, is the larger world of
fishing—deep fishing. Here is a sport that can make a woman or a man
look up, to see beyond water, fin, scale. Or to look beneath the current,
under the rocks, where life moves. An expert fly-fisher is forced to see
more; he or she may even become (like Sara Jane McBride) an entomol-
ogist—may come to know that the metamorphosis of a mayfly lasts a
year, that it changes from burrower to clinger to crawler to swimmer;
that duns are the newly hatched adult mayflies that emerge from the
water and fly to the foliage along the stream; that after depositing their
eggs, the females fall from the air in a spin to the water, a "spinner fall"
of magic and beauty. The fly-fisher uses little nets to scoop life from the
water and scrutinize it for its luck, and must know of the caddis fly larvae that build their own tapered submarines from the finest of plant ma-

MARGOT PAGE

terial, must know that golden stonefly nymphs crawl en masse from quick waters into shallows in the late afternoon and in the dark. The deep-fishing angler must be intimate with water itself, must know the feel and mood of riffles, runs, pools, flats, eddies, pocket water, and edge water, and must sense or know even the relationship of the life cycles of plants on the bank and fields beyond to that water and the fish in it.

Women anglers aren't the only ones to notice this.

Bob Scammell, of Red Deer, Alberta, author of *The Phenological Fly*, explains the concept of phenology. The word is derived from the Greek, phaino, meaning, "to appear." Phenology is the science of appearances of things in nature, of "making the connection between appearances of flora and fauna, specifically connecting the appearance, or flowering, of certain streamside wildflowers to the appearance, or hatching, of those insects that produce the super hatches so interesting to both trout and anglers."

He describes the super hatch, the experience of being at the right place and the right time when insects fill the air and big trout attack the angler's artificial fly. Zenlike, he asks: "Is any hatch super if no fly fisherman is present?" He dismisses the tendency "for people with little time to develop any art . . . to rely on. River hotlines, computer programs, newsletters, and informal networks of anglers with cellular phones that announce sudden hatches." These shortcuts are, he says, "substitutes for real knowledge derived from personal observation and experience" and lack sensitivity to the "vexing variables." And they create what he calls human super hatches: "Everyone goes to all the same places, all at the same time."

Ruminating on how distant from natural observation some anglers become, he recalls: One season, while in his office, he received a call from an angler who was standing next to a stream. The fisherman, calling by cellular phone, told Scammell that two river hotlines had provided conflicting information about hatch conditions on Alberta's North Raven River. He wanted Scammell's expert advice. Looking out of his sixth-floor window, and wishing he were on that river, he did his best to be helpful:

"Are the marsh marigolds out? " I asked.

"What?"

"Those clumps of bright yellow flowers down at the water's edge."

"Oh, yeah."

"Then you should see some Western Green Drakes starting about noon. Is the wolf willow blooming yet?"

"Don't know that one."

"Well it smells real spicy, sweet, like burning incense . . . if it is out, you could get Brown Drakes, starting at dusk."

That, he wrote, was a short, sharp illustration of phenological connections.

The combinations he recommended to the cell phoner for the North Raven would probably not work on Henry's Fork of the Snake where "I have also fished Green and Brown Drake hatches on the same day. I do not recall ever seeing marsh marigolds along the Henry's Fork or smelling wolf willow on Brown Drake evenings there. Rest assured, though, there would be other wildflowers native to the area blooming along or near the Fork when those hatches occur."

But when streamside phenology—involving an understanding of bugs, bees, bluebonnets, berries, and the barometer—becomes almost intuitive, second nature, what is it? More than the sum of the sciences, more than craft. Scammell writes: "The first intimations of phenological connections to fishing came to me when I was a child in the 1940s and '50s. There were folk-ways, old wives' tales, if you will, and wise sayings that guided us: 'Pickerel run when the cotton blooms and blows' (from the Cottonwood), or 'Gold-eye run when the wild roses bloom.'" Thinking like this, the angler enters the realm of cultural dream, beyond logic—into gut, almost genetic, knowledge, with unlimited complexities.

Margot Page says that women fishers have been taking the time to smell the flowers—and that this makes them better anglers.

"Why restrict this idea of fishing intuition to women?" I asked.

"I'm not. I'm just saying that women tend to be more aware of this connection—they use it more naturally, maybe because their egos don't get in the way."

If this is an argument, it's one that no one and no sex can win. But it does point men and women in the right direction: toward a deeper immersion in nature during the incidental act of fishing. Margot says women are writing about this more than men. I don't know about that, but it's a useful discussion. Margot's grandfather and his generation (and a good number of today's male fly-fishers) figure they're bringing civilization to the rude and crude, or at least protecting it. Now, Margot and many other women anglers figure they're refeminizing the sport, bringing (or reawakening) a deeper sense of nature, intuition, and magic.

↬ WE WALKED TOWARD THE DOOR, she opened the cage next to it, and two ferrets undulated up her arms. Outside, the weather was changing; the heat had given way to cool, and the clouds were lower over the valley of the Equinox.

"Oh, I forgot to tell you about something," she said. She described a different kind of women's fishing organization: Casting for Recovery, a nonprofit group that, when we met, was just over a year old. It teaches fly-fishing to breast cancer survivors. Though she has never had cancer, Margot serves on the board of advisors.

Here is something else that women are bringing to fishing. The idea of fishing as therapy is old; the creation of fishing-therapy *groups* is new.

"Sometimes the sport can be very selfish," she said. The ferrets made little chirping sounds as they played in her hair. "So this is a way of giving back." Most of the women who join Casting for Recovery, she explained, have never fly-fished. "You should see these women's eyes as, out in the natural world, they learn to cast—that graceful, mesmerizing, hypnotic thing of beauty." Forget catching fish; the casting is mantra. "These women have been in sterile rooms with veins opened up to poison, and you see their eyes shine with discovery." Some of them are very ill. "When they return to that chemo room, to the hard time, they'll have a place to return to, in their minds, and it might give them a moment of peace." The doctors on Casting for Recovery's advisory board believe that the benefits are both physiological and psychological. "The casting helps muscles that have been frozen, nerves that have been severed. Some women get frozen shoulders after they have mastectomies. The physiological motion of casting helps to loosen them up. The instructors have been trained to help adapt the casting motion to whatever circumstance the patient finds herself in."

I told her that many anglers had told me that fishing was healing.

"I almost hate to say *fishing*. I'd rather call it water treatment. Yes, it's about the line and these wild flashes of light you see in the stream, but it's really the water that we go to and the water we've always gone to. For some kind of solace, for understanding, for cleansing, for rebirth. I think we're drawn primarily by the water and then by the wild things that inhabit it. We need the power of the ocean and the power of a small stream. Beyond that I can't say why fishing is healing. It's irresistible. When you become more familiar with the creatures that inhabit these bodies of water, you are drawn to *see* them, to connect somehow. But it starts with the water."

"By the way," I asked Margot, "is your daughter a fly-fisher?"

"Yes, she is. She turns out to be an absolutely fantastic caster. And she will find her own way."

I said goodbye and shook her hand. It was a strong handshake, like her daughter's.

Industrial-Strength Fly-Fishing

ON THE FINAL DAY of the Vermont visit, I headed to Orvis central, down the road from the American Museum of Flyfishing in Manchester. The compound serves as both Green Mountain retail outlet and national headquarters. As I drove up, I was surprised by how small it was.

In front, the retail store is a long, one-story structure, faux rustic and red. Two canoes thrust out and upward from the front, which houses a fairly typical Orvis outlet—shelves of practical or dream gear: Clearwater Breathable Waders, Deluxe Forceps/Scissors, Battenkill reels, Easy Poke Fly Threader, Orvis High-Beam Hats (battery included), and so on. Next to the building is a picturesque casting pond. Orvis is the most famous commercial name in fly-fishing, the Starbucks of angling. The company has set up outlets in just about every fly-fishing region in the country, sometimes to the consternation of the local Mom and Pop fly shops—though few of the owners of these small stores will talk about their angst publicly; they want to become or remain Orvis distributors. The company makes a good chunk of its profits selling outdoor apparel (outdoor in the sense that a Ford Explorer is off-road) but fly-fishing is still the core, the soul of the company.

In 1874, C. F. Orvis invented the prototype of the modern fly reel and in 1876 founded the company. In 1892 his daughter, Mary Orvis Marbury, age twenty, took charge of the Orvis company's commercial fly-production department. Sixteen years later she published the first definitive reference book on American fly patterns, *Favorite Flies and Their Histories*. With more than five hundred pages and thirty-two color plates of 290 different regional patterns, the book standardized the names and patterns of American flies—and, for the first time, provided professional fly-tying companies with a method to sell, by catalog, the known patterns.

When she died in 1914, Britain's *Fishing Gazette* ranked her, among women in the sport, second only to Dame Juliana. She was the midwife of the modern fly-fishing business.

Kim Champine, a 22-year-old rod-shop tour guide who also works in the rod painting room, gave me a tour of the fly-rod factory, if it can be called that. It's more of a large artisans' shop. The workers, men and women who are part of a manufacturing crew of eighty or so, looked more working-class than any of the anglers I had yet seen in Vermont. The place was surprisingly intimate, not perfectly clean, and far smaller than I would have expected.

"Please wear your safety glasses," said Champine. She handed me a piece of milled bamboo.

"Our bamboo comes in to us from China," she said, with an efficient but pleasant tone. "There are actually about one thousand different species of bamboo and the best is from China. It's Tonkin cane. It comes in a twelve-foot section and we cut it into two six-foot chunks. We're going to put a split down the length of it, and this is why: It is a grass and not a tree; it is very porous, it holds a lot of moisture. If we don't put that crack down there it's just going to split while it's in storage." She went on to describe wormholes, watermarks, discoloration, density, and nodes. "For coloration, we put it in a fourteen-hundred-degree rotisserie oven. The more it rotates through the oven, the darker it's going to become."

How long does it take to make a thousand-dollar rod, and how long does it take to make a hundred-dollar rod?

"The only thousand-dollar rods we have are our bamboo rods."

OK, a five-hundred-dollar graphite rod.

"One of the Trident series? From start to finish, it'll probably take two weeks."

Of constant work.

"Right. In batches of thirty."

What about your least expensive rod?

"Our Clearwater series? About one hundred and fifty dollars. It's not going to take as long because it's not painted, for one thing. It doesn't go through a lot of the inspection stages that the other more expensive ones go through. So maybe about a week."

Most of the difference between rods is aesthetic, the way it's wrapped, the wood of the handle, the paint, she explained. But the highest-end rods are indeed technologically different. "The Trident series uses a dampening technology that affects the action dramatically."

I told her I was surprised that the rod factory was so small.

"I couldn't believe it when I first started working here, that it was so small," she said.

That's what's so striking about the fly-fishing industry, how small it is, almost as delicate and diminutive as those Tunghead Hare's Ear Caddis and Disco Midges you find in the catalogs.

Randy Carleson, president of dealer sales, is trying to change that. His nondescript office's most dominating feature is a campaign map. Carleson, thirty-eight, is a solidly built man, a bit soft around the edges but not the eyes, with neat hair and moustache. He wears aviator glasses and an Orvis polo shirt.

In 1992, *A River Runs Through It—the movie—*"turbo-charged the industry," he said. In the next few years after the movie's release, the industry experienced an astonishing thirty-five percent rate of growth, the demand grew faster than the industry's ability to supply its products. After the euphoric economics of '92 and '94, the business cracked along at a good twenty percent annual growth rate; by 1997 it had flattened out to five to ten percent. Orvis compensated by selling more clothing.

The growth in the number of women fly-fishers has helped. So has greater ecological awareness.

"Just got back from Martha's Vineyard, myself," he said. "The culture on that island is based around fishing." No trout streams there, of course; it's all saltwater fishing, and saltwater fly-fishing is hot, commercially. Fifteen years ago ninety-five percent of the people who fished on the island did so with conventional tackle, spinning gear. "Today, if you go out on the beach during June, seventy-five percent of the people will have a fly rod in their hand." This fishery is an illustration of how tied a business can be to ecology, and its management. The Vineyard has become a Mecca for the saltwater fly-fisher, due to the resurgence of the striped bass in the Northeast fisheries.

Orvis donates five percent of its pretax profits to conservation efforts, and has raised millions of dollars to lobby to protect the striped bass fisheries, and for restorations of the Blackfoot River in Montana and the South Fork of the Snake River in Idaho. These are markets to protect and grow.

I asked Carleson to define the current and emerging ecocenters—the ecological and economic targets—of America's regional fly-fishing cultures. He walked briskly to a map of the United States and picked up a pointer. He exuded a sense of command, kind of like a young General Schwarzkopf.

The striped bass fishery in the Northeast, of course, is an emerging market region, he said. So is the Gulf Coast. "From the Appalachacola River right at the bend where the Florida panhandle begins, all the way around to Port Isabel, Texas, Louisiana, Mississippi, the Texas coast, all the way down to the bottom edge of Texas. We target that. Within that area there's probably five different sub-fisheries."

The Ozarks? "The rivers of the Ozarks are typically flatter, slower water—tail water fisheries, cold water flowing deep behind dams. But the Ozark region is growing in importance to the fly-fishing industry without question."

Now for the established ecocenters. The pointer moved quickly. *Snap.* "The Catskills, in south central New York State, is a very important area. Steeped in fly-fishing tradition. Town there called Roscoe; they have a sign as you enter town, says 'Trout Town U.S.A.'"

He tapped Pennsylvania. "South of Harrisburg, very rich agricultural area, strong in limestone deposits and a tremendous amount of quality spring creeks rich in nutrients."

His pointer slid across the Appalachians, across the upper Midwest. "Working our way across the country, the next stop would be the Rocky Mountains." *Snap.* "Colorado, west of Denver." Denver is Orvis Ground Zero. "Close to twenty fly shops in the city of Denver itself. In the suburbs, even more. Greatest concentration of fly shops in the country."

His pointer circled Yellowstone, then drove northwest to Washington and Oregon. "Inland, fine trout fisheries. But when you think Northwest, typically you're thinking steelhead fishing, migratory fish coming out of the ocean. This center also dips down into Northern California's coastal areas."

Snap. His pointer flattened Los Angeles. "There's not a lot of fishing close to there. But those guys have the Sierras, a four-hour trek from Los Angeles. High population, high ability to travel, high income. Our biggest domestic dealer is near Los Angeles, out in Fullerton."

Now his focus zoomed back across the map.

"Let's face it, no city other than New York has a better and more varied amount of quality fisheries within a three-hour drive. You can go to the Adirondacks, the Catskills, to Pennsylvania. Great saltwater fishing in Jersey, the Long Island Sound and out toward Montauk. Vermont is only four hours away. With New York, you've got eight million potential customers."

He lowered the pointer, and slapped a hand over New York City, splaying his fingers over New Jersey and Connecticut and several other Eastern seaboard states. Orvis hegemony was his.

↜ BUT NOT QUITE. A few weeks later, I attended the International Fly Tackle Dealer Show in Denver. Once a year, for three days, this show is the center of the known fly-fishing universe. This is where East meets

West, where the best fly fishers and the wannabes connect, where the big guns of fly-fishing commerce go head to head with the smallest startup companies.

Saint Joan had headed West too; had flown from the New York Catskills. Wulff is probably the most famous living professional fly-fisher. She and her husband, Lee Wulff, who died in 1991, were charter members of fly-fishing's pantheon, which includes Theodore Gordon, George LaBranche, Harry and Elsie Darbee, Walt and Winnie Dette, Art Flick, and others. I met her an hour before the show opened. She was sitting on a high stool in the Winston Fly Rods booth, alone. Straight out, let me say she's the kind of older woman—she's in her 70s now—for whom a younger man could develop quite a crush. She exudes a dancer's grace, even when perched on a high stool, as she was now. Her hair is now steel gray. On this day, she wore a scarf held by a clip depicting a trout leaping for a fly. She's also an extraordinarily nice person—that's another phrase people use to describe her.

She invited me to sit on a folding chair in her booth. After we began to talk, I forgot all about the living legend stuff, and just enjoyed myself. That is, until she gave me a fly-casting lesson—but we'll get to that.

I asked her about her introduction to fly-fishing.

"My father was an outdoorsman, had an outdoor store," she said, rocking slightly on the stool. "Everything was hunting, fishing, and dogs." She smiled. "I remember my very first fishing experience. I was four or five and my father wanted to fish for bass with a flyrod on Greenwood Lake in New Jersey. My mother was rowing the boat. My mother was not a good rower and all night long my father was correcting her, saying she was too close or too far to where the bass were. In spite of this he caught some fish. At the end of the evening my clear thought was that it was better to be the fisherman than the rower."

Like Margot Page's grandmother, Lady Beaverkill, Wulff calls herself a fly-fisherman. "I'm old enough to remember when mankind was all of us."

When she was ten, her father started teaching her eight-year-old brother to fly-cast, but didn't teach her because she was a girl. Joan had other ideas. One day, with her mother's permission, she borrowed her father's rod and walked to the local pond, and inadvertently cast the tip section of the rod into the pond. A neighbor pulled it out of the water with a rake. After that, her father decided that if she was going to cast, she was going to do it correctly. He began to teach her to fly-fish, along with her brother.

"Fly-casting, more than catching fish, is always what turned me on," she told me. "I loved casting because it was so physical. I started dancing and casting at the same time, ended up becoming a dancing teacher and having a dancing school for eight years. Through dancing, I learned how to use every inch of my body to cast accurately. When that fly line goes out you see it and feel it; it's both the seeing and the feeling. It's like when you're wading in a river, you're part of the river."

Indeed, an extraordinary 1952 photograph shows Wulff tournament casting from a dock, her body in a perfect arabesque, her weight on one dancer's leg with the other behind her, straight and taut, toe touching the dock; her arms on a plane, one hand holding the rod, the other arm in a straight line behind her. Energy seems to travel from the tip of her toe, up her leg, through her body and arm, grip, and out to the very tip of the flyrod.

How she grew, and what she learned, changed the face of fly-fishing. Before she turned thirty-four, Wulff had won an unprecedented seventeen national casting titles and one international casting title; had set a women's record distance cast of 161 feet (the record was unofficial, she says, because there were no distance events for women); and was the first woman to win the Fisherman's Distance Event against all male competitors. Her book, *Fly Casting Techniques,* is considered by many fly-fishers the most important casting book ever written. "She has done for casting what Stephen Hawking did for physics," declared *Fly Rod & Reel* in 1994.

The biggest change in fly-fishing that she has witnessed is the trend she pioneered: the movement of women into the sport.

"The big rush of women into fly-fishing came after *A River Runs Through It.* It wasn't the movie that did it, it was Robert Redford saying this is something special," she said. "But of course the women's movement had a lot to do with it. When my fishing school opened in '79, we were lucky if twenty-five percent of the students were women; they were usually dragged there by the husband, and probably never fished after they left the school. But during the past two years I've had more women than men students. These women are arriving on their own or with a woman friend, paying their own way, buying their own tackle."

Still, a lot more women will enter fly-fishing when the tackle business gets its act together.

"Very few women in my generation fly-fished, in part because heavy and cumbersome waders were made of canvas and rubber and the companies only made them for men. You might have been able to get a boy's hip boots, if you could find them in your size." Lighter, more flexible nylon, neoprene, and Gore-Tex waders are a vast improvement, and women's waders are now widely available. "The main thing was that the tackle was always too heavy. The trout flyrods, made of bamboo or glass, weighed roughly four ounces. When I was young I would have calluses

JOAN WULFF IN 1952

and burns on my hands, and if I fished more than a day and a half, I hurt too much. It wasn't until I met Lee Wulff in 1967—and he was using a two-ounce, six-foot rod—that I learned I could cast for as many days as any man could. Emancipation! When graphite came along in the mid-'70s, we had lighter rods than ever, but even with graphite, rods can be heavy for women."

She has advised Winston and lent her name to a rod with a handle (which she designed), incorporating a thumb groove, shaped for smaller hands. The rod is marketed especially to women. She handed me one. The grip felt good in my hand, comfortable, weighted carefully.

The convention hall was beginning to fill with people. Some of them, walking the aisle, stared at Joan Wulff; they'd seen her somewhere before.

"I probably learned to fly-cast all wrong," I said. "No lessons."

To my surprise, smiling broadly, she offered me a fly-casting lesson. I said: I'll be back.

Out on the floor, the booths were alive with the eagerness of the sell. No one from the street, no regular customers were allowed on the floor; only dealers were, and fly-shop owners, manufacturers, distributors, and other members of the industry.

A majority of the companies represented here were startups, small fish in a big pond, offering anything you can imagine involving fishing: rods, reels, lines, flies, fly boxes, fly-tying tools, feathers, nets, luggage, boats and floats, eyewear and knives. Even art. Out of one booth, Joseph R. Tomelleri, with the Cimarron Trading Co. of Kansas City, Kansas, offers the Trout Collector Folio, an exquisite series of paintings of trout, including, as his promo literature says, "Pure Volcano Creek Goldens . . . now found mostly high in the headwaters of the South Fork of the Kern River." Another company, called Reel Women, sells tee shirts that say, "Reel Women Like Long Rods." The company, out of Victor, Idaho, also markets fly-fishing trips geared specifically toward women, and they're here to tell you about it.

Despite the weight and force of Orvis (both admired and resented by many of the companies here), the fly-fishing tackle business is one of the last manufacturing industries in which you can make money through the labor of love.

In fact, most of the entrepreneurs here don't dream of becoming an Orvis; they have the Thomas & Thomas model more in mind. Thomas & Thomas is arguably the industry's premier flyrod builder, a company with mystique. Tom Dorsey, white-haired and debonair, about to turn sixty, is one of the two Thomases who founded the company in 1969. At his large, stylish booth, he told me of the origins of the company.

I was a musician during my college days, jazz bass player. I went away to school in Ann Arbor, Michigan. Good trout-fishing there and I used to fish a lot. My father was a cabinetmaker, and I had a feeling for making things, so I began making rods for myself.

My brother-in-law and I decided to do it as a small business, and we used our first names, Thomas and Thomas. But then I went away to get my undergraduate degree and decided to be a college teacher. Between that and playing music, I thought that would be the great life. But I began to see professors get tenure who wore a jacket and tie because the chair of that department happened to dress that way. That life, it's not quite as free as you might think.

My brother-in-law was working for General Electric. He was an employee relations executive and he hated what he was doing. So he went to Kent State to continue his schooling, the year they shot all the students. Those were bad times. When the guns started going off at Kent we felt a little discouraged and confused about things. We decided to go away from all of that, to Montana. Fly-fishing was so pure. Fly-fishing didn't argue with itself. We knew we could make rods. We didn't know if we could make a living at it. We put our first ad in *Fly Fisherman* magazine and were immediately overwhelmed with orders and have been ever since, and here we are today, back-ordered.

Thomas has earned enough industry stripes to become a bit curmudgeonly. He sniffs with impatience at "vanity rod makers," the rod makers "who just buy blanks and parts and have things made with their name on them." To Thomas, that's not a rod maker. "I feel about rod making the way I would have felt about violin making. If you're really a rod maker you want to do it from the bottom up. There aren't many rod makers like that around, who do it all, and I don't know of any newcomer companies doing it. The ones I do know who do this are individuals. There are some fine young bamboo rod makers across this country, working on their own, in their homes and garages." He said he doesn't like to fish with people in the trade. "I don't like people who score; I don't like competitive fly-fishing. I like to fish with people whose company I enjoy. I don't care if they're particularly good fishermen, but they have to have a lot of enthusiasm about it and not take themselves too seriously. After all, it's just fishing."

Expecting him to say something profound, I asked him: What has fly-fishing and rod-making taught you?

"It's taught me that I should not have been afraid to charge more money for my rods."

I walked on. At the beginning of the arc that Thomas had completed is the C. A. Harris Company. Its owner and proprietor, Greg Harris from Hazel Park, a suburb of Detroit, appears to be in his thirties. He is a slight man with dark-rimmed glasses and a quiet, intense demeanor. He was standing in a one-man booth over a small display case of fly reels. He said, "I did two things as I grew up. I knew I was going to be a fly-fisherman; my dad started me when I was five, and I knew that I was going to be a tool and die maker; I started working in the shop when I was seven. I have both trout and tool steel running in my blood."

After Michigan's manufacturing meltdown in the '80s, Harris turned his tool and die talents—specifically, as a gauge maker—to trout. He learned quickly that starting a fly-tackle manufacturing business is very capital-intensive. "You have to have another business that you can build it out of. That's what I did. I would tell anybody who wanted to get into making things in fly-fishing, it's the old joke: If you want to make a small fortune in the fly-fishing business, start with a big fortune." He stuck at it. Now his five-year-old, four-employee company makes a fine reel called the Solitude.

Harris doesn't count on selling his reels in the Orvis stores: He'll rely on the independent shops, a plan with some risk, given the precarious health of many of them. He said:

> There are hundreds of small companies in this building. Most of the people here, they love to fly-fish and it led them into this. That's why American fly-fishing tackle is regarded as the best in the world. When we build something, it's damn good because it reflects our own personality. All those little gadgets, in the booths and catalogs, there's somebody behind every one of those. That's not true for bass-fishing. Because bass-fishing and the general sportfishing market is dominated by much larger companies. In fly-fishing, there are big companies such as 3M, Scientific Angler, Orvis, but even when you look at their total sales and compare it to people in the bass market, it's minuscule. The fly-fishing market is a lot more personal.*

---

* Greg Harris isn't entirely correct about the bass-angling world. At a boat and tackle show in San Diego, I met Ron Buhler and his eleven-year-old son, Cody, who started Edge Products with even fewer resources. Buhler, a thirtyish jeweler from Huntington Beach, California, showed me a squeeze tube of his product, called Hot Sauce. "What it is, it's a fish attractant that smells and tastes like fish. It's like a hand lotion. It's a real natural product. There's a lot of attractants on the market commercially that smell like garlic or licorice or some odd thing and I thought, 'You know what, there's a better way to do this.' So I spent two and a half years working in the kitchen with my wife's Tupperware and stove and blender and ground up crawfish and all manner of things. I started with six local stores. Today, this product is in three thousand stores." His son helps bottle and label the Hot Sauce. He also collects live critters, from which his father creates molds for poured plastic baits. "This one here . . ." he held up a green

He picked up one of his nearly spherical reels, turned it in his hand for me to see. He spoke softly, no hucksterism in his voice—only pride of craftsmanship. "There are great differences in reels. Look at this design. The sphere is the strongest shape known to man. We can make the wall thickness thinner and lighter because of that." I opened his brochure and read his company slogan: "Solitude. It's what's next." Is anybody else making that spherical reel design? I asked. No, he said. What would he do if someone tried to rip off his design? He smiled. If they do, he said, he'll just have to kill them.

⤳ THOUGH ENTREPRENEURIAL HOPE springs eternal, and individuals— from Joan Wulff to Greg Harris—can still make an outsized impact on the industry, this year's show was taking place in a troubling context.

Yes, fly-fishing is chic, still gaining enthusiasts, as the fastest-growing adult sport in America, but tackle sales are down, the market is flattening out, according to a study by the North American Fly Tackle Association, NAFTA (an ironic acronym given what I was going to learn). Trade leaders suggest several theories about why this is happening: One is that the initial excitement caused by the movie has faded; another has to do with bad weather in the late '90s—blame it on El Niño. And another possibility is that anglers have already saturated their garages with fishing gear, and their spouses are giving them the eye, or that, especially within the fly-tackle world, the gear is too good. Much of it is so lovingly and carefully manufactured that it breaks infrequently, and when it does break, it's likely to be covered by a generous lifetime warranty. Snap the tip of a St. Croix flyrod off in your car door, for instance, and the company will replace it free, no questions asked.

Among the manufacturers, there's not much talk of changing the warranty policies, but there is talk of new horizons. "What we're concentrating on," says Jerry Wiant, NAFTA administrator, "are ways to widen the market, to new demographic areas and new fisheries." That's good news, making fly-fishing more democratic. But the industry is also changing in ways that could ultimately drain the culture of fly-fishing of its localized personality, its intimacy.

At the show, a thirty-foot balloon trout hangs over the entrance to the great room, above all the Gore-Tex waders and fleece and wading vests and Japanese bipolar neoprene stocking foot waders with "special lining

---

plastic crawfish, "this one Cody caught in the drainage ditch behind the house. Now that crawfish is replicated all over the United States—most realistic claw there is! By the way, on the Hot Sauce bottle I wrote, 'You gotta get bit.' Because getting bit is where it all begins."

that reduces sweat and moisture buildup" featuring "anti-microbial treatments."

Sure, bamboo is back in, but, as *Esquire* magazine reports, "The piscatorial upshot of defense downsizing is a whole new wave of high-end fly rods and reels that are the talk of the industry." High-end rod companies, some of them previously unknown, are applying extraordinary and expensive Cold War technologies. For instance, Orvis offers what it calls a "stealth" antivibration technology. Sage, a high-quality rod builder, pushes something called the "reverse compound taper."

Higher technology isn't necessarily the enemy of the small entrepreneur: Harris, with his low-overhead, computer-aided designs, knows that. New media can help, too. At a booth promoting Internet publishing, Sharon Eastman says the Internet is changing the fly-fishing culture for the better, making it even more personal. She works for a company that publishes *Fly Fish America*, a magazine distributed to 1,450 fly shops, now with a version on the Internet.

"You order from a major company through the Internet, and they don't deliver in time, or they send you the wrong thing, somebody gets in a chat room and everybody in the world can see that," she said. For the little guy, the Internet increases access. "Anybody who has a guide service or other fishing destination business, if they're not on the Web, they're lame." Guides and lodges are experiencing a serious uptick in business because of the Internet. "It used to be difficult to find out about little shops and little guides, where to go and who to know." Not any more.

Nonetheless, the local may yet be subsumed by the global.

↪ ALWAYS SOMEWHAT INTERNATIONAL, fly-fishing is now a business with no borders. A Japanese rod manufacturer tells me he's set up shop in America because in Japan, where fly-fishing is popular, he finds the culture too restrictive, creatively. At another booth, Shandra Tibrewal hawks fly-tying vises made by Bhagwati Impex (Pltd.) of Calcutta, India, but he's not pleased with the American way of doing business. "We have the very good vise like the Supreme Vise," he said, "which is selling very good." He complained that American retailers are harder to deal with than Europeans, "because in Europe, they plan for the year; in the United States, they plan for the week."

Dorothy Hobbs-Kunkel and Gene Kunkel had traveled to Denver from West Liberty, Iowa, to represent the Hobbs Feather Company, Inc., probably America's largest suppliers of hackle for fly-tying. Behind them, on the booth's high display panels, hung an impressive array of bagged rooster wings and necks, some natural color, others brightly colored. Dorothy, the company's president, looks like a church secretary, with peroxide-blonde hair and darkened eyebrows. Her husband, Gene, wears a white western shirt. His face is furrowed; his hair is slicked back in something approaching a 1950-era jellyroll.

Dorothy and Gene are mighty pleased to meet you, and mighty proud of their hackle operation. Dorothy's parents started the business in the '40s. She says it was the first of its kind. Her father was a processor of turkeys, ducks, and geese. "He had produce, and the byproduct was feathers, for bedding, pillows, and later for fly-fishing." Before that, she speculates, fly-fishermen "plucked their own" or bought hackle from the farmer down the road. Neither Gene nor Dorothy fish ("Never got around to it," said Gene), but a hackle wholesaler's business is birds, not fish. High-end necks, fans of feathers still attached to strips of scalp from genetically cultured roosters.

The birds are handled with special care to keep their feathers pristine; they're gassed to avoid blood staining, and because of this, the meat is unmarketable, so it's processed and fed back to other birds. One little scalp of fine rooster feathers can sell for $125. Hobbs, like most other hackle companies, doesn't raise its own birds, but buys them from processors.

While many of the birds are raised in the United States, especially the Midwest, an increasing number are grown and skinned in China, and then sent to the United States for washing, dying, and packaging. Dorothy explains: "Some people prefer Chinese birds because they have narrower feathers." Turkeys, on the other hand, are grown in the United States but exported to China for processing—then shipped back to the United States for packaging and wholesaling. "We've got the turkeys, but China's labor is cheaper," said Dorothy. Amazing: all that shipping back and forth, until the final product is packaged and sent to the fly shops. Sounds expensive, to me. "Yes, but there's a lot of feathers in a pound."

"Deer hair, especially belly hair, has a unique feature," Gene said. "It's hollow and it floats. The dry-fly fisherman wants that." He grinned. "That reminds me of a little anecdote. We were on a selling trip up in Montana three summers back, calling on shops. We ran across this fellow who said the best material he's found for dry flies is dog hair. He said, 'I've got two great big dogs. And when I'm tying my flies they're looking *awful* ratty. But necessity is the mother of invention.'"

Never judge a small business by its owner's bouffant. This was one sophisticated international operation.

Next stop: the fly-sellers—and a surprise.

Like most anglers, I had thought of fly-tying as an American cottage industry practiced by tweedy New Englanders or true cowboy artists

DOROTHY HOBBS-KUNKEL AND GENE KUNKEL,
FEATHER MERCHANTS

high in the Rockies. But, as I learned, most of the fly-tying industry moved offshore in the '90s. One fishing industry advertising executive calls this fly-fishing's "dirty little secret."

Today, nearly all of the flies used by environmentally conscious, upper-income American fly-fishers are made in Sri Lanka, Cambodia, Thailand, Kenya, China, and Colombia. Some of the women, and possibly children, who work in these factories earn as little as $3 a day. The trend is unlikely to do anything drastic to the trade imbalance, but it's a sign of the times. Most of the merchants and manufacturers I spoke with at the show saw nothing wrong with offshore fly labor. Wandering over to the booth of one of the nation's major fly distributors, I asked a company owner how many of his flies are made in the United States. "Very few," he said, tapping his fingers next to a rack of Blue Duns and Royal Wulffs and other delicate flies. "A lot of things stop people from making volumes of flies in America," he said. "Government regulation. Cost of labor. Tying a fly is time intensive; you just can't make a machine that will tie a good fly."

How long does it take to make a fly?

"Average from two to five minutes each."

Who makes them?

"Workers basically in good conditions. Is this for an article?"

At another booth, a fly salesman explained the situation this way: "There's no employment in some of those places anyway. What would they be doing? They'd be walking through the jungle trying to pick up sticks for firewood. America employed child labor here for many years while we got our feet off the ground as an industrialized nation. Let's be a little realistic. We also employed black slaves and whipped them. Now we're saying to these developing countries, 'Oh, no, you can't do that. It hurts our feelings as Americans.'"

Quality control in other countries, however, can be a problem.

Martin James, the best-known fishing personality in England, overheard the conversation. "This one guy gives me three nymphs," he said in his thick Cockney accent. He was leaning on a cane. "Each one, the body slipped down to the bend of the hook. The dealer said, 'That's the trouble with the ones made in the Far East.' Well, I asked, 'Why don't you buy American products?' He answered, 'They're a lot dearer.' And I said, 'It's better to pay more and have a good fly than bloody rubbish.'"

Here's the odd thing, he said: Serious fly-anglers think nothing of spending $250 to one thousand dollars on a good-enough rod, and never mind all the other expensive gear and tours of Chilean rivers. They can't afford an extra quarter per fly? "Bloody *rubbish*," repeated the Brit, then he lurched toward the seminar rooms.

Some parts of the U.S. industry remain. American tiers continue to turn out specialty flies for select clientele. Design also remains an American domain.

Ken Ligas, of Belgrade, Montana, cowboy hat pushed back on his head, told me how he took his designs to Johannesburg, with the help of two South African entrepreneurs. "A year later we were producing ten thousand flies a day." His workers: three hundred women of the Xhosa tribe, who wore scarved headpieces and spoke a language punctuated by clicks. As they sat there tying the flies, "they sounded like castanets."

John Bailey, owner of Dan Bailey's Fly Shop (and Robert Redford's consultant on *the movie*) said his Livingston, Montana, business kept a U.S. factory going long after it became unprofitable. "That was a mistake." Bailey is currently setting up production in Bhutan, where "people start weaving when they're five, so they're good with their hands." Fly-tiers in Bhutan make more than doctors, he says, "because the doctors work for the government." He visits his factory now and then and sneaks off to do a little trout fishing in the surrounding Himalayas. Do the Bhutanese—his workers—fly-fish there? No, he said, "those people work all the time."

Joe Brent, a big, crewcut, balding, bearded guy from the eastern plains of Colorado, is one of the few American individuals left who makes a living tying flies. He's a rugged man, wears a prohunting tee shirt. He said his company, Brenton Marketing, also serves as an agent for a handful of other small-time fly-tiers.

Can you support yourself tying flies in the United States?

"There are ways to do it," said Brent. "There are a lot of people who develop a reputation as a fisherman and then they put their name on the fly. A lot of the local shops have people who tie part time. There are a lot of American flies produced. There are more than people are aware of. Because a lot of it's done mainly on the hobby basis. My guess is it's around 15 percent of the total. If you think about it, that's a lot of flies. You just don't hear about guys like me."

The problem that the fishing-tackle business faces, particularly the fly-fishing business, is the same problem that smaller-scale business faces all over America. Despite a relatively good economy, the creators of niche companies—especially these very personal enterprises of the heart—feel they're squeezed by larger forces. They bend or break.

∽ I SLIPPED OUT OF a positive-thinking seminar to the hallway to take a break. I ran into Martin James again. He was holding court.

"Call me Martin," he said, in that thick accent.

Martin is one of the true world-class characters of fishing—kind of the Roland Martin of fishing in Great Britain, except that the analogy isn't perfect. First, there's no real fishing TV there; Martin is a twice-a-week radio personality with millions of listeners. Second, he comes from a fishing culture that is at once the birthplace of fly-fishing (if one accepts the English version) and an angling culture so different that it illuminates our own. Martin is about five feet seven inches tall, with perfectly combed black hair, the posture of a rooster, and, I'm sure, probably one of the most infectious grins that side of the Atlantic.

A group of anglers and public relations folks who had fled the seminar were clustered around him, laughing and shaking their heads as he regaled them with stories about his travels in America, about his adventurous past (". . . and I was with British Special Forces down in South America, working with your DEA guys back in the '60s. I've been around, kicked a bit of ass here and there . . ."), and about his popularity with women.

He is one of those men who, despite the braggadocio, you like immediately.

I promote America and Canada like no other countries in the world! I've brought fourteen hundred anglers over here, with one travel company alone, in the last three years. I bring over twenty, thirty couples every time I come across. I have a tremendous amount of women listeners who don't fish. People love me accent, me enthusiasm, me love for life. I'm sixty years of age, I've had multiple sclerosis, I've been in a wheelchair for eight years. I'm out of me chair but I use a stick and I use a walking frame. Me hands and arms, me legs are ever so painful. I'm on the river and I could cry with the pain but I don't give up. You never know what's going to happen. One time I'm in Oregon, and I say to the radio audience, "You've joined me on the Deschutes." I was there with a guy fishing and we stopped for lunch, set up a table. And underneath the table there was a rattlesnake. And I actually put the microphone on top of his rattle and you can hear this guy saying, "Be careful Marty James, that's ready to strike!"

Women love me, see, because I talk about the countryside, I talk about the environment, I catch them up in the spirit of it, I describe the kingfisher zipping up the river, I describe the bobber slowly going away. One afternoon I'm sitting on the river and I'm saying, "It's four o'clock, usually the time for tea and cake. I'm just going to have tea today because I haven't any time to bake any cakes. Living on me own as I do, fishing takes the precedence." And lots of women bake cakes and send them to the studio for me! Lots of women, when we meet on the street, say to me, "Where are you go-ing next, Marty James? Do you want somebody to carry your bags?" And my wife says, "I've already got the job!"

Too many people go out and they're too serious. I always say, if you're out there having your string pulled and your stick bent, you got to be having fun.

After his fans wandered away, I asked Martin what he was doing at the show. He shifted his small backpack around on his shoulders; it was filled with odds and ends and recording equipment. He leaned on his cane with one hand, held a microphone with the other, which he was placing under the face of anyone who would talk.

"Gathering stories, bloke," he said, and thrust the microphone toward me. I laughed. No, I said, I'm interviewing you. I asked: What's the dif-ference between the cultures of fly-fishing in England and America?

"More catch-and-release in America," he answered. "You're more careful of the quarry. You care about the environment a lot more than we do. I've been coming to America for six years now, spent a lot of time with the fish and game boys." He was taking some of our ideas home.

"The second difference is we like coarse fishing, which is to fish for fish like carp and bream. Carp's the number-one fish in Europe, and fish-ing's the number-one participant sport. Anglers spend thousands of dol-lars on carp-fishing equipment, from electric bite indicators to the latest fourteen-foot rods and bait-runner reels, to special bivvy beds to put next to the waterside for two or three days at a time. Specially designed beds that fold up small but they're comfortable."

They *sleep* there?

"They sleep by the waterside. Some guys will fish for carp four, five months on end. Nonstop."

Do they fish while they sleep?

"Oh yeah, they've got $150 electric bite alarms, one per rod, and they usually fish with three rods, so when the fish picks up the bait the bite alarm will sound and they'll have a loudspeaker inside their tent that wakes them up."

As I learned later, the tweedy English anglers chum with corn, bait balls, or maggots—which they deliver with a slingshot or something called a baiting spoon, a long-handled spoon that they use to flick the bait far out over the water. The most bizarre method of chumming, though, employs remote-controlled model boats that drop the bait when the angler flicks a switch on shore.

Do they eat carp? I asked.

Martin looked at me with an expression of horror. "No, no, they're *revered*. If somebody was to kill a carp I think they'd string him *up*. There's more catch-and-release for all our coarse fish than all the other species. Most of our coarse fish are hooked in the scissors, in the corners of the mouth, what we call the scissors area of the mouth. I've never known anybody to gut hook a carp. We use finely tuned rigs—it's a science. All coarse fishing is a science, an art. Trout and salmonid, the ones with the adipose fins, mostly they're killed. People will go and catch a dozen Atlantic salmon in a day and they will kill them all."

The two cultures, British and American, so close in so many ways—the enthusiasm for fly-fishing, for example—are far apart on this one. One countryman's fish is the queen of freshwater, another man's fish is trash. "In England, people sell them, move them from pond to pond. The big old stocking carp are worshiped, even *named*—they're famous! I tell you that a twenty-pound carp for stocking a pond will cost between fifteen hundred and two thousand dollars."

Indeed, individual carp, like the famous Clarissa, the largest carp ever caught in England, are venerated. Chris Ball, publisher of the British weekly *Carp Talk* magazine, named his home *Cyprinus carpio*, the carp's Latin name.* "This," Ball tells an American reporter, raising his index finger, "this is the finger which touched Clarissa." Celebrity carp, demigods really, are caught-and-released so many times that they give recidivism a good name. One of them, named Brazil, has been caught at least forty-five times during the past two decades.

He raised his cane and pumped it up and down with excitement. "You've got gold mines swimming around in the Willamette River valley, I tell you!"

⌐ MARTIN JAMES SUGGESTS that Americans bone up on carp. One reason: It's another way the fly-fishing industry could cast a wider net for more money.

An intriguing idea, fly-fishing for carp. As a teenager I spent more hours fishing for carp than I did for bass, sitting with no shirt on a dock, just inviting future skin cancer. My buddy Pete and I would cast big balls of dough bait squeezed around treble hooks as far as we could into deep water. The base ingredients of our secret carp bait recipe were Wheaties, molasses, vanilla, cornmeal, flour, and other classified additives. (Pete and I passed the secret recipe on to our sons a couple years ago.) The fish averaged seven pounds, and often reached fifteen and twenty pounds—

* This is the Latin name for the edible freshwater carp.

occasionally even larger. When a carp picked up the bait and ran with it, we knew we were in for a fight that could last thirty minutes to two hours.

We caught hundreds of the fish. We collected their air bladders, dried them in a lengthening row on a hot limestone ledge. We used their carcasses for garden fertilizer, or stacked the big ones in our freezer, where they remained for years.

We figured we would learn to cook the big, bloody, bony things someday. We heard distant rumors of people who had developed techniques to transform or disguise the flesh, including recipes for smoked carp and fillet de carp. Someone knew of someone's uncle who made carp jerky. And it was known that African-Americans, who fished under the bridges in and near Kansas City, knew how to tenderize them with a pressure cooker. My father, being a chemist, experimented with this technique. A vague recollection of an explosion and flying carp paté sticks in my mind.

In our family, there was no clear line between carp and the garbage can.

Martin James is right: Do a beauty makeover, transform the carp—like the New Nixon—into a fish of class and grace, worthy of a nymph or even a caddis, and you'd be accomplishing a heroic feat. We're talking about a major economic opportunity here. Until now, in America, the carp was simply a fish before its time. This being the age of catch-and-release, the inedible carp's moment may finally have arrived.

As Brad Jackson might say, enough with our shame already.

Here's a quick course on carpology: In 1876, the U.S Congress encouraged the importing of carp as a food supply for the growing immigrant population. Carp were sent by rail across the land, thrived everywhere—even in the foulest water—but failed miserably as an immigrant staple. Nor did they catch on as a sportfish. Some writers suggest that the reason is cultural—that in America, a fish must be a fierce predator to get respect. More likely, carp are disrespected because a), they were originally associated with poor immigrants, b), they became associated with race, and c, they're bottom feeders in often unprotected, polluted waters. Today, the U.S. Fish and Wildlife Service doesn't even list carp in its surveys of sport fishers.*

---

* An omnivorous bottom feeder, the carp is essentially a large minnow, indigenous to Asia, and the most widely distributed freshwater fish in the world. It can grow to immense size. In England, where the carp arrived around 1450 and became known as the Queen of Freshwater Fish, the record is forty-four pounds. But in September 1998, an Austrian angler caught the world record carp, a monster that weighed over eighty-three pounds, in a Romanian lake created by the communist dictator, Nikolae Ceausescu. After deciding that he wanted his own

Nonetheless, an increasing number of new immigrants from Asia and Eastern Europe are fishing for carp. British and French anglers—who consider America the last carp frontier—fly to North America, where they can catch as many carp in one day as they do in a week back home. And Americans are catching on to carp. In 1993, a mixture of English, Canadian, and American carp enthusiasts battled for the first North American Carp Championship, holding an annual Chicagoland Carp Classic on the Chicago River. Contestants came from fifteen states, from England and Canada, to challenge such players as Bernie Haines, who runs America's only carp guide service—on the St. Lawrence River. The organizers poured one thousand pounds of cooked corn into the river over a two-week period before the tournament. Though the Brits were horrified by the crude tackle used by the Americans, the Yanks did well in the competition—and continue to improve.

Tackle dealers see an opportunity. In 1998, an American importer, Hans Knaevelsrud, who lives outside Seattle, told a reporter for the *Providence Journal-Bulletin* that he's counting on American attitudes to change. "Sooner or later, carp-fishing will take off." His company, H.K. International, has introduced a carp-fishing starter kit for sixty-five dollars. He's also importing a line of telescoping carp-fishing poles and British tutti-frutti "boilie" baits. Soon to come to a tackle store near you—five-hundred-dollar European twelve-foot graphite rods with electronic strike sensors, special landing nets, handling sacks, and inflatable bank mats to protect the carp while it's unhooked, weighed, and photographed before release.

The biggest growth of carp-angling will likely be among fly-fishers. One reason: If you're a fly-fisher, you don't have to think about maggot-flingers or chum-hauling remote-controlled model boats. Another reason: Trout waters are rare and difficult, but carp live in most every farm pond, county lake, and river, muddy or clear. And though the carp consumes plant life, it also has a taste for insects and minnows.

Just as it took the old communist-fighter Nixon to open China, fly-

---

version of the Panama Canal (this was around the time that he made his dog an army colonel), he flooded the Danube Valley and unintentionally created his only good legacy: some of the best carp fishing waters in Europe. Asians continue to prize the fish; Tokyo University now offers lessons in crucian carp-angling. Assistant Professor Hiroaki Kanehisa says that carp fishing is deeply rooted in Japanese culture. The professor says he hopes to "incorporate environmental and social issues, and human relationships" into the carp classes. The *Daily Yomiuri*, a Japanese newspaper, explains an ulterior motive, "Teachers at the university started offering unusual courses in 1970 to improve relations between students and teachers, which had been damaged by student-led demonstrations against the Japan-U.S. security treaty." Clearly, the carp is a political animal.

fishing icons must go to carp. At least two fly-fishing heroes have done just that. John Gierach, author of such classic fly-fishing books as *Trout Bum* and *Sex, Death and Fly-fishing*, defends the carp as a sportfish. He entered a fly-fishing carp tournament and even has a bamboo rod he uses especially for carp. And he's written for *Outdoor Life* about the joys of fly-fishing for carp in Montana. *Carpe diem!*

↜ I HEADED BACK to Joan Wulff's station.

The crowd was drifting away, and she was sitting on that high stool, alone, a serene expression on her face. I asked her if the fishing-tackle industry expressed any concern about, say, working conditions of overseas fly-tiers. "No," she said. "You would think that somebody would have asked that question.

"Ready for your casting lesson?" she asked.

We walked through the thinning crowd. She carried a Winston rod, with standard grip, to one of two long and narrow casting pools at the middle of the hall.

I mentioned what Margot Page had said about women being better anglers than men. Wulff smiled and shrugged. It's not quite that simple, she said. "Men start at zero minus X. You have to get rid of a man's preconceived notions. Men are brought up to believe that they should be able to do anything without instruction. But remember, the man has almost twice the upper-body strength of a woman, so he can cast badly and still get his fly line out there. A woman has to use her lesser strength more precisely."

She demonstrated a couple of flawless short casts, nothing special, and yet the line even then seemed an extension of her slender fingers. I asked her if she is aware of every inch of her body when she's casting.

"Absolutely, sure. It's a thing of feeling. Your body motion helps with the timing; it also increases the length of your stroke. At my tallest I was five feet five inches. I only have so many inches of movement in my arms, but if I drop one foot back and then shift my weight back, I gain another ten to twelve inches' stroke length. So my body movement becomes very important."

How does that feel?

"I feel connected to something alive. The fly line has energy. What you're doing is transferring your energy—you're 'impulsing' the rod. When your body is moving, the energy shifts from your hand and into the rod; the rod magnifies what you do and transfers energy to the fly line. We call it loading a rod, loading spring energy; you bend the rod from the tip downward by the weight of the line and the speed of the

JOAN WULFF

stroke. Then when you stop the butt, the tip flips over the spring and projects the line. So all of that is alive."

I hoped to feel the same. In her book, Wulff delivers a poetic description of a fly-caster's search for perfection: "A perfect cast is . . . like a note of music extended and held. In all other sports the moment of impact separates you from the very thing you are projecting in beautiful flight, but the execution of a perfect cast can be seen and felt, from its inception until the fly touches down on the water."

She handed me the rod, and stood directly behind me, hard on my elbow. Flex your thumb on top of the grip, she said—not tipped or flattened, but flexed. I had held the handle in my fist, no thumb holding. Ineffective, she said. I flexed my thumb and placed it just so. She explained her screen-door analogy for the forward cast. "At the end of your cast, pretend your hand is operating the mechanism of a screen door handle—push with the thumb, pull back with the lower fingers."

She explained all of this and more. But, in the hands of Saint Joan, my casting was desultory. My line kept slapping the water like a poorly aimed whip. I couldn't quite grasp the concepts—at least not out in front of all those passing professionals. I tried to feel the line through my entire body, but she kept grabbing my elbow. "There now, you've got it," she said, but I think she was trying to make me feel better.

Maybe I could chalk up my ineptness to the public setting. Or maybe
I was just at zero minus X. She finally patted me on the arm and said I'd
catch on soon, and she drew the lesson mercifully to a close.

⌐ I WALKED OUTSIDE to look for a cab. The air had that peculiar chill
that slides down the eastern slope of the Rockies in September. I
thought: What have I learned about the future of the industry? Women
are the future, of course, along with a wider marketing loop to bring in
blue collars and new collars (UPS drivers, 7-Eleven managers, and the
like), and harder-edged methods of commerce, new ecocenters, new target species, and a widening internationalism. And I'd learned that, Saint
Joan aside, the little guys face an uneasy future, particularly the true be-
lievers.

The plainsman, Joe Brent, saw me waiting at the corner and offered
me a ride. We walked across the street to his dented Toyota pickup. He
pushed a pile of papers and boxes off the seat. The back of the truck was
filled with a jumble of his wares. As we rolled through downtown Denver, he told me how he came to the fly-tying business, and survives.

Before starting his company, he studied engineering, worked for a
7-Eleven, and bought a soft-drink distributorship for RC Cola and
Canada Dry in northeastern Colorado, where he lives now. "I ran that by
myself for five or six years, then I had a health problem that put me in
the hospital for a month or two. When I came out of that I had been
forced to sell my soft-drink business. I had been tying flies part-time, so
I just went into tying full-time." He's forty-seven now, lives in a little
town called Otis, and he's making a go of this business. He markets his
own flies, and the flies of six other friends, two women and four men,
who live in Colorado and Wyoming. He hopes to increase his clients to
thirty or forty within the year. "I teach my friends to tie to my specs; one
product will be their own creation, the other one is something I can
wholesale commercially."

So how do you do it? I asked.

I'm very cheap. I keep my overhead low. A good fly-tier, if he's
managing his things carefully, his materials shouldn't be more than
20 percent of the price he sells his fly for.

If you tie a thousand dozen flies a year, you're talking in the
range of from five thousand to fifteen thousand dollars' worth of
gross. That's what you would be able to wholesale the flies for. If
you retail the flies you'd make double that, but retailing takes a
whole lot more work. In terms of time, if you tie a forty-hour week,

you're looking at fifteen thousand dollars to twenty thousand dollars a year, wholesale. Do networking and work with a few other people, and work sixty hours a week, you can do more. That's basically what I do. For my wife and my son and my daughter and I, the fly business is the bulk of our income. The four of us tie around five thousand dozen a year. Then there's the agenting. And I also wholesale for a hook company and for some other tackle resources and materials companies.

You got hidden costs, though. On the books it looks like we're horribly, horribly broke. We don't make a ton of money but we like our lifestyle.

He drives across Wyoming and New Mexico and Utah and Nebraska to supply his customers. Joe is a Westerner and accustomed to long distances. "It works out. I paid fifteen thousand dollars for my home. That's five acres of land and a house with a well, all of that and I'm totally independent out there as far as those kinds of expenses. That's less than what a lot of people are paying for a used car."

Sounds like all of this fits into a general philosophy of life, I said.

"It does for me. I was raised on a dry wheat farm in eastern Colorado. When our wheat was cut in the middle of the summer, we could take off to the mountains and fish. I fell in love with fishing when I was very small and wanted to do it all my life, and it worked out to where I got the chance and I took it. It's a blast. It's a great way to live."

But the foreign competition, the cheap labor undercutting him? Or the growing corporate competitors like Orvis? That doesn't bother him? He shrugged. It's called free trade, he said. He's all for it. Freedom.

"The thing that's going to explode on somebody sooner or later is that a lot of the sweatshops in Red China have political prisoners in them, from what I've heard. Most of your reputable brand names in fly-fishing tackle are probably not going to be doing that. That's the only thing that I would be upset about, if there are political prisoners involved. Other than that, we should compete with the world on a fair basis and I think there are ways for American labor to compete."

He drove through the old inner-city neighborhoods of Denver, ethereal in twilight—the Victorian gables, the turned columns with elaborate brackets, the bands of fish-scale shingles, all held by the twisted branches of old trees. The plainsman wanted to tell me something else, because I was a member of the media. He spoke casually, but beneath his words was subtle intensity. He wanted someone to hear this:

"Fishing is the last personal involvement with killing on a level that's politically acceptable," he said. "If you believe in evolution, then every step that is taken is an attempt to progress through time, including what we do with animals. Likewise, if you believe in God, then there's a plan and we're part of it, and we're here for a reason, and our needs count. Either way, we have a right and a reason to use animals to survive."

He continued to talk, his words coming faster, and somehow they formed a direct link between fly-fishing and creationism and self-employment: He believes in all three. I was enjoying this philosophical monologue. But then we found my friends' house. He parked the Toyota, the engine shuddering and gasping. I got out and turned and stuck my head back in and shook his hand. He smiled. "Good talkin' to you," he said.

"You too, Joe. Good luck to you."

He banged the truck in gear, waved quick, and smoked down the street toward the plains.

Lodge Life

⌒⌒

Fishing is a world created apart from all others, and inside it are special
worlds of their own—one is fishing for big fish in small water where there
is not enough world and water to accommodate a fish and a fisherman.
—Norman Maclean, *A River Runs Through It*

MONTANA FLY-FISHING offers a weird mix of trout, biology, history, literature, business, and a lesson in the meaning of service . . . especially if you spend a few days at a luxury fishing lodge.

Montana is physically the fourth-largest state in the Union, but near the bottom of the list in population and per-capita income.

Now that so many rich outlanders are moving to the state—some of them are fly-fishers looking for the dream painted by Norman Maclean—the lower-income residents are struggling with the Montana paradox. On one hand, they're glad to see the newcomers, who bring money to a relatively poor state. On the other hand, some of them resent the outsiders, because in order to tap into that cash, the locals have to serve all those movie stars, computer zillionaires, and strip-mall magnates who show up, slap on a new bull-rider Stetson, buy up the ranches and streamside property, and lock their gates to some of the best hunting land and fly-fishing water.

I had been invited to join a group of overachievers who meet here to fish every year—with occasional turnover of members. They call themselves MF2, or Masters of Fly-Fishing. This year's assembly included fourteen anglers, among them the executive vice president of Tenneco and a former postmaster general of the United States. My invitation had come from the group's leader, Bert Berkley, chairman of the board of one of the world's largest envelope companies, Tension Envelope Corp., of Kansas City, Missouri.

Dancing rain was drifting along the wide horizon of southwestern Montana, a big anvil of a cloud dark blue above, with smaller thunderheads stretching across the range of vision, dark tendrils hanging down. The lodge I would be staying in was a low, gray structure, part of it under construction. It was hunkered down alone on a long, grassy hill. The wind swept the grass in green and yellow waves. Late afternoon sunlight came flying across the plains from under the clouds. A gravel driveway curved down and around two ponds where trout were rising. As the Ford came to a stop behind the lodge, Jay Burgin, one of our hosts (along with Mary Jacques), walked briskly toward us. A dog—or was it a coyote?—sat off to one side, watching us.

Lodge life. This would be a new experience for me.

I was not accustomed to such expense or luxury on a fishing trip. In the past, my definition of fishing luxury included forgoing the back of a cold van for a night in a roadside motel.

Many of the higher-end lodges, like Five Rivers Lodge, offer gourmet evening meals served by candlelight and streamside lunches with cloth napkins, real cutlery, a vase of fresh flowers, and (as one nearby lodge provides) an inspirational quotation of the day tucked into the daily picnic basket. All the accommodations of a five-star hotel, and more. These new lodges are definitely not your grandfather's fishing camps.

Five Rivers Lodge advertises itself, truthfully, as providing "comfortable elegance in a region considered to have the last uncrowded blue-ribbon fisheries in the U.S." Fly-fishing options include "day floats on the Jefferson and Big Hole rivers, float or private access to the Beaverhead River, wading four miles of private access water on the Ruby River, private ponds with large trout, and three and a half miles of private spring creek with big browns that love hoppers!" Also included: gourmet meals "served on your schedule," one guide per two anglers, airport shuttles and laundry service, and a library with more than ten thousand books—many of them about fly-fishing. Typical price: seven nights, six days with guided angling: $2,295.

Jay Burgin showed me to my room. Burgin is a tall man in his fifties, with a thick swatch of dark hair. He is a former building contractor whose demeanor encourages instant familiarity.

The guest rooms stretch out in a long, two-story arm of the lodge, each room with a magnificent view of the plains and mountains. My assigned roommate had not yet arrived, nor had the other members of the party, but they would shortly.

"Enjoy yourself in the meantime," said Jay. He pointed in the direction of the pond. "We have some fine rainbows in our ponds. Feel free to fish them."

⤳ I THREW ON my fly vest, assembled my St. Croix, and walked down the hill through the tall grass to the ponds. From this vantage point, you can see the Pioneer Mountains sliding gracefully out of the prairie into the big sky, the Tobacco Root mountains in the northeast, and the Ruby Range to the east. The prairie here remains almost entirely empty.

Looking at that expanse, I could better understand Norman Maclean's religious devotion to the state. By the time he wrote his haunting recollection of fishing and family in Montana, he was in his seventies and still alert to that passion. *A River Runs Through It* moves the heart in a way that is difficult to explain.

Long before the movie came out, like many men (and not a few women) I had already given away nearly a dozen copies to friends. In 1977, the Pulitzer jury for fiction selected *A River Runs Through It* for the prize, but the oversight board decided against awarding it the fiction prize that year—some say because it was a book about fishing and the West. ("Too many trees," one East Coast editor is said to have commented, when rejecting it for publication.) Before that, Maclean, who died in 1990, had had a relatively obscure career as a professor of literature at the University of Chicago. His former students, who included Philip Roth and Supreme Court Justice John Paul Stevens (who said the best way to prepare for the law was by taking Maclean's poetry course), remember how, during his intense lectures, he would sometimes start talking about Montana.

"He would look out the window. He always played with a piece of chalk, he would juggle a piece of chalk in his hand, and he would look out the window and just start talking," one of his students recalled. "He had a very gravelly kind of voice, a very rough voice. He would just drift away, talking about some aspect of the West, or life in Montana or fishing." One time, he became so caught up that he threw a Zippo lighter out the classroom window, thinking he had just lighted his cigarette with a match.

Since then a lot of Americans, maybe too many of us, have discovered Montana's cold magic.

The pond was dark under the anvil. At the other end of the pond, I saw a man with white hair casting expertly. I tied on a caddis and began to ply the water. Immediately, a large trout rose, blipped at the fly, and disappeared. I fished for another half hour. Nothing. I watched the man with white hair catch a couple of nice-sized rainbows. He watched me, too. I walked around the edge of the pond and asked him if he had any advice. He opened a fly box and handed me a nymph. The same type he was using. I thanked him for the fly, tied it to my tippet—the end of the leader, which, if light enough, it tapers to near-invisibility. I worked my way around to the other side of the pond.

Suddenly my rod nearly folded in two. I lost the fish. And then another one struck, and after a couple of long minutes and a fight, I brought it in; it was fat and slippery and escaped my grasp and flopped around in the grass, where I wrestled with it. Suddenly I noticed two legs a few feet in front of me. It was the white-haired man.

Quietly, he told me I should use a heavier tippet and bring them in faster, and not tire them out so much. "They're fragile fish." Something in his voice made me feel foolish. Knowing how to catch a fish is one thing; knowing how to bring it in and release it so that it survives to bite another day—that's an entirely different skill. In the excitement of the catch, it's an easy one to forget.

I let the trout slip through my hands into the water. The white-haired man walked away and headed up the hill.

A half hour later, the mosquitoes on the pond were thick and the light was fading, so I walked back to the lodge. On the grassy expanse in front of it, I saw the white-haired man leading a dozen other men in a fly-casting lesson. Their lines laced through the air. The CEOs were doing a kind of synchronized dance. The white-haired man turned out to be Doug Swisher, one of the most famous fly-fishers in America, hired to spend the week with the execs. I had been shamed by the best.

⌐ THE REST OF the guests had arrived, stashed their suitcases and flyrod tubes, practiced their casting, showered and shaved, and assembled in the great dining room, windowed on all sides, with the mountains silhouetted in fading light. The storms were gone. I met my roommate, Bob Colnes, of New Salem, Massachusetts. He's in his late seventies, a kindly man with whom I felt an immediate kinship. He is a retired businessman. He now lives in the country and tends an apple orchard. I sat next to our host, Bert Berkley, who is seventy-three. We'd met a year or two earlier, when I was on another writing assignment.

He's a fascinating character, a no-nonsense Ross Perot type—a lean, happy man, one of those people who energizes everyone around him, or else. Bert is the kind of corporate chief who truly cares about his community's problems and does something about them.

Right now, though, Bert was focused on fishing.

He stood up before the happy group and gave a little speech.

"You're going to have excellent fishing, you're going to learn a lot from Doug Swisher. . . . Everybody here is well-known in their own communities in their own right. But we do have some famous people here tonight, so I'd like to just say a brief word about them. First is Doug Swisher, who as you all know is one of the leading professional fly-fisher people in the country but is reputed to be by far the best instructor of fly-fishing in the United States. And with him, Sharon Chaffin." He was referring to Swisher's companion. "She's considered to be the best female fly-tier in the country. Why are you shaking your head, sir?"

One of the execs laughed. "Sexism, sexism. The best *female* fly-tier?"

"The other individual is Paul Carlin, a former postmaster general and one of the most knowledgeable people in his field."

Bert moved on with announcements. "The guides get here tomorrow morning at eight o'clock. Breakfast is served at 7:30 but we have coffee about 6:30. There are two people to a boat. I suggest that tomorrow you fish with your roommate. After that you can trade around and fish with whom you want to fish. Jay will pass out your license application. Tomorrow morning you're going to go to the Sunrise fly-fishing shop. Your application will have been faxed over there and your license will be ready. Remember, the state does not accept credit cards, so pay cash or check. I may also mention that you don't have to carry your wallet and get it all wet. Leave it in your room. There's no question about anyone taking it. You might want to take a MasterCard or a Visa for anything you want at the shop."

He smiled impishly. "I realize that practically everyone here has more fishing gadgets than they could possibly use over a lifetime. Because we want you to save thousands of dollars over the rest of your life, I have a very special gift for each of you. You will note that there is a rope attached. This is a fly-retrieval device." The men and a lone woman applauded and laughed.

The Tenneco executive vice president, Stacy Dick, and his attentive wife, were sitting next to me. He seemed impossibly young to serve in such a position. I asked him why he fished. He thought for a moment, and said quietly, "All fishermen have to eventually resign themselves to the futility of what they do, to the unknowability of why fish do what they do. All of us who fish come to realize our limitations. Fishing is more than just technique. It's an understanding."

Bert leaned over his salad and said that learning to be a good fly-fisherman can make you a better businessperson. "A trout will take the steel in its mouth and feel it and spit it out. If you don't set the hook in that second, then you miss the fish. You must concentrate exclusively on what's happening in the water. You must think about nothing else."

Then why is it, I wondered aloud, that I tend to catch most of my fish when I'm daydreaming?

"You are unique, sir, you are unique!" said Bert.

Jay Burgin flew around the room during dinner, snatching plates from the tables, kneeling to talk privately with some of the guests, laughing loud and long, and then he disappeared into the kitchen. His partner, Mary Jacques, was moving even faster. She was shyer, and very serious.

The Tenneco executive suggested another way to look at the fish/business analogy. "A guide in New Brunswick I know, he believes that the fish, the Atlantic salmon, is evil. It's a Moby-Dick thing. The fish is out to get you, to punish you for everything you've done wrong. The slightest mistake in your technique, and they will find it and they will humiliate you for it. You must strive for absolute perfection, and bow to their ability to find your weaknesses."

He added that he thought that was the wrong approach to fishing, "The guy has projected his paranoia onto the fish. You can tell a lot about someone by the way they fish. People who change flies all the time, I think it's very telling."

"You do it all the time!" said his wife, laughing.

"Sometimes." He laughed. The goal, he said, is to understand what a fish is thinking, and this goal is unreachable. "We don't really know what a fish is thinking, any more than we know what our dog is *really* thinking. We have theories. That's part of the great mystery. The surface of the water is the separation between two worlds. The world of the fish is something you intrude upon but never really understand."

Of course, said Bert, anglers aren't always easy to understand either. His sister-in-law's son, for instance. "He's a professional bass fisherman. He must change baits rather frequently in order to find the perfect bait—so he took a little file and sharpened and serrated one of his front teeth, so that he could cut the line more quickly when changing lures."

"Someone should tell him about fingernail clippers," someone said.

"Too slow, way too slow," said Bert.

He's a tournament fisherman, big bucks are at stake here, I offered.

"That's right!"

↪ AFTER DINNER, I relaxed in a kind of parlor, furnished with two couches and blessed with a sweeping view of the mountains. I was already learning about the different pace and rhythm of lodge life, the bondage of empty time. What would it be like to own and operate such a lodge? I wondered. More than a few anglers have entertained the fantasy—along with that of becoming a guide.

Jay Burgin, taking a break, walked in and sat down. He told me about the reality.

"Mary and I started with $250. That was our total down payment on the house. Everything we've earned we've put back into the business. All that was here was an old, abandoned house. People called it 'the dark house.'" In the beginning, to defray some of the cost of rehabbing the structure, he and Mary planned to offer writing seminars and photography workshops. Then a fly shop approached them and asked if they were interested in taking in fly-fishers. "I said, 'Not really. Do they pay anything?' We've never advertised, it's all been word of mouth. Eight years ago, our place was a twenty-seven-hundred-square-foot house and it's now thirty-two thousand square feet."

Today, as competition has increased, opening a fishing lodge can demand a huge monetary investment. Jay says that the operators of several Montana lodges have spent as much as $4 million each just to open their doors. "If you're opening a lodge to make money, I would suggest you put the money in CDs or some sort of investment, live off the interest, and go play. Because it's not a money-making operation. Everything goes back into the lodge. Everything."

Sweat equity can be equally demanding. From April to October, Jay and Mary work eighteen to twenty-one hours a day. They attend to every detail.

The lodge staff includes twenty-four employees, not counting guides, and a professionally trained chef. "A lot of people want to buy a lodge and just use it as a toy, and they hire a manager. Those lodges generally do not work. Managers are transient. Most people want the stability of coming back to people they know." Most lodge owners are also the outfitters, the provider of guides—even work as guides themselves. "I don't know how you can do that and be ready to take care of the guests when they return to the lodge." So Jay contracts with a local outfitter.

Where, I wondered, did he learn to give such service? "Both of us grew up with it," he said. "My dad was in the oil business in Texas. My parents entertained quite a bit and my dad was probably the ultimate host. He was German Swiss so meals were a very important part of our life." A wealthy family? "Fairly, yes." Much of Mary's preparation for lodge life came, he said, from being a professor at the State University of New York in Albany, and then dean of the graduate school of social work at the University of Cincinnati. As an academic leader, she was required to entertain—and to move carefully through the marshlands of academic politics.

This is a process, not a hotel. "For instance, we make sure that the visit *builds* for our guest." By that, he means that the first dinners are relatively sedate events, but as the week progresses, Jay includes more lotteries, contests, gag gifts.

Of the two thousand–plus guests they've entertained over the past eight years, only one could be classified as the guest from hell. "A miserable person, with a miserable life, who made everyone else miserable. But if somebody is a little bit difficult to deal with, our philosophy is, instead of getting upset and just shutting him off, we work that much harder."

So what is the upside to owning a lodge? "The fantastic people we meet. If you go back to the root word of recreation, it means to *re-create*. That's what we feel we're about, to help people re-create themselves so they can continue on."

They work hard to weave that life into the lodge experience. Mary is also, in fact, an Episcopal priest. Jay met her at a religious retreat. She was responsible for six parishes, covering some 15,000 square miles, in West Yellowstone, Jefferson, Virginia City, Sheridan, Dillon, and Deer Lodge. "She was the most refreshing priest I'd ever met: no collar, no notes. I had just been divorced after twenty-seven years of marriage and was absolutely wiped out. Mary had an opening for a lay person in her ministry so I applied for it and went to work for her and fell in love with my boss." Do the people who visit you at the lodge ever ask for a service? "We've had a couple of services. I'd say probably 40 percent of our guests are Episcopalians. The Episcopal church is not large in number but it's large among the movers and shakers in government and business. And of course we don't advertise that she's a priest. People would think that they're going to have the Bible quoted to them. People would come expecting that they couldn't cuss, couldn't swear, couldn't drink, or that someone's going to try to convert them. We don't do that."

During the coldest winter months, Jay and Mary "hole up and fill ourselves back up with sleep." And they travel, often staying with the more frequent guests of the lodge. "Some of them will rent a private club or host a cocktail party or dinner in their own homes, with Mary and me as their guests. It's a good chance for them to talk about fly-fishing and introduce some of their friends to it." And to lodge life.

↜ DURING THE NEXT three days, life took on rhythm that was both soothing, within the lodge, and exhilarating, on the river. The other world beyond the rivers faded away. One morning I sat outside with out-of-breath Mary Jacques, who was perspiring in the cool air. She had been rushing around, setting out a buffet from which the anglers would assemble their own box lunches. When I turned on my tape recorder, she fumbled around with one of her own—perhaps because she had been burned by a recent newspaper account that described her as an ex-nun, something she is not. She's even more careful than Jay to make sure the lodge doesn't get pegged as some kind of religious retreat.

Still, God is never far from Mary's mind and heart. She remains His servant.

The people who stay at the lodge, who come back year after year, tend to be committed to the "total experience," as she called it. How does she define the total experience? She took a deep breath. "I don't do well on definitions . . . I would say it's enjoying the many gifts that we have and that we're part of. . . . Paying attention to the wildlife in the area, or learning about the geology." She said she and Jay fly-fish, but do not count, keep, or even measure their catch. She finds herself more interested these days in what lives beneath the rocks along the waters.

People, including an increasing number of women (who sometimes come with husbands who don't fish), come here to "rest and relax," to "do things that fill them up again." I asked: Is helping people re-create part of her ministry? "It's not because I'm ordained . . . it's what I am called to do. I do not separate the secular and the sacred. Anything to do with life and living is sacred."

She looked out at the mountains, purple in the early morning light.

"I think that people find spots that they feel are . . . special," she said. "Some people have called this area the Tibet of the West. You look out at those mountains—people find spiritual spots, and that crosses any kind of religious line. I heard a quote, I don't know the origin of it, a friend passed it on to me: 'There's a difference between religion and spirituality. Religion is for people who are afraid of going to hell, spirituality is for people who have been there.'"

⤻ ONE EVENING, I noticed Josh Dickinson sitting outside on a deck, alone, looking at the sun slide into the rip in the sky where the mountains ended. I joined him in the fading light. He was, I had already learned, an especially accomplished fly-fisher, a man from the older, tweedier times. We talked for a while about lodge life, and he said many of the people who come to lodges like this are "fly-golfers." By that he meant that they come to network more than to fish. He grew quiet.

"My wife and I used to sit out on this deck," he finally said. He sat for a little while longer, then slowly got to his feet and walked inside.

⤻ DOUG SWISHER AND Sharon Chaffin were working downstairs in the fly-fishing den. Most of MF2 had collapsed into bed after a long day of fishing and a four-course dinner. Doug was doing paperwork and keeping Chaffin company as she tied flies.

They split their time between their base in Hamilton, Montana, and Naples, Florida—and spend many weeks during the fishing seasons of both states catering to well-to-do fly-fishers at lodges like this. Doug is known as an innovative author, and his books include *Fly Fishing Strategy*, *Selective Trout*, and *Backcountry Fly Fishing*. He works as tackle consultant, fly-designer (Sharon is his primary tier), lecturer, fishing-school operator, and fresh- and saltwater-guide. He's one of the few fly-anglers who makes a complete living from fishing. I wanted to know about the pantheon, the top fly-fishers. Who were his peers?

"Depending on how famous you think these people are, there are probably five to ten who are the real big ones. Lefty Kreh, he's considered one of the premier casters. Great at giving presentations. He's not much of a fisherman, he's more of a demonstration fly-caster," Doug said. "A great ambassador for our sport, he gives a lot of fly shows. Dave Whitlock, of White River, Arkansas, is the other one. Known him for thirty years. He's been here at this lodge." Whitlock is multitalented, "a pretty good fly-caster, a hell of a fly-tier, and an artist so he illustrates all of his books rather well. People pay pretty good money for his artwork. He's a real down-to-earth, great guy." He named a few more, including Joan Wulff.

> Most of the people who work in the sport have something else they do. Lefty Kreh, for example, has been an outdoor writer for the *Baltimore Sun* for many years. He recently retired, but that was kind of his main income. My buddy and writing partner Carl Richards was a dentist and still is. Dave Whitlock worked for years for Phillips Petroleum; he's been involved with various companies down the line, as an angling advisor, and then he went to Bass Pro. Another guy's a biology professor, and one's a medical orderly in some hospital.
>
> Everybody's got to make an income some other way. I'm about the only one who really gets it all from different aspects of fly-fishing. We're having the world fly-fishing championship in a few weeks in Jackson Hole. I was hired by the Tasmanian team to be their coach. Just all kinds of crap. I'm kind of the maverick in the whole bunch, I'm the only one that's never been involved with any big company. I've refrained from doing that.
>
> The reason is I used to fish with a guy named Joe Brooks. He's been dead since 1978 or so. He was one of the greatest fishermen I've ever met. He was the fishing editor of *Outdoor Life*. His writing is the reason I came to Montana. Over and above that, he's the

DOUG SWISHER

greatest man I've ever met. I used to think he was God, and he was. He told me one day, he said, "I know you get a lot of requests to do things for companies, but if you can hold your own it's better."

I don't have to say "this is the best rod" or "this is the best fly line." The other one who might be totally independent is Joan Wulff. I think her whole income is just from doing fly-fishing, as mine is. I have a mail-order business, I'm a captain in Florida, I'm an outfitter here. I've never heard of anybody who has both of those.

"Doug used to guide on the rivers in Montana," said Sharon, magnifying glasses down on the end of her nose, looping over a beautiful grasshopper fly designed by Doug. "Two trips a day, a hundred trips in a summer. I used to worry about him, he would get up and meet his clients at 5:30 in the morning and run one run, and meet the next bunch of clients about 3:00 in the afternoon and take them on another float. He was putting in two eight-hour floats a day, come in totally knocked out."

Doug shook his head. "I quit that. That was stupid."

Later in the week, I noticed that some of the local guides were not particularly kind when they referred to Doug. They made fun of how he moved when he cast, crouching and pointing to where the fly was going to fall. One of them called him a California caster, because he made so many false casts, or at least they claimed he did. They considered him something of a showboat.

But there's always resentment from local experts toward more nationally recognized experts on any topic. And Doug Swisher is deeply dedicated to the many arts of fly-fishing, and justifiably proud of his independence.

↩ HOWARD THOMPSON, of Ennis, Montana, is the quintessential slow-talking westerner—by way of Minnesota and Washington. He was our guide for the day and was waiting for Bob Colnes and me at a campground on a high, wide sweep of the Big Hole, the water sliding fast through high barren crags. Howard is a tall, lanky man, and appears to be in his late fifties or early sixties—but in retrospect, I am unsure of his age, because guiding ages men quickly. He has a thick gray mustache. He wore wraparound sunglasses, with side guards, fastened with a braided cord around his neck, an Orvis vest, and a ball cap. He talked slowly and quietly as he rigged our flyrods for us, as is customary among many guides—but I never got used to this. After rigging us, he backed his trailer, with a driftboat on it, into the river.

SHARON CHAFFIN

The boat was uplifted on each end, perhaps fourteen feet long. The guide sits in the middle and mans the oars—a job that demands considerable skill and strength—and the anglers sit at each end on raised seats with backrests. The middle seat is a hazardous position, particularly if one is with neophytes; that's one reason the guides appreciate barbless hooks.*

We were beginning the float at about fifty-eight hundred feet above sea level, Howard explained. "We've had rain and it's discolored the water. The higher up you get, the better water you're going to have. You try to get above the tributaries." Bob and I climbed into Howard's boat. This was Bob's first time to fly-fish. He had decided to take it up in his seventies with good-natured courage. Howard took his position at the oars in the middle, and then we were out into the river, riding the current. He rowed fast to move us into proper position, and as we came around a slowing bend, stared out over the swirling eddies and smooth runs, as if reading tea leaves. He said, "The hatch starts, the insects are transitioning from pupae to nymphs, and they're trying to break through to get on top of the water. That meniscus builds up like a brick wall, takes a lot of energy for them to break through that covering, to break a hole in it and crawl up to the surface. So they float around underneath the surface. That's what's happening right now." Trout, he explained, are eating machines, their bodies requiring constant nutrition just to stay in position—pointed upstream in fast current, facing the food as it's swept downstream. Howard instructed Bob and me to "cast using the center line of the boat as a reference point, ahead at about a ninety-degree angle from the side of the boat. That angle is going to change as the water velocity changes."

---

*Some driftboats and fly-fishing river rafts today are inflatable, made of tear-resistant nylon, Dacron, or Kevlar, and coated with neoprene or other synthetic materials. The inflatable oar rafts are, it is said, safer for unskilled passengers and children, but the dories or driftboats are more maneuverable and more aesthetically pleasing—and the boatman must be highly skilled. But many driftboats are still made of wood. These simple, elegant boats can be works of utilitarian art, especially when made of wood—usually fir or pine framing and fir plywood—with zinc-plated or stainless-steel fasteners, storage trays, casting platforms, and three oars (one extra) made of ash. Nearly all rafts have one or both ends upturned. The ends are upturned in order to shorten the length of boat actually in the water; the shorter the waterline length, the easier it is for the oarsman to pivot and maneuver the boat. Their ancestry is richly woven into American history. Zane Grey owned one, from which he fished on the Rogue. The Northwestern strain of driftboats, or river dories, was developed mainly on two Oregon rivers, the Mackenzie and the Rogue, and these evolved from the nineteenth-century log-driving bateaux of the Penobscot River in Maine, migrating to Oregon through the Adirondacks and Michigan. The ancestry of these boats probably stretches back to French and English colonial days. Now, instead of herding logs, the driftboats carry anglers and chase great browns and rainbows and steelhead and salmon.

I cast and my line immediately made a U-shape on the water, and the leader created a V in the water as it was pulled.

"We're starting to get some drag there. What that means is that the current is pulling the fly in an unnatural way. What you want to do is fish it in a dead drift and to help that happen, we're going to mend the line—we're going to roll the line up and over and keep it upstream from the fly. What that does is it allows that fly to float for a longer period of time." Mending was my weakness.

John Holt, author of an elegantly written guidebook called *Knee-deep in Montana's Trout Streams*, writes that the Big Hole deserves its reputation as a world-class fly-fishing river—known for its beauty and wild and fast rises and big browns and rainbows and the natives: cutthroat and mountain whitefish (looked down on in these parts, but thrillers nonetheless). The Big Hole is the last river in the contiguous United States to contain graylings, *Thymallus arcticus*, a strange and beautiful fish, with turquoise patterns on silver background and a large sail-like dorsal fin. Meriwether Lewis described this fish as a "new kind of white or silvery trout." It was common on the Missouri River and many of its tributaries until loggers and developers killed it off. Holt writes:

> The Big Hole really is a great river, even with its off days, but gluttonous water usage is seriously damaging the stream for much of its more than 100 miles of length. Some ranchers in the valley believe that because they were granted water rights decades ago before the value of the trout resource was recognized, they have the inalienable right to use every drop entitled to them, regardless of need. This greedy, shortsighted behavior needs to be legislated back to the dark ages where it originated.

As the stream slid lower, the land would flatten out from time to time; across the lush expanses we could see the outsized spidery, loom-like structures used to collect Beaver Slide Stackers. They convey loose hay up a wooden structure and dump it onto the stack.

Howard continued to patiently educate us. And he talked about growing up on a farm in southern Minnesota, fishing for bluegills and bullheads and bass, and how, when he was "all of seven or eight," he read an article about fly-fishing. "I became so intrigued by it that I went and borrowed my sister's biology collection of insects and went down to the lake and took those bugs out of the display and put them on a hook. Problem was, they'd crumble on the hook."

There, he said, that mend was just fine.

He pulled on the oars hard now, to straighten the boat like an arrow pointed down a narrow path, smooth water slicing through bow-snapping boulders. As we passed on, I saw the peculiar flat stillness on the upstream side in which trout often lie; I dropped a caddis directly on the slick as we passed. A blur of patterned gold blurped the surface and I yanked a ten-inch brown from the water and yelped with joy. Howard grinned, leaned hard into the pull of his right oar, and Bob pushed his rod high in the air and cheered. The first fish of the day. It would be a while before we caught another.

Again the river slowed, the incline softened. We drifted slowly now.

Howard took a thermometer from his vest and dragged it in the water. Prime temperature for feeding trout is below sixty-five, he said. Above that, the oxygen content begins to fall and the trout become lethargic. The water temperature today was sixty-eight degrees.

"When you've guided a river for a long time, as I have, especially the Madison, you know the mood of the river. And you're not going to forget that river and your fondness for that river is not going to go away. Even though the fishing may not be what it once was, you're still gonna have a love affair with that river. It's in your heart, it doesn't die, so to speak."

We passed through fast water now, with lots of boulders, not easy water to fish because, as Howard said, "When you're going so fast, like, you don't always get a chance to reach your target. First cast has got to be right or you probably won't get another chance."

The land and the bankside glides and the runs along fallen trees and the riffles and eddies mesmerized me. I began to notice more boats, most with one guide and two anglers. On such a float trip, the world seems tilted, and then slowly flattens until there is no tilt, and you awaken from the hypnosis of the current. You feel a growing sense of regret at the missed strikes. The flying leaves gust across mossy rocks that you will probably never see again. But then something taps your line and everything changes. Reincarnation is possible. You get up the next morning and you take another run at it, this time with a different guide—offering different lessons.

In the boat, moving over one more fast white rapids, we glided onto a glassy, leaf-dotted pool. We caught a few trout, but nothing spectacular. During our float, Howard had taught Bob and me with patience and gentle humor, never at our expense. It occurred to me that his role, perhaps the role of many guides, is something like that of a father, taking his kids fishing. I mentioned this theory, and he said, "I understand that. I have a lot of fathers who bring their sons or daughters and ask me to teach them. A child will probably be more attentive to the guide than he would be to his own dad. It's like when a husband tries to teach his wife

how to fly-fish: It never comes out very well. It's better for a wife to learn from a professional guide and instructor."

Bob and I had missed bite after bite all morning, and now we drifted downriver through a long, discouraging dead spell. Bob was mending his line poorly, catching branches. Our laconic guide bent over the oars, squinting at the riffles. We kept casting.

Suddenly, Bob shot the tip of his rod high in the air, and it bent nearly double.

He had hooked a nice brown trout that turned in the water, its spots flashing like visual Morse code. He got it up to the boat and then the fish performed what the local guides liked to call a "long line release," and it disappeared into the dark green current. But the old man was ecstatic. He was shaking and grinning. I was grinning. The guide was grinning.

"What *is* it about hooking a fish?" I exclaimed.

The guide turned the boat farther out into the current, head bent down, and smoothed his mustache with his finger. "Well," he drawled, "it *changes everything.*"

I laughed. "Do you mean that literally or metaphysically?"

"Well," he said, "both."

It changes everything. That's what hooking a fish does for some of us. In that moment, the past is irrelevant.

⮑ THE NEXT DAY, the experience was quite different in tone. At breakfast Swisher was irritated, but resigned to the fact that none of the guests had shown up for his 6:30 A.M. casting lesson on the lodge lawn. Further proof of the lowly state of casting. This time, our guide on the Big Hole was the outfitter who hired all the other guides, Lyle Reynolds. He's forty-four, but he looks older; the skin of his face and hands is lined and furrowed from the sun. He does not use sunscreen, which he regards as a nuisance.

He's handsome, a tightly built man. Lots of sinew and lean strength, straight ragged dark-blond hair. He moves quickly, never stops, and leads with his shoulders.

Unlike most of the other guides, Lyle was born and raised in Montana, right in Melrose, with a population of perhaps one hundred, a few buildings right out of *High Plains Drifter,* now with his Sunrise Flyshop—with a weathered bar next to it, where the guides unwind.

Lyle and his family live in a small trailer there, next to an old log home under an ancient, craggy cottonwood. This was his childhood home. Built in 1885, it used to be a mortuary. Rusty spring traps hang on its side. Its stained-glass windows remain intact. An outhouse sits askew next to it. This is not an easy part of the country, at least not for some.

On the way to the high Big Hole put-in, I asked about his background, and he told us his story:

I was number fourteen of fifteen kids. We were pretty much raised on hunting and fishing around here. We ate a lot of fish and wild game when we were growing up. That's how I come to do it, the guiding. I've been doing it since 1982. My mother come out of Canada, her name was Wilburetta Antoinette Goyette, about as French Canadian as you can find. My dad come out of Idaho; his family moved up here and worked the mines in Butte for years.

There was never fifteen of us home at one time, only seven or eight, so that made it easier. There's twenty-five years between the youngest and the oldest of us. We're a Catholic family. Back then it was common to have so many children. By the time I was born, some of them were already gone and married. There's fifty-four grandkids in the family. I have one nephew that's older than I am. I've got one sister that's got thirteen kids. I have two boys, fifteen and ten. They both like to fish, the oldest one he likes to hunt; he started hunting when he was twelve and after three years of hunting he's got three elk already. One of the guides, his family has eleven or twelve kids, then there's another with about ten.

My dad, he got silicosis and lost one of his lungs in his forties, so he had to quit working the mines. He had to support his family. So he trapped during the winter; that's how he pretty much supported all the kids. He'd trap coyotes, fox, muskrat, beaver, marten, bobcats—all the fur-bearing animals. Did beaver for damage control for a lot of the ranchers, coyotes as well, when they were killing sheep. He'd have to go high to trap, up to seven thousand feet for bobcats and martens. He usually went alone. He hauled the furs down to Rexburg, Idaho. A lot of times, some of the older kids would go, too. I trapped with him. He got along pretty good with one lung; he smoked until he was sixty-some years old, then he died when he was eighty.

I trapped, myself, for quite a few years. That's what I'd do during the winter months after the hunting season was over. Like my dad, I did damage control for some of the ranchers but I've pretty much given that up. I haven't done it now for four or five years. The fur trend went out of style and the Russian market started selling stuff over here. A lot of environmentalists were not big on it. Now the fur trend is starting to come back and maybe you can feed more people with it now. If prices ever get back up there, I still got all the trapping equipment and I could get right back into it. When you're trapping, it's a daylight until dark situation. You get up at daylight to start running your trap line and you cover one hundred miles.

You go up and down the mountains, here and there, constantly checking traps and resetting and skinning. By the time you're done, it's a long, long day. Daylight to dark, just like guiding.

With guiding, the day don't start the minute you pick up your flyrod and head to the river because you've got two hours' preparation getting your boat all cleaned up, making sure the lunch is ready, getting ice in the coolers. At the end of the day you've got to put your stuff up, get ready for the next day—so you're working two or three hours after you've dropped your clients off. My day don't usually end until 10:30, 11:00 at night. It makes for a long day sometimes. But guys wouldn't be doing it if they didn't enjoy it. I still enjoy watching somebody else who's just learning how to fish.

It's changing, though. A lot of outfitters now, they're school-teachers and then in the summer they're guides or outfitters. I make a good living at it but the only reason being is because I do hunting and fishing both. By the time September rolls around and the leaves start changing, you get kind of tired of the fishing and get anxious to go hunting. After five weeks of being out every day hunting, fishing looks pretty good again. That and having a fly shop, it blends together.

I don't plan on getting rich doing this. My wife helps; she's worked on a brush crew and a chain-saw crew for ten years, for the forest service. During the fire season she goes and fights fires. She stands about five-seven and weighs about 110 pounds, tall, thin, hair down to her waist. I don't know how she does it. She's tougher than I am.

We caught more fish that day. I practiced not yanking the fly when I had strikes, and it helped.

We moved along a smooth and biteless passage, and I wondered what Lyle really thought of the outlanders from moneyed lives, men and women who come to his harsh domain in order to relax, to soften—men who, probably from his one-lunged father's perspective, lacked sufficient sinew.

Now and then, in the lower stretches of the river, we saw large vacation houses, freshly built—rather stupidly built close to the bank, in the flood plain—by the incoming wealthy. Do local people like Lyle resent these new structures, particularly their disruption of the ancient view?

"It's not the sweetest thing to come around a corner and see a house staring you in the face," he said. "That's what's happened on the Madison River. I don't even like to go over there. Every corner you go around there's a house. Years ago, it used to be pretty good fishing. Then it self-destructed, I guess, with the whirling disease."*

Whirling disease, and the crowding of the rivers—and something else, the gentrification of guiding, the import of smoother guides with more social grace and education—must make Lyle nervous about his future.

Next to his fly shop, there's that dark and basic bar where the guides gather, especially the noncollegiate locals. I can imagine them delivering bitter sermons into their beer about the rich idiots they encounter on the stream. You got to tie their damned flies and kiss their wimpy ass and tell them when to set the hook. Hopeless. But a man's got to support his family, don't he? So we build their subdivisions and untangle their wind knots and tell 'em that's a fine fish.

Or at least that's how I'd feel if the boot were on the other foot.

꩜ LATER, AT THE lodge, Jay Burgin described the old-school guides and the new-school guides, in particular the tension between the cultures of those who stay the winter, decade after decade, and those who visit.

> In this area and in most remote areas in the West, the guides who grew up here have a way with them. There is no gray, it's either white or black and that's the only way people here—ranchers, for instance—could survive. If there is any gray, if they vacillate, they can lose the ranch, their life, their spot—like when it was forty-three below and they were out calving. Most people living some-where else would say, "Maybe I won't get up this morning; it's awful cold out there." A rancher has no choice. "If I stay in bed, I lose my ranch." It's that way all the way down the line. "I'll do it by myself, I'm very self-sufficient, and I expect other people to be self-sufficient."
>
> That's the way of the Old West and those values are not held anymore by a lot of people. These guys are abrasive, like the heroes in *Lonesome Dove*.
>
> Most people in this area don't take advice very well. If they feel

---

* Whirling disease, a parasitic condition so-named because it causes fingerling trout to spin in circles until they die, was brought to the United States via European fish around 1950. Although originating in the East, the disease spread westward into Colorado, Idaho, Wyoming, and Montana as streams were stocked with sportfish. This worm-carried parasite kills 90 to 100 percent of the fingerling trout it infects.

they have to have advice it kind of hurts them, gets them thinking they can't do it themselves. I don't necessarily condone their attitude, but I understand why it's that way. Very few will ever make much money at what they do, including ranchers. But the ranchers and guides grew up hunting and fishing, and they love the outdoors, and things that you and I might consider a hurt, they don't.

Most people who come here don't have the foggiest idea of what it was like growing up here, as a young person. Two bedrooms, no heat. The bathroom was an outhouse. How many people can even relate to that? A lot of lodges bring in college kids who don't know diddly about the river, they don't know diddly about life, but they can relate to people. It's very rare that a guide can do both and those that can make an awful lot of money and are in big demand. There are very, very few of them, I can count maybe three in this whole area.

We're all a product of our environment. People expect somebody to have all the skills of guiding, be a wonderful human being, shed everything that has formed them, and have the ability to relate to everybody. That's not a realistic expectation.

But now we moved down the river with Lyle. We were wearing on him. Bob was missing strikes and Lyle, who is known as a good but tough teacher, began to snap at him for his slow reactions.

The day before, Howard Thompson had patiently tied our flies, untangled our lines, but Lyle said, "Three strikes and you're out." Three tangles: That's all he'd do. Only way we'd learn, he said. Bob struck out quickly—and looked ashen when Lyle chastised him.

Nor did Lyle have patience with my flaws—especially my awkward mend, rolling the line back to position it in the current. "Mend! Mend! I give up." Some of the critique was indirect. "California caster," he said when he saw a man in a nearby boat making numerous false casts before letting his fly settle on the water. "You can always tell people from California 'cause they make so many damn false casts."

I'm from California, I reminded him. He said nothing. I made a few extra false casts.

Once, he pointed to a fat brown trout up against the shore and I cast to it and the fish rose, but I mistook a floating leaf for my fly, and missed the hit. Lyle's frustration flooded his banks. "Damn! Watch your fly!"

I tried again and this time I got a nice thirteen-inch brookie, then a fourteen-inch cuttbow—a cutthroat-rainbow cross. Meanwhile, Bob was having a difficult time. In his late seventies, his reactions were understandably a bit slower, but Lyle continued to tell him what he was doing wrong, with an edge to his voice. If this was fathering, it was a harsh brand. He was upbraiding a man nearly twice his age. Apparently some men—especially those who are powerful in business or politics—prefer a stern taskmaster on the river, and some guides are even rougher on their clients. These guides, I surmised, are the fly-fishing corollary to the French waiter.

In truth, Lyle is not unlike the people he's guiding. I imagined what would happen if roles were reversed, if Lyle entered the corporate domain. I doubt he would be treated with care and nurturing. I suspect if he were to spend time with his clients in *their* dominion, he might find them harsh, patronizing, and with little patience. Power depends on the domain. On this river, it was clear: Lyle was the master.

In any case, his mood had turned dark, perhaps from exhaustion. He had worked thirty days straight, with no time off, but I was fed up.

"Lay off Bob," I hissed, after we climbed from the driftboat to walk the shore.

Lyle looked at me with apparent disdain. "How do you expect to learn?" he said, shrugged, and grabbed his rod from the boat and walked off up the river, to do some sullen fishing of his own.

↩ LYLE'S OLD WEST isn't the only way of life that's going to be crowded out, if things continue as they are. The upside is this: The more anglers on the waters, the more people who care about water pollution and watershed destruction. The downside is that the West is following the East toward more privatized water, for two reasons: because of the avarice of the wealthy, and also because of those who want to preserve fine trout waters.

The wealthy are buying up ranches along some of the best trout streams of the West, particularly Montana—along the best rivers, including the Beaverhead and the Ruby, where the new landowners are putting up fences to keep people out. Anglers—some of them locals who have been fishing these waters all their lives—have been yelled at, photographed, and have even heard warning shots fired as they floated past private land. Some of these new landowners are either ignorant of or resist the fact that fishing the rivers is legal as long as anglers remain within the high-water marks. Says a fisheries biologist for the Montana Department of Fish, Wildlife and Parks: "I suspect they didn't do their homework before they bought land. This is America, not feudal Europe."

Public rights to the water were underscored in 1984, when the Montana Supreme Court unanimously concluded that navigable rivers were Montana's first highways of commerce (even as far back as Lewis and

Clark) and they should remain so. In 1985, the Montana legislature approved the state's stream access law, which seemed to settle the issue. But now the outlanders buying up river property for new developments and summer homes have formed something called the Montana Streamside Protection Association, which is raising money to challenge the law—promising to take the case to the U.S. Supreme Court, if need be.

Some landowners want to rescind the public's right of access, at public bridges, to the streams. Cordon off those points, and public access—except by boat—is virtually ended.

In terms of the quality of fishing, the argument to limit public access cuts both ways. Local residents and businessmen say the strangulation of public access on the Ruby has caused fishing to plummet, during the past decade, from about ten thousand angler days per year to three thousand to four thousand. Good news, say the new landowners: Less pressure improves fishing. Reid Rosenthal, the landowner leading the efforts to restrict the Ruby, explained his position to *Fly Fisherman* magazine in 1997: "The quality of the fishery was declining rapidly. The issue on the Ruby is not access; it's the quality of the fishery. The landowners I represent are preservationists."

Bad news, say the locals whose businesses rely on fishing tourism—and who resent the fact that the province of fishing is increasingly for fee-paying customers of private waters controlled by private lodges and other landholders. Jim Short, the owner of a bar in Sheridan, spoke well for the locals: "A lot of local people grew up hunting and fishing on the Ruby. It was a way of life. Now that is gone; our kids no longer can fish the river. The closure has hurt the town, and businesses are up for sale." If the wealthy landowners win, he said, "we'll lose public access everywhere. A way of life that we all enjoyed will be gone, and fishermen everywhere will be the losers."

Interestingly, two years later Rosenthal was in Canada, negotiating with southern Alberta farmers for exclusive access to stretches of what the *Calgary Herald* called "the most bountiful trout rivers in Canada." Rosenthal, who charges up to six hundred dollars a day to stay at his Montana lodge, told the *Herald* that privatizing access preserves and improves a fishery: "If you want to fish, you have to be a guest." He added, "Canadians understand what a sustainable resource is; Americans do not. They think it is their God-given right to harvest . . . if it swims or walks it should be harvested."

Trout Unlimited Canada executive member Tim Hamilton had this to say about that: "Conceptually, it is a great concern to us." Canadian fly-fishing guide Vic Bergman said: "The scary thing is if he ties up enough property it will make it hard for the local guy to get down to the river to fish unless he has a boat."

Most Westerners would never admit they're following the lead of Easterners, but that's what they're doing. Meanwhile, the East is re-affirming its preference for private waters.

In 1994, guides on New York's Salmon River had the right to float through private property and fish as they moved downstream. In 1997, after a group of ten guides tested their legal rights to anchor and fish, New York State's Court of Appeals reaffirmed the state's long-held legal position on riparian property rights: Landowners own the bottom of the river. Fishermen may float through the water but they may not anchor to fish.

In fairness, understand that fly-fishing and trout preservation organizations often use some of these same arguments when they lobby states and localities to mandate fly-fishing-only or barbless hook stretches of water. That's a restriction to access, too—cultural access—by bait fishers. In 1996, when the Oregon Fish and Wildlife Commission opened eleven rivers and lakes to anglers using lures and spinning rods (part of the idea was to encourage kids to fish), angry fly-fishers "emerged like Deschutes salmon flies," wrote *Oregonian* columnist Bill Monroe. They argued that allowing such gear on the river leads to overcrowding and makes steel-head and salmon easier to catch and kill. As a result of their protests, the Fish and Wildlife Commission rescinded its decision.

One angler's restriction to access is another angler's definition of conservation.

John Holt, writing in *Fly Fisherman* magazine, put it well:

> The Great Land Grab is on one more time in the wild West, es-
> pecially in Montana. Hordes of people seeking refuge from the
> increasing madness, violence, and general frenetic pace of city life
> are storming the state's borders, buying up chunks of land at an
> ever-accelerating rate. Both local and out-of-state developers are
> purchasing hundreds of thousands of acres of agricultural and
> undisturbed country. These individuals and businesses—often of
> questionable reputation—are constantly seeking zoning and build-
> ing-code variances in order to circumvent regulations aimed at con-
> trolling growth. In fact, in many cases in Montana those in charge
> of formulating, adopting, and enforcing regulations designed to
> protect prime country are often realtors and developers. Hardly an
> ideal situation for preserving unspoiled landscapes. . . . You cannot
> have world-class water when it's surrounded by a 522-unit subdivi-

sion. Life doesn't work that way. . . . Montana hasn't been discovered, it's been pimped.

There are more pernicious kinds of restriction. A few bait-fishers, lodges, and rich landowners buying up access rights is probably small change compared to the larger issue: what large-scale development is doing to the watersheds, and not only in God's and Lyle's country.

Fishing with Papa

⤳⤳

ON MY NEXT-to-last day in Montana, I stayed off the river. I had other plans. Having arranged for a rental car, I drove to Bozeman to meet one of Ernest Hemingway's sons.

I drove across the Montana plains, past the wide and winding Jefferson River. Everywhere, I saw abandoned log structures, cabins and sheds, their rear ends burrowed into the rocky hills for protection from the wind and cold. Snow was still on the mountains, high up. Near White Hall, by the Tobacco Root Mountains, I saw the empty space where most of a mountain had been, before it had been sliced away by strip mining.

The fields here are irrigated by long pipes mounted on huge wheels that are pulled across the land. Much of the foam seen on the rivers is fertilizer runoff. A few days earlier, Jay Burgin had been driving home to Five Rivers Lodge along this road and plunged off into a ditch. He had been so exhausted from tending his guests that he fell asleep at the wheel. Fortunately, he was not hurt.

There was a sign on the highway for the Church of Christ. It said, "Auditorium is prayer conditioned." West of Bozeman, not far from the East Gallatin River, is the beginning of suburban development, tennis courts, a golf course.

Patrick Hemingway, and his wife, Carol—a retired professor of theater and playwright—live in a white ranch house on the edge of town. The house is surrounded by a high hedge of trees.

Carol met me at the door, invited me in. Hemingway, 69, looks a lot like his father. His head turned slightly toward me. He was sitting under the horned head of a kudu with narrow white stripes across the back and long, twisted horns. The easy, high-pitched laugh, even the cadence of his speech, reminded me of what I knew of Ernest Hemingway.

How strange, I thought, to be the son of such a man, who once said, "To be a successful father . . . there's one absolute rule: When you have a kid, don't look at it for the first two years."

Patrick, one of Ernest's three sons and a big-game-hunting guide and conservationist in Africa for three decades, has accomplished much in his own life. But right now, Patrick was talking about how Papa taught him to fish.

His earliest memories of fishing with his father are of saltwater fishing. He walked to a bookcase, bracketed by reproductions of art that once hung in Ernest's house, paintings now donated to museums. He picked up a photograph. Here's a picture of his mother holding up a rather big fish. "I think it was a pike that she had caught." He was imprinted with fishing at a very early age. "You get that early experience, and it's part of your earliest feelings about people and the family."

Some of Patrick's earliest memories include fishing for bluefish, which he didn't particularly enjoy at the time. "Children have a better sense of smell—the smell of gasoline, that general ocean smell—so I was just seasick all the time." He remembers how, in Key West, people would wait for his father on the dock when they returned, not because Papa was famous (he wasn't in the '30s, Patrick insists), but because they were hungry.

"The strongest image of him was later on when I must have been eight or nine, maybe a little younger. I was there the day he caught a tuna which he fought for eight hours. He was having buckets of water thrown on him. It was dark by the time it was over. He lost, I think it was fifteen pounds, through dehydration. It was something."

He remembers nothing remarkable about the talk on the boat that day; most of the talk was quarterback talk. "He was the first person to land a tuna like that in tropical water. In fact, they said it was impossible, but he did it." I asked Patrick if he was worried about his father then, about the ordeal of it. "No, you never worry about anybody as a kid." The closest Ernest came to writing about that experience, says Patrick, was in *Islands in the Stream*, where one of his sons fights a big fish.

Today, Patrick, who fly-fishes on Montana's stretch of the Missouri River, takes a dim view of most fly-fishers. "Most trout fishermen are like golfers: Their interest is in how they cast, how they tie their flies, it's really not learning about nature at all. Most are interchangeable with golfers and vanity is the main drive. And competition." Nonetheless, some of his sweetest memories of his father are of fly-fishing at the L Bar T dude ranch.

"He fished with wet flies and he had all this equipment he had brought over from England." I told him I had seen Ernest's flyrod at the American Museum of Flyfishing in Vermont, right next to Babe Ruth's rod. "Oh, yes, it was a very nice bamboo rod."

His father took good care of his gear. He recalls the silk line that his father would strip out and meticulously dry. "Usually he'd fish together with his wife, they'd fish two sides of the same stream, casting out and letting the current swing the fly around to the bank. They'd fish downstream. Actually there's a picture here, this is from that time."

He took down a small, framed photo of a pretty, short-haired woman sitting next to water, wearing fine waders and boots. "That's a picture of my mother with all that gear, taken about 1935."

Was your father happy when he was here? I asked.

"I guess the answer to that one goes back to good ol' Tom Jefferson. It's the pursuit of happiness, isn't it?"

The pursuit.

At the other end of the room was a bust of Ernest Hemingway typing on his small, manual typewriter. The bust was surrounded by stacks of books. And on the other side of the bust was a humming Macintosh computer and several stacks of paper. Patrick saw me glance at the Mac and said that he was working on a book, something to do with his father. He could not tell me anything more about it because his publisher had sworn him to secrecy, but later I learned that he was editing his father's final, unpublished novel.

I asked him about his father's influence on fishing and hunting literature.

He smiled. "A couple of generations were forced to read *The Old Man and the Sea* in high school. I don't know whether that had an influence on people or not; it's hard to say." Hemingway's writing about hunting and fishing was part of a larger fascination with animal behavior. He would write about it indirectly, even when he described the play of his house cats.

Ernest Hemingway's legacy to his son is a certain brutal honesty—an uncomfortable clear-sightedness. For instance, on the issue of catch-and-release:

> On the Missouri River, pelicans have learned to follow the guide boats. The fishermen make a big thing of putting the fish back, holding them in the current for a while before letting them go. But the fish are vulnerable for a few minutes and that's when the pelicans can get them. If you really want to release fish and have them survive, you have to play them very quickly. That means you have

to use much heavier tackle. In other words, there's an antithesis between the desire to release and the desire to feel how good a fisherman you are by landing a fish on light tackle. By landing a fish on light
tackle, you automatically are making it unsuitable for release. In a
long play, the fish is truly desperate and it goes into sort of what
people who have childhood diabetes go into. They start mobilizing
every type of energy reserve that they can. They've exhausted their
glucose and they're starting to metabolize protein. If this process goes
on past a certain point, it's fatal. The fish are fighting for their lives;
it's no sport to them. That's an illusion on the part of most people.

One of the things that my father was very conscious of was the
anthropology of hunting and fishing. Among primitive people, any
acts of killing animals involved fear on the part of the hunters, and
they knew they were depriving that animal. They identified with the
animal, and out of respect, would beg its pardon—which sounds a
little phony to do nowadays because it's so remote. It's disturbing to
me to see the lack of respect people have for dead things other than
ourselves. To see an animal, especially a big animal, a deer for example, which people will run over time and time again, never having a thought that it might be a nice idea to take it off the road.
Among the vivid memories I have of the early fishing days with my
dad was the cleaning of the fish—seeing the internal structure, being very conscious of the gills and that little area along that back-
bone that's just filled with material you sort of clean out with your
thumb. I didn't have any idea of physiology but I was very aware of
those innards. On the outside, the fish is so perfect and on the inside is all the *stuff.*

True, I thought. The meaning of *stuff.* My kids don't clean fish.
They've seen me do it only a few times. But like Patrick, one of my most
vivid memories of my father is when he would clean fish on the boat
docks in the Ozarks—the ritual of it, opening the stomach to see what
was in it. Looking at that strange bladder filled with air. But also watching him throw the guts on the bank and seeing the snakes slide up for
dinner. I had remembered that, only yesterday, when I had watched a
water snake attempt to consume a whitefish. Perhaps as fishing becomes
more environmentally sound, it loses some of the experience, some of
the relationship. It becomes more like golf. Fly-golf, as Josh Dickinson
had called it.

Patrick nodded.

"More like a game, that's right. One of the things I think people have to accept is that things just don't last forever. We wear out. Things are dying all the time."

I suppose that a person would have to think like that in order to make a living as a big-game hunter, that is—to think realistically. So it is with fishing, as well. I asked him: As a hunter, and as a fisher, what about the differences between hunting and fishing?

> One of the fundamental differences is the sentimentality. We somehow believe that the fish is the more primitive form of life. The implications of killing and an animal's suffering don't seem to connect with fish as much as with other animals. A deer, for instance, is a very developed mammal with a good nervous system; they can certainly feel pain. Fish have a nervous system too, and they do feel pain.
>
> The truth is people don't have much feeling for people that they don't know, so why would they have any feeling for a deer? We don't really care what happens to the North Koreans; it's pretense. I heard a wonderful remark by a mathematician on that subject. He said, "Microbes undoubtedly have a vision of a world made safe for microbes."
>
> One of the things that people must face up to, if they really consider animals to be important to them, is that the most awful thing that we have done to animal life is to take away their land. Human beings have increased to the point where there really isn't room for anything else, OK? That's the problem, not whether we shoot or don't shoot a squirrel. This is the problem for the California moralists with their deep ecology. I'm not against it, but the greatest damage that is done to the natural world is because of the increase of human population without any desire to stop it. When I was born, the population in the United States was 120 million. So the number of people in the United States in my lifetime has doubled. And I can see the difference.
>
> If I believed that human beings truly wanted to do something about their own population growth, their appropriation of land and water from other animals, then I would give up any killing of animals, absolutely. But until I see any desire to do this, I won't.

Are you a catch-and-release fisher?

"Not particularly. I'll do it if it's required, otherwise I eat them. I don't believe catch-and-release is a moral issue. I believe that if you're going to have a lot of people fishing in an area, that's the only way the fishery can

PATRICK HEMINGWAY

be maintained. That's it. In fact, catching and releasing is torturing animals for your amusement."

I mentioned that People for the Ethical Treatment of Animals (PETA) has targeted fishing recently.

"And rightly so. Catch-and-release fishing is indefensible, from the standpoint of putting an animal in absolute fear of death. They don't know they're going to be released!

"Carol and I don't take more fish than we can eat, we don't keep them for a long time in the freezer because they aren't good then. And we know how to clean fish and how to prepare them so they're good to eat, right? It isn't some stinking thing that we'll throw in the garbage can."

Later I asked him about his father's suicide. He rejects the armchair psychoanalyzing, the assumptions that his father was mentally ill. "I saw sometimes some extraordinary behavior, but he never struck me as the classic portrait of having bipolar disorder." Most of the time, his father was simply fun to be around.

Still, suicide runs in the family, and, he says, his father's drinking did rise like a slow tide. The place in the universe that his father loved the most was Cuba. His little house was there, and his boat. "They fished, but there were also little harbors where they could fish, completely un-inhabited areas where they go in and anchor the boat and be in calm water. I think the prospect of his life without that was very grim. He'd had such a wonderful life in that respect, which he created for himself. But to live a sort of suburban existence, or urban existence, was just unthinkable to him.

"The Bay of Pigs was in April of 1961, OK? And my dad shot himself in July of '61, OK? And the Bay of Pigs really was the end of any hope of him getting back to his home."

I stood up to leave, and noticed I was standing on the remains of an antelope, a kudu's skin. On the wall was a painting that Patrick did when he was a boy, of a cat.

"Is that one of the cats he wrote about?"

"The cats in Cuba, right. He had a lot of cats."

⤳ THAT NIGHT AT dinner, back at the lodge, some of the men stood to give happy toasts. MF2 was in a terrific mood: Plaques were handed out, men slapped each other on the back and acted like boys again. And then Josh rose to his feet, tall and commanding, and raised his glass.

"To my dear wife," he said. She had come with him to this lodge every year for over a decade and had died a few weeks before, of cancer. He began to give a little speech about her, but his voice broke. He held the glass in the air for a moment. The members of MF2 raised their glasses too, and then they drank.

⤳ ON MY LAST day in Montana, I hooked the trophy fish of a lifetime.

It was bright and sunny, not the best conditions for fishing. My fishing partner was Bert Berkley, wearing sun-protection gloves, red scarf, and his thrilled-to-be-here expression. Our guide was Justin Jones, twenty-four, one of the new breed of guides. Some of the younger guides, Justin told us, are the sons of guides. Many of them are attending college and return to the waters in the summers. Justin grew up in Bozeman, and is studying accounting and computer science. He learned most of what he knows about guiding from the older guides, but his style is different. He looked like a California surfer, with his shorts, baggy tee shirt, and wad-ing sandals, which he wore instead of the traditional wading boots. He bounced around with eagerness. He didn't act like a father, he acted like an excited son—glad to be introducing Dad into his domain. Bert and I liked him immediately.

Justin doubts most of the young guides will return to guiding, or even to this state, once they graduate. "You only get to live in Montana if you make a lot of money."

Any chance he would choose guiding over accounting and computers?

"This is definitely a pretty good place to have your office. Out here, overtime isn't really a big deal to me. I've thought about doing the accounting for a lot of these different fly shops."

We were standing on a stretch of crusted cheat grass next to a crude boat ramp. The edge of the river was thick with willow trees. As Justin prepared his inflatable driftboat, he began to chuckle.

My buddy and I never fished the major rivers, still don't. We have our secret places on the tributaries, in the mountains. One time me and my buddy were up high there, and man, the fish were biting. Not a soul in sight. My buddy gets snagged in a tree, and he climbs up to retrieve his fly, and he falls out of the tree.

Busted his leg bad. You could see the bone pushed up under the skin; he thought he had broken his leg, but it turned out he had just separated the bone from the muscle. He was lying there and he says to me, "Justin, you've got to go get help." So I left him there and headed down the mountain. It was going to be a long hike. But along the stream, you know, those fish were really rising, and I kept looking at those fish, and walking, and looking, and walking, and looking. Finally I couldn't stand it anymore. I stopped and did some fishing. Good fishing, too, until I had a hit, and pulled up hard, and the fly flew out of the water and buried itself in my cheek. Barbed hook. Couldn't get it out. So I cut the line—had this hook in my cheek with a foot or so of tippet dangling from it. I kept fishing. But after a while my conscience got the better of me, so I headed downstream again. I finally found help, and we hiked back up there.

I followed the bend of the stream around, and there's my buddy. He'd dragged himself to the bank. He had his leg in the cold water to make it feel better. And he was lying there on his back *casting*. He looks up at me, sees that fly in my cheek—couldn't hardly miss it with that line hanging down—and he says, "Goddamn it, Justin, I *knew* you stopped to fish! So how was it?"

The Beaverhead was crowded. We passed a boat every few minutes, or they would pass us. Even large pontoon boats and flat-bed paddle boats were on the water. People looked vaguely unfriendly, and I could imagine how tensions could flare.

The Beaverhead flows north through pastureland, bracketed by rolling hills, rugged rock formations, and bushes so thick and water so deep, in most places, that wading is impossible. Lewis and Clark once believed that the Beaverhead, and the river system to which it belonged, might be the Holy Grail of waters, the passage to the Pacific. Today, the Clark Canyon Dam, built in 1964, creates the deep, cold water necessary for the largest trout. What makes fishing the Beaverhead tough "is the knowledge that literally tons of trout are present in periods of adequate water flow at every mile of water," according to Jim Holt. "A ballpark figure would be twenty-five hundred pounds of browns and fifteen hundred pounds of rainbows per mile." One overgrown stretch of bank is, for the most part, dead to anglers. "I asked one biologist if he'd ever caught a fish there and he said, 'No.' But when we have to shock [an electric shock is used to stun fish, bringing them to the surface for counting] this stretch, no one wants to handle the net. It's not possible to bring to net all of the fish. Your arms will give out." The density of the population of the largest fish has fallen in recent years, but still, this is the place to hook a big trout.

Which is what I did.

Bert and I had each caught a nice brown trout, and we were passing through ranch land that Justin said Bill Gates had recently bought. "Huge ranch," he said.

As he rowed, Justin was talking about what he called "the Utards," the local term for anglers from Utah "who tend to put spinning reels on fly-rods and use worms," which is legal on this stretch. We were fishing with deep nymphs, two to the line, and the puff balls Doug Swisher called "bobbers."

I was . . . well, daydreaming about . . .

Suddenly the bobber disappeared in a deep pool. I set the hook hard and felt the size of the fish immediately. It felt me too, and headed south, downstream. Bert gave out a yelp. I held the rod high and the fish kept going. My reel screamed—no better way to say it—as the line disappeared, down to the backing. I gradually applied more tension to the line, and the fish stopped.

I pulled the rod back to turn the fish's head; it went deep, to the left, then, opposing my directions, turned right, leaped into the air, once, twice—*my God, I had never seen a trout this big*, a brown trout, golden in this light, reflecting the sun as if it were the sun itself. I was alternately releasing line and reeling it in. Justin was leaning into the oars, rowing hard, a big purple vein standing out on his neck. He pulled us upstream toward the fish. Then the fish headed for us. Justin jumped up with the net. I lifted the rod and the fish came up, so close I could have reached down and touched it.

"Holy shit," said Justin. It was, he said later, the biggest trout he had seen at the end of a line in the three years he had guided on the Beaverhead. I stood, knees quivering. The trout seemed to study us for a fraction of a second and sounded, dove so deep we couldn't see it anymore: He went under the boat, and I pulled the line around the bow.

The fish headed straight for the thick brush, and the tangle of roots in the water. Justin chased it, arms a blur. Five feet away, I saw it again, rolling slowly, shaking its head.

This was it, I thought. Just keep it out of the brush. But the fish had other ideas.

"The hook's out," panted Justin. The fish's head was freed from the first hook, and the dropper fly was lodged in his tail, the tippet wrapped around the fish. The current and Justin's expert rowing moved us past the trout, but I could no longer turn its head. I brought it near the boat once more, Justin made a wild swing with the net, and it flew from his hand and floated downstream in the fast current. The fish was now in complete control, and it turned downstream. The line disappeared from my reel again. Boats were on each side of us, the anglers staring. *Grab the damn net*, I thought, as it slipped past one of the boats, *and net this fish*. Instead, one of the anglers made a long cast over my line. I tasted bile, and yelled (in a voice I am not accustomed to), *"Do NOT cast over my LINE."*

My task was to keep the fish out of the fast current directly in front of us: If it reached that zone, the current alone could take the fish from me. Now I saw the trout, five boat lengths away, roll on the surface. Once, twice, seeming to tire—but it slid into the zone of no return, and suddenly my rod snapped back. Limp.

I was limp, too. I sat down, stared at the line in disbelief. I felt ill.

"You fought him just right," said Justin, the generous son.

Bert shook his head and said, "You're the hard-luck kid today."

I snapped at him, reminded him that I had caught one more fish than he had that day. My heart was beating, there was a foul taste in my mouth. Fishing does change everything, and right now it had changed me into something I did not particularly like.

Bert and Justin were silent as the boat drifted listlessly through the gauntlet of other anglers.

After a while, another feeling filled me. Gratitude. I would not forget that fish. I was glad that it had escaped.

When that long line goes out over the water, our greater intent is to bring back a good story. The stories are what we teach and trade and tell, and we compete to see who can tell the best fishing story. It's an endless competition no one ever wins. When the old man, in Hemingway's story, caught his huge marlin, and strapped it to his small boat for the long trip home, and then watched helplessly as the sharks devoured his catch of a lifetime, the sharks were creating the story.

"It's not the fish that you catch that you remember," Justin said. "It's the ones that get away, they're the ones who stay with you."

Near the end of our run, we floated through a clear, shallow tributary. I looked down and saw two fish, rainbows as big as my brown, drifting slowly along the rounded stones, on their sides. One was already turning belly up. They were dying.

"Probably killed by worm fishermen," said Justin. "Gut hooked."

But I knew better. I could sense Patrick Hemingway and Doug Swisher looking over my shoulder. I had fought my fish too long and too hard. It was probably deep in the river, exhausted, staring blankly, tilting to one side, losing its life.

Ghostwaters

❧❧❧❧❧❧❧❧❧❧❧

Don Quixote and Sancho reached the river Ebro, and the sight of it was a great delight to Don Quixote as he contemplated and gazed upon the charms of its banks, the clearness of its stream, the gentleness of its current and the abundance of its crystal waters; and the pleasant view revived a thousand tender thoughts in his mind. Above all, he dwelt upon what he had seen . . . for though Master Pedro's ape had told him that of those things part was true, part false, he clung more to their truth than to their falsehood, the very reverse of Sancho, who held them all to be downright lies.

—*Don Quixote*

Nick Raven and the River of Heaven

Hungry to return to a more proletarian culture of fishing, I called my friend Nick Raven, a New Mexico farmer/carpenter/woodworker and former Marxist (now a born-again Christian) and suggested we spend some time wandering around New Mexico.

Nick is the son of Tadeusz Raven, a Polish immigrant and musician who wandered the country toward California after World War II. When his car broke down and he ran out of money in Clovis, New Mexico, he settled there and eventually opened a music shop. Tadeusz took a different route from his brother, Jay, a social worker before he joined the Abraham Lincoln Brigade in the Spanish Civil War. Ernest Hemingway described Jay Raven in a 1937 newspaper dispatch from Spain, a description of a field hospital. In the story, Jay Raven tells Hemingway how he lost his face helping rout fascist troops. He is optimistic about his wounds, and expects his eyesight to return soon, and hopes to get back into battle. Later, Hemingway learns that Raven had lost both eyes and that it was the partisan troops who had been routed, not the fascists. Nonetheless, Hemingway admires Raven and writes, "This is a strange new kind of war where you learn just as much as you are able to believe."

Nick describes his uncle, who died in 1969, as a committed communist, a true believer. Such stubbornness is a trait that Nick shares. In the 1960s and early '70s, while others of his generation took drugs and joined communes, Nick became a serious student of Marxism at Eastern New Mexico University, then headed back to the nineteenth century. He and his wife, Isabel, and two children settled in a nearly deserted old Spanish farming valley called Puerto de Luna, in eastern New Mexico, population less than one hundred. They bought six acres and a century-old, one-room adobe house that was half-melted back into the land.

The Pecos River runs through Puerto de Luna. Right up the road is the place where, by some accounts, Coronado, searching for the seven cities of Cibola, crossed the Pecos in 1541. In the mid-1800s, when the village was the Sumner County seat, a thousand people lived in Puerto de Luna. Billy the Kid was held at the local jail; he broke out, killing two men. Two beams in Nick's adobe house came from that jail. Today, beyond the mesas of the valley, self-flagellating Penitentes, an ancient Catholic offshoot, still meet in hidden adobe chapels on holy week to "crucify" an honored member, hanging him from a cross with leather thongs; until the 1930s, nails were used in some parts of New Mexico. The irrigation ditch that runs through Nick's land has been attended by major domos—ditch riders—whose job it is to clean and tend the wood dams and locks. The ditch has functioned since the 1850s.

Nick became a chili farmer, and he covered a wall with everything written by Marx and Engels, Emerson and Thoreau, and various depressed Eastern European thinkers, and waited for the apocalyptic end of capitalism.

Instead of the apocalypse, he got appendicitis.

One afternoon in 1980 as he was chopping wood he fell violently ill. His wife hauled him in their 1952 Chevrolet pickup truck fifteen miles to the closest hospital, in Santa Rosa. My wife, a nurse practitioner volunteering for the summer in that hospital, diagnosed him and then held his hands as the less-than-competent doctor sliced into him, using local anesthesia. Tough guy, said my wife.

At the time of this unpleasantness, Nick had removed the west wall of his house and was making adobes to extend the one room into two. The appendicitis hit in late August, and he was running out of time before the cold weather arrived. I had time on my hands that month, so I offered to do the heavy lifting. For the next few weeks, he and I made adobes, mixing the red New Mexico clay with hay and water from the irrigation ditch and an occasional shovelful of pig manure. Nick needed to heal, so we took frequent breaks under a big cottonwood, ate chili and smoked pipes (he gave me one of his corncob pipes), and as his geese and pigs ran past, we argued politics and religion and fishing until we'd worked up a sweat from the debate and the chili, and then we'd head back to the adobe pit to take out our furies on the earth.

The next summer, when my wife and I came to visit, Nick baptized me in the Mora, a northern New Mexico stream that winds through a green valley under the dissolving tower of an abandoned adobe church.

The banks of the stream were high and leaned over the water, which was dark and smooth with deep pools. The stream slipped alongside a red rock cliff and disappeared under a canopy of thorn bushes and willows.

He led me into the water and handed me one of his beat up flyrods, this one with an automatic reel. He was wearing ancient jeans and rubber farmer boots with holes in them that let the water run straight through. I don't think he'd ever seen an Orvis catalog. But having grown up fishing all the streams of New Mexico, Nick was and still is the best fly-fisherman I have ever met. As we waded, the stream became darker and deeper and the canopy leaned over us. He showed me how to do little roll casts under the thorns. I found myself grinning like a fool.

I held Nick's rod above my head and pushed my chest against the current, and flipped my fly out ahead of me, and saw the flash of spotted gold as a little brown trout rolled in the water and took the fly down deep, and my rod tip followed it into the water.

"Now you're a fly-fisherman," said Nick. "Which is the only thing better than being a Marxist."

So NOW, a few years later, Nick met me at the Albuquerque airport. I hadn't seen him in three years—the last of several times we had gone fly-fishing together. Since our most recent visit, Nick and Isabel had decided they could not make it as farmers and they had left their property under the care of people from a family that had lived in the valley for 150 years. They moved to Espanola, on the highway north of Santa Fe, where Nick worked as a self-employed carpenter and craftsman woodworker and Isabel went to work for the state. Nick converted from Marxism to Catholicism. (I've never asked him why.) Their farm in Puerto de Luna remains their one true place and they return to it whenever they can. They plan to die there.

Typically, he was wearing a flannel shirt, an old straw hat with additional ventilation, and those same old rubber calf-high boots that seem to slosh even when dry. He had replaced his Jurassic jeans with a pair from the Cretaceous period. His beard was big and blond, his face hardened by wind. A pipe was stuck in his shirt pocket. He ambled confidently through a field of cell phones and gave me a bear hug.

We headed for the parking lot. He had given up his truck for a city car, a 1982 Chevrolet station wagon with a patina of dust and oil. The back was filled with fishing gear and sleeping bags; the dashboard was laden with various tools, flyboxes, and scribbled measurements for cabinets he had yet to make. We traveled past the endless Jiffy Lubes and fast-food outlets of outer Albuquerque and toward Santa Fe. We passed an incongruous scene of a huge water slide and amusement park set out in the barren high desert. This scene set Nick to talking about the preciousness of water, and why it's time for outsiders to quit moving to New Mexico.

"Last year, we had such a terrible drought that there were ordinances passed against smoking outside in Albuquerque and Santa Fe. Didn't have the water resources to waste on somebody lighting a fire." Nick took out his pipe and, while steering with the heel of one hand, tamped down some ready tobacco. The air rushed past the station wagon and he snapped a match to life and held it over the bowl. "In Espanola, where we have an irrigated acre, our irrigation ditch only had water in it two days a week. That was rationed and Santa Fe had an edict against watering at all in the daylight hours. All the water is used up, being diverted to Texas or just drying up. All of the underwater basins—the biggest one in New Mexico is out in the east and runs through Kansas and all the way up into Nebraska—they're dropping. I've talked to ranchers who drilled their first irrigation well back in the '40s; they only had to drill forty or fifty feet deep to hit water. They're now pumping water at two hundred feet or deeper."

How does the water crisis affect the fisheries, especially the trout fishing, I asked. He contemplated this most serious of issues.

"My guess is that it doesn't have too much effect because most of the trout streams are in areas where it's the mountain runoff. They don't have any dams; the dams are downstream."

So, I asked Nick, do you think the lack of water will keep population down in New Mexico? He puffed furiously on his pipe. (He had promised his wife he would cut down or quit, but fishing trips are to be taken out of the context of time.) "It doesn't seem to be doing it. This last year has been a good, wet year. Santa Fe and Albuquerque are growing like mad again. But this water thing will catch up with us sooner or later. There is no free water." He pulled the pipe stem from his mouth and pointed with it over the steering wheel at nothing in particular. "The only way New Mexico can take on more population is to take that water from other uses—from farming. The money in development in this state is a lot more than the money in agricultural. My bet is that there's going to be more and more attempts to take water from the small asequia systems—the old Spanish irrigation ditches."

What's even worse, he said, placing his pipe on the dashboard to let it cool, is that the trout streams are starting to crowd up—maybe not as bad as in Colorado or Montana—but he can definitely tell the difference from when he was a younger man, when the streams were his. This

NICK RAVEN

crowding, with people who bring their expensive equipment and their Range Rovers to the distant streams, offends Nick's sensibility of spareness, thrift, life stripped to the essential. About the only thing that could slow all this down would be a devastating drought or an uprising of the older populations, particularly the Hispanics—who don't fish in great numbers, certainly not with flyrods, but who know the value of the asequia.

You can't separate fishing from culture and economics, says Nick.

As we entered Santa Fe, to pick up my fishing license and a few extra flies at the High Desert Angler fly shop, Nick told me he refuses to drive vehicles with air-conditioning. He said he's planning to run for governor so he can outlaw air-conditioning, "which is the only reason there's so many people here. Make people live in 117-degree heat in the asphalt cities; now *that* would bring the population down to what the state's water can support. I'm not sure my kids are going to vote for me, though."

Nick was pinching snuff now.

"That's terrible for you, Nick; that causes cancer, too."

"You should never give up one vice without picking up another," he said.

᳓ HIGH DESERT ANGLER is located across from an old rail yard on South Guadalupe Street next to a shop called Body Décor, under the horizon of the Sangre de Cristo range. The building is in the Territorial style, Nick notes—adobe topped with brick, windows and doors trimmed out in wood. Jan Crawford owns the shop. She is a tall, thin woman whose posture seems slightly curved, like a cattail in a windy marsh. She speaks very softly. A brilliant smile emanates from what seems to be a private soul. High Desert Angler is the only fly shop in Santa Fe—surprising, considering the proximity of streams and wealth. But Orvis is on the way, with plans for a franchise store here. Jan isn't worried. She figures she'll bend with the wind just fine.

Her manager, Bill Orr, a former elementary schoolteacher and native of Sheridan, Wyoming, worries a little more about Orvis. "I'm concerned how it will affect the guiding part of the business. Orvis is good at getting lots of private water lined up—private fishing water on private land. We haven't been real good at that. We only have a couple sections of private land where we can take people to fish and not compete with anybody else. That's my concern."

It was closing time, so Jan locked up the shop and we sat in the showroom on folding chairs. With some coaxing, she told me her story—how she worked in the computer industry for twenty years in Minnesota, and when her husband died she asked for a transfer to the West, to a place and a state of mind she had always dreamed of. She ended up buying the fly shop in Santa Fe in 1986 from a "fellow with a trust fund who didn't need to make a living at it and couldn't make a living at it; he kept all his accounting records on bits of paper in a paper bag, never had any money for inventory, and he'd just close the shop and go fishing when he wanted to." These days, she doesn't get to fish as much as she'd like. But she's made a name for herself as a fly-casting teacher, as a booster of women in the sport, and for her conservation work. If you meet her on the water, you'll know her: She wears a very feminine straw hat with dried flowers ringing the band.

She said she began her career as a poacher. "I grew up on a Minnesota farm in very watery country, lakes all over the place, and I fished for bullheads and panfish and pike and walleyes. When I was seven, eight years old, I'd steal fish from the commercial fishermen's nets. Those fish were neat to see and good to eat. We mostly took walleyes because they were the best. My outlaw days are quite a ways behind me, though."

Her early career gives her a certain understanding for the angling outlaws of New Mexico, a state that probably has more than its share of poachers.

A fairly large element of the New Mexico culture is into outlawry relating to fish and game regulations and land use. It's not that far from the Wild West here, in some places. New Mexico has been very sparsely populated for a long time, so that kind of outlawry was probably tolerated more because there were fewer people around to resist it. It still persists. If you go out and talk to people that live on the Pecos River, you'll find that two of the top problems are littering and poaching. Machismo is associated with poaching—it's something to brag about if you take home sixteen fish. Some of it is thumbing your nose at authority. Some of the Pecos, for instance, is regulated artificials-only. But it's common to find people out there fishing with bait. They know they're not supposed to. A lot of this is tradition; the people have always had big fish fries on Friday night for their whole extended family, so they're always going to do that.

Some fishing is simply beyond the state's ability to license or regulate. Jan told us of religious records "that show that some of the first fishing that was done in America was done by the Spanish coming to the Pecos. There was Spanish culture here in the Southwest before English culture came to the East Coast. So people were fishing for trout here before Europeans were fishing for trout anywhere in the country. With baskets, mainly, I'm sure. No evidence of fly-fishing. The poachers still fish this way."

Mary Orr, Bill's wife, joined us. She's a federal biologist and has worked for the U.S. Forest Service in Colorado, Wyoming, and now New Mexico. Her specialty is charting the effect that development has on fish habitat.

She described a father and son loading garbage bins with trout out of a stream with a two-fish limit. "The biggest impact is on the small streams," she said. "I remember going fishing with Bill on a stream we knew well, with a six-fish limit—which should be enough for anyone—and we couldn't get anything. We didn't even see any fish. Then we saw a guy crawl through the bushes with a string on his back with twenty, thirty fish. And we went, 'Oh, well, we might as well go home.'" The state offers an 800 number to report poaching, but New Mexicans are hesitant to use it. The "culture of lawlessness," as Mary calls it, "crosses all ethnic lines."

She didn't mention Jan's girlhood poaching.

She'd like to see, across the country, a greater resistance to poaching and disrespect for angling regulations. "Talk about it, speak up, that's what I want people to do. If somebody comes in and brags to you about how many fish they took and you know it's way over the limit, you tell them 'here's the limit, and you're violating the rules' and explain to them why what they've done affects everybody. It's a corrupted attitude, but somehow it's been glorified or made to appear cool and acceptable. It's like notches on a gun."

I mentioned the explanation of poaching I had heard from San Diego's lake manager: "They're the 'king's fish'—a lot of poaching has as much to do with defying authority and resentment of wealth and power as it does with a desire for food or recreation."

"They're not the king's fish, they're the people's fish," she said vehemently. "The founding principles of the American game management system are totally different in Europe. If you want to go hunting or fishing in Europe, you have to either buy into some club or be the landowner. You just don't have any other opportunity otherwise because it's a different system. Here, the point is to make sure everyone will have the chance to pursue game if they want to."

↪ NEW MEXICO IS a textbook example of how nature shapes culture and then, how cultural conflict reshapes nature. As in Montana, the wealthy have a different vision of that relationship. Some of the newest

and most powerful arrivals represent the new class of high-tech entrepreneurs and their retinues.

Huge growth of wealth in the high-tech world has, as *Field & Stream*
reports, produced a breed of the ultra-wealthy that "has turned its attention to buying trophy ranches in the West." By 1998, Ted Turner had
snapped up somewhere around 1 million acres of New Mexico's most
pristine ranchland and forest, including the Vermejo Park Ranch on the
border of New Mexico and Colorado, with legendary fishing and one of
the largest elk herds in America. As *Field & Stream* reports, "any would-
be sportsman has to be prepared to pay big money to set foot there."*

Old-timers catch the fever, too. Even as Nick and I were wandering
through New Mexico, C. S. Cattle Co., the owner of one of the state's
major fishing lakes, Eagle Nest Lake (where Nick and I had fished), was
refusing to renew its lease to the state unless the state decided to buy it
for more than $10 million. This is a lake that accommodates more than
10 percent of the trout-fishing in New Mexico.

At the same time, the range of native trout is shrinking. In New Mexico, Rio Grande cutthroats—northern New Mexico's only surviving native trout—are especially endangered by cattle grazing. Today, the trout
inhabit less than 5 to 10 percent of their original range. They're increasingly isolated in small populations in high-altitude streams and lakes.
"This is due in part to irrigation and the building of roads, which increase sediment in the streams," said Mary Orr. "We get around thirteen
inches of rain a year up here, but we can get ten inches at once—and
that causes serious erosion when it runs off. If you have all your vegetation eaten down, there's nothing to stop it. High siltation clogs the in-
terspaces in the gravel and suffocates eggs and fry. Even in adult fish,
high siltation interferes with gill action, by extracting oxygen out of the
water."

Unmanaged grazing cattle trample riparian areas—river banks—making the streams wider, warmer, and siltier. She described the factions on
the cattle issue: old-time ranchers who insist on grazing their cattle in
the same way they have for generations, with no regard for the condition
of the waters; "environmentalists who come along and say, 'We want all
cows off the national forest land, no matter what'; and then the people

* *Field & Stream* also reports: "What makes Turner's ownership of Vermejo particularly galling
to New Mexicans is that both the state and federal governments dropped the ball on a chance
to buy it in the early 1970s for the comparatively paltry sum of $26 million. Just a few years
later, the federal government gave former owner Pennzoil Corporation a tax break of more
than $20 million in exchange for donating 100,000 acres—just 20 percent of the original
ranch—to the Forest Service." Ben Neary, "Another Paradise Lost?" *Field & Stream,* October
1998, p. 42.

in the middle who say, 'We just want good management'—but when you say good management, everyone has a different opinion of what that is."

Indeed. One organization, the Forest Guardians, is perhaps "New Mexico's most pugnacious and effective environmental group," as the *Christian Science Monitor* calls it. The organization's leader, Sam Hitt, is passionate and poetic about this region of the country: "You can't believe what an artery of life the Rio Grande was at the turn of the century . . . the sturgeon, this eight-foot-long fish, used to swim (some 1,500 miles) up from the Gulf of Mexico all the way to Espanola. We even had a freshwater eel that came up all the way from the Gulf. Now, basically because of overgrazing, levees, and pollution, the Rio Grande is dying." Through a series of court cases, the Forest Guardians has stopped livestock grazing in riparian areas; forced the Environmental Protection Agency and the state to set water quality standards for rivers; and halted all logging in eleven national forests for eight months as of this writing. It also leased grazing land from the government to keep livestock away from streams. The U.S. Bureau of Land Management has agreed to bar cattle from about forty miles of streams in northern New Mexico, settling a 1996 lawsuit by Forest Guardians.

All of this sent many cattle ranchers in New Mexico into apoplexy. Hitt has been vilified, physically threatened, and hanged in effigy. But he's as stubborn as those sturgeon used to be, saying, "We want a new Magna Carta for water in the West that protects endangered species and ecosystems." Hitt is currently suing the federal government and six states over water compacts, some written as far back as the 1920s, before environmental laws. "We are facing the consequences of those decisions, because there is little water left for the rivers. Urban run-off, agricultural run-off, grazing damage, and toxic metals have befouled and changed the rivers."

Some environmentalists want as much of the West's open spaces and its wildlife off limits as possible—including severe limitations on fishing. "What does it mean to the economy of the world if a handful of ranchers belly up and blow away? Absolutely nothing," Jim Cooper, a retired fisheries expert with the U.S. Forest Service in New Mexico, told the *Los Angeles Times.* "On the other hand, what does it say about us as human beings if we have to sacrifice the living things around us just so we can live a certain way?" What he and many other environmentalists want is a network of wilderness reserves, from Canada to Mexico, absent most human activity, and to return as much as possible to the biodiversity of the continent before the arrival of Columbus. But James Brown, a University of New Mexico biologist, points out: "For thousands of years before Europeans got here with their cows and sheep, there were vast herds of grazing animals and people manipulating the landscape."

And far more habitat "has been destroyed to provide water for cities, subdivisions and irrigated agriculture than by even the heaviest grazing pressure." He says that keeping the West's ranching culture intact is the most serious challenge the West faces; at least a ranch is, by definition, a wide-open space, with no allowance for subdivisions and freeways.

Not long ago, I ran across this quotation in an issue of *BioScience*, a journal published by the American Institute of Biological Sciences:

> Stressed ecosystems are characterized by a "distress syndrome" . . . that is indicated not only by reduced biodiversity and altered primary and secondary productivity but also by increased disease prevalence, reduced efficiency of nutrient cycling, increased dominance of exotic species, and increased dominance by smaller, shorter-lived opportunistic species.

Apply this statement to the ecosystems and human cultures of New Mexico and the West, and you've got a pretty good idea of the difficulties Orr, and others, face. It's enough to make a person just want to forget about all this for a while—and go fishing. Which, after saying goodbye to the good folks at High Desert Angler, is what Nick and I headed out to do.

On the way, we met a river witch.

River Witching

We drove north, to where the land expands into high plains between mountain ranges.

The light was fading, and I found myself feeling melancholy. Since that summer I made adobes with Nick, New Mexico has represented something dependable to me. Something about the dust and waters of this part of the country feels older—different. A park ranger in northern Arizona once told me, "Nowhere on earth is so much of the past so close to the surface." That goes for New Mexico, too. We urbanites and suburbanites are drawn to fishing because it puts us in such places, where fast current means slow time.

Like so many people who find themselves living and working in Southern California—or for that matter anyplace in America that looks like Southern California (and doesn't most of it these days?)—I have fantasized for years about moving somewhere with real trees, and front porches and . . . well, maybe it doesn't exist. But I still wonder: What am I attached to in Southern California, other than good friends, good work, and the weather? Certainly it's not most of the man-made environment, a landscape sliced and diced beyond natural recognition. When I drive east into San Diego County's mountains, through Mesa Grande and the little town of Julian, I know that these places have entered my heart. They have a distinct mystery. But then always, always, a voice in me says: Most of this will soon be stuccoed over and gone—so don't get too attached.

Fishing transports us to the earliest meaning of a sense of place. Some places "have an attraction which gives us a certain indefinable sense of wellbeing and which we want to return to, time and again," as writer John Brinckerhoff Jackson puts it. "So that original notion of ritual, of repeated celebration or reverence, is still inherent in the phrase. It is not a temporary response, for it persists and brings us back, reminding of previous visits."*

When I fish with Nick every year or so, I feel like a poacher sneaking into his domain, tapping into his sense of place.

As long as it lasts.

Heading north on Highway 84, we passed the Cities of Gold Casino, glowing in the dusk, all spangled lights and fake adobe.

"The name of that pueblo is Pojoaque," said Nick. "When I was a kid the Mafia ran the numbers racket and the government ran the jails. Today, the government runs the numbers racket and the jails are turned over to private industry." He laughed. "I'm not sure exactly what kind of progress that is."

Nick was quiet for a while.

"You know, I used to poach," he said. "Isn't there a statute of limitations on this? We're talking '70s now. But I did, I poached when we had no money and there was no meat."

One deer a year.

"There were some years I took none, but it was as illegal then as it is now. It was something that you did; you went out in the evening and waited for them to come up to the alfalfa along the posque—the woods."

We approached the lights of a little town, and passed it into the dark.

"Moonrise over Hernandez."

Pardon me?

"The famous Ansel Adams photograph." I recalled it. A magical image: old crosses glowing in moonlight, a few adobe buildings, and the vast desert under a nearly full moon. Now all you can see is lights and trailers and mobile homes, no graveyard in sight, but a full moon was drifting along behind us. The trout on the San Juan would be feeding tonight.

↪ WE CROSSED THE BORDER into Colorado and entered the trendy town of Durango, where we stopped at Arby's. The young Indian fry-cooks were playing a recording of a war dance in the back. We ate and found a motel. In the morning, we drove ten miles west of Durango to the crossroads village of Hesperus and waited for Corey Sue Hutchinson at the Hesperus One-Stop convenience store. The One-Stop was faux western

---

* John Brinckerhoff Jackson, *A Sense of Place, a Sense of Time* (New Haven, Conn.: Yale University Press, 1994).

in design, with a false front and pine porch. We fed popcorn to a friendly pit bull while we sat on the bench. Nick noticed that the bench was chained to the store and said, "See? It's even come here." A sign in the window said, "This property is under video surveillance. Daylight cameras, all activity is being recorded."

Corey arrived at the One-Stop Market in a spray of gravel. She was driving her F-150 Ford pickup, with its side panel advertising her company: Aqua-Hab Aquatic Systems.

She bounded out to meet me with a hard, strong handshake. "Call me Corey Sue."

At thirty-eight, she's tan and hard-muscled, her arms scarred from physical labor. On this day, her hair was woven into a long braid. She wore designer sunglasses, earrings, jeans, work boots, and a stylish cotton ball cap with the message "No B.S." stitched into it.

She was, as Nick said later, "a credible witness," which was his way of saying that she was a fine-looking woman. We followed her to the La Plata River, which she plans to move.

When Corey Sue was a sophomore at Northern Michigan University, she decided to become a marine biologist, packed a bag of clothes, jumped on her bicycle, and with only four hundred dollars in her pocket, rode some two thousand miles to Oregon State University— where she learned she was prone to violent seasickness. She shifted to watershed management. In 1989, she accepted a job as a biologist in southern Colorado's San Juan National Forest.

"I wanted to make a difference, to protect the environment," she said. But she grew impatient with government's habit of "having meetings to plan meetings, and accomplishing little." So in 1994, she gave up her plum job and generous pension and set out to join the growing number of private river restorers in the West.

Over the past century, ranchers and developers have dramatically altered and damaged rivers like the La Plata, removing the thick vegetation, allowing cattle to collapse the banks with their hooves, encouraging erosion. One rancher even bulldozed this stretch of the La Plata into a straight line, making it more ditch than river.

Now some of the newcomers have become riverkeepers. The family that bought this land, through which the La Plata runs, hired Corey Sue to return it to a natural, winding pattern.

As she waded through the cheat grass and ducked under the willows that line the bank, swinging a walking stick made of a broomstick and bike handlebar grip, she talked of the river as if it were a person. She likes rivers more than she does most people. Rivers are easier to get attached to.

"I'm a vagrant, I've moved all across the country," she said. "Oregon was my home before this. My parents split up and they're in different parts of the country so there's no home town. Home is where I am." She's married to a man who builds adobe houses.

"Real adobe?" asked Nick.

"Real adobe," she said.

We passed a mound of boulders, ranging from four to eight feet long. She buys her stone from a private landowner near Durango. "The smaller ones I'm going to be using in the banks, on top of the logs that will stabilize the soil. The bigger ones will go in the river." The rocks cost her about thirty-five dollars each, including transporting costs. She's brought in four hundred boulders for this piece of water.

How interested in fishing are the people that hire you? I asked. Do they want you to create a stretch that's going to hold fish?

"That's usually the objective."

Is it unlikely that these rivers would be reclaimed if there wasn't that interest in fishing?

"True. I have done some bank stabilization and that kind of thing where it's eating away their property and it has nothing to do with fish. But most of the people who hire me want healthy fish habitat."

For the next hour or so, we walked the streamside through the timothy and smooth bromegrass, past a cluster of narrow-leaf cottonwoods and what she called coyote willow. She explained how she pores over old photographs, especially aerial photos, of the way the river once was—and then hypothesizes what the river would have been like by now, if left to its own devices.

Every detail counts. She gathers information on gradients, the steepness of slopes; she graphs the flood flow recurrence interval to estimate the size of "the hundred-year flood" that could occur tomorrow or a century from now. "This stream right now is flowing at about twenty cubic feet per second; the most common flood flow would be 500 cfs, which would fill this flood plain bank to bank. But the hundred-year event would be about 2,000 cfs."

Corey Sue's work is part science, part art—she calls it "hydrologic voodoo." She combines her education in water flow with her intuition about a river; therein lies the art. "I have a pretty good background, but I operate more off my gut feeling."

So you're a river witch? I said.

She laughed.

After learning all she can about the river's past, and projecting as far as she can into the river's future, she goes to work, sometimes with a small crew of men, but usually alone.

COREY SUE HUTCHINSON

She builds grade-control structures, creates vortex weirs, stabilizes banks with native bank protection of cottonwood logs, root wads, and willow and rolls of excelsior matting—a biodegradable cloth to keep soil and seed in place until the plants sprout—over the dirt on top of the bank to hold it down. She hauls in boulders to reduce erosion. She operates the heavy equipment herself. "Clients seem to get a kick out of that, a little gal in the big D-9 bulldozer who actually knows what she's doing."

Essentially, she speeds up geological time, accomplishing in a few weeks what nature might take a century or more to do. Accelerating the process—if only by fifty years—can potentially prevent the permanent loss of some species of a watershed in the meantime.

Her understanding of the river's desire is sometimes eerie. After she began the La Plata project, the river flooded. "To my surprise, a new channel cut right where I was planning to put one. This stream is trying to get back to where it wanted to be. It's already starting to cut into the bank. That's encouraging, when it happens. I had drawn the design for a channel and then we had a big spring flow and it's like, 'Whoa—I don't have to move that water!'"

That must be a weird feeling, I said, to be able to know the river well enough to know what it wants.

She nodded, leaned over to see where the bank was being cut. "But

humility is a requirement for this job." A couple years ago, the Animas—
El Rio De Los Animas Perdidas, "the river of lost souls"—a river she
worked hard to save from dumped cars and collapsed banks, shifted on
its own and washed out everything she had done. "Sometimes Mother
Nature has other ideas."

She's done fifty-three river projects like this in four years.

For the mile-long stretch of the La Plata she's reviving here, she'll be
paid close to sixty-five thousand dollars. Ninety percent of that will go
for machinery and material.

No doubt about it, she's making a difference—at least in the short
run. Restoration lowers the washing of sediment into the river, improves
water quality, creates habitat for migratory birds and a stable spawning
area, nursery, and good living conditions for trout—and, not incidentally,
reduces land loss for riverfront property owners. "We're all working in a
relative microcosm of geologic time. A decade is a very narrow window.
To get high and mighty about what we do because it lasts a few
decades—well, it's all still temporary."

Sometimes, in order to return a stream to a more natural state, she
must intentionally kill the fish in it. "When I worked for the Forest Service, I worked on a project similar to this one. We killed the brook trout
that had taken over the stream, improved the habitat, and then stocked
it with a native Colorado River cutthroat."

She won't plant native fish in the La Plata, not only because the property owner hasn't commissioned it, but because Colorado River cutthroat—remnants of the native population that graced these mountains
eons ago and still live in a small number of isolated, high forest
drainages—would not survive long here. Without natural barriers against
browns, rainbows and other non-native fish, the more delicate cutthroat
would be decimated quickly. "That's the tragedy of losing a species like
the Colorado River cutthroat. The rivers are all connected; it's almost
impossible to get them back."*

---

* John Gierach points out that, in Colorado, many of the highest lakes, which are now populated with cutthroat, were fishless when European settlers first arrived. The fish there were
planted later by bucket-hauling private clubs or Johnny Appleseeds on horseback. The current
cutthroat populations in Colorado are mostly mixtures of Yellowstone cutthroats, native to the
region but not the state, and other strains. The cutthroat-rainbow hybrid—the cuttbow—is
widespread. But here and there native Colorado River cutthroats can still be found. Then
there's the greenback cutthroat, which, Gierach writes, was thought to be extinct by the late
1930s, until a legendary professor at Colorado State University found a small, pure-strain population in high headwaters. The greenbacks have now been introduced into a few lakes,
streams, and beaver ponds in and near Rocky Mountain National Park and can be fished for on
a strictly catch-and-release basis, and "presumably, few people now living know what a greenback tastes like." *In Praise of Wild Trout*, Nick Lyons, ed. (New York: The Lyons Press, 1998),
pp. 35–43.

She does suggest that her clients plant more recent species of what she calls "generic" cutthroat, "a kind of homogenized strain, but at least they're similar to the originals."

And she also recommends to the landowners that they keep the beavers, because they build dams and create ponds and wetlands where fish and other wildlife flourish.

After completing a project, she returns often to monitor it. After a high flood, especially, she'll go out and take photographs, to "see how nature works on what I did," to see if nature approves. Sometimes she even fishes the streams she saves. "But I get all tangled up. I'm not that good a fisherman. The fishing months are a very busy time for my business, and I have a husband and a house and we have our property and we ski in the wintertime. And I just got a Harley."

She does, however, dress up as a fish from time to time.

"We had a parade in my town two years ago and I have a big trailer we used for a float; I made a mountain stream on the trailer. So, I was a fish and I had three troutettes—women friends of mine—and we danced. We won second place. I made these big, elaborate, foam costumes with sequins and big eyes, they looked great. Since then, I've worn the troutette costume a few times."

She was already pushing ahead through the grass, heading back to her pickup.

⌐ ON THE WAY to the San Juan, Nick and I detoured back through Durango and stopped to see Nancy and Jerry Freeman, who operate a guide business on the San Juan called Anasazi Angler. I had seen their web page and had written them, and they were eager to talk about the big change in their lives. Nancy and Jerry, like Corey Sue, had rejected established careers in favor of a new one—and had found their bliss.

Jerry ushered us into his modest suburban house and we sat down at his dining room table. Next to it was the Freeman fly-tying table, with a row of vials filled with dead bugs that Jerry had pumped from the stomachs of trout. "People will always ask the wrong person what to catch fish on," he said. "I say, 'Ask the trout.' Don't ask other fishermen, ask the trout."

For twenty years, Jerry was a pilot—mostly of corporate jets, and then the company sold its planes. "I asked myself the question, 'What would I do if I knew I couldn't fail?' I'd fish," he said. At forty-nine, he's fit, tan, bearded and balding, with an infectious laugh. He's clearly a happy man. "I started looking around and my hobby was fly-fishing. Nancy's too.

Here's the San Juan, it's a year-round tail water, I saw other people making a living at this and I thought I certainly could."

That was nine years ago. Nancy, with a degree in accounting, worked
a nine-to-five job for years, but this year she's devoting all her energy to
Anasazi Angler. "I'd always wanted to find a business we could do together, and it's either now or never for us," she said.

They met in Durango in 1978. Nancy was born and raised in Lawrence, Kansas; Jerry grew up in Bastrop, Louisiana.

His father worked at a paper mill; when he began at the mill, most
work was done by hand—by the time he retired, he was in charge of the
mill's computerized automation. "He made paper for forty-three years.
At the same mill," said Jerry.

I asked Jerry if he grew up fishing. He smiled, and launched into the
story of Lucky 13.

> I remember the very first fish I ever caught. It was one of those
> vivid type of memories. All your senses are involved, what things
> felt like, how they smelled, sounds. It was on a swamp lake. I had a
> cane pole and I remember it being heavy. I mostly put worms on
> the hook and the plastic was red and white and my dad would
> throw it out for me and then hand me the pole. I lost a lot of fish.
> Finally, I got one and I drug him up fifty feet on the bank and he
> was flopping around in the dirt and I remember running and grab-
> bing him so he wouldn't get away. I picked him up and his spines
> were sharp and he was covered with dirt. It was slimy, it had that
> fish smell, from living in the mud. It was perfect.
>
> When I was a kid, I always wanted to bass-fish. But my dad was
> a bait fisherman. He would say, "Son, fish don't want to eat plastic
> and wood. They want bait, they want food." Good concept. He was
> a bait man and just didn't believe in plastic and wood. One time
> when I was eight or nine, we were out fishing for bluegill and cat-
> fish, and my hook got snagged on something on the bottom of the
> lake; I pulled up this old steel bass reel. My dad said, "That's just
> junk, throw that thing back!" I said, "No way!" I rarely would op-
> pose anything my dad told me to do, but this time I did. "No, I'm
> keeping this!" I thought I'd hit a gold mine; my heart was pounding
> the rest of the day.
>
> I took this reel home and took it apart and cleaned it up, put it
> back together, and it still worked. It was stainless steel. I put some
> line on it and I went down to Western Auto and I paid three dollars
> for the cheapest rod they had, and soon I was out in the backyard

throwing that thing. I had every subscription to *Field & Stream* and *Outdoor Life*—all those things that create all those dreams, even the ads spurred something in you. I definitely had dreams. I told my dad after I got pretty good throwing that thing, give me a lure, I'm ready for a lure. I showed him how well I could cast and he was impressed.

So we went up to the gas-station bait store and they had these rows and rows of beautiful lures in packages. He was going to buy me one—just one—and I could pick it out. I picked out a Heddon River-Runt. It looked like a fish, had scales on the side. He said, "No, you're not having an underwater lure. You'll make one cast out there and lose it first time." He said I could get a top water lure. So I got a Lucky 13, a big, old-fashioned wooden plug. I took it home. I slept with it.

I just couldn't wait. A friend of ours was going bass-fishing and he said he'd take me out. I went out there and the first cast, I can see it today, I don't even have to close my eyes to see it, I can see it zinging down the cypress trees. It landed in a splash, the bass actually saw it in the air and was under it and grabbed it before it hit the water. My first cast!

It pulled harder than anything I had ever known.

When I finally went fishing with my dad again, he hated having that rod and reel of mine in the boat; he was against anything having to do with lure fishing. Nothing was biting, we were just sitting there, it was hot and humid. I said, "Hey, Daddy, can I make a few casts with this?" He grumbled and said, "I guess so." I went back to cast and I stuck the Lucky 13 on the top of his head. Three treble hooks, brand new, razor-sharp things, stuck in his head. I got these needle-nose pliers and I started pulling these things out and every hook was hooked into his head. Right then I realized I had to go to a lighter tackle.

Afterward, he didn't yell, he just said, "Put that rod down!" But I already knew bass-fishing was over.

Not too long after that, he bought me a flyrod. A friend of his told him he should buy one. So he bought the whole family flyrods, my brother, my mom, me. I still have the fly reel that was on that rod.

So that's how I came to fly-fishing.

I asked him if he ever went fly-fishing with his dad. No, he said, his father never did learn to use a flyrod—he used the flyrod for bait-fishing, with monofilament line—and Jerry never got a chance to take him. He died in 1987, at the age of seventy, still preferring bait-fishing.

The afternoon went on, and Jerry regaled us with more stories and a few theories—the most interesting being something he calls "rivertime."

I noticed that his hands were heavily callused, darkly stained, and cracked. The calluses, he explained, were from rowing his clients; the dark stain was from using a fishnet with an aluminum handle; the aluminum oxide rubs off. "You get some tremendous medical consultation on the river, because you guide doctors. This surgeon saw a big crack on one of my fingers and he told me to Super Glue it. He said he uses Super Glue in surgery. The glue kills all those little nerve endings so the pain stops instantly." This same surgeon is one of Jerry's classic Type A clients, one of the ones that Jerry introduced to "rivertime."

> Jack leads the pack as far as Type A, so he comes out here and I fish for a week with him and I'll do whatever he wants. He says, "Jerry, I know you're taking the day off before I get there and you'll take the day off after I leave." I'll be out there saying, "Jack, I can't see the fly anymore, it's dark." And he says, "One more! One more!" It's like this for several days and finally I get him into what I refer to as rivertime. To get to rivertime, you first must reach a certain state of fatigue. The last time I had Jack, he was getting grumpy and I said, "Jack, it's taking me too long to get you on rivertime, what's going on?" He said, "Oh, I've gotta go back to the real world." I said, "What do you mean?" He said, "I've gotta go back to work, the real world, this is my last day." I said, "No, you're leaving the real world." He looked at me and said, "You've got a point."
>
> On his last day, he settled down completely. See, for some of my clients, I act as a kind of therapist. I give them the understanding of rivertime. One person I had, he was smashing trout and didn't even enjoy playing the fish. "That one's only sixteen inches, get him off and let's get another one." So I told him, I said, "Do you know what the real purpose of fly-fishing is?" He said, "To catch fish." And I said, "No, that's the most misunderstood part of the whole thing. The whole point is the alpha- and theta-wave production in your brain." He was a doctor, so he got that.
>
> We had lunch. It was shady on the river and after a while he said, "You're right about those alpha- and theta-waves. I think I'm just going to sit here and take a nap." He just lay down in the shade and it was 100 percent theta-wave production for about an hour and then he got up and he was just a different guy, refreshed.

Rivertime is the zen of fly-fishing, though you could be a bait fisherman and still achieve it. The mechanism that creates rivertime is one-point concentration. Especially if you're nymph-fishing, where you're watching the indicator on your line, or if you're watching a dry fly. It's a repetitive behavior. You're casting and presenting the fly over and over and over, watching it. After a while the physical part becomes mechanical; it's not the product of conscious thought. A thousand times, the same motion. Your mind empties of other things; that single point of concentration doesn't let you think about anything else. It diverts all your thoughts to this one single point, for hours. You get out in the middle of the river and do this repetitive behavior and watch a fly or strike indicator for hours, and suddenly, without knowing it, you're on alpha wave time, rivertime.

I've run in marathons, and I know the runner's high, but this is different. Rivertime is the combination of single-mindedness and being immersed in nature. You could be walking the shore, studying the insect life to understand what the trout are eating, and even that repetitive action can draw you into rivertime. It's just another way in. Every time you turn a stone over, you're deeper into it.

Have you ever heard of doodle socking? Jerry asked. Is that like noodling? I asked in return.

Yep. In the South, if you get a chance, you need to talk to a doodle socker. You won't believe it when you run into a real hard-core doodle socker. If you're down in the South, I'll tell you how you can recognize one of them without them saying a word. From his elbows down, he's filled with scars and puncture marks, scars all over his hands. Catfish get in hollow logs and muskrat holes, and doodle sockers actually go down and wade out and reach into these hollow logs and grab these catfish.

But I'm talking here about trout doodle sockers. They exist, too. I once had a client, he was an Indian, and I said, "What happened to your arms? Did you get attacked by a bobcat?" He was a doodle socker. Those people have had to arrive at something that I don't understand. This guy could reach down into the river and pick up the trout. He'd never been to the San Juan before but he understood something about these fish that I didn't perceive. He'd reach down and in less than a minute, he'd pick the fish up out of the water! I looked at that and I said, "Give me that flyrod, I'll hold it. Show me that." He said, "Here's what you do." He would reach down and pick another one up. He tried to teach me. "Put your hand down here, next to the fish, and just leave it there for a while and he'll get used to it and he'll come up a little closer. Try with the tips of your fingers to touch his belly. Once you touch his belly you've got him." I tried it until my hand was numb—forty-three-degree water, I just couldn't understand it. Couldn't do it. It was one of those ways of being in rivertime, but one that goes beyond my understanding, something you only learn or experience from direct knowledge.

That sounded more like "guddling," what the Indians taught the first European settlers.

Well, whatever you call it, it's direct and immediate. That's one of the basic things people really want, to directly experience being alive. But life is getting to be like watching a ballgame; you're not really playing ball. Your life's going by and you're just watching these games. Direct experience has been replaced by electronics. You almost believe it's real. You finish the day thinking you did a lot of stuff and really you did nothing. You're sitting in front of a screen or punching buttons, but as far as life, you didn't directly experience anything. What's the saying about most men living lives of quiet desperation, about being in the arena with the dust and dirt? That's the reason I became a fishing guide. Life was becoming too easy for me, too detached. The boss came by one day and said, "I'm going to give you a raise. How much money do you want?" Too easy. But it was a scary move for me, moving from flying to fishing, from being a professional pilot where the money was good.

Some guy asked me once, "What do you think is the number-one quality of a guide?" I told him, "Adaptation to poverty." Material things just fall where they may. Your rewards are the experiences in your life, more than building a bank account. The lifestyle is the reward. When I decided to change careers, one of my rules was never pursue anything that you couldn't pursue with passion. Flying was like that, now fishing is. The second rule was Buckminster Fuller's. He had this theory that money flowed around the world from place to place, like blood in arteries, so the closer you get to this higher flow the easier it is to make money.

That's why Jerry located his business near the San Juan: high traffic, high yield, and more clients who are doctors and lawyers than you could

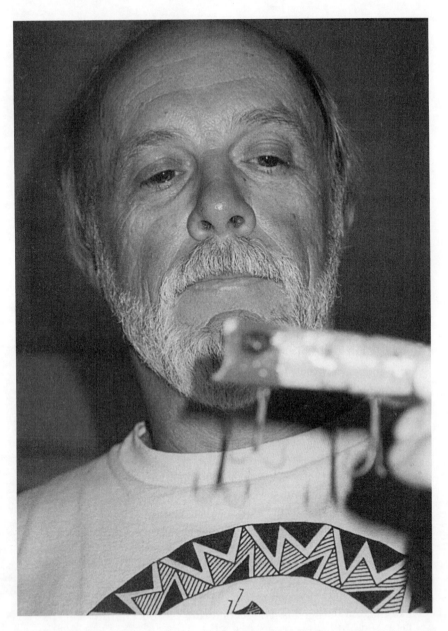

JERRY FREEMAN AND LUCKY 13

shake a six-weight at. I asked him which was harder, being a commercial pilot or being a fishing guide. He paused and thought—the longest break from talking he had taken since we sat down. He stared straight ahead.

> I think it would be harder to become a guide and remain a guide. If you're a pilot, that's a definite career with money incentives. With being a guide, it's something that's hard physical work, the days are long. Even though the people are enjoyable, it's a high demand on your services. You really learn, you understand what giving is all about. There's not really a monetary incentive. It comes down to, "Do you like to live like this?" Do you want to get up before daylight, come in after dark most days? That's a long day. But I think I'm wealthy now because of what I have and the experiences. That's living life more directly. There's no security, the river could go dry. Catastrophic things beyond my control could happen, but that's true, too, in the corporate world. For me, the hardest part is when that alarm goes off and it's still dark. Getting up before light, there's something wrong with that. But what happens is, I'm driving to work drinking coffee and eating a doughnut, to pick up my clients—and suddenly I realize I'm observing the morning star. The natural world is waking up, and you're waking up with it.

The other elemental question a prospective guide should ask is, "Do I like people?" and Jerry and Nancy figure they do. One customer had cancer. He was dying, and his family asked him what he wanted to do and he said he wanted to go fishing one more time—just one more piece of rivertime. The family called Jerry.

"We said we'd comp the trip," said Jerry. "He died the day before he was coming. You never know."

I said it was getting time for Nick and me to go, and we stood up, but before we knew it, we were swept up in one last Jerry Freeman story—the one about the opposite of rivertime.

> One day I showed up to pick up this client, rich guy from Chicago, and he says, "See that woman over there?" And I said, "Yes, sir." He goes, "That's my wife. The only reason I've hired you is because I don't want to hear her whine. I want her to enjoy this sport so I can go fishing more." So he goes out and the fish were really biting and he's hammering these fish almost every two or three casts. She's sitting in the back reading a book. He says, "Honey, get that rod, the fish are biting and I want you fishing." She says, "No, I just want to finish reading this chapter." I said, "Let me catch you one."

I'm trying to mediate between the two, trying not to have him ruin the thing. I said, "First I'll cast, and then you can bring the fish in." She said, "But then it's your catch." And I said, "Well, there's two parts of the game. First thing is what are you going to do to get the fish on, and the second part is what are you going to do after that? You'll learn the second part of the game first."

So I'm fishing and I hook a big fish. I handed her the rod and she plays the fish, lands it, a big twenty-inch fish. They take pictures of it, I put the fish back in the water. She lays her expensive rod down, and her husband yells at her, "Pick up that rod! Dammit, I want you fishing; people fish all their lives for a fish like that. I want you fishing now!" I said to her, "Here, let me hook you another one." She said, "No, he's not going to be happy if I'm not fishing—so let me cast."

So she picks up the rod and on her first cast hooks him right in the tongue, right in the tip of his tongue, he's wagging it at her. And he's really upset and he throws his own really expensive rod down on the bottom of the boat and he's yelling at her, his mouth is bleeding. And so he's got this hook hanging out of his mouth, his lips are red with blood and he's still yelling at her. I can give him first aid but you have to ask permission if they're conscious and I'm saying, "Would you like me to pull that hook out of your tongue?" He's making these noises and I say, "I'll take that as a yes." I'm thinking the usual hook method with the leader and the loop wouldn't work because it's too flexible so I get a napkin out of the lunch kit and grab his tongue and I'm thinking, "I've never had ahold of a guy's tongue in my life" and I got these needle-nosed pliers and I just pulled it out like it was a trout. I had to resist saying, "Did that hurt?"

Jerry went over to his fly-tying desk and whipped us up some special worm flies—his own design, a variation on the classic San Juan worm, which he calls the Anasazi worm. He loaded them into a medicine container and gave them to us, no charge, and spent a while telling us how to fish the river. Just before we left, he opened a small drawer in the fly-tying desk and carefully took out a rectangular box with the Heddon logo on it. It was brown with age. He opened it and took out a chewed-up red and white wooden bass plug. He held it up for us to see.

"My Lucky 13," he said, with a smile as big as the western sky. "See? Still in the original box."

⌐ AND SO, THAT NIGHT, we finally reached the river of heaven—the San Juan River, in the drier lands of northwestern New Mexico. We stayed at

Abe's Motel & Fly Shop, a simple compound of cinder block and frame. Abe, who is a plasterer, had created swirling designs of trout swimming across the front of the whole fly shop, which had bars on the windows. This is an extraordinary piece of tail water, famous worldwide for the size and quantity of rainbows and browns—as well as cutthroat and cuttbows.

I called my wife from the hotel and said, "This is the river all good fly-fishermen go to when they die."

"It must smell pretty bad," she said.

But it's true. In the quality water below Navajo Dam, surveys show over ninety thousand trout averaging seventeen to twenty inches. The dam provides a constant flow of water at a perfect forty-two to forty-three degrees. Because of the extraordinary biomass, the abundant hatches of midges and mayflies, trout here grow as much as a half inch a month, until they reach sixteen inches and then they begin to add more girth than length.

One can wade this river and see large fish splayed out ahead by the dozens. The New Mexico Game and Fish Department rule of the river is: no "intentional shuffling," no kicking up the bottom with your boots to unleash aquatic food, which draws the trout to you. Some will even follow you, swim between your legs—even bump the back of your legs with their nose—in hopes of food. (This rule is enforced mainly through the expressed wrath of other anglers.) Jerry Freeman's advice was to take advantage of the trout's lack of fear:

> San Juan trout have become desensitized to a close approach, so use this to your advantage. Position yourself with the rising fish quartering downstream. Successful dry-fly-fishing techniques on the San Juan often require a downstream or across and downstream presentation instead of the normal upstream. Determine whether your fly can be best seen with the light coming from behind you or if fishing into the glare with the fly silhouetted offers the best view. *Get close.* Approach the rising trout carefully and stealthily. Cast the fly above and across the feeding lane and with an upstream lift of the rod, skate the fly into a position about two feet above the trout and *between his eyes.* Drop your rod tip and let the fly drift *drag free.* Give the trout time to close his mouth on the fly or porpoise down before tightening the line.

For the next three days, we fished this river. As with many tail-water fisheries, it's not the prettiest river on earth. The dry hills and bluffs above are spotted with short New Mexico junipers and bear grass and grayish-green sage and clumps of chamisa bushes, with the beginning of a yellow bloom that signals the end of summer. High sunflowers turn to the sun. The bank is lined with willow thickets laced with game trails; deer emerge from the willows in the evening.

The river alternates between deep holes (the most productive one is called the Texas Hole), riffles and rapids, and shallow flats—particularly the Kiddy Pool (because it's easy to get to and fish), and Beaver Flats, which stretch for hundreds of yards, where the fish are the most visible.

I spent hours the first day studying the trout behavior. When the trout took food, I could see white flash from the inside of their mouths. They were territorial, positioning themselves hierarchically in the feeding zone. The dominant fish held the prime spots at the head of the pool or in the lower current where the water slowed and curved in on itself, and where the food—mainly little curled worms mixed in drifting moss—funneled into a narrower, slower range. The other fish were required to expend a good deal more energy holding themselves in the harder flow in the middle of the pool. If a smaller or less aggressive fish moved into another's zone, the dominant fish would attack it—almost savagely—and chase it away.

Angler behavior was similar. The river was crowded. The fishermen waded the shallow shore at the head of the Texas Hole, jockeying for the best positions. Nick was a politely dominant fisherman; early in the morning he positioned himself in the middle of the river, in the shallow current right before it rushes into the deepest part of the Texas Hole, and stayed there most of the day, casting to the side and then drifting his nymph downstream.

He hauled in one trout after another. Anglers would ease up beside him, but when he held his position they backed away.

Downstream a bit, some of the fishermen defined their own zones by casting in an arc that marked their territorial border.

The fish were plentiful, but picky. Jerry Freeman had served us well, stocking us up with his Anasazi worms—made of a little strip of dyed shammy—which the trout much preferred to the traditional San Juan worm pattern, a hook wound with chenille.

Because the fish are so visible, they begin to take on a personality—in the angler's mind, at least. At one point, a lunker trout remained a few feet from me as I walked. I would take a step, it would move an equal distance, but no more. Though I presented cast after cast to it, the trout would take no fly.

After a while, I was standing in water up to my thighs and tying on another Anasazi worm. I stumbled in the current and I dropped the fly. This one was my last Anasazi. "Damn." I watched it sink and disappear.

I was putting on another fly and I looked down to see that the fish had moved in close, inches from my feet. It was hovering just above the muck, munching on the worm fly. As it chewed, I could see the end of the rawhide moving outside of its mouth. The trout seemed to be contemplating the taste. Its eyes wobbled and it chewed some more and pretty soon swallowed my last Anasazi.

﹏ I WANTED THIS trip to last forever. Good friend with a fast net. Good, slate-green water, clear with fingers of moss. Finally, rivertime. A gaggle of Canada geese flew over. The fisherman next to me looked up and counted thirty-one. For an hour, I fished next to a fat, focused beaver. It was hauling aquatic plants and stashing them somewhere under a brambled overhang. It seemed unafraid. I waded within fifteen feet of it. Nick told me later that he had been wading close to the shoreline, in ankle-deep water, and suddenly plunged to above his waist. He did that two or three times and realized he was walking on top of submerged beaver dams.

During one of our days on the river, we counted seven driftboats out on the water. A blonde woman who seemed to be in her thirties was out there having a wonderful time with her male guide, who was patiently teaching her, and smiling a lot. We saw Jerry Freeman in one of the boats, rowing hard and grinning. He waved at us, and later gave us some extra Anasazi worms. I ran into Jan Crawford of High Desert Angler fishing the flats, with her straw hat decorated with dried flowers. I half expected to see Corey Sue Hutchinson walking along swinging her walking stick, studying the native bank protection.

On our last afternoon a big thunderstorm came up, bringing sudden sideways rain and close flashes of lightning. Most of the anglers ran for their trucks but a few stayed out in the current, with the crack of doom right above them. Nick stayed out at his spot at the head of the Texas Hole in the driving rain and so did I, following him like a fool.

"If it's going to hit anything it's going to be those bluffs," said Nick.

"Graphite conducts electricity," I said.

"I have a cork handle."

So did I, so I stuck around. We stood there, drenched and freezing, hoping for one more bite.

After the rain ended, I fished the flats for hours while Nick took the deeper water. A couple dozen anglers were out on the flats, evenly spaced. Somehow they seemed as natural as the willows. Jan was out there again, in a quiet cocoon. I watched her and realized what she reminded me of, with her tall, thin, curved-over posture. A tall bird, a

standing heron, picking up each leg slowly and putting it down, watching the water, ready to spear a trout. The anglers were almost always
kind to each other, asking how they did that day, sharing their flies. Sure,
sometimes they displayed a bit of territorial behavior, just like the trout,
but heaven is a tolerant place.

As I waded across the flats, I cast my nymph out ahead of me and
watched the graceful, dark-backed rainbows and browns splay out ahead
and make patterns in the water. I saw them clearly, so beautiful in their
detail, their mouths flashing white as they ate. I saw how the sun shone
through the clouds and how the clouds made shadows on the water and
then moved on, and how the willows shook with small breezes, and how
the fly-fishers stepped carefully in the quiet river.

But there was one disturbing detail.

A trout, perhaps eighteen inches long, moved up and down and
across, darting this way and that, behaving differently. I watched it for a
while and then, as it passed close by, I saw that its lower jaw was dangling—trailing under its belly as it frantically looked for some way out of
this heaven. Perhaps a fisherman had pulled too hard in his enthusiasm
as the fish leaped in terror. I could not think of any other way such a
thing could have happened.

This was not something I wanted to remember, but I couldn't get the
image out of my mind. Fishing is a strange sport, if it is a sport, in which
you learn just as much as you are able to believe.

⌐ THE VALLEY OF the San Juan is changing slowly. It now contains a few
trailer parks and some other fly shops, guide services, and the Sportsman's Inn, a tavern and restaurant and pool hall with western decor
packed with the day's fishermen. This is where Nick and I celebrated our
trip. The anglers around us were sunburned and happy. In one booth, the
blonde woman and her guide were sharing draft beer; her eyes were
bright, perhaps with premonition. This is a moment she'll remember, I
thought.

"The one thing we didn't do was go back out that night and fish with
woolly buggers in the full moon," Nick said. "I think we both lost the opportunity for two or three twenty-seven- or twenty-eight-inch fish because we wimped out."

He and I are so different and so alike, I thought. He is a rough man
who is gentle inside; I guess I'm a gentle man who is rough inside. I've
always been overprotective of my children; he believed that he must
teach his children directly about the harshness of life, about reality. He
told me this story: When his children were small, his daughter came

home from school one day, home to the adobe farmhouse with the ristras and the asequia, she found her favorite goat—one that followed her everywhere—skinned, gutted, and strung up in the barn. This was a time when the Ravens were short on shoes; the meat they ate was meat that Nick butchered or shot with his gun. But finding that goat was a terrible moment for his daughter. Nick says he has no regrets, but he has told me the same story on several fishing trips.

"She was hurt, but she knew from that moment on, and will for the rest of her life, where the meat that she eats comes from, and that meat is not born plastic-wrapped." This is not the kind of direct experience I would have wanted for my children, but then I have had a different life.

On our fishing trips, we always end up in an argument about something, usually politics or religion.

This time, in the anglers' tavern, I was moaning about the lack of emphasis that Americans, especially my fellow Californians, seem to put on education—that they tend to favor investments in large-scale public-works projects like sports stadiums (for corporate benefit) over investments in the intellectual infrastructure. Nick rubbed his beard as I ranted, and then leaned over and said, "What's your precious education going to do for me and people like me?" By that, he meant what used to be called blue-collar workers. As a carpenter/farmer/woodworker, Nick looks at what education (or at least what we consider education these days) has wrought, and finds it wanting.

"You think you have to prepare all these kids for the high-tech future? Is that future what you really want? Look at the way of life you Californians suffer from out there." Freeways that clog like arteries filled with pasta; cell phones, which cause our driving to be on par with that of drunkards; answering machines that talk to answering machines; interchangeable housing-unit pods in which people sue each other over basketball hoops. If this is the twenty-first century, he prefers being retro-Victorian. Or more precisely, Jeffersonian. Where is the joy of fixing something, instead of throwing it away? Where is the feel of dirt, the knowledge of place? Where are the roots of life, clinging deep, in this life that education (as we know it) has wrought? When is there time to *read*?

"No, friend, if this is the kind of life your education is bringing us, why subsidize it? Besides, there's no profit in it for people like me, who work with our hands. It just replaces us. And you wonder why we might prefer a little beer and football?"

What he said made some sense.

"Besides, it's asinine to expect a big solid voting group to support more spending on education. Which education? The Christian fundamentalists hate schools because of the values debate; leftist feminists hate public education for the same reason; people into science think the schools should teach more science. People into the arts think they should teach more arts. The home schoolers, whatever they believe, don't want to have anything to do with the schools. The teachers hate the administrators and vice versa. So why would you ever expect a political consensus?"

A few beers later, I mentioned that it bothered me to see the changes in New Mexico, but at least the rate of change is slower than back home.

"Well, Isabel and I know we're lucky," he said. "A change that takes three years to happen in California probably takes thirty years in New Mexico. But we don't know anything other than the rate of change we know. So it's hard for us too."

Nick mentioned something he'd noticed about all the people we'd met on this trip. They all had gone through or were experiencing some kind of midlife change, or late-life transition, whatever.

These people that we talked to—like Bill Orr: Bill was a schoolteacher a few years ago when I met him and he changed to tying flies and working in the fly shop full time. And then we went up to meet the Anasazi Anglers and Jerry had been a pilot and when he was forty, he changed and started his guide service and he's happy rowing a boat. His wife made the switch to full-time with the guide service and she's happy. And then we went and met Corey, who had a wonderful job with the Forest Service but she had worked up in the hierarchy to the point she had lost the hands-on experience, so she quit it and started doing the streams for private people, and she was happy with her new job.

It built my spirits up a little bit to hear about all these people that made these midlife job changes. Of course they were all into fishing but they all seemed real content about it. In fact, at the motel in Durango, the gal that was behind the check-in desk, I got to visiting with her and she had worked sixteen years for the city and she quit and had been working now for a year as a hotel clerk and she was so happy because she was meeting all these people every day.

I've been a carpenter for twenty-five years. That's how I started paying my way through college and I ended up not using the degree and staying with the carpentry. Two weeks after I get back from this trip I'm going to start school to get my teaching certification so I can teach social studies in New Mexico.

Hey, I said, what about your dismissal of education? He laughed and waved it off and referred to something Thoreau had said: "Foolish consistency is the hobgoblin of small minds." And from Aldous Huxley: "The only truly consistent people are dead."

> You know how it is, you've done something and reached a level of competence in a field, and you're familiar with the tools of the trade. You know 99 percent of the stuff you need to know. You may never have done laminate work, but you can see a guy do it and in an hour you know how to do most of it yourself, too. But the teaching, two things: One is I've worked almost all my life in fields that are almost exclusively male. I haven't worked with women. And since the Army I've never really worked in a big organization that had all this standard operating procedure. I know it's going to take a while to learn those types of things. When you're older, at least with me, I don't have quite that same "I'll get out and learn that" attitude that I had twenty years ago. I'm a little more humble than I used to be, I guess, about my abilities to just do something new.

Later, I learned that Nick and Isabel, now empty-nesters, had moved back to their one true place, the farm in Puerto de Luna. They both had new jobs at the new medium-security Guadalupe County Correctional Facility seventeen miles away: Isabel is in charge of the prison computers, Nick is the prison's director of education.

They car-pool together, drive down the old road that was recently paved for the first time, much to Isabel's displeasure. "There was a meeting to talk about naming it," she told me on the phone. "The hell with that. A name means it'll be on a map. That means people will know how to get here." That's not the only change for the Ravens. Nick installed an air conditioner. He claims it's because he had sunstroke a while back, and his wife made him put one in, otherwise he wouldn't have one.

I told Nick: I believe you. Really. So when are we going fishing again?

The Giveaway

ᏑᎵ

ON ARRIVAL IN THE NORTHWEST, I decided I needed an education in the ways of salmon and steelhead and human beings, so I did something I usually try to avoid: I went to a conference. A conference about a war.

Canada, the United States, assorted Indian tribes—or First Nations, as Canadians more gracefully call them—were locked in a fight over the rights to salmon likely facing extinction. Representatives were up on the stage flinging platitudes.

Just when the audience seemed ready for synchronized snoring, Billy Frank stood up. He looked like a cross between Chief Dan George and Studs Terkel: distinguished and gritty at the same time, Frank is the man who forced the U.S. to honor its fishing treaties with the Northwest tribes. "I'm still looking for who the hell is in charge here!" he barked. "Soon we're going to be arguing about the last fish!"

That month, the Canadian province of British Columbia had sued the states of Washington and Alaska for violating the Pacific Salmon Treaty (signed in 1985, after fourteen years of negotiation), accusing the U.S. government of breaking a treaty that governs an annual $300 million industry. British Columbia premier Glen Clark charged that the United States had "been overfishing with impunity," and in retaliation revoked a lease to the United States to test torpedoes in a bay near Vancouver. In addition, more than one hundred Canadian fishermen surrounded an Alaskan ferry in British Columbia and held it hostage for several days. Senator Frank Murkowski of Alaska threatened to call out the Coast Guard to protect American fishing boats.

The war was even fought with biological weapons: Someone, probably a disgruntled American commercial fisherman, introduced voracious, parasite-carrying northern pike to Canadian salmon waters.

From a distance, this might seem like a missing chapter to *The Mouse That Roared*. However, the threat of salmon extinction and the near disappearance of steelhead are deadly serious to people whose way of life is threatened—and almost as serious to sport anglers. The theme of this forum, timed to coincide with the annual Seattle Salmon Homecoming Celebration, was "Moving Salmon Up the Political Agenda."

The immediate dispute was over the Pacific Salmon Treaty's "equity principle," a complex formula to measure the benefits of salmon to the United States and less-populated Canada. Looking at fish-harvest statistics, the two sides saw entirely different numbers. Differences in the two political systems posed an added problem: While Canada negotiated with one voice, the U.S. side contended with fractious states and a multitude of bureaucratic jurisdictions.

With the bearing of an offended Mountie, Canadian treaty negotiator Bud Graham pointed to complicated charts of "total salmon interceptions" and demanded that the United States acknowledge the imbalance between the two nations. "Interception" was the key word. Salmon fail to acknowledge international borders, and each country accused the other of "intercepting" the other country's fish runs, as the official language terms it, and catching more than its fair share. Iona Campagnolo, a former member of the Canadian Parliament, huffed, "In a global society, the U.S. will face many more transnational disputes over natural resources. If Canada and the U.S. are incapable of agreeing, who else in this world will agree?"

They weren't going to agree today. James Pipkin, the weary U.S. special negotiator for Pacific salmon, announced that "all efforts to resolve the dispute have come to naught," and that if negotiations didn't start moving, the United States would "take a look at whether there is any real reason for the U.S. to remain part of the negotiation."

The representatives who made the most sense represented the fishing cultures that preceded borders. The Indians, from both sides of the border, had heard enough talk of interceptions and "pieces," the bureaucrats' word for fish.

"If we get caught up in trying to count fish as they run over the border, we'll never resolve this," said Fred Fortier, chair of the British Columbia Aboriginal Fish Commission. Billy's right, he said. "We really will be arguing over the last fish."

⌒ THE TRIBAL LEADERS were being insufferably holy, I thought.

They're commercial fishermen, albeit with a special cultural relationship with salmon. The Indians' critics, among them many sportfishers, say the Indians' proclivity is for netting every salmon and steelhead in sight. So it's logical that they would play down their own culpability and wish to shift the debate from how to divide a shrinking resource to how to increase the total number of salmon—by improving the habitat of fish runs. That's ultimately the most important tack, though dangerous: It challenges development, big agriculture, and the hydroelectric and timber industries.

I fled the auditorium and ran into Chris Zimmer in the lobby. He is communications director of Save Our Wild Salmon Coalition, a Seattle-based conservation organization and one of the sponsors of the forum. He also is a self-described fanatical steelhead angler with long, wild black hair. His tee shirt said, "Walk softly and carry a big fish." He, too, had lost patience with the droning, so we sat down and talked.

This notion of intercepting fish is a strange, new concept to me, I said. Maybe they should be issued green cards.

"The thing you have to understand is the sense of ownership people have for these fish," he said. "The Northwest isn't like the rest of America. Salmon and steelhead are part of the psyche of the place, not just for sport fishermen. Nowhere else do you have the tribes who have depended on salmon and steelhead for spiritual and economic sustenance for thousands of years. It's hard for us to think what the salmon mean to the tribes. A good analogy: Imagine taking cars away from white people."

Zimmer paused. "Actually, that's kind of a blasphemous way to put it."

He pulled a stack of reports out of his knapsack and dropped them in my lap. "Read these, you'll get an education."

Here's the short version. Wild Pacific salmon have existed more than a million years. Their migration from small inland streams to the ocean and back again is a majestic rite of nature. At the beginning of the century, 15 million wild salmon moved through the waters of the Columbia Basin every year. Today, less than 2 percent of the basin's wild salmon population remains. In only two decades, the count of adult wild salmon on the Snake River has dropped from more than twenty-eight thousand to fewer than four thousand, according to the Army Corps of Engineers. In 1994, only one sockeye salmon returned to the Snake River.

Over the millennia salmon have adapted to floods, El Niño, and earthquakes, but these fish are not equipped to survive human economies based on cheap hydroelectric power, subsidized irrigation and navigation, natural-resource extraction, and big agriculture. Dam-building, logging, grazing, and suburban subdivisions have blocked their migratory pathways and destroyed the habitat that salmon need to survive. In the Columbia River Basin, dams kill many times more salmon than fishing, commercial or sport, and all other human activities combined. Juvenile

Chinook or King salmon must travel hundreds of miles along the Snake and Columbia rivers, through eight hydroelectric dams. Between 70 and 90 percent of these fish are killed by hydroelectric turbines, predators, or other means as they attempt to make their way to the sea.

So, said Zimmer, some of the dams have to go.

"We don't have to eliminate dams altogether. We just need to change the way dams work. One thing we can do is run more water over the spillway to dump juvenile fish over the dams instead of running them through the turbines, where they can get chewed up or get stunned, to where then they're easier prey for squawfish or birds. On the lower Snake dams, though, the science shows that for recovery efforts to be effective, they need to go."

For several years, an ambitious plan to save the salmon has been pushed by Reed Burkholder, a fifty-year-old musician and piano teacher, who wants the government to bypass four federal dams on the Lower Snake. His proposal calls for carving a new river channel around them. The rationale: Nearly as much money is spent every year on efforts to restore the salmon population as it would cost to create the new channel. This would mean, however, that a 150-mile stretch of river would no longer be navigable. Hundreds of millions of dollars in products, such as grain or paper pulp or petroleum, would have to be carried by truck or rail, costing two to three times as much. The Army Corps of Engineers is seriously studying the new channel plan, but the Northwest's most powerful lawmakers, more beholden to business than to fish, are unlikely to go along with the proposal.

What about closing the rivers to anglers—no more sportfishing?

"At times, in certain stretches, that is flat-out necessary. But then that constituency will fish elsewhere and many of them will no longer care about the stream you closed," Zimmer said. In other words, anglers equal political power; remove the anglers as a political constituency and you lose the fish.

⌒ BACK IN THE AUDITORIUM, Billy Frank was on stage again. "For too many generations to count, tribes have gathered in this spot. There's a site about a mile north of here called West Point, which archeologists have determined to be four thousand years old. They found lots of remnants of salmon, so the salmon has been here for a long time. Tribes have always been caretakers of the salmon." He introduced the next speaker by naming her ancestors and family: "With no further ado, grandfather, first governor of the Yukon, James Ross; grandmother, first woman admiral in the British Navy, Katherine Furst. Parents Barbara Ross and

Peter Furst; husband John Platt, children Amanda and John, it's a pleasure for me to introduce from Washington County, Oregon, and Washington, D.C., Congresswoman Elizabeth Furst, first district."

She talked about home.

"As Northwesterners, we really have a lot of reasons to care about fish. They are the icon of the Northwest; we can't imagine the Northwest without them," she said. "Their presence is what tells us that we are or are not healthy. On a personal level the reason the salmon mean so much to me is that they have such a sense of home. The salmon know how to get home. They know where they came from."

I was moved by what she said. If Americans are looking for anything, it's a sense of home. We leave home to find home, and wonder why we never seem to feel at home. Developers build gated communities with ersatz Mayberry architecture (one is actually named Mayberry) offering the illusion of home. But without the context of nature, a sense of connection to land and water, all is just plasterboard. The Northwest, by force of nature, has retained this connection more than many parts of the country. Seattleites tend to let you know that they're special, but they're not: They're blessed. They live in a part of America where the salmon come home.

Furst's statement seemed more important than all the droning numerical talk, more to the source of things. She talked, too, about Billy Frank, and about her hope that all the parties involved could do the impossible and save the salmon and steelhead.

> I was raised in South Africa; I did march in the first demonstration against apartheid in Cape Town. I was there when Nelson Mandela went to prison, and I was there on the glorious day in Pretoria in 1994 when Nelson Mandela was sworn in as president of South Africa. We had those three factors: leadership, will, and vision. And in 1969, very shortly after I had come to this beautiful place, there was war on the river. I went down to the Nisqually River to a little spot famous now around the world called Frank's Landing, and there I met a leader. Billy Frank sat down with this woman who had come from Los Angeles, who asked what happened, and he took the time to tell me. He was being arrested night after night and it was impossible, impossible that they would ever, ever secure their rights. And the impossible became the possible because of leadership, vision, and will.

Nelson Mandela and Billy Frank almost in the same breath; now that deserved looking into. An hour later, I met Billy Frank in the lobby. At sixty-eight, he was the chairman of the Northwest Fisheries Commission. He insisted on being called Billy. Not yet familiar with his history, I asked him about what Furst had said. He was sitting on a straight-back chair. He slapped his thick-fingered, net-scarred hands on his blue-jeaned knees and laughed.

"Oh yeah, yeah, that was back in the '60s and the Boldt decision was actually February of '74 in a district court in Tacoma, Washington, and from that point on we, the twenty tribes I represent, were comanagers with the state of Washington. We got 50 percent of the salmon, the state gets 50 percent—and we just had a decision handed down here a year ago where the shellfish come up the same, 50 percent for tribes and 50 percent for the state. We did all kinds of fish-ins in the '60s, and Marlon Brando was up here, a lot of actors, Jane Fonda. We took advantage of all opportunities to get the United States government's attention. Elizabeth was part of that. People from Seattle came down and actually watched us getting beat up on the rivers. We were exercising our treaty rights."

Though many Northwesterners, including many sportfishers, detest Billy Frank, familiarity with his history breeds respect. He was arrested more than forty times, labeled a "renegade" leader by a Washington governor. Billy and the members of his tribe, the Nisqually (the same name as the river they had fished for generations) were considered outlaws—worse, poachers! His first arrest was by two game wardens when he was fourteen, as he cleaned chum salmon in the dark. "Like his father before him, Billy Frank lived like an outlaw, fishing at night and always on the lookout for men in uniforms. Indians all over the Northwest lived the same way," writes Alex Tizon, a *Seattle Times* reporter.

The Nisqually Indians, devastated by smallpox, murdered by settlers, and a series of imposed treaties that sliced away at what remained of their ancestral land, held tight to their relationship—spiritual and physical—to the salmon, who always came back to them. Then, in 1889, state legislators—in the name of conservation—closed six rivers to salmon fishing and eventually banned net fishing in all rivers, except the Columbia. Over the decades, non-Indian commercial fishers caught millions of tons of salmon at sea, and the salmon runs declined. The state blamed the Indians. But the real reasons, as researchers have now concluded, were commercial fishing, logging, dams, and damage to the watersheds. In the '60s, the Indian fishers, who at most were catching 5 percent of the harvestable salmon, rebelled; they staged "fish-ins."

The protesters, led by a crewcut former Marine with a ninth-grade education named Billy Frank, overtly defied state fishing laws, as they had been doing since before the turn of the century. Again and again, the state attacked Frank's Landing, the family riverfront property where most of the fish-ins were staged. Game wardens used high-powered boats and surveillance planes, tear gas and billy clubs and guns. Marlon Brando was arrested at a 1964 fish-in, saying that he was just "helping some Indian friends fish." A state boat rammed Billy's canoe, carved by a friend, and he nearly drowned: The canoe was confiscated. One Indian activist was shot in the stomach while fishing, by white vigilantes, he said. And in 1970, helmeted police brutally beat, shot at, and arrested fifty-nine protesters on the nearby Puyallup River.

That year, the federal government, on behalf of the tribes, filed suit against the state of Washington. The central question: Could the state regulate the fishing practices of tribes that had signed treaties with the U.S. government? The wider issue at stake: If Indians lived in "nations," just how sovereign were they? The three-year trial was presided over by District Court Judge George Hugo Boldt, a conservative Eisenhower appointee who had once denied bail to Billy and five other protesters. Boldt also was a dedicated sportfisher, which didn't bode well for the Indian cause.

The case came down to how each side interpreted this sentence in the treaty: "The right of taking fish at usual and accustomed grounds and stations is further secured to said Indians in common with all citizens of the territory." The state took "in common with all citizens" to mean that Indians, like everyone else, were subject to state control. The Indians argued that their oral histories, dating back to what they considered the beginning of time, proved that these rivers were their "usual and accustomed places" to fish. On February 12, 1974, Judge Boldt handed down his 203-page decision. To everyone's surprise, Boldt had interpreted the treaty in what he believed were the definitive terms of its day. He had relied on an 1828 edition of *Webster's American Dictionary* that defined the phrase "in common with" to mean joint ownership—the Indians, he said, were entitled to half the harvestable salmon running through their traditional waters. This was an astounding decision—1 percent of the population would now be joint owners and comanagers of all the salmon runs. This time, the Indians had won.

The decision, ruling in favor of tribal sovereignty, represented a political and economic breakthrough not just on the rivers of the Northwest, but across the country—helping create the legal context for tribal casinos, online tribal lotteries, and increased tribal police powers. But the decision also meant that Indians could become powerful champions for the environment—or at least share in the spoils.

Later, the Muckleshoot tribe stopped the city of Tacoma, Washington, from building a pipeline along ancestral Green River fishing grounds— until Tacoma agreed to build a tribal fish hatchery and hand over one hundred acres to the tribe. In New Mexico, the Isleta Pueblo, which manages the watershed of the Rio Grande River, forced the city of Albuquerque to spend $300 million to clean it up. And as a direct result of the salmon decision, the federal government ceded regulation of endangered species on Arizona's White Mountain Apache reservation, including a native trout, to the tribe—which already was doing a good job of preserving them.*

Commercial and sportfishers have thus far challenged the ruling without success. Billy doesn't have much use for sportfishers. "Indians don't play with their food," he told me. But sportfishers aren't that much of a problem to him. "When the salmon goes home, he has to have a home— clean water, watersheds." To Billy, the habitat—the *home*—is the most important thing: Improve that, save that, and fish will come home for everyone, Indians and anglers alike.

"Maybe everybody should stop fishing. If we don't have a scheme, nobody goes fishing, the sportsmen don't go fishing, the commercial people, nobody goes fishing along the Pacific Coast. That forces us to come to a scheme."

With that, he headed back to the auditorium.

In 1916, a Washington state Supreme Court justice wrote: "The Indian was a child and a dangerous child. Neither Rome nor Britain ever dealt more liberally with their subject races than we with these savage tribes, whom it was generally tempting and always easy to destroy." The justice, of course, had not met Billy Frank—who was eventually awarded the Albert Schweitzer Prize for Humanitarianism by Johns Hopkins University.

---

* Billy Frank had an unseen and probably unintentional partner in his fight: Richard Nixon. Though aboriginal peoples of Canada like to call themselves the First Nations, Indian tribes in the United States have always had more sovereignty—at least on paper—than the Canadian tribes, according to Stephen Cornell, codirector of the Harvard Project on American Indian Economic Development. That sovereignty was guaranteed in treaties that, though seldom honored by the U.S. government, explicitly recognized a kind of Indian independence. "In Canada, the legal process was much more destructive," says Cornell. "The U.S. government didn't grant sovereignty to Indians, it just never fully extinguished it." As he points out, treaties are—by definition—agreements among nations. True, the definition was obscured. In the 1830s, an ambivalent Supreme Court Justice John Marshall described Indian populations as "domestic dependent nations." The United States discouraged expressions of Indian independence until Richard Nixon became president. Nixon replaced the antisovereignty approach with a "self-determination" policy, recognized by Congress in 1975. The result: a burst of court decisions that turned back legal challenges to the sovereign rights of Indian tribes to salmon, and essentially exempted reservations from the rule of federal gaming laws. Complete independence was short-lived: The Indian Gaming Regulatory Act, passed by Congress in 1988, now regulates reservation casinos. Indeed, some Indians view the rise of gaming as a net loss of sovereignty, because it forced them into negotiation with the states. But in a sense, Richard Nixon was the father of Indian gambling casinos—and Billy Frank's unintended coconspirator.

↜ MANY STEELHEAD ANGLERS do blame the tribes for some of this loss. One long-time salmon and steelhead angler from Oregon told me:

"The Boldt decision is killing our fish supply. The Indians have basically unlimited rights. The Boldt decision gave the Indians half of the fish, but the Indians assume that means unlimited rights." Essentially, the tribes remain the last commercial fishers for wild steelhead; their treaties protect them.

"On the Columbia River over the past two decades, Indians have probably killed 100,000 to 150,000 wild steelhead," says Frank Amato, publisher of several fishing magazines, including *Salmon-Trout-Steelheader.* "During that time in Oregon, sport fishermen were only allowed to catch-and-release and only Indians were allowed to kill wild steelhead. It's still legal for them to kill them. So, if wild steelhead are going to be killed, they'll be killed by Indians."

The tribes, he says, should be able to fish at the dams with their dip nets. "If they use dip nets directly out of the ladders, they hurt fewer fish, catch more, and it's easier that way to release the wild fish. I have no problem with Indians taking their percentage of fish, but what I do hear many complaints about is that they accidentally kill a lot of wild steelhead, the ones that go into Idaho on the Snake and Salmon rivers. On the Columbia, the Indians have their own expert biologists. They know what they're doing, but they don't talk about it. To tell the honest to god truth, they're mainly interested in numbers, and if it's numbers you're concerned with, then you have to support hatcheries." Amato agrees with Billy Frank that the ultimate issue is the watershed and sees some progress being made to improve habitat. "But the dams aren't going to be torn down—and even if a law was passed to tear them down, a lot of folks in eastern Oregon and eastern Washington and Idaho would probably pick up arms. It's pie in the sky to think we can bring back wild fish in numbers great enough to fish for them commercially. So it makes sense that the Indians are the biggest supporters of the hatchery fish."

If you listen closely to some of the Indians, some of them share the sport anglers' view that the tribes are taking too many fish. But that's a distinctly minority position among the Indians.

↜ THE NEXT DAY, I walked from the hotel down the hill in a light mist to Seattle's waterfront. The Salmon Homecoming Celebration, a four-day outdoor event that verges on the sacramental, was under way.

Two Indians in stained jeans and flannel shirts, with black hair flowing down their backs, stood in the back of a pickup truck. They were up to their knees in salmon. They hefted two of them with gaffs for the passersby to see.

The men's elbows were straining above their shoulders; the salmons' eyes were at the level of their chests, the tails nearly touching the bed of the pickup. The flanks of these magnificent fish were silver and sleek and reflected light even in the mist. Blood trickled from the gills of one of the fish and ran onto the shorter man's shirt.

"King salmon. This is the last of them," he said. "Take a good look. You're not gonna see no more of these."

He was grinning oddly. The passersby clumped around the pickup. A woman wearing a stylish Seattle rain parka reached out and touched one, and then wiped the slime on the truck. The shorter Indian laughed.

I moved along with the crowd and into the festival grounds. In the tents and canvas shelters, sellers—many of them members of Northwest tribes—sold Indian jewelry, wooden salmon fetishes suitable for hanging, buffalo skulls (one hundred dollars each), and the furs of red fox, beaver, and badgers. PETA was not in attendance. I wandered through the tents and walked up to the railing at the end of a wharf and breathed in the thick, wet marine air. A man standing next to me said that if I watched the water carefully, I would see the salmon coming home. We watched the water for a few minutes. "There's one," he said. I saw a flash of silver, and then it was gone.

The man's name was Ray Fryberg. He is a member of a fishing tribe called the Tulalip, who live on a reservation up the coast. His tribe mainly fishes Puget Sound and around the Strait of Juan de Fuca and the Strait of Georgia. His hair was pulled back in a long braid. He had a mustache. He was strong, muscular, but with a rounded belly. We sat on a bench, feet on the railing. He said that he's one of his tribe's historians. He described the netting process:

> We started out years ago as families beach-seining with a net hooked up to winches. We towed rope away from the beach like that and set this seine net out and make a half horseshoe and then we'd circle around the fish and bring it to the beach. We'd have a lead line on it and corks and it would be pulled in to the beach and the fish would be caught in a pocket in the shallows. When I was nine or ten, my grandfather would ask me to go out and hold up the corks as the King salmon thrashed around in the net. It was exciting. We lived on the beach and every family had a different section of beach that was their own. All along our shores, we lived in tents; I had a pet seal and a pet deer that lived at camp with us. Somebody

found out about the pet seal and they came to transfer it to one of the zoos. But the deer lived on the beach with us, up above us on the bank, and he was tame. We had a collar and bell on him. He stayed with us until he started developing horns, little nubs in the fall.

Everybody worked together. It was really exciting to pull in a big load of fish. We'd set the net out and come around and pull fifty, sixty Kings to the shore. We've moved along since then. There's hardly anybody who beach seines anymore.

How big were the King salmon? I asked.

"They were big, I've seen King salmon up to sixty-five pounds," he said. "That was probably forty miles north of Seattle."

We put up a lot of salmon, preserved salmon for the winter and traditionally that's what the whole thing was about for our people. That would sustain us for the winter months. Our people during the winter lived in longhouses out here, historically. During the spring months certain things were indicators, when things happened. There was a type of butterfly that came around and when it did, our people knew that it was time to go out for the King salmon. The King salmon was used for trade and for barter. Some of the ways we prepared our fish were valuable and unique to the Indians across the mountains, so we traded with them. All of our people still fish. I just put up sixty jars of salmon for myself and my family. There's a very distinct line between a recreational fishery and people who use it for sustenance.

Fryberg is a commercial gill-netter now. The gill net, he explained, is laid in the water in anticipation of a run of salmon. When the salmon hits the gill net, it makes a quick surge and pushes its head into the web past its gills, and then cannot back out. Most Indian fishers are gill-netters. His fleet hasn't yet moved to purse-seining, a method used to capture fish at the mouth of rivers before they can move inland to spawn. "It's too effective. We catch too many fish."

I talked to Billy Frank yesterday, I said.

"He's a good man."

A lot of recreational anglers are angry at Northwest Indians, I said. Are Indians angry with recreational fishers? No, he said, anglers aren't to blame for the dropping salmon and steelhead runs any more than Indians are.

"Right now the salmon are having a hard time, and I don't think it's because of management or commercial and sportfishing, but because of environmental degradation. You can have all of these practices and laws in place to protect the environment, but you might as well not even have them if you're not going to enforce them."

He told me the significance of the Salmon Homecoming Celebration, that the dancers here dance in celebration of all things, and that this brings people from different backgrounds together to share their respect for the salmon, and hope that the salmon can be saved.

One by one and collectively we can make a difference for the benefit of the salmon. Bringing this type of awareness to the people is very important. A lot of people don't really know what's going on, or the newspaper still has a tendency to play up this distress between the tribes and the state, when actually we've been working pretty good together. There's a lot of development, and it's happening real rapidly in and around this area. All the clear-cutting and the gravel mining and the pollution change the water, and the salmon can't handle it. They're a resilient animal, but some of these things are new and they can't adjust to them that fast. Siltation because of the clear-cutting covers up their eggs. The loggers cut right down to fifty yards of the stream; they're taking away all of the old growth and the mosses that served as natural filters for the river systems. People are building right up to the streams; they throw stuff over the banks and cover up the streams, block the salmon's ability to travel upstream. Salmon don't just occupy the main rivers—they occupy the little, tiny tributaries and the little creeks, and all of those losses add up. You think, "That's just a little creek," but it might be a home for a couple hundred salmon. Those are the things that really impact the salmon.

Fryberg fell silent. He leaned forward and stared down at the water.

In this area, our history is completely oral; everything is handed down through stories and legends. Our teachings are about a being that transformed us. Before we were transformed, we were brothers with all of the animals, and all the animals spoke the same language. We know that every creature has a spirit. So when we take the salmon out of the water we realize that if we do it in a proper method and we do it with respect, we're transforming him to his spirit world. If we treat him right and we treat him good, he will give himself to us freely and generously because he knows that we use him for the benefit of our families. We say that the salmon, when it comes back to us, it's time for his giveaway.

Every year we have a salmon ceremony. When we bring in the first salmon we make an elaborate ceremony to welcome him. The person who catches him is not allowed to eat him. We sing songs about him welcoming him; he's well respected, almost like a chief. After he's prepared to be eaten, then the bones and the rest of him are taken very carefully and placed back into the water so that he can go back as a messenger and tell the other fish that when he was here he was treated well and with respect. If you don't do that and you lay the bones on the ground and a dog gets a piece of that back-bone, then that fish would go to the spirit world crippled. So you have to make sure all of his bones are placed back into the water the way that he came out.

All of the fishermen's first catches we give away to people—to elders that don't have people that can fish for them, to widows, to people that just don't have access to the fish. We always have a big giveaway. We bring in several fish, the first ones, and give them away. And when it's time for us to die, our family has a giveaway, too. You have to be prepared, you have to save all your goods and items so you're prepared for that time. We have these giveaways to pay respect to all of the people. We give many things, blankets, everything. We give as much as we can to as many of the people as we can.

The fishing season starts in July or August and ends in December. The Indians fish in skiffs from fourteen feet to forty feet long, and the work is dangerous.

"Oh yeah. I lost my dad fishing when I was eight years old and my un-cle, I've lost an aunt and an uncle, there's been several people in my fam-ily I've lost fishing."

Do you have kids of your own? I asked.

"I have five kids."

Are they going to be fishermen?

"Oh yeah, all of them fish with me right now except my youngest daughter, she's only eleven. But my boys, they all fish with me. I have a son that's fifteen and one that's twenty-two and another one that's a lit-tle older. They help with my boat and sometimes we'll fish four or five days in a row without coming back to land."

How did your father die? Was it a storm?

"It was a storm, yeah. In a smaller wooden boat. The boat tipped and there weren't very adequate motor mounts in the boat and the motor slipped off its blocks and crashed into the side and the boat sunk. It was in November, and these waters are cold."

Is that part of the giveaway, too?

"It is, yeah, it's our connection to the water."

≈ I WANDERED AROUND the celebration, poked my head in the booths, bought some souvenirs for my kids and a shell necklace for my wife. I briefly toured the Seattle Aquarium, next to the celebration. The aquarium is one of the sponsors of the homecoming. In one tank, a cloud of Chinook fry swam, seemingly looking up at the sky, in a swirling, clinging school—almost one animal. Hatched in the fall of 1996, they were scheduled for release in the spring of 1998, and those that survived would come home in the fall of the year 2000. Some of you reading this may be there to welcome them. Downstairs, children were making paper salmon. Elizabeth Furst was right, I thought. This is the fish that shaped the Northwest's human cultures—and continues to shape them. In the Seattle-Tacoma airport, a recorded female voice, pleasant and with a touch of humor, announces: "This is a nonsmoking airport, you cannot smoke cigarettes, cigars, pipes, or salmon."

Back at the celebration, I watched competition powwow dancing. People came from all over the West, some of them small children wearing feathered, beaded costumes, hopping on one leg, then the other. A circle of men sang and beat on a single drum, and their beat was hypnotic. One young singer lifted his chin to sing, and the vibration of the song could be seen in his neck. Another singer's jaw hung loosely, his lower lip quivering with the song. He was an old man; he was sitting in a wheelchair, wearing a cowboy hat, and his singing was the strongest.

Even after the singing and drumming stopped, I could feel it—as if my own bones were striking stretched leather.

Later, the man in the wheelchair gave the invocation: "As we look around this morning, we honor and give special recognition and privilege to all of our grandmothers, each and every one. All of you that are mothers. All of you that are daughters, aunts, and nieces, that which we call the power of the Grandmother Moon. On our man side, the ones we call the protectors and the providers and warriors. To our grandfathers we raise our hands. . . . In the fire of our hearts we make that expression of gratitude and thanksgiving for each and every one of you here today. . . . The drums, they are like our grandfathers, they are like our teachers. . . . Let us pray. Our God and our Father, the Great Spirit of our Indian people, who created all good things. . . . Let us pray for the singers, for the drummers, for each of the ones who are outside of that circle and for the homecoming of the salmon."

And then the Homecoming Queen was crowned, a shy teenager who blushed beneath a halo of feathers.

Kenny McCloud stood beside me. He was one of the men on the truck holding the King salmon. We had watched the ceremony together. He had something to tell me, he said, so we sat down. He began indirectly.

"That King I showed you. It weighed about thirty-five pounds."

Do you ever use a rod to catch fish? I asked.

"Yeah, we use fishing poles, we use bows. Some people still dip on the Columbia. A dip net, it's just a hoop on a line pole, they stick that into the water. Wait for the fish to come by and when it hits the net, just pull it up. They fix it so where the net will close up at the end of the hoop and the fish will be inside of it."

Everybody should stop fishing, he said. "We're catching too many. Catching too many and not letting enough go by. The last ones to catch the fish are the natives, so they're the ones that need to stop first." He lowered his voice. "That's my opinion, just how I feel. Long time ago I felt like I was catching too many fish. Like you have a school of ten thousand salmon come to this river and you're wiping out eight thousand and there's only two thousand going back out, there won't be ten thousand going up again . . ."

So that's probably not a popular view.

"No, it's not."

Do you stand up in meetings and say that?

"No, I don't go to meetings. When we were kids we used to chase fish all over the place, but you can't do it no more. All the fish are dying out through all the streams, all over the world. Not because of just overfishing, it's the whole world itself, it's the way we're living now, I think. There'd be a lot of fish for everybody if everybody slowed down a little bit. Maybe we don't have to stop all the way. We're catching the fish with gill nets, we're catching forty, fifty to one hundred fish in these nets and if we used a dip net we're only catching two or three or four or five at a time. But everybody wants more fish, more money, and that's not right. Our life is changing. The world wants us to be like them and we're changing into their ways, and it's greed. I don't believe in money, I don't believe in catching all the fish in the world."

He wasn't smiling anymore. He was looking at his hands. They were scarred like Billy Frank's.

"I live in a country town, all westernized, cowboys and Indians. They try to keep us alive by pictures and posters and murals, that's their way

KENNY MCCLOUD

of looking at us. But we see ourselves different. You don't see Indians nowhere until you come to a gathering. To me, we're kind of like the invisible race. They talk about the Native Americans, they talk about Indians—do you see them? Don't see them nowhere. Only in a place like this. You might see Indians and you might think they're Orientals from another country. But we're still here."

Did you bring those big King salmon here to sell? I asked.

"No, I brought them to give away. You have to make an offering so you can catch more fish next time."

Who did you bring them to give to?

"Mostly people I know that have big families. They'll eat the fish instead of wasting it. I try to take care of the fish."

Do you give them only to Indian families?

"Oh no, to anybody, it don't matter. I brought eight or nine. I gave a couple away already."

I told him about the conference, and how someone had said the reason that so many people in the Northwest feel deeply about salmon is that salmon come home. I asked him if he thought that was true.

"I can't really explain how it is to us. Salmon need us and we need the salmon, just like all life. We need all life and all life needs us. We need them to survive and they need us—they're here for us. It's the circle of life."

Fishing for Ghosts
(or, Sasquatch of the Stilly)

⌒⌒⌒

I HAD FISHED for steelhead once before coming to Washington.

My brother, Mike, a teacher and fierce fisherman, had taken me steel-heading on the Mad River, near Eureka, in Northern California. The day was cold and gray and misty. Five or six men stood on our side of the slate-green river. They wore heavy parkas and ball caps. Most of them were bearded. They were loggers and mechanics and they were seri-ous—dour, even. We couldn't see the steelhead, but we knew that they were coming home from the sea, moving up the river and biting out of irritation and territoriality. The men, using bags of salmon eggs for bait, with attractors made of bright feathers tied above the bags, had been standing out there for hours—some for days—waiting.

Another fisherman came walking up the river on the other side. He was younger than the rest of us, dressed lightly in tight neoprene waders and a short vest. He was hatless. He carried a flyrod. He moved up the river and stopped just below the bearded men across the water. Accord-ing to the unwritten etiquette of steelheading, he was almost but not quite invading their space.

It began to rain. The bearded men pulled down the brims of their hats and watched him. Meticulously, ignoring the rain on his bare head, the fly-fisherman placed his line on the river and pulled it back high. Then his rod arched down. For twenty minutes, he played the fish. His face told of no excitement, no dread, only efficiency and concentration. The big fish broke the surface three times, and then the fly-fisherman grabbed it by the tail and turned and walked up the bank. The fish was as long as his leg. He put the fish on the ground, knocked it out with a rock, and then continued fishing. In all of this time, he never once looked at the men on the other side.

They watched him grimly, barely moving. After a while, the fly-fisherman left. The bearded men remained, their heads pulled a little tighter into their parkas.

I recalled something Jim Brown had told me, something about "lining." Steelhead swim upstream, mouths open. Some fly-fishers are skillful at drifting their line into the fish's mouth, then pulling it up so that the line runs through the mouth until the hook catches. Essentially, they're snagging the fish, which is illegal. High-class poaching.

"Most fly-fishers don't do that," said Chris Zimmer, the Save Our Wild Salmon Coalition director, when I related the story to him. "I don't do it." But what I had seen on the river that day was fairly indicative of the cultural gap between gearheads, as Zimmer called them, and fly-fishers. "There's way too much animosity there."

Steelheading. Even the sound of the word conjurs a feeling of difficulty and magic.

"Steelheaders are probably the weirdest fishermen out there," added Zimmer.

Celebrated by many anglers as the West Coast's premier freshwater sport fish, steelhead are rainbow trout that migrate to the ocean and return to their home waters to spawn. "Some steelheaders spend their every waking moment thinking about steelhead—and I'm one of them," Zimmer said. "They follow the fish runs like some people used to follow the Grateful Dead. Some of them live in vans and mobile homes, and move from river to river, just following the fish. These guys fish in the worst weather, and they'll catch one every week maybe, and sometimes they'll go three months without catching one."

The fewer steelhead that come upriver, the stranger the pursuit; fishing for steelhead is getting to be like fishing for ghosts. Or Bigfoot. "Just the pursuit of steelhead is something you have to experience," Zimmer said. "You should check out the different subcults—the gearheads, who throw spinners or eggs, versus the fly-fishers. Man, if you have the chance, go steelheading."

The objective facts about the steelhead trout—with its steel-blue coloring along its head and back—are impressive enough. The steelhead is a seagoing rainbow trout, but more than that. Often referred to as a rainbow on steroids, the fish is among the fiercest of fighters. Though northwesterners claim the Pacific steelhead as their own, its native range extends from the Alaskan Peninsula to Southern California. Before dams were built on the Columbia River, steelhead migrated inland over fourteen hundred miles to spawn in their natal rivers and streams.

Still, the salient fact about steelhead is that they're hard to catch and getting harder, because there are—depending on which river you're on—

fewer of them. Instead of becoming discouraged and moving on to other species of fish, the steelheaders dig in and become even more obsessed.

I asked Michael Checchio, the author of *A Clean Well-Lighted Stream*, who stalks steelhead in Northern California, why steelhead are such prized sportfish. Again, the objective facts:

"This is a fish that was born in a river and after a couple of years it swam out to sea and spent four years there. It survived the trawlers; it survived the seals; and it's come back to spawn. It's a great torpedo of a fish, with all the power of ocean fish and all the craftiness of river trout. You're getting a fish that's still bright and powerful from the ocean—often with sea lice still clinging to it—but it's as difficult to catch as the cleverest river trout you've ever encountered."

Stocked steelhead also live in the Great Lakes before returning to their spawning waters in the rivers and streams. Some of the original Great Lakes steelhead became Midwesterners by accident, when an 1876 shipment of what were thought to be generic rainbow trout from California's McCloud River contained eggs from steelhead. Steelhead are raised in hatcheries in the midwest, but over the last one hundred and twenty years, many strains, including the McCloud River immigrants, have combined and evolved into Michigan's own strain of wild steelhead. Another good steelhead fishery exists—five hours by car from New York City—in the Salmon River, which feeds into Lake Ontario. These fisheries, and their proud steelhead cultures, deserve a chapter of their own, but space and time prohibit that.

"There are steelhead bums who really are like Kurtz; they've gone too far up the river," said Checchio, referring to Joseph Conrad's story, *Heart of Darkness*. "Their life is steelhead, it's as if nothing else exists. Some of these guys have marginal or seasonal employment, and they just spend their time traveling, chasing steelhead. Most of them are single guys, I'm sure, and they'll live on cigarettes and a bunch of bananas and coffee to get them through the day, and they'll stand in icy water day after day after day, waiting."

THE FULLY-EMPLOYED CAN qualify as steelhead bums, too. An Oregon elementary school principal and steelhead gear-fisherman e-mailed me when he learned that I was interested in his angling culture. He informed me that steelheaders, "who mostly roam the northwestern United States, Canada, and Michigan, are a strange lot with some strange traditions and superstitions. For example, we never make love the night before fishing. Seriously. We rub strange lotions on our hands to keep fish from smelling us."

I had met him before, in his unrelated capacity as a principal, and he had seemed mild-mannered, reputable, solid. So I called him and reminded him that he had written something in his e-mail that I thought was funny—about not having sex the night before. It sounded to me like an Indian purification ritual.

Apparently it's not just steelheaders. I was talking to a fly-fisher in his twenties who lives in the Smoky Mountains—good guy, well-educated, works in the computer industry. I mentioned, "I'm hearing some really strange things, like steelheaders, they don't have sex the night before." After a pause on the other end of the line, he said, "Well, I don't touch my wife the day before I go fly-fishing for trout."

Why?

He said, "Well, because I get that sweet smell on me and the fish stay away."

The principal didn't have a firm grip on the sex thing, either. Some of his fellow steelheaders wear latex gloves to mask their human odors. "And you know the smell thing is almost an obsession now in the fishing industry.

"You can't talk to a fisherman now without talking about the issue of smell—this tube of bass attractant, catfish attractant, trout attractant. I think the odor must have been the origin of the sex thing. Or maybe it's just superstition, maybe some guy was out on the river and got laid the night before and got skunked."

So when in doubt, choose the fish?

"Exactly. I can remember with my wife, my ex-wife, I'd get so excited thinking about fishing in the morning, I couldn't sleep. I'd lie there, and I'm saying to myself, 'Oh God, do I dare touch her? Because if I touch her I don't have any chance of catching fish.' I don't know which one to choose. My buddies are the same way because they'll come hauling in from a night of making love and we'll meet at the café and of course the conversation around the table is, 'So tell me, Tom, did you get laid last night?' Everybody checks up on each other. This is probably where the concept of safe sex came from."

Safe sex and tight lines.

"There you go."

He figures steelhead fishing broke up his marriage.

I think there was an understanding in that when the rivers are in, when they're at their prime time for fishing, everything else ceases to exist or happen. The phone call from the office would come in: "Guess what?" "What?" "The river's in and fish are in." And I'd look at my watch and say, "Oh God, it's ten after four, I'm supposed to be to dinner at six with the in-laws, how am I going to do this?" And I'd figure out a way to lie, steal, and cheat my way. "Oh, I'll make it up to you, I'll make it up to you! I'll only be gone an hour."

The best method was after my wife introduced me to her cousin. And we were sitting over at a family reunion and I was bemoaning the fact that I was sitting here on a beautiful day looking at the water with no fish pole in my hand. And I was commiserating and one beer led to the next beer and he says, "Well, hell, I fish." And of course the friendship began. So we decided that this was all a bunch of crap and we had to figure out what we were going to do. So we conspired and I said, "Tell you what. I'm new in the family but I know I'll get on the good side if I tell them that I need to do something because of you. They'll really understand." You can imagine what happened. Every time it came time for a family meeting, here's what we'd tell our spouses: I'd tell my wife, "Well, you know Uncle Hubert is your cousin, and I really don't want to have to leave early from chicken dinner to go fishing, but God, he's your relative. What can I do? How can I get out of it?" At the very same moment, Hubert was telling the same story to his wife. So we would tell the same story and both of the families would feel sympathetic to us. And Thanksgiving would come, and we would hurry up through the meal so we could go on our three-day jaunt, right? We'd always be real sad around the family: "I should be with the family, but what can I do?" Well, we'd get in the car and we'd both just howl all the way to the fishing hole.

This worked for twenty years, until I got divorced.

I started feeling guilty about making excuses to go fishing, so I just decided to go fishing. I guess that's when my marriage went to hell.

Part of the attraction, as with other fishing, is the camaraderie. "I guess you could call my steelheading buddies the equivalent of a gang," said the principal.

I called Mike Checchio about the salmonid-and-sex theory.

"I never heard that one about steelheading," he said. "But I do hear it increases the libido."

↩ FAITH ROLAND, KNOWN as one of the best steelhead fly-anglers in the Northwest, expresses a devotion to steelhead that goes beyond male superstition and into the metaphysical. While in Washington, I floated eight miles down the Skykomish River, east of Seattle, with Faith. She educated me about the ways of the Steelhead Gods.

Faith, a game warden's daughter, now works for King County buying up land along the watersheds in order to protect the rivers. She doesn't accept the sex theory, but when she fishes, she *must* wear one of her two purple fishing hats. She uses a purple wading belt. Recently, her husband gave her a fine purple Abel reel. She believes in being color coordinated on the stream.

She was twenty-three when she caught her first steelhead—using metallic lures called casting spoons—a seventeen-pound buck. "When I caught it, and then let it go, I felt a sense of assurance that I could catch another one. I always assume it will happen again. It may be two years from now, but I am sure that I will catch more steelhead in my life—because I put the first one back, and the Steelhead Gods smiled on me after that. Two months after I released that fish, I had a terrific thirteen-day, twenty-two-catch season—and five of those were over twenty pounds." She laughed. She said she doesn't take the Steelhead Gods totally seriously. But almost. Then she told me this story:

> My best fish isn't my biggest, but it's the one that's more metaphysical to me. This was back when I was having a relationship with a fly-tier. I didn't feel I could fish by myself; in fact I was really struggling with my general sense of independence. I had an interesting sister-in-law who had four dogs and liked to come visit unannounced on Sundays. One afternoon I didn't have the patience for her or for her four dogs, so I said to my partner, "Take me down to the stream, drop me in, and pick me up in a couple of hours." We had this little one-person boat. He dropped me off at the Hazel drift of the Stilly. He planned to pick me up at the Seapost bridge a couple hours later, about two and a half miles downstream. I proceeded to fish the hole at Hazel. I hooked a fish and lost it. I was on the next drift and I stopped, pulled my boat over and I walked down and stood in ankle-deep water. I made this cast and hooked this pretty little hen. I swear I felt someone watching me. When I looked up in this tree, I saw an eagle sitting up there. He's looking down at me—and I assume it was a *he* because he was looking very proud of himself. It didn't occur to me that it was a female eagle. So I've got this pretty little hen fish, probably the smallest I've ever caught. But it was at that moment that I realized something. You know what? I realized that I had rowed the boat myself and I had made all those casts by myself and I had tied the fly myself and I had rigged my gear myself. I realized in that moment that I was totally self-sufficient at this steelhead thing. Because up until that point I really wasn't, or hadn't let myself be or nobody had let me

FAITH ROLAND

be. This was that moment when everything changed. I had hooked that fish and then I let it go because I could, I wanted to. Didn't need to, but I wanted to. This eagle was watching me the whole time and he and I somehow communicated. We said a few words to one another. That was the fish that made steelheading all mine as opposed to somebody else's. That was my metaphysical fish. That was my best fish. Still is.

↜ TECHNOLOGY, NOT METAPHYSICS, was on Tim Bohlin's mind as he drove us in his Toyota 4 Runner to the Sauk and Skagit rivers, about eighty miles northeast of Seattle. Bohlin is thirty-three years old, tall, handsome, brilliant—the quintessential Seattle techie. He's a new-economy worker, an independent contractor with AT&T specializing in cellular-phone fraud. He's doing quite well at this; one piece of evidence is the sprawling reproduction farmhouse he shares with his wife (and soon, their first child) in the woods outside Seattle. We stopped there briefly to pick up his sixteen-foot jet sled—essentially a johnboat with a forty-horsepower Yamaha engine. Another piece of evidence is that he gets to go steelheading just about any time he wants, which means a lot. Being attracted to the finer things in life, he's fascinated—fixated, he ad-mits—by steelhead; because they're rare, because catching them on a fly demands extraordinary fortitude, patience, and precision; because Wash-ington's steelheaders are a tight community, which includes older men from whom he can learn; and because steelheading is *not* high-tech.

As a teenager fishing with his father, he started out as a gear fisher-man, angling on the Olympic Peninsula, and the Deschutes River, and the Stillaguamish River, which has summer steelhead in it as well as sea-run cutthroat.

"My parents live down on the Washougal River, which has a good hatchery run." As a kid, he fished for years using what he calls "corkies and yarn" rigs using steelhead roe or salmon eggs for bait, before he caught a steelhead. Today he's a fly-fisher, and a good one, but even dur-ing the best winter's fishing he ever experienced, he only caught seven-teen steelhead. But the word "only" is relative in this fishing world.

Many weeks can go by when an angler won't catch a single steelhead, he said. He knows guys who have been in the river every weekend for *months* without landing one. Tim figures a good day steelheading is when you've had one on, and lost it. He doesn't like to talk about num-bers. True steelheaders are like that.

"I don't think that's universal, I think there are people who are very much into doing the math," he said. "They keep a fishing log not so

TIM BOHLIN

much to remember the experience as to maybe measure how they think they're doing, like a golf score. I guess that's OK but it's not for me. If the goal were to catch as many fish as I could possibly catch, then I'd be fishing differently. I'd go to the same place every time, one that I know produces fish; I'd go where fish concentrate, which is also where fishermen concentrate. But I'd rather focus on experiencing the different rivers, knowing that by doing that I'm not optimizing my chances of catching as many fish as I might otherwise."

We entered the scattered town of Woodinville and passed a wrecking yard that specializes in Ford Mustangs, called the Mustang Ranch, with a sign that said "acres and acres of pony parts." We were headed into the subdivided woods now, north on Highway 9, leaving the denser suburbs behind. Tim said the steelhead community of the Northwest is smaller than people think. For instance, the community of hard-core fly-fishers for steelhead is composed of only fifty people or so in the Seattle area.

A ways down the road, he pulled into the parking lot of Forecasters Pub, a restaurant and microbrewery. Inside, we ordered sandwiches and dark Redhook beer. I looked around. Now this was different. Microsoft Central. We were surrounded by the affluent young workers of a booming economy, packed in under the rough wood rafters, wearing their Orvis chinos, black tee shirts, their heads shaved—the works. This is the new Northwest.

Hey, Tim, I asked, have you given much thought to the relationship between fishing and, well, computers?

I expected some kind of enthusiastic description of the growing number of fishing web pages, but I was wrong. Tim squirmed a little and scowled. From the expression on his face, I realized that I'd touched a nerve.

"You have to understand where a steelhead fisherman would be coming from," he said. "The idea of automating fishing via the World Wide Web is the antithesis of what you would want to have happen. Some people think the World Wide Web is a good way to purvey all kinds of fishing information. For example, you can find detailed fishing reports, river flow levels, and diagrams of where to fish certain rivers. It seems obscene to me. Maybe it's because I do that during the day, and just want to get away from it."

But his reasoning was more complex than escapism, and more interesting.

A true steelheader, Tim believes in the value of secrets.

This fishing club I belong to, guy named Ralph Wahl was a member. Ralph died recently. He held some of the state records for fly-caught rainbow trout back when *Field & Stream* didn't draw a distinction between a rainbow trout and a steelhead. Of course, he was catching twenty-pound fish. He wrote a book called *One Man's Steelhead Shangri-La*. He had this place on the Skagit River and I won't tell you the name of it because he wouldn't. He believed that if he went around telling people his secrets, then they wouldn't have the thrill of discovery. I think he had it figured right. At our meetings, at the Washington Fly Fishing Club, we're supposed to stand and give a fishing report. One of the men serves as a gillie—a gillie is somebody who typically assisted an Englishman or Scotsman fish the Atlantic salmon rivers. At the meetings, if you didn't reveal where you caught your fish, if your report is too vague, the gillie walks up to you, holds out a net, and you're supposed to drop a quarter in. Ralph was the kind of guy who, the moment he stood up to give his report, would pull out a quarter to pay his fine in advance, because he had no intention of ever telling anybody where he was fishing. He kept this place a secret for years. Then, eventually, when it was wiped out by flooding, he wrote a book called *Steelhead Shangri-La*, and he still didn't disclose where it was. He would never tell where it was. Ever. So that's why I'm offended by this whole idea of telling everything, of automating and posting all the fishing information—the notion of instant gratification—rather than being willing to go pay the dues.

This was an understandable explanation of what some people might consider the elitism of steelheaders. Here I am surrounded by the worker bees of Microsoft, with a man who taps my cell phone—I'm wearing a cell phone, he initially tracked me down on a cell phone—in a universe of increasing connectedness. And yet, steelheading is still a world with secrets.

I asked him to imagine a fishing world in which fishing technology was maximized. He resisted, looked away. I asked again, and his analytical mind began to wrap around the idea of the automated angler.

"You could easily figure the analysis to make the catching of a fish a very measurable event."

Tell me more, I said.

OK, but it kind of sickens me to do it. If you're going to take it to the extreme, you'd put data collectors on the river, measure when the fish are in the river—a little electric-eye beam that would beep, beep, beep as they're moving through Puget Sound into the river and when they pass certain checkpoints. You'd then know that, say, ten thousand fish went above Concrete, Washington, and only two thousand went above Rockport, so guess where they all are? They're between Concrete and Rockport. Now we've isolated where the fish are, and we know they're fresh entries because we're looking at the chart on the Web that's showing us that all of these fish came in last Wednesday. The electric eyes would remove the need for your own judgment. Your understanding of natural cycles and the effect of weather on fish would no longer be needed. Now that you have a calculator you don't have to know how to do arithmetic.

The second piece of it would be that all the people who catch fish would agree that they're going to sign on and contribute data. So after a day on the river, you'd go back to your cabin or house, you pour yourself a little malt Scotch, and sit down in front of the terminal—and report how your fishing went that day. You plug in water temperature, fly color and type, entomological patterns. If you take this to its extreme, you're getting into virtual fishing. Why not just send a robot out to the river and have it collect data?

All of this is conceivable because of our instant gratification concept of technology—the belief that we should always take things that are hard and make them easy. Sometimes there's value in having something be hard to do. I can't explain why we choose to spend so many days on the river without catching much, if anything. It's not the opportunity to hook that one fish that motivates us—it's a lot more than that. I can't fully explain it. But start introducing technology into steelheading, and you've lost it. At what point do you no longer need to use your own judgment? At that point, any moron could catch a steelhead—if there are any left by then.

This sounds like cybersex, I said.

"Yeah, right. Anybody who's got the password and is willing to spend the monthly expense can sign on."

He shuddered. "Know what the fallacy is in all of this? Fishing, like a lot of things in life, is all about participation. Information is old the moment it occurs, so it's completely irrelevant that somebody had good fishing in a certain spot yesterday—or that the fish went through an hour ago or even fifteen minutes ago. You could read the Web in the morning, get there by noon, and a variable has changed. Information also raises expectations, so you're more likely to be disappointed, and less likely to participate the next time. So what's the use of that information? Hell, my wife and I don't use the World Wide Web at home enough to keep it. And we don't even have cable TV at home."

He finished his beer quickly, and we headed for the road.

⮌ TIM WAS TAKING me to see his good friend Walt Johnson, one of the pioneers of steelhead fly-fishing. Walt lives in a kind of gingerbread house deep in the woods. Tim clearly loves the old man and finds solace in the male-only world of his fishing club, which has a membership of about 200 and was founded in 1939. We were driving past Lake Stevens, north and east of Arlington. On our right was the Stillaguamish River. Its banks were heavily wooded. Now and then I could see old cabins—steelhead fishing shacks—weighed down with moss, on their way back into the earth. Our destination was the Darrington vicinity, and just past it. Many loggers and ex-loggers live in Darrington; the culture is definitely more backwoods than high-tech.

I could see mountains ahead, the Cascades, their peaks covered with snow or hidden in clouds, their flanks scarred by clear-cutting. "That's White Horse Mountain, the snow-capped one you can see in the background," Tim said. We passed over Deer Creek. "When you first brought technology and fishing up, it made me uncomfortable," he said. "It's a sore topic. My fishing club is made up mostly of older members. The old-timers refer to the younger members as Young Turks—in a positive way. Recently, some of the Young Turks decided we needed to create our own Web site for the Washington Fly Fishing Club. I opposed that. It's a male-only club, and the last thing we need is additional attention to that fact. Some guys had these grandiose ideas of publishing fishing reports, and all that. I was the one saying, 'I'm not sure this is where we want to spend our time.' Some of the older members didn't know what to make of the idea. But I lost; now we've got our own Web site."

So tell me about the male-only thing, I said.

He rolled his eyes and smiled—actually, it was more of a grimace. "I'm not a right-wing wacko, at all, but men definitely act differently when they're around men. Everyone knows everyone's quirks. About a third of the club thinks we ought to invite women. I've decided that I'm all for equality in the workplace, but that there are some parts of your life that just don't need to be political or commercial. This is one of those issues that you almost wish never came up—because it can be so damaging."

We turned onto an unpaved, muddy road, and Tim drove into a cluster of old-growth cedar and hemlock—dark, wet moss hanging from the limbs. In the middle of this grove a few shafts of light illuminated part of the roof, the front door, and walk of a cottage. Tim was right. It looked like the gingerbread man's house. The cottage was green with white shutters. Flowering dogwoods and a short, white picket fence surrounded it. The portico and window shutters were ornate. We parked and walked through a rose arbor, up a short, curving cobblestone walkway to the door. The Sasquatch of the Stilly was waiting for us.

That's Walt Johnson's nickname. Stilly is short for the Stillaguamish, the river Walt favors. His fellow anglers gave him that name a few years ago. They would see Walt on the river, look away, look back, and Walt would be gone; he would have faded into the woods like Bigfoot. For several years, he avoided other anglers, even his friends. Tim thinks it was because Walt was heartbroken after the death of his wife, of throat cancer. Walt, he said, is a particularly sensitive man.

He lives alone now, out in the woods. White-haired, slightly stooped, his face filled with light, he was glad to see us. It had been a while since his last visitor. He's known across the country for tying exquisite steelhead flies in the tradition of classic Atlantic salmon flies, ornate and artful. Some old Atlantic salmon flies sell in the range of fifteen hundred dollars; Walt's flies are collector's items, too, but they sell for under one hundred dollars. Now and then, he hands Tim a new fly.

Inside, sitting on Walt's French Provincial settee, I looked around. The ceiling was high. The room looked like an eighteenth-century French parlor. The life-sized images of butterflies were painted all over the walls. High on one wall, among the butterflies, was a mounted coastal cutthroat—a trout that spends part of its life in the sea, like the steelhead.

Starting almost in midsentence, Walt handed me an article he wrote in 1948, about planting wild steelhead in nearby Deer Creek. "Most of the upper river back then was trout and a few cutthroats," he said. "We used a bucket brigade and a truck. The fingerlings were so wild that they wouldn't stay in the pools. They were always jumping out, so we had to cover the pools with tarps." He told me how, back in the early forties, the Washington Fly Fishing Club convinced the state to close a stretch of the Skagit River to any type of fishing except fly-fishing. They accomplished this through a letter-writing campaign and personal political connections. The closure was one of the first times in the western United States that a river was reserved for a single kind of sportfishing. Gear fishermen were incensed. "They said, 'If we have fly closure, where are our kids going to fish?' They used every argument."

So where did the kids fish? I asked.

"I suppose in some of the creeks, maybe some of the lakes around here. Ponds, whatnot. The thing is, they were catching downstream migrant summer steelhead in the Skagit. They didn't realize it. We needed to stop that from happening."

Even then, in the early '40s, you knew that these were rare fish?

"Oh, yeah. Needed to be protected. And we knew that fly-fishing would protect them more than bait fishing."

I noticed stacks of letters on tables, on the floor, on the chairs, all of them from his fishing associates around the world. Walt's generation still believes in the power of a letter, still views the world as a network of individuals. His was a generation that actually believed that one letter to the editor could change the world, or part of it.

Nonetheless, Walt is finding it difficult to hold back the tide. He mourns the loss of solitude on the streams near him, or at least his definition of solitude, imprinted in 1939. "There's too many fishermen for the pools. These guys are in there at dark, they wade out there and stay there all day in one spot and they don't move." Definitely impolite, to steelhead fly-fishers at least. Some anglers are now using Spey rods— sixteen-foot, double-handed rods that originated in Scotland more than a century ago. "They've found out they can catch steelhead that way. They can throw the line all the way across the Skagit or some of these other rivers." He shook his head. The farther the fish from the angler, when hooked, the harder and longer the fight will be, building up lactic acid in the fish. Therefore, Walt believes Spey anglers are harming the steelhead population; the exhausted fish die later, out of sight.

Other changes lap at the shores of his shrinking world. "I hear these chainsaws going at about eight in the morning, buzzing like bees. They're logging all the way to the point." He hears the clear-cutting up on the mountain, and sometimes the logging companies show up at his door asking if he'll sell the old grove that surrounds his house. The more they offer, the more he resists. "Now that the big corporations own half the mountain, they've been logging behind me all over on that side. They were supposed to leave a greenbelt between the rivers, but they don't do that. The dollar sign is all they notice. They take our trees and ship them to Japan. Where's the wildlife, where's everything else going to go? Their habitat is being destroyed." He reached forward and inserted a videotape into his VCR. Here was a speech he had made a few years ago to the club, on the occasion of his eightieth birthday:

> Back in the deep woods of the north fork of the Stillaguamish River lived the Sasquatch. He had passed great hordes of silver creatures leaping from the water as they migrated upstream. Although he didn't understand their behavior, he accepted it. But now . . . he wondered what had happened to all those silver crea-

tures . . . On crossing Deer Creek in years past he had seen these same creatures as they lie on the bottom of the deep pool. He had assumed that they had been on a long journey and had returned to this their home to rest. But now these same pools are filled with dirt and debris, and their habitat destroyed. Sasquatch stopped to sit on a log and rest, feeling very depressed, contemplating all the things he'd witnessed . . . Lo and behold, one of those silver creatures he remembered seeing in the distant past rose from the depths and raced downstream in an effort to escape. Sasquatch followed as fast as his lumbering gait would allow . . . He gently removed a feathered object and allowed the silvery form to swim away. He felt a deep sense of gratification that these native creatures had survived. Would there be more or was this the last of its kind? . . .

Walt, I said, would you ever consider giving up fishing if you thought it would help the steelhead?

He said, quickly, "Sure, sure." In fact, he hasn't been steelheading for three years. The waters may be too fast and deep for him now, anyway. He got up slowly and led us into his fly-tying room. His vise and table faced a window with a view of the Cascades, through cedars, and several birdhouses raised on eight-foot stakes.

On the wall was a picture of Tim holding a steelhead caught in British Columbia on a fly that Walt loaned him.

"I told Tim, 'When you get up there, everybody's going to be trying to throw across the river. The fish are lying in front of you, twenty feet.' Tim walked out there and the first cast, he gets this one over nineteen pounds. On my fly." Tim smiled broadly.

"Oh, and here's something else," said Walt, reaching with quavering hand to touch a small, delicate bird's nest on a shelf. A fly was hanging from it, the line woven into the nest. "See, the hackle in the back is a badger hackle," said Walt. "That's the pattern I caught my first steelhead on." He had found the nest along the river, the fly in it, a fly he had lost while fishing years before. He smiled at the poetry of that tale. As we were leaving, I asked Walt if he believed in Sasquatch.

"Well you know, it's funny, because living here in the woods, I don't see people unless they come to visit me. A couple times during the night, I heard—"

He knocked on the wall hard, twice.

"It was on the wall to my bedroom. 'What the dickens is this?' I look around out there, can't see anything. Some time later I heard—"

He knocked on the wall three times. Harder.

"Of course, my friend Dale lives down the road; he says it's a female Sasquatch who's come calling for me."

The Sasquatch of the Stilly said goodbye, and we headed east.

⌐ AS WE DROVE higher into the Cascades and farther from people, Tim said, "Did you notice how Walt read to you from that article about the science of fish sight?" Tim's theory is that Walt's generation truly believed in what they called scientific angling, that American men of the middle part of the twentieth century held deep faith in the goodness of technology and science.

"Back then, technology wasn't invasive, not yet. That was back in the days when technology was still somewhat gentle, at least in daily life. Remember I told you about Ralph Wahl, and his secret? I spent hours sitting in Ralph Wahl's basement eating bologna sandwiches listening to tape recordings that he'd made on Mystery Lake while fishing with his friends. He'd actually take a reel-to-reel recorder out in the boat with him. Now and then, on these tapes, you can hear the scream of fly line leaving a reel as a fish ran, then someone would say things like, 'Gee, Ralph, nice fish—it was sure great coming out here. Too bad they're not biting; too bad we had to drive one hundred miles from your house to get here.' And you could tell they were sticking total red herrings in there, to keep the location secret." He laughed. "But they believed in technology . . ." His voice trailed off.

I mentioned those stacks of letters to Tim, and said: So many of us now perceive the world not as a social network of friends and acquaintances, but as a mass culture too large to be personal.

"Exactly. People my age often have a sense of hopelessness," said Tim. "We see something like what's happening to the steelhead, and we try to get involved—but then we learn where the power really lies, in the hydroelectric dams and development, the commercial interests. So we withdraw into tunnel vision."

Ironically, Tim, a master of one corner of the technological universe, feels less powerful than the Sasquatch of the Stilly.

What happens, I wondered, when a generation loses hope and belief—the sense of personal power? "Then the million letters that would have made a difference never get sent," Tim said, a little sourly. "I'm looking forward to fishing."

He drove, and talked about the cultural distance between the fly-fishers and the goo chuckers—as gear fishermen are sometimes called by the fly-fishers. "Don't get me wrong, though, fly-fishers don't have a lock on taste or sanity." He described some of his younger fly-fishing friends.

One of them recently proclaimed himself the Steelhead God. Another fishing partner believes in Sasquatch and in hexes. "He draws the witchy evil eye in the sand to ward off other fishermen from his favorite spots on the river." This same guy booby-traps trails that lead to the good spots on the rivers "by, well, crapping on the path. I guess he's marking his territory."

This is strange country.

"Up there, that's where the Bulgarian wild man lived," said Tim, pointing to the slopes of Whitehorse Mountain. I looked up at the frigid peaks, alpine and moody, caked with ice and snow and beaten by clouds as dark as your worst nightmare.

For years, residents of the small towns near the mountain had reported thefts and break-ins by a kind of real-life Sasquatch who would slip invisibly into cabins. He would steal canned goods, clothing—whatever he needed to survive, but nothing more. Once, he took a pair of socks and left his own, reports the *Seattle Times*. One woman would leave food out for him, but he never took it; he avoided occupied houses. From his fingerprints, police said they knew the suspect's name, Mincio Vasilev Donciev. Details about his past were sketchy. A former policeman, he was apparently convicted of murder in 1954, served a five-year sentence in his native Bulgaria, then worked as a shepherd. In 1966, he killed a villager he caught stealing lambs and was sent to a work camp. Four years later, he escaped from Bulgaria and found his way to the United States. He lived with a Seattle woman, but when she kicked him out, police say, he tried to burn down her house. Then he disappeared into the Cascades.

Twelve years later, a few days before my trip with Tim, the sixty-seven-year-old fugitive was finally tracked down by Joel Hardin, fifty-eight, a retired Border Patrol officer.

Later, I called Hardin, who had been hired by the frustrated Snohomish County sheriff and the U.S. Forest Service. Hardin is a legend himself, one of the nation's best trackers or sign cutters, who learned the art of tracking in the '60s and '70s tracking drug smugglers and murderers and AWOL Marines, from the Mexican border to Riverside, California. He tracked one man one hundred and twenty miles through the harshest, hottest back country before he caught him. A modest man, he told me, "Tracking the Bulgarian was nothing special." But consider this: Hardin relied on bent twigs, flattened plants, or a footprint from which he could tell that "the man walked with purpose, in a measured manner, and he was very patient." He could also tell that Donciev often carried a seventy-five-pound pack ten miles up and down the mountain. "A misconception about tracking is that signs disappear quickly. But some of the signs the man left were five years old."

Hardin tracked Donciev for one hundred hours. Police planted electronic sensors on a trail Hardin had found. The Bulgarian tripped a sensor. Then the officers moved in with a police dog that attacked Donciev's legs and tore off two toes and part of his left foot.

Hardin remains puzzled by the spareness of Donciev's lair.

The hole was six feet by eight feet and lined with logs. The roof was covered with tarps, dirt, and brush. The distance between the floor and ceiling was only thirty inches. He had dug a smaller hole in the dirt floor so that he could sit on the floor and put his feet in the hole and have three inches to spare above his head. "He could sit there and almost touch all four walls." Donciev kept two loaded guns. Hooks on the walls held flashlights, most of them with dead batteries. Everything was dry, neat, almost militaristic. To Hardin, the most mysterious wilderness was the one inside Donciev's mind, where the wild man moved in darkness. "I felt admiration for him," Hardin said. "To be able to live that way for so long." And yet, Hardin is haunted by one fact. "We could find no evidence of any craft, any carving, anything that would have occupied his head and hands." One thing that Hardin did find were spears that the wild man was probably using to catch steelhead and salmon in the rivers I was to fish.

Tim and I spent the next two days fishing on the Sauk and Skagit Rivers, using strong, 8-weight flyrods and sinking line and brightly colored flies to match the strength of the steelhead we never caught. Tim knew these rivers well, drove the jet sled fast over water both rough and smooth. He drove standing up, watching for snags. He drove as fast as he could through the shallow waters, to keep the boat up on a plane, so that it was drawing only three or four inches of water. Tim had built his own rods. I noted that he was using a reel made in the 1940s.

On the first afternoon, in fading light, while wading in quicksilver-colored water with the Cascades cold above us, Tim became agitated. "Look!" he said. The steelhead were "rolling," he said. Which meant that a rush of them had come around the bend of the river and were heading east from the saltwater. The way they rolled, Tim figured they were fresh fish coming in from the sound, perhaps with the sea lice still clinging to them. One curved over the surface of the water feet from me, its side as bright as chrome. "That's a kind of 'fuck you,' when they roll over in front of you like that." Whatever the intent, it was a beautiful sight.

That evening, next to the river, we sat on the tailgate of his Toyota and watched the quicksilver river grow darker.

"Sometimes you care more than others, and today I cared," said Tim, staring at the water. "I wanted that fish. Three days of fishing last weekend, it was a wonderful experience, but it starts to build and build and build and there comes a time when you want to catch a fish. Sometimes you can almost get depressed about it, and begin to doubt yourself."

He reached into a satchel in the truck and pulled out a bottle of fine malt Scotch and two cups. This is a traditional steelheading ritual, he said. "At the end of the day."

We settled back on the tailgate and listened to the boat slide against a rock. Down the river, I could see some camper trailers with their lights on, people moving slowly inside, and I could smell the smoke from a campfire. An osprey flew along the surface of the river and picked up a fish and flew into the trees. Not a single cell phone could be heard.

He raised his cup. "Here's to the Sasquatch of the Stilly."

"And to the Bulgarian wild man," I added. I lifted my cup.

"And to steelhead," he said, "wherever they are."

↜ SINCE MY TRIP to the Northwest, some things have changed. The undeclared war between the United States and Canada is over. In 1997, at the Salmon conference in Seattle, the two governments, commercial fishermen, and assorted Indian tribes were locked in a furious, fish-flinging brawl—and the chief negotiators remained frozen in pessimism and platitudes. Now here's the good news. Mother Nature and human beings seem to be on the same wavelength, for once. On June 30, 1999, after five years of negotiation, Canada and the United States signed a new agreement aimed at protecting and building up the dwindling runs.

The ecologically complex document essentially comes down to this: Canadians and Americans can't catch and keep fish that were spawned in the rivers of the other country. That solution won't be easy to enforce. Wild salmon and steelhead are difficult to track, but hatchery fish, tagged by clipping a fin, are identifiable. So, if a Canadian catches a U.S.-tagged fish, he must let it go or face a stiff penalty. The same is true for U.S. fishers who catch Canadian fish.

The second change involves U.S. law, which severely restricts fishing. Since 1991, twenty-four wild salmon and steelhead runs, spanning 157,000 square miles of the Pacific Northwest—that's nearly twice the area protected for the famous spotted owl—have been listed under the Endangered Species Act. Most commercial fishermen aren't pleased with these restrictions. And most Indians in the United States, under treaties signed in the 1850s, will probably continue fishing as they have in the past. "But from the sportsman's point of view, this is all great news," said Frank Amato, the *Salmon-Trout-Steelheader* magazine publisher. Though sport fishermen also face restrictions, at least they'll still be able to catch an occasional salmon or steelhead.

The most important edict, however, came from Mother Nature. "El Niño is over, and the biologists have discovered—by studying documents going back to the time of Lewis and Clark—that the salmon-steelhead runs ebb and flow in twenty-year patterns," Amato said. "We're now entering a twenty-year upswing in cooler weather, which favors these fish. On some rivers, we're already having some of the best salmon runs in years." Nonetheless, salmon and steelhead remain endangered by development, pollution, and—in the future—global warming. As good habitat is destroyed by development, hatchery fish displace wild fish, and the gene pool shrinks.

In mid-1999, a suburban teenager who had heard tales from his grandfather of fish as long as his leg, walked up San Mateo Creek in the rough country near Camp Pendleton in San Diego County, and found a run of little southern steelhead, a species thought to be extinct since the 1950s. Somehow, now that wet weather has filled the streams again, the southern steelhead had come home.

As it turns out, this fish, which is native to the relatively small biological zone of San Diego County and, possibly, of Baja (where my son Jason and I had fished, early in this journey), from which some biologists believe all rainbow trout emerged tens of thousands of years ago—this species of steelhead is thought to hold the oldest and hardiest genes of any seagoing rainbow trout, genes that have allowed it to survive droughts, higher water temperatures and perhaps long-term global warming. If the other, more recent strains are diminished or destroyed in the future by rising temperatures, only the most genetically diverse steelhead will be able to withstand the changes.

Ironically, California's fish—not the Northwest's—may someday be the last steelhead.

City Waters

~~~~~~~~~~~~~~~~~~~~~~~~

*What squire in the world is there so poor as
not to have a hack and a couple of greyhounds
and a fishingrod to amuse himself with in his
own village?*

—Don Quixote

A Trout Grows in Brooklyn

$\backsim\!\backsim$

ALONG THE EAST RIVER, the junkies have decapitated the streetlights. They split open the fixtures and pull the copper wiring out, and sell it.

At an iron railing below, fishermen huddle in their overcoats, their hands covered with blood—the oozing red fluid of an unsavory bait called the bloodworm. These men, Dominicans, Puerto Ricans, Russians, and others, catch big striped bass, perch, bluefish, and fine crabs. The city posts signs warning anglers not to eat more than one fish a month, because of PCBs and other pollutants. But most of the men ignore the rule. Some of them need the food. And besides, the river is cleaner these days.

You learn a lot about America while fishing. It's a better America than the one the headlines or those headless streetlights suggest.

"You think this is such a cold city, but people care about their fish, and about this river," said Angel Franco, a photographer for *The New York Times* who grew up in the South Bronx, East Harlem, and Brooklyn. "They'll run you over with their car, but don't mess with their fish. They got priorities, man!"

Franco, forty-seven, still considers himself a man of the streets, but three years ago he became an avid fly-fisher. His hair tied back with a strip of cloth, he walks the rocky shore of a river island across from the South Bronx. At 240 pounds, he's an imposing presence. For the past hour, Angel had driven me along Harlem River Drive, my first guide to this unexpected world of urban angling in New York City.

"Look there, about four hundred feet, there's an abandoned firehouse, and people manage to climb down behind it and catch good fish there. Now look at this, this is all fishing area here. Look at this, these guys are here in the early morning, waiting for the tide to start coming in. Poor folks come from those projects to fish here, to take the fish home to eat. See there? That's the police department's harbor unit, OK? You see how it narrows? On the other side of that, I fish right there. I wade, man—I use waders out there." He laughed, knowing that would be an odd sight to those uninitiated to the charms of fly-fishing the East River. "It's a couple of feet deep. You can walk across when it's low tide."

The whole river?

"The whole river! Not this side but the narrow side, to the Bronx. Now look at this." He had driven over a bridge and parked his car on Randall's Island. He took a high-priced Orvis flyrod out of his trunk, re-moved it from its aluminum tube, and assembled it. We walked to the dark rocks along the East River where the brownish-gray water swirled under an overcast sky. Across the river was the South Bronx. When An-gel looks at red brick buildings of the South Bronx, he doesn't see the broken windows and rubble. "I stand here and I see the light change, man, and I see the paintings of Edward Hopper.

"I meet people out here I don't have anything in common with out-side of the fact that we're human and we fish," he said. "I'm a pretty big guy, but some of these guys cast a shadow on you, and you think, 'Oh, shit, I'm going to have to fight my way out of here.' The guy goes, 'Hey, man, what kind of bait?' And you go, 'Oh, all right, bro!'"

The river is cleaner than you might expect, with a healthy population of striped bass and bluefish. Through the efforts of the Riverkeepers and other environmentalist groups, the river is improving—but those PCBs are here for a few angling lifetimes.

"Several years back, Mayor Giuliani was talking about fishing in the city, and he came up with an undersized striped bass. I called City Hall and said, 'That was an undersized bass, he was supposed to throw that back!' Every person that fished knew that that was an undersized striped bass and they called him! What happened? He had to 'fess up to, 'Hey, we bought this fish dead and we put it on a hook and I walked over and pretended to catch it.'" Angel threw back his head and laughed. Laugh-ing seems to come as easily to Angel as breathing. He was using a fly he had made, for bluefish, with an epoxy head. He was wearing an Orvis cap and wading coat. His girlfriend gets on his case because he buys all this expensive fly-fishing gear to wear. He tells her he has to dress down all week because he's a street photographer, so when he goes fishing he likes to dress up. He carries his flies in a Dominican cigar box: *Reserva Especial*.

He made a long cast and watched his fly drift in an arc. And he began to tell me his story.

My father died when I was nine. He was an alcoholic; he drank himself to death. He was a Puerto Rican radical—very political. He was a merchant seaman, so he used to take us down by the waterfront. I fished once with him. He bought me a spinning rod and I caught my first fish in Central Park, what we call Castle Lake. I caught a little sunny, I still remember that. I remember the light, I remember what the fish looked like. I remember the fishing rod was yellow and red. Remember how they used to have those funny colored rods?

I remember going with my father and my older brother to this weird store on some side street somewhere, right, to buy this thing. My mother and father were separated and we came back with these fishing rods and my mother said, "Son of a bitch never gave you anything and he's taking you fishing?" She kept trying to break them and I guess they were fiberglass or plastic and they just kept going, bending. Finally, when they broke, it was a stringy break, but it was still together and she got even more frustrated.

We grew up from the *barrio* across the river, which they called Spanish Harlem. When my dad died my mother—she couldn't read or write—had to go on welfare because I started a grease fire cooking at the restaurant while she was working. The city came in and took us away and said to her, "If you do not become a mother, you'll never see your kids again." So what do they do? They gave her a welfare check and she had to stay home, and we got to come home. As soon as that check came in, she would take it, pass it on down the (he makes a slapping motion at my face). . . . She would go down the line of her nine boys and say, "This is not what we came here for. We didn't come here to receive a check, we came here to bust our asses." My mom's in her seventies. She'll kick your ass.

He laughed hard, and moved up the bank to cast to the boil of the incoming tide.

My mother always taught us: "If you get busted, hold your head up high because if you did it, admit it. Do what you have to do, make up for it, but hold your head up high. Don't ever lower your head to any problems or any issues. Attack! If you're a criminal, when the judge finishes with you, I will kick your ass." Exactly that. The other saying was, "Above me, only God and airplanes—because I can't control them." The other thing my mother did, which was cool, I got baptized a Mormon once, right? We're baptized in all kinds of religions, because if you were baptized in a religion you'd get a free apartment from that church for a while. If you became a born-again Christian, right, and you were down and out and you had children, they'd say, "We'll save you and get you an apartment." It's a payoff. We used to get baptized. It's a whole survival technique, man! So we would move from place to place. . . .

Now here I am, covering the streets for the *Times*—I can deal straight across from here to the White House, man. Not a problem. I've been to all those places. Sometimes I am sitting in someplace like that, and I say, "This is not bad being Anna's son."

"She's got nine boys, man."

Did any of them get in trouble?

"Not a one, not a one."

He said growing up poor made him appreciate the city, because he was in it, not above it. "You found things," he said, "like fishing in this river. It's there. If you wait for it to come to you—well, James, you ain't gonna get it, you know? But like Mom said, if you throw your ass out there and expose yourself to the world, then you find all these great things."

You know what's great about fishing this river? If you fish and you catch a fish, people will stop and applaud. Earlier this year we were out at Sunken Meadows state park and this spinning guy came out and has this huge striped bass. People were applauding this guy, right? He cast out again, caught another one! He's bringing them in and this little old man is standing there. So he takes the rod and he hands it to this old, old guy in his seventies, you know, and the guy's battling the fish and he brings it in. And he says, "It's your fish," and this old guy barely has the strength to pull it in. Then everybody starts to applaud again. It was great!

When people see me out here fishing and they look at me funny, I say, "Look, this is why my mother came to America, so I could fly-fish, I can play golf!" And it's great. As a matter of fact, this morning, there's a British guy that lives next door to us and I say, "Hey man, do you fly-fish?" He says, "No." Meanwhile he has the jacket on, the whole British look, right, and he's on his way to work and I'm thinking, "There's something wrong with this!" I say, "Look, you gotta learn how to fly-fish." All of a sudden I realize, here's a Puerto Rican guy, first-generation American, going to teach a British guy how to fly-fish. I mean, that's what this place is like, New York City.

He fished a little while longer. I had forgotten my flyrod, so he handed his to me and I cast for a while. "If you walk up the river, you'll see some Puerto Rican fishing—sometimes the method is a Budweiser can, monofilament line, and a weight and a hook at the end, and that's the way you fish on the island," he said. You hold the can and throw the line overhand. "But on the island you have this ring, a steel ring, which now they sell in hard plastic. Put all this line on it, take it and stand here and, just like David and Goliath, cast it out and pull in this huge fish! The Puerto Rican guys that live in my building, when I'm working with my rod they say, 'Man, where's your can! You traitor!' Because I'm walking around with a flyrod: 'That's not fishing, brother, go get a can and put some line on it and cast it out!' I tell him that's why I came to America— to fly-fish."

We walked to where the river widens out and the point of the island faces Hellgate. A black couple was parked there, necking. Angel walked down a slope and, balancing carefully, walked along the large granite riprap rocks to a man who looked like he was in his sixties. He was a bait fisherman, using bloodworms, with a heavy rod and a bell on the line. He wore a Super Bowl '96 cap. I followed and Angel translated.

"He lives in Cypress Island in the Bronx," said Angel. "Says he's been eating the fish from here for the last thirty-five years." He teased Angel, told him he should put a bell on his flyrod. He offered us some blood-worms. We declined. This November week had been unseasonably warm, but now the wind was getting colder. Upriver, a group of black guys were breaking up firewood and stuffing it in an oil drum. They lit it.

"Now, these are guys that if you normally saw them walking down the street, they look like big, tough guys, right?"

I walked over to them. They were looking at a big osprey sitting in a small tree. Two feet tall, beautiful cream belly, gray wings. The leaves were shaking in the wind. The grass around the tree was littered with beer bottles. The osprey watched us. One young man with gold earrings was stoking the fire. A teenager had caught a small bluefish; it lay gasping on the bank. "That's a beautiful fish," I said.

"We've been trying for about a week here. Trying to hook up on some of the last blues that are around," said the fisherman. "They end in the fall, when the water gets cold they head south. Basically just fish for stripers until December 15, and then you can't keep the stripers any-more until March 21." His name was Carlos. He said he bakes the fish he catches here, because "when you bake 'em you got 'em in your alu-minum foil and all that water just drips down into the pan in the bot-tom. When you fry it everything stays in the oil, so you're just cooking whatever's in the fish."

Carlos said the four of them fish here often, except for the sullen one who was feeding the fire. "He just tags along once in a while. When he's bored."

What's the biggest fish you've caught out of here?

"Two summers ago, it was a thirty-seven-inch striper, nineteen pounds . . . look at that!" Carlos got up quickly and walked to his buddy's line. "He's getting a hit over there and he's got his back to the line. I watch everybody's rod, everybody's!"

On the way back to the car, Angel said that he often sees the osprey in that tree, watching him as he fishes. Pulling away, we passed the car where the couple had been necking. Now they were under a coat and the coat was heaving up and down. "Brother getting down, got a down coat!" said Angel, laughing his generous laugh. "Where else but in America can you go fishing and get a porno show at the same time?"

Angel was headed for work, back over the bridge. On the way, he dropped me off at 96th Street next to the river and told me that was the "Mason-Dixon line." Walk toward the lower street numbers along the river, he told me. "Don't turn left, it gets dicey up there." We shook hands and he drove away.

I turned left, toward Spanish Harlem. I wanted to see what they were catching up there.

✿ AMERICA ISN'T IN the headlines, it's in the details. Walking up FDR Drive into Spanish Harlem, I watched the clouds move over the East River, changing the color of the water from light brown to dark olive. Above 96th Street the complexion of the neighborhoods changes, too, from boutique pastel to housing-project brick. I stopped and talked with a tall man wearing a tattered coat, striped violet pants, and a stocking cap. His rod was held to the railing by a bungee cord.

What's biting?

"Bluefish."

He's from the Dominican Republic. He led me to a cooler. "Bluefish," he said, again, lifting a three-pounder. "Yeah, yeah, yeah. *Boom, boom, boom!*"

He was talking about how bluefish bite, but right then four cars stacked up in a rear-ender behind us. *Boom, boom, boom.* The fishermen rushed over to look. On the other side of the railing, two drivers—upscale young guys—leaped out of their cars, took a look at the less-than-fastidiously-dressed anglers, and flipped open their cell phones. They had a "Beam me up, Trump" look in their eyes. I kept walking.

A dozen blocks into Spanish Harlem, past a project surrounded by ra-

zor wire and park benches with people sleeping on them, wrapped like
mummies in the cold, I saw a pier and walked out onto it. I met Sal
Quintana, who came here from Puerto Rico when he was seven years
old. He was fishing with his twelve-year-old son, Julio. Tall and gentle,
Sal wears an Indiana Jones hat, with a strip of leopard-patterned material wrapped around it, trailing down his neck. He takes his son fishing to
keep him away from bad company.

Despite this worry, he said life is getting better. "They clean it up, this
river. Four years ago I catch trash. Bicycles, car chassis, mattresses." The
once-crumbling pier has been refurbished, too. Sal and his buddies even
fish here at night. "So far, nothing happens."

He pointed upriver. "You see that car under the bridge, the person
walking away there? One day that was years ago when my daughter was
little, I went that way home and I caught a thirty-six-pounder, a striper,
a striped bass. It was bigger than my daughter, it was like this tall."

I noted an intricate pendant around his neck.

"That's Jesus."

I told him it was beautiful.

"I don't like gold, I like silver. I don't like gold because they sold Jesus
for gold and I don't like that. I'm very religious."

Jesus was a fisherman.

"Yeah, yeah, he was a fisherman. He was a carpenter but he used to
fish, too. Hey, this my friend Bobo, another fisherman." Bobo was going
through the trash cans, collecting the aluminum cans. Now another man
approached us, wearing a Miami Dolphins jacket and a black beret.
"That's my friend George. He don't let nobody litter."

George works for the city?

"No, he does it on his own. He takes a broom and soap and cleans the
whole pier." Sal pulls a crab trap up and baits it with pieces of fish.

"On the pier, we share everything. You see another fisherman in trouble, you gotta help him. It's a rule."

A homeless couple—a black woman and a white man—live on this
pier. Their shopping cart is parked a few feet away, neatly packed with
blankets, a rolled mattress, water bottles, a bag of briquettes and a grill.
The fishermen save their beer and soda cans for the couple, and sometimes they feed them. The other day, Sal took a bluefish home and
cooked it, Puerto Rican style, and brought it back to the couple.

"Nice people," he said. "My son comes down here just to see them."
Julio nods. Sal frowns. The couple has been gone for three days. "We
don't know where they are." The fishermen guard the cart. "We don't let
nobody touch it. Everybody respects it." Then Sal brought up the World
Series. "Hey, you from San Diego, that's the home of the Padres. Four

SAL QUINTANA

games in a row, man. They beat Atlanta! They beat Houston!" He didn't even mention the Yankees, who beat the Padres in four straight games. The Yankees go without saying, I guess.

"See that tall building out there? I work right next to it. I'm a cutter. I cut any kind of material, leather, plastic, whatever." He said this proudly, and he told me that he used to be a body-builder. "I competed. I won Mr. New York State. I've been in the magazines." His eyes were honest; I believed him. "I knew Arnold Schwarzenegger. I met him in 1969, when he first came from Austria and couldn't speak good English."

He smiled, leaned over and looked at his line curling down into the water. His son leans over with him. One man went to Hollywood, the other man fishes. It's America.

~ THE NEXT DAY I took the subway over to the Urban Angler Ltd. fly shop on East 25th Street, between Park and Lexington: third-floor walkup. This is where the smooth dogs in red suspenders go to buy expensive fly-fishing gear. Angel Franco had suggested I look up Edwin Valentin, his fly-tying and urban angling hero.

Edwin was splitting his time between fixing some plumbing pipes and tying some of the finest flies to be found in New York City. He's getting famous for these flies. He's thirty-five, about five feet four inches tall, Buddha-shaped, with shaved sidewalls and a flattop, two earrings in one ear. He started fishing when he was nine, introduced to it by his aunt, who took him to Coney Island. When he was fourteen, his stepfather gave him a flyrod and he'd go by train from the rough Brooklyn neighborhood of Bushwick to Central Park to fish for sunfish and bass. He would drop by the Urban Angler to stare at the racks of flies. Steve Fisher, the dry-witted owner of the Urban Angler, loaned Edwin fly-tying books, and Edwin began to tie flies by imitating what he saw in the books. He also began to turn over rocks in the park and take bugs and flies home to study and copy them.

Edwin cannot read or write and, according to Steve, is probably dyslexic.

"He hung around the fly shop so much," Steve said, standing behind a counter holding expensive reels, "that we figured the hell with it, he might as well work here." The title Edwin uses for himself at the shop is "tier, stock boy, take people out fishing." Steve calls him the resident urban expert and considers Edwin something of a genius—a fly-tying savant.

I asked Edwin about his neighborhood.

> I don't want to be there. I take you someday, you and me in the
> day. Not at night, I got shot a couple of times. Right in my hand,
> you can see the dot right here. I grabbed the gun. I'm a lucky guy. If
> I didn't have this job right now, I'd be in jail or dead. Shootings, you
> see people die. Can't do nothing. I ain't playing no hero, no. You see
> it, you keep on walking. That's the rules over there. You don't open
> your mouth, you're OK. You open your mouth, you'll be the next
> one. "See anything?" "I ain't saw nothing." I like fishing and pigeons.
> I got a coop. I used to have a thousand pigeons. Nice ones, not rats.
> The pigeons on the street that you see, we call them rats. They eat
> anything. The other birds, we feed them corn; nice. It's a hobby. My
> friends who see me in the fishing catalogs say I'm lucky. They think
> I'm all on drugs but no, I'm fishing, fishing. I'm trying to get some
> money to move over here.

Right there in the Urban Angler Ltd. catalog, you can see the flies he
creates, with his initials next to them: March Brown, Split Shuck
Emerger, Snow Shoe Rabbit, Bass Clouser, Eelworm, and the Bushwick
Special—appropriately named. He calls it a "bushwack" special. "These
guys come in three-piece suits and treat him like the guru of fly-fishing
and fly-tying," Steve said. "It's really very interesting."

Steve and his wife and Angel Franco have offered Edwin a reward—
to take him fishing in the Rockies or Alaska—if he'll let them teach him
to read. "So far, he's just a little too macho," said Steve. "Plus, he's too
loyal to the city. He's really not interested in fishing beyond here."

Steve explained the curious makeup of New York's urban anglers:

> Here in the local fisheries there seem to be two distinct groups,
> for the most part, split socioeconomically. There's a bunch of fly-
> fishermen in the higher end, and spin-fishermen; they're in it for the
> sport. Then there's the guys lined up with their sinkers, for food—
> probably the vast majority of people out there are out there for
> food, no question, whether they know about the rules on eating fish
> [or not]. More than anyone I know, Angel Franco lives in those two
> completely different worlds. There's very little interaction between
> those two groups. They just tolerate each other. "They're all fisher-
> men so they can't be that bad" is more or less the attitude. Edwin is
> unique in that he crossed completely over from one culture to the
> other.

There are angling wonders here, too.

I have fished all over the world, and I get such a kick out of fishing locally. New York City, Brooklyn, Queens, the Bronx. I go out with this fellow Joe Shasta in the harbor in a nineteen- or twenty-four-foot center-console boat. You can go out at sunset; it's like you're fishing in the middle of the Land of Oz, with all the lights on the buildings. Last spring, Edwin and I fished one day in Central Park; it was a cool, windy day, but everything was in bloom and the colors were intense. It's hard to believe you're in the middle of New York City, out there in a rowboat surrounded by spectacular beauty. Of course, two days later a guy was murdered nearby. But it can be spectacularly beautiful, particularly on the harbor at night. I took my wife and my daughter and my future son-in-law out in July, and we stayed in a drift from the UN building down to 14th Street, catching fish. The sun set in back of the Manhattan skyline, then it got dark and all the lights came on and it just blows you away.

Let's say we get on a subway and go up to 86th Street with fly-rods to go fishing at Gracie Mansion. We'll get all kinds of comments from people. Gracie Mansion is the dividing line. Gracie is at 90th, if you get above 96th Street, that's part of the danger zone. What I find shocking is the number of people who ask us questions, like they've never seen people fishing in New York. Don't they ever open their eyes? You can't possibly drive along the East Side or the West Side and not see people fishing almost any time of year.

Maybe it's because the anglers tend to be poorer, economically.

You're absolutely right, no question about that. But we've gotten more and more people involved in higher walks of life. The future of urban angling will depend on whether the city opens access to the reservoir. The city isn't using the reservoir in Central Park anymore, because they're worried about terrorists poisoning the water. If they ever pull the fence around it down, that'll open up a tremendous resource.

Poachers do fish the Central Park reservoir, though, sneaking over the fence at night.

"Kid drowned in there a while back," said Edwin. "And in the lake there, where you can fish, people catch ducks for dinner in there, in the nets.

EDWIN VALENTIN

And them Asian people catch bluegill, open them up and eat them right there. Sushi." He made an unpleasant face. "Oh yeah, the tail is still moving. They cut them up and eat them. I tell them they're sick. I tell you straight out, crazy people. They ask me for the fish I catch, they can't believe I'm releasing them. I tell them, 'Catch your own fish.' I give them a hook and line. They're crazy."

Steve laughed. "He doesn't have a great tolerance for cultural differences."

Edwin led me to a counter and picked out one of his flies—a long, delicate saltwater minnow creation—and gave it to me. Then he went back to work on the plumbing, whistling bird calls.

↬ I MET JOAN STOLIAR at her Greenwich Village apartment, and her husband drove us to Brooklyn. Because of Joan, a trout grows in Brooklyn. Make that over four hundred trout. They're coming of age in a classroom at Intermediate School 318, where they bump and dart around. A cluster of seventh-graders attend the fry. They hover over the little piece of ersatz stream and wave their hands like parental fins.

"It's important that kids get exposed to the lifecycle," said Stoliar, the fairy godmother of this scene, who appears to be in her sixties. She said she's survived two types of cancer, and I can see why. Joan never stops smiling. She often travels the streets of New York on a Lambretta motor scooter while wearing high heels. The heels are for safety, she said. "Nobody dares hit you if you're wearing heels."

She's also an important player in the tweedy world of New York fly-fishing; Stoliar was probably the first woman to join the old, distinguished Theodore Gordon Flyfishers club. She talked the club into sponsoring New York State's trout-in-the-classroom program—with the help of Trout Unlimited, the National Fish and Wildlife Foundation, Hudson River Foundation, and Catskill Watershed Corp.

Such programs—which began in California—have been springing up around the nation over the past decade. Their goal is to bring biology alive and to connect kids to nature. That's not an easy thing to do these days for inner-city kids or even for many suburban kids, who prefer the universe of electronics to the earthier or more watery world of bugs and frogs and fish. The trout-in-the-classroom concept has now reached the East Coast. The New York effort is particularly noteworthy because it matches city kids with country kids, in what Stoliar calls "a social experiment in creating sensitivity at both ends of the water tunnel." Several hundred students in ten inner-city New York schools and eight upstate schools work together to raise the trout and replant streams.

"This program gives city kids an appreciation for nature, but also teaches them about the source of their drinking water. They become watershed children," she said, her fish-shaped earrings bobbed this way and that.

That first October, each school received several hundred fertilized brown trout eggs from the state's Department of Environmental Conservation; the hatchery director even gave the kids his home phone number in case anything went wrong.

Students placed the eggs in tanks designed to recreate the habitat of a trout stream. In Brooklyn's eight-foot piece of stream, a pump pushes water over rounded rocks and aquatic plants and routes it through a chiller to keep it at a steady forty-nine degrees. Above the water, in a canopy of screening, insects hatch, rise, and fall. A "trout-cam" above sends magnified images of the fish to an adjacent TV.

The students care for the trout almost constantly, checking water temperature and pH level and other factors that can kill the eggs or fish. This is a lesson in nature, but also in nurturing. Stoliar calls it "instant parenting."

By the following January, the kids reported their progress on their class web page: "We saw a caddis fly larva eating a dead trout [and] we found a large fry with a trout tail sticking out of its mouth—it probably ate a smaller fish. Lot of dining action! About forty-two fish have died in 1999 but we still have over four hundred fish."

As the trout grow, the rural and urban kids trade letters and e-mail on their progress. "We hope they remain friends for years, and maybe even fish in the same streams together someday," she said. The kids are bused north to a stream in the Catskills in the spring, where they meet the rural students, and together they release the fish into the wild.

An eighth-grader named LaToya, who had helped with the trout last year, said, "Up there you don't smell anything like toxic waste. I never saw a reservoir before. It was so beautiful, so clean."

Vasily, a Russian immigrant, remembered fishing with his grandfather in the Ural Mountains, but he said he doesn't spend much time in nature now. "My father's allergic to animals," he said.

Fish, too?

"No, not fish. We just don't have time for fishing, I guess."

After visiting the Brooklyn classroom, at Stoliar's suggestion I reread *Trout Fishing in America*, which somehow captures how the kids feel about the program. In one chapter, author Richard Brautigan describes a visit to the Cleveland Wrecking Yard, where he buys a section of used trout stream.

" 'We're selling it by the foot length,' the salesman said. 'You can buy as little as you want or you can buy all we've got left.' It's not a big stream, he added, but it's very pleasant. And the trout? 'They come with the stream' said the salesman. 'Of course it's all luck. You never know how many you're going to get or how big they are.' "

Exactly. Even in Brooklyn.

I WAS SHIVERING FROM COLD in my leather jacket as I flagged a cab late that afternoon and headed to Harlem.

There, on 125th Street, also known as Dr. Martin Luther King Boulevard, Harlem's main thoroughfare, was the Apollo Theater, where, according to the marquee, the *Roseanne Show* was taping. I paid the driver, got out, and walked toward the Hudson River, past Inner City Meat Corporation, Newman Meat, a radiator and body shop, and the Cotton Club—a re-creation, not the original.

In the shadow of the elevated Henry Hudson Parkway, I saw men fishing along a fence. They were standing with shoulders bunched up, and wore stocking caps, army coats, bright parkas. I walked to the fence and looked over the top railing at the brown swirling water, which was deeper and more powerful on this side of the island. I stood next to a black man who appeared to be in his sixties. He was wearing a black skullcap, black tennis shoes, and his beard was white. It was a little harder to get a conversation going on this side of the island. He didn't take his eyes off his line, which angled straight out into the water. His hands were bloody. I asked him about the river—how it had been cleaned up.

"Yeah, you rarely see any waste floating down now."

You mean trash?

"Lot of stuff floating down, including bodies."

Really?

"People drowned, people jump off the bridge up there and stuff like that. Do crazy things." He pointed at a distant bridge without looking at it. "That's the George Washington. They had a couple of people jump off of there. Sometimes bodies come all the way from around the other side. You don't see as many of those bodies now."

I looked across the broad river, toward the Palisades, and then at his hands again. What do you use for bait? I asked.

"Bloodworms." He opened his hand. Coagulated blood filled the deep creases of his palm. "That's the blood." He bent down, still without looking at me, and picked up a small cardboard box, opened it and pulled out a bloodworm. It looks like a cross between a centipede and an earth-worm and secretes a red liquid that looks like blood. "It *is* blood," he said. I wasn't going to argue.

Walter Morgan was more talkative. Morgan lives on 147th Street and works as a drug-rehabilitation counselor. He started fishing as a kid in Central Park; he'd collect bottles, cash them in, dig some worms, and go fishing. Now he comes to the river.

As a social worker, he's interested in the role this spot on the Hudson plays in people's lives. It's been a favorite place to fish for at least a century. He said he's always noted a camaraderie among the men, and oc-casional women, who gather along the banks.

"It's usually the regular crowd—you know who's who; you know the faces after a while. They do look out for each other, give each other bait. It's also, for some of them, a place to talk. Especially some of the old-timers who have been coming here for decades," he said. "They have their favorite spots." He pointed to two older men, one with a rod, the other leaning back on his car—except when he jumped up to make a point—who were debating who it was who had ruined the country.

"Those guys like that spot, they've been coming for years. They get in terrible arguments, but they're back the next day just fine."

He listed the unwritten rules of etiquette. Don't hog the space, don't cross anyone's line. Don't touch anyone's pole or gear. "A lot of foreign-ers—Japanese, Chinese—especially if you fish down by Battery Park, they'll walk up to you and pull your line up to see what you've got on." His fishing partner, Chris, added, "Someone coming up and pulling out your line is like me coming up and putting my hand in your pocket." Walter shrugged. "I think they're curious, which I understand. But you've got to give people their space."

Walter takes his clients upstate to fish. "It's therapeutic for them. Oh, the smiles on their faces. People that didn't talk before opened up, I'm doing eight trips this summer. And I get to fish, too—on company money." One of these clients is schizophrenic, as well as a crack addict. "He caught eight fish back-to-back and he's still talking about it." Walter likes seeing kids fishing here, though there aren't many. "My son would be here now but he's somewhere in the house playing Nintendo! He goes with me every weekend, mostly here." He looked at his watch. He said he should have gone home a while ago. "My ol' lady had some fried chicken. But here we are, shivering to our bones. But one more cast, you know? There's always one more cast."

I wandered along the fence and met Mack and Everett. Nobody was offering their last names on this side of the island. Everett was standing next to the fence. He looked vaguely Native American, with gray hair

WALTER MORGAN

and white mustache and fair skin. His nose was pushed in—a fighter's nose. He seemed to be in his late fifties. Mack was much older, black, and not fishing. He was sitting on the hood of his Buick Skylark, giving everybody advice and offering political commentary.

"If I had a dollar for every fish I caught I'd be a millionaire," Mack was saying. His voice was raspy. "I love the water. I'd buy me a boat and stay on the water. I was in the service, drafted in 1943. I wanted the Navy and they gave me the Air Force! When they were drafting me, I was doing mechanic work, so they put me in the hangars by the planes. I wanted the Navy 'cause I loved the water but they said *noooo*, I had to do mechanic work. I didn't do no fighting 'cause if you're in the Air Force, you don't have to do no fighting. We had a .50 caliber and a Thompson machine gun because we had to defend the airport, so we didn't need all the stuff the infantryman had. The M-1 and all that shit."

He crossed his arms and watched Everett, who was lighting a cigarette. "You got a goddamn bite there."

Pause.

"It's the current, Mack." He coughed hard into his fist.

"The politicians are the biggest bullshitters in the world," Mack added, with no segue. "All of 'em! Every damn one in there is nothin' but bullshit! They talk about Clinton telling a lie, all politicians lie!"

Everett turned around, pulled the tip of his rod up slightly to test for a bite.

"Tell you one thing, they make this country free, though," said Everett. "Freest country in the world, man."

"Well, my grandparents, they helped to make it free," said Mack, sourly. "Make it better for me. 'Cause they were slave. They come here, they was slaves. It makes it better for me, it makes it better for you, too!"

He looked at me. "Are you a Jew?"

No.

"Italian?"

No, I'm kind of mixed.

"We all mixed!" he said. He made it sound like a challenge. "When I went over there in World War II and seen Africa, they were the blackest men I've ever seen in my life! But in America, they're not that black. We got a couple of them like that but the rest of 'em, it's not like that. Everett there, he's part Mohawk."

Everett hauled in a two-pound snapper. He's been fishing here since 1956. This is his spot. He was wearing an "American Veteran and Proud of It" ball cap. The Korean War was his war. He's worked with his hands his whole life. He was a boxer for fourteen years. That's what happened to his face, he said.

Mack was clearly in a bad mood. "Since the water cleaned up, the last three or four years, the fish ain't like it used to be," he groused. "Fish was bigger back then."

I asked him how large his biggest catch had been.

"I caught a fifty-pound striped bass. Down on 158th Street."

"You caught a fifty-pound striped bass? When was that?" asked Everett, disbelieving.

"That was two years ago. It couldn't fit in the trunk of the car."

Everett turned away and baited his hook with a bloodworm. Mack talked about when he fished as a boy, "with a cane pole, then. All over, North Carolina, South Carolina, Georgia, Mississippi, Alabama, all that shit. We liked to move around. I was born in 1920. When I was teenaged down South, running down the goddamn road. In the creek, and in the river, bigger than this. I caught me a sixty-three-pound gar once. When I was a kid, my father helped build the Harlem Tunnel."

I heard a big sigh come from Everett's direction. Mack launched into another political speech. "The politicians, they made this country into shit, they made our kids stupid, won't do nothing. The politicians. Your kids ten, eleven years old, you can't hit 'em because they put the law on you and the law lock your ass up. When my kids were coming up in the '50s and '60s, I whupped their ass, make 'em do what I say, and right there, and ain't none of them been in jail."

"Oh, please, don't blame it all on politicians," said Everett. He was hacking and wheezing now, hand over his mouth and nose, coughing so hard tears were in his eyes.

"We're all looking for excuses," said Everett, when he finally caught his breath. "My pop used to get a whip from a tree, use branches and braid 'em. He'd whip the shit out of me. Sometimes I deserved it, but a lot of times I didn't deserve it. It was my brothers, I'd get the ass-whipping. Let me tell you something—a lot of parents got carried away with the shit. Breaking the kid's arm, ribs—come on. I got a fourteen-year-old daughter, man, I never laid a hand on her. Sometimes I want to grab her around her goddamn neck, she's got a nasty mouth on her."

He turned around to tend his rod. He didn't want to talk anymore.

The light was beginning to fade. The river looked surly. During the next hour or so, I learned that Mack had been a mechanic, a carpenter, and a plumber and had picked cotton.

"You know, I could die today, tomorrow, I don't worry about it. People worry about dying, but I don't."

You look pretty healthy, I said.

"Yeah, I'm healthy. I go and have my examination. You're born to die, when you come out of your mother's womb you die. That's right. You're in there for nine months, once you come out you begin to die. Once you understand that you aren't afraid to die. We got a problem with the white population, they're gonna be here forever! They're afraid to die."

You may have a point there, I said.

"Ain't no point, I know it! People like you they're gonna be here forever, they don't believe they're gonna die. You could live eighty years, you could live one hundred, but you got to go!"

Now Everett turned around, took two steps toward us. His face was red. He'd left his rod against the fence.

"What were you born for?" he said.

"Nobody knows," said Mack.

Everett turned to me. "What were you born for?"

"I don't know."

"He don't know," said Mack.

Everett's eyes were filled with fierceness and pain.

"You're born to *create*. Not to destroy but to *create*."

"Good answer," said Mack.

"Not 'good answer.' The only answer."

His fists were balled up.

↪ I TALKED TO Walter and Chris some more, but after a while they packed it in. Walter grinned and handed me his box of leftover bloodworms. Just what I needed. Mack had left in his Buick Skylark, apparently in a huff. The city's streetlights were coming on in the gray dusk.

Everett was standing with his hands in his pockets, the red hood of his sweatshirt pulled up over his veterans cap, looking at the river. I walked over to him and asked him if he'd like me to send what I wrote about him.

"No. I'm not gonna be here long enough."

You mean you're moving?

"Nah. I got lung cancer."

Lung cancer? When did you learn you had that?

"About a month ago. I was told fifteen years ago to stop smoking but I never did."

He tapped a cigarette out of a Winston pack, and watched where his line disappeared into the water. I looked at the box in my hands. "You want some bloodworms?"

"Sure," he said.

Down the Potomac

THE DISCOVERY—or rediscovery—of urban angling may yet save fishing and our waters.

In 1985, the federal Fish and Wildlife Service conducted a survey that discovered that about 60 percent of American anglers lived in urban areas. The latest studies indicate that figure is now closer to 75 percent, despite some Americans moving to small towns and less-populated states, such as Montana. This demographic shift may be one reason why the sales of fishing licenses have lagged behind population growth in recent years. But there are some surprising benefits.

Nation's Cities Weekly, the journal of the National League of Cities, ran an article with this headline:

AS URBAN FISHING CATCHES ON,
PEOPLE CARE MORE ABOUT POLLUTION

Now there's a twist, but it's true. Ethan Rotman, of the California Department of Fish and Game, "has found a way to dramatically increase the concern of Oakland, Calif., citizens about their polluted lakes and streams—he's got them hooked on fishing," the journal reported.

Rotman enthused: "If I had known how effective fishing would be in hooking people into environmental issues, I would have done it years ago." Rotman is the San Francisco Bay–area coordinator of Fishing in the City, a program designed to teach people how to fish and protect the health of urban waterways. Naturally, the average Oakland resident won't worry about preserving remote salmon runs. But the fish running through the creeks of their back yards? They care about them, and the more they fish, the more they care about the quality of water and watershed.

Rotman has formed a coalition of clubs, tackle shops, and public and private agencies to teach urban angling. Locals are given twenty hours of training in watershed issues; they pick a nearby stream or pond to study with their students and test pollution levels in the water.

Members of Rotary International go into the classrooms to teach Fishing 101.

Students get a free tackle box and head to Lake Merritt, in downtown Oakland, which was badly polluted for years but is a lot cleaner now. The kids learn about urban runoff and how untreated toxins enter lakes and streams through storm drains.

In California, the Department of Fish and Game has made a conscious shift toward promoting urban angling. In 1991, its biologists began compiling a list of potential recreational fisheries—more than sixty lakes—within urbanized Los Angeles, Orange, and Riverside counties. Half of them were stocked with trout. Similar programs were created in the Sacramento and San Francisco area. The money comes from the Federal Sport Fish Restoration Program, paid by anglers as taxes on fishing tackle, motorboats, and other fishing items. California's Urban Fishing Program is exploring habitat improvement projects such as (in true West Coast style) Crappie Condos and Catfish Houses made from plastic fencing and pipe.*

Urban sprawl is probably the most serious challenge to fisheries and watersheds. The environmental organization American Rivers says that urban sprawl around Atlanta, Seattle, Chicago, and other cities is posing new risks to the nation's waterways. Atlanta is growing so quickly that new dams are being proposed on the Coosa and Tallapoosa rivers that would threaten marine life. Sewage and runoff in the Chicago area—one of the nation's prime urban and suburban fishing regions—are polluting

---

* Urban waters come in strange forms. There are hundreds of thousands of private lakes, ponds, and other waterways across the country. These aren't reservoirs, but the "water features" created by private developers, ranging in size from small ponds in condominium projects to lakes of several acres, increasingly marketed as amenities in large residential communities or office parks. Some of these developments dump as much as eight hundred pounds of algaecides, often copper sulfate or chlorine, into a one-acre pond. The Environmental Protection Agency considers copper sulfate a "priority pollutant." Yet anyone can buy copper sulfate by the ton at pool-supply shops. Fertilizer runoff from surrounding green areas pours added nutrients into the artificial lake, which feeds the algae, which encourages the dumping of more chemicals into the water, including blue dye to mask the problem. Biologists call it the Tidy Bowl effect. The toxins eventually make their way into storm drains, the water table, or other bodies of water, including fisheries. Ironically, the chemicals aren't necessary. A careful use of aquatic plants and animal life can clean the ponds naturally and almost as cheaply.

the Fox River and threatening drinking supplies for some two hundred thousand people.

Not that progress hasn't been made in recent decades. The relative comeback of the Hudson, due to the work of Riverkeepers and other organizations, is encouraging. So is the re-emergence of the Potomac River. The Potomac has gone from a virtually unfishable garbage dump to one of the best smallmouth bass fisheries in the country. And from the Chain Bridge to the Chesapeake Bay, the Potomac is one of the ten best places in America to catch largemouth bass, according to the Bass Anglers Sportsman Society. Humility is in order, though. Because of farm runoff and bacteria from poultry farms and cattle feedlots, American Rivers placed the Potomac on its list of the ten most-endangered rivers in 1998. Even so, population growth is the most serious threat to the Potomac.

↶ WHAT'S MOST STRIKING about the Potomac and many rivers that flow through large urban areas is how beautiful they still are, or could be. That's what Dave Roland impressed upon me when we floated the Potomac one spring day.

Roland, a documentary filmmaker and former broadcast executive, is a member of the Potomac River Smallmouth Bass Club—a powerful group of about two hundred anglers, including some of Washington's leading lawyers and bureaucrats. Roland says these anglers consider themselves the stewards of the river—with a little prior help from former President Lyndon B. Johnson, who called the 383-mile Potomac "a national disgrace" in 1965. The passage of the Clean Water Act a quarter century ago was a vital part of the comeback of more than a few waterways, including the Potomac. The Potomac River Smallmouth Bass Club, by its presence on the waters and its political contacts, intends to clean it up even more.

Tall and intensely intellectual, Roland spoke with an almost mystical reverence for the river as we drove to where we would launch his canoe. What urban waters give us—though it's rarely noted—is a main line into our country's history. "When I fish the Potomac, history is palpable, it's physical," he said.

> My favorite stretch of the river . . . is a long stretch about seven miles from my home that was part of the original Potomac Canal that George Washington built. And the blocks that were hauled in two hundred years ago are still visible. I stand on those rocks and can't help feeling that this is someplace special.
>
> When we're out walking the river or out in the canoes, we talk

about it. Inevitably, somebody has a story that someone else didn't hear before. There's a stretch just below the Cabin John Bridge, which is the beltway bridge that crosses from Virginia to Maryland. A few years ago, in the fall, a number of us went on a trip of about seven or eight miles. We went under the bridge and passed through a stretch where hundreds and hundreds of years ago—I have no idea how far back—there were fish traps built by Indians. When the water is low, if you know where to look, you can find them.

They're just rocks, piles of rocks that were put in the streams to create dams so that the fish would gather in the pools created by the dams. The Indians would lure the fish in there and probably spear or net them. Shad and striped bass probably ran then, smallmouth bass didn't. Smallmouth are a different story; they didn't come until the mid-nineteenth century.

You can see physical history all along this river. There's a quarry on the Maryland side from which the sandstone for many of the important buildings in Washington was cut, including the Smithsonian Castle in the 1850s.

The majority of the battles in the Civil War were fought within one hundred miles or so of these waters. From the river, along the high banks overlooking Washington, there are remnants of forts that were built by the Union forces to protect Washington. Farther up the Potomac, Confederate snipers would sit on the bluff on the other side of the river—on the Virginia side—and take potshots at the Union troops.

Putting my boat in the river one day, I looked up at the bluffs where, in midsummer 1864, those snipers hid themselves and fired on the island where I would cast my fly. The hills are still there, the water probably looks exactly like it did, the rocks probably haven't moved all that much despite the floods. Squinting into the hot summer afternoon just a bit, there I was, 130 years ago, in the middle of a Civil War battle—wondering whether some Confederate sniper was going to take a shot at me in my boat.

We stopped along the river and hiked the bank where George Washington once walked. There, you can see the stone remains of a canal built in 1785, by a company headed by Washington, to improve the Potomac River for access to trade with the western frontier. There was a depression in the ground, partially filled with water. A plaque read: "The agreement that Maryland and Virginia share the river for their common purpose led to further meetings, Annapolis, 1786, and Philadelphia, 1787, then to drafting of the U.S. Constitution." Washington hired Irish immigrant laborers to build the canal, and they probably line-fished the river from the rocks below.

We put the canoe in and floated downstream. I was astonished by the beauty of the river. Even as we passed dense suburbs, the river seemed wild. This is partly because residents are prohibited from improving their views by trimming the forests and foliage. With few exceptions, you see no buildings or freeways. The banks are thick with sycamore, silver maple, wild cherry, and oaks, and the star grass grows high. Hawks, eagles, and vultures circle; now and then a black bear will wander down to the edge of the river from less-populated areas. On an island in the Potomac in Maryland, elk once grazed. As the story goes, the elk had escaped from Arthur Godfrey's wildlife preserve and become a naturally breeding population.

Dave Roland is right: Float this river and you move backward in the current of time. Like gliding slowly into a major urban area by passenger train, floating on a river reveals an America unlike the land of malls, condos and high-rises glimpsed from a freeway. If the riverside is protected or, in some cases, forgotten, you see the way the land and water once were. You may even see a hint of the creatures that once lived in abundance where the city now spreads. On stretches of the Potomac, the city ceases to exist, even as the current flows into the shadow of the nation's capital.

The river was a half mile wide, and then it narrowed. We got out and waded a pool. I had seen only one fish rise, and we had caught nothing. We had, in fact, started the float on a disturbing note. The day before my arrival, Maryland's freshwater fisheries biologist had told Dave some bad news. He had just spent a week electroshocking the water—stunning fish—at various places along the river for a fish count. His preliminary assessment: The smallmouth population seemed to have disappeared below Harper's Ferry all the way to the Chesapeake Bay. "He believes that, unless the fish are there and just hiding and they can't find them—and the fishermen aren't finding them either—then the two floods and hurricane of 1996 really must have taken their toll," Dave said.

Several environmental organizations also suspected another culprit: the region's chicken industry, which produces tons of waste. When heavy rains come, nitrogen and other nutrients in the manure flow into the surrounding watershed and lead to microbial outbreaks. What's called "nonpoint" pollution can consist of anything from lawn herbicides to runoff oil residues from city streets to seeping hog waste held in "lagoons" the size of several football fields. This kind of pollution is emerging across the nation as a more insidious problem than urban industrial pollution or run-off from waste-treatment plants. The Clean Water Act, as currently written, isn't particularly effective when it comes to nonpoint pollution, which is more prevalent and harder to pin down in areas of urban sprawl.

Dave Roland, however, is skeptical that the fishkill on the upper Potomac was due to pollution. "What killed or weakened them were those two floods of the century."

In a side channel of the river, Dave and I got out of the canoe and waded the pools. We both caught some fierce bluegills. Finally! Back in the canoe, Dave said:

> I'm convinced that there is some primal connection between the fishing part of our brain and the survival part—the reproductive part. I can fish all day long and catch a fish every two hours and every time it's like falling in love all over again. Or it's like when you were eighteen years old and the girl of your dreams just left you and you go without a date for a couple of months, and then a new gal turns her head in your direction, and the world is new again."

Farther downriver, after we passed below an area called Seneca Breaks, we began to see huge bloated carp floating downstream or lodged in the brush.

The wind came up off the water. "So the Potomac has gone from a great smallmouth river to a poor smallmouth river and within five years, if we don't have any more cataclysmic events like the floods of '96, maybe we'll be back to a great smallmouth river again," Dave said.

At the end of our run, as we pulled the canoe out, a sudden, surprise storm ripped into the river. It blew up like a tornado, sending leaves flying and stirring whitecaps on water that seconds before had been smooth as the back of a spoon. Within ten minutes, the temperature felt as if it had dropped twenty degrees.

As we drove back to Dave's house, he veered around fallen limbs. A transformer, hit by lightning, was on fire. Car alarms were going off. And he talked about another gift that urban waters give us: the lesson of humility in the face of nature, especially combined with our own overconfidence.

> Sometimes it takes a zero day on the river to remind you of just how good a fifteen-fish day feels. I don't think there's any finer gift than the sense of possibility. But we all walk a fine line between great success and utter failure, between riches and poverty, happiness and unhappiness, health and the alternative—maybe it's just because I'm fifty-three years old and I've seen more now and pay attention to it more than ever, but I think more about these things. The economy is a lot like the Potomac. We forget how close we are

HERON ON THE POTOMAC

to things going awry. Whoever would have thought that two floods in one year would occur and would have done this to the fish. I don't think we really understand the odds of success and failure. Part of the American dream is people convincing themselves that the odds are in their favor, no matter what the reality. Lewis and Clark certainly thought the odds of finding something worthwhile far surpassed the risks that they were going to face—having no idea what the reality would be.

"Well, we did catch some nice bluegill," I said.

Dave began to laugh.

"God bless the bluegill," he said. "First fish I ever caught and maybe the last. Reminds me of an old line: 'Small favors gratefully received, others in proportion.' The lesson of the river—God bless the bluegill."

Saltwaters

༄༅༅༅༅༅༅༅༅༅༅༅༅

In truth, captain, the manner in which you have related this remarkable adventure has been such as befitted the novelty and strangeness of the matter. The whole story is curious and uncommon, and abounds with incidents that fill the hearers with wonder and astonishment.

—Don Quixote

Captains of Florida

⤳⤵

As I DROVE UP Interstate 95 after midnight, I couldn't see much land or water. Only clusters of light and the shine of the road ahead. I felt a vague sense of dread.

As a kid, I idealized Florida: The state was *Jungle Jim* and *The African Queen* and *Treasure Island* all wrapped together. I dreamed of exploring the lost water roads of the Everglades. I bought a mail-order, five-foot Indigo snake from a reptile farm in Florida—Florida! On my bookshelf, I still have a battered copy of *Adventures with Reptiles: The Story of Ross Allen*, published in 1951. A self-taught herpetologist, Allen wrestled alligators in the crystal waters of Silver Springs, Florida. Now and then I recall a little poem, recorded in that book.

Inhabitants of Okefenokee Swamp recited this jingle in order to remember the difference between the poisonous coral snake and a similarly banded but harmless king snake:

Red touch yellow, kill a fellow;
Red touch black, good for Jack.

Growing up in the Midwest, I had no practical reason to retain that knowledge, but it remains—even as a good portion of the multiplication table has departed.

I turned off Interstate 95 at Exit 61 to the town of Stuart, and drove down a nearly empty thoroughfare, past a darkened shopping center and low, pastel buildings with tin roofs and screened-in porches, and then along the water to a village called Jensen Beach. I turned into the driveway of a cluster of cottages, a fish camp called River Palms, on the bank of a lagoon. Someone had tacked a note on the office door for me, directing me to my unlocked room, where I gratefully collapsed into bed.

The room's air-conditioner groaned all night. A revolving fan turned above me. Humphrey Bogart would like it here, I thought. *Red touch yellow, kill a fellow . . .*

I drifted to sleep.

⌐ HOT SUNLIGHT POURED through the window. A fist banged on the door.

Captain Rufus Wakeman—owner of River Palms and a well-known Stuart guide, called out, "Awake?" I was now. "I'll meet you under the cabana," he said. I dressed quickly and headed out into the nearly solid wall of heat and humidity. I'd been directed to Rufus by Karl Wickstrom, publisher of *Florida Sportsman*. Rufus would provide a good introduction to the high-end, moneyed fishing culture of Florida, Wickstrom advised.

And he'll educate you about the art of being a captain.

Sitting under the palm fronds of the cabana, Rufus was wearing shorts and a turquoise fishing shirt, sleeves rolled up, vented underneath the arms. He also wore a cap with the initials DOA stitched into it. He was tall—about six feet four inches—with a black beard, and a round, sunburned face. He was barefoot. He looked something like Popeye's nemesis, Brutus. He loves his little Eden, the cabins the colors of old Florida. His wife, Melynda, seeded seven acres of grounds with ninety-three types of edible tropical plants. "See that bird out there?" he said. "That's a great American egret." The bird, three feet tall with long stilt-like legs and a thick dagger of a beak, lifted into the air and landed twenty feet from us. In mincing, slow-motion steps, it approached. "His name is Pete. Sometimes he'll eat from my hand."

Born and raised in Palm Beach, Rufus Wakeman II has lived in Florida most of his thirty-seven years, except for a stint in a Connecticut boarding school. He attended Florida Institute of Technology, where he studied outboard motors, boat handling, and celestial navigation. He also went to Duke University's Marine Biology Laboratory for two summer quarters, where he studied invertebrate zoology and marine biology—making him one of the more appropriately educated captains. "The Wakemans landed in Westport, Connecticut, in 1632, and Rufus Wakeman I led the Connecticut militia," he said. "I am the only son of an only son of an only son, four generations of only sons. I bore the first Wakeman girl in two hundred years, and boy is she tough. I pity the poor fool who messes with her. She's hard on equipment right now; she's five and a half years old and when she turns up the heat, she brings my wife to her knees." His great-great-great-grandfather was John Deere, founder of the John Deere tractor company. He doesn't advertise this. But he does like to be referred to as *Captain* Rufus.

"That's the custom."

To become a captain is a daunting endeavor. Before taking a U.S. Coast Guard test, boaters must document 360 days of sea time, pass a drug test and physical exam, have letters of reference from three people, undergo a background check for drunken driving convictions, and be fingerprinted. The paperwork can be overwhelming. So can the Coast Guard exam, a selection from twelve thousand questions on everything from safe boating practices to federal requirements for reporting oil spills. The process—the courses and paperwork—can easily consume a thousand dollars and thousands of hours of study and practice.

The license buys you a certificate suitable for framing, a shot at one of the rare maritime jobs, and a certain status. "Not quite as big a deal as being a doctor, but it's up there."

Captain Rufus described the pecking order.

Among Florida captains, the people who reign supreme are the offshore captains who run custom boats, ones like *The Merrit*, made down in Pompano Beach. That boatyard produces the crème de la crème. Each boat is hand-made, takes about three years to build, and costs millions of dollars. They're works of art.

The captains who run those big custom boats walk down the docks proud, knowing that they're being paid a thousand dollars a foot. If the boat's sixty feet, they're making sixty thousand dollars a year, plus benefits. A boss man, not the captain, owns the boat. The boss man can be anyone from the CEO of Mobil Oil to a sports figure. The boss man fishes when he wants to, whether it's two days a year, ten days a year, or a hundred days a year. On the off days, the boat sits, but the captain still gets his check. A limited number of captains are allowed to play in that game. Maybe a hundred of them in Florida. If the boss man sells the custom boat, the captain goes with the boat. The captain goes as part of the package, and if not, as soon as another job becomes available on another custom boat, that captain usually gets hired. You're at the top of the list. Once you run a custom boat you tend to always run a custom boat.

Then come the offshore captains who run your big plastic boats—your Hatteras and your Betrams, for example. They're beautiful boats in their own right but they don't have the woodwork or the teak chairs. After that, you've got your guys who run smaller outboard boats offshore. Some of those, like Bob Trossett and Ralph

Delph down in the Keys, are setting world records. Trossett and Delph are two captains who are each responsible for over one hundred world record catches. When they walk down the dock, they walk with their head tall.

Then you get captains like me, who fish offshore, inshore—from a 31-foot outboard—and also fly-fish from a smaller flats boat.

The universe of the boss man and custom boat captains—and sometimes the others—is associated with trophy fishing and saltwater tournaments and a betting system called the Calcutta.

"These are heavy-hitting people, these folks that play these tournament games—we're talking an entry fee that can be ten thousand dollars, twenty thousand dollars. He who catches the big fish, usually a marlin, of the day can win three hundred grand." And what's a Calcutta? A marginally legal system of side-betting. "That money can be in the millions of dollars." Florida isn't the only place such betting occurs: The Big Rock, a forty-year-old billfish tournament held in Morehead, North Carolina, reached a million dollars in side bets for the first time in 1998, according to *The Post and Courier* of Charleston, South Carolina. Most of the high rollers still prefer off-the-record betting, because they pay no taxes on their winnings—unless they're caught. "The tournament angler can enter the Calcutta, too," said Rufus. "So it's not uncommon for one guy to have one hundred thousand dollars tied up in a tournament, between the entry fee and his bet." Some players open offshore bank accounts, just for the game. "If you're going to fish the Bahamas Billfish Championship series, you better open up a bank account in the Bahamas. God bless you. Anything to beat the system, you know?"

Does anyone make a living through Calcuttas?

"No. Most of the people who play that game have a huge pocket to begin with. These are the big offshore guys, the CEOs of big companies, people of that nature. You've got a boat that's cost you a million or two or three. Then you've got a sixty-thousand-dollar-a-year captain. You've got to keep that boat at a marina, which is charging you one thousand dollars a month. You've got insurance on the boat. So your annual upkeep can be $250,000, and you haven't even left the dock yet. Then you start burning fuel; some of these boats burn one hundred, one hundred and fifty gallons an hour. You're going to burn one thousand gallons in a tournament, in a day, easily. And then you're going to get back to the dock and you've got to fuel up for the next day. The money is staggering."

The water in front of where we were sitting suddenly erupted. What was that? I asked.

"A bunch of mullet, maybe twenty or thirty fish, got attacked from below by one of the predators," he said. "Probably a snook. The predator will come up beneath the school and the bait fish will scatter—we call it a shower." The egret turned its head to look at the water, then looked back at us. Maybe he was figuring the odds: wild food versus a handout from Captain Rufus.

↩ I HAD RESISTED coming to Florida. As an adult, previous visits had led me to believe that Florida is the bellwether state in all the wrong ways. The state's population jumped from 528,000 in 1900 to 2,771,305 in 1950 to some 14 million in 1996—and is expected to reach 32 million by the year 2010. In the '70s and early '80s, a massive new drug trade brought riches and corruption. With its overdevelopment and walled housing tracts, Florida seemed to be what America was becoming—a place not of magic, but of excess. Certainly not the kind of place I could imagine going fishing.

Here's the rub. Though Florida is the fourth-most-populated state in the nation, half the region is uninhabited—or uninhabitable. The separation between water and land is ambiguous; the state has 7,800 lakes, 54 major rivers, 1,700 streams; countless natural springs; and 1,300 miles of coastline—more tidal shore than any state except Alaska.

This is perhaps the biggest fishing hole in America—and, as I was about to find out, probably the most threatened.

↩ A FEW MINUTES later, Captain Rufus brought his boat around to the shallows just in front of the cabana and stopped a dozen feet from the manufactured River Palms beach. He was ready to take me and his languid, slow-talking sidekick Donald out fishing.

Rufus threw me some neoprene wading shoes, which I used to walk through the thick and stinking muck that clung to the bottom here. I pulled myself up on the side of the boat. "Take the wading shoes off," Captain Rufus commanded. The deck of his boat was clean, shining, with the look of Teflon. Donald sat impassively, in loose bathing trunks, no shirt—older than Rufus by a few years, but Rufus was clearly the Alpha angler. Rufus rooted around in a shallow compartment, and then turned his attention to the engine. This boat is a twenty-one-foot Maverick Master Angler, he said. Similar to a bass boat, it was nearly all platform—a sleek, fast, floating dock.

"This is called a flats boat; there's no obstructions, it's all open deck, it's very popular for saltwater fly-fishing," he said. Above the engine was a polling platform, a high table where the captain stands and shoves the boat along with a twenty-two-foot pole, usually made of composite graphite-fiberglass. Other than wading, this is the best way to get around the shallows—the flats, as they're called—far from shore. The platform allows the guide not only more leverage, but better visibility. Rufus's boat is equipped with a two-hundred-horsepower engine, with a seventy-gallon gas tank that allows the boat to go 150 miles before refueling. "The flats boat and the bass boat emerged in the early '60s at about the same time. But they came from opposite ends of the universe."

I told Rufus how I had joined a bass tournament on Lake Erie, and fished in Texas with Sugar Ferris of Bass'n Gals, and how I had come away from that world admiring it more than I thought I would, because of its democratic nature. Anybody can join. And joining doesn't take that much money, at least not at first.

"Exactly. But saltwater tournaments are for the big boys with deep pockets. BASS and FLW, people are making a living at that, that's what they do for a job, that's their job three hundred days a year. But saltwater tournaments are where the big boys *play*." And some of them play rough. "It's a cutthroat business. There've been accounts of sabotage. People have unscrewed propeller nuts, and when you pull away from the dock and put your boat in reverse your props fall off. There've been people who have unplugged aeration systems to kill all the live bait, and people have unplugged battery chargers to make sure the batteries don't get charged. We used to joke that you could go through Tradewinds Fish Camp in Homasassa and wipe out half the tarpon fleet by throwing one circuit breaker."

He cranked up the engine to a slightly raised purr. It skimmed across the water. I looked at his cap. What's DOA? I asked. "It's a Stuart-based lure company called DOA, Deadly on Anything." Below DOA stitched lettering spelled out: "The unfair advantage."

We zipped over open water far from shore. The banks of Indian River Lagoon were dotted with houses and docks, but palms and mangroves hugged them so tightly that they seemed on the verge of disappearing. We passed a series of long flat islands entirely covered with mangroves. The humps, called spoil islands, are man-made—the side product of dredging. Traversing this water is tricky because of the numerous flats—islands or sandbars that peak just below the waves.

Suddenly and without warning, Rufus swerved the boat in a tight arc. Donald and I hung on to the guard rails. In a swirl of water, the boat nearly on its side, he circled a piece of debris, a big piece of flat Styrofoam.

"Get it, Donald," he yelled.

Donald reached down and grabbed a corner of the Styrofoam and hauled it into the boat. Rufus idled the engine and began to break the

CAPTAIN RUFUS

Styrofoam into smaller pieces. He stuffed the chunks into the live well.
A few minutes later, we approached a white sand shore and he stopped
the engine. We drifted. This shore was empty of human habitation and
rimmed with Australian pines and red mangroves, an estuarine tree with
exposed, spidery roots that serve as a nursery for small fish and other

life. Rufus handed me a heavy spinning rod with a jig. Nothing fancy today. Just vertical jigging for snook. "Its Latin name is *Centropomus
undecimalis*. The snook is probably the number-one game fish in the
state of Florida, along with the speckled sea trout, which has a much
wider range." He already had a rod in hand and his jig was arcing out
over the water. "You just want to dead-stick drag it and every now and
then give it a little pop of the rod tip. The snook are down there facing
the current. Around here, they run up to twenty pounds. The all-tackle
world record is fifty-seven pounds, caught in Costa Rica."

We were moving fast in the current. I snagged a random thought and
asked him about drug-running captains.

That was back in the '70s. In the Keys lots of the captains knew
the waterways. People would run a load of pot or cocaine and get
paid one hundred thousand dollars for a few hours of work. You
can't beat that kind of money. Some guys made a million dollars in
a month. Granted they risked everything, but money like that is
tough to pass up. If they were being chased by law enforcement, the
guys would start throwing over the bales of pot and they'd get
away. Bales of marijuana were floating all over the place. The square
grouper, that's what they were called. The square wave. Sentencing
got tougher, though. Which is good. So they're not running drugs
through the Keys like they used to.

Donald was casting at the other end of the boat, and Rufus barked a
couple suggestions to him about how to play the rod. Rufus shot his rod
up and it doubled down; he hauled in a strong snook. It was a juvenile,
of about twenty inches. The fish looked something like a striped bass,
long and sleek and silvery, with a dark strip down each flank, but its
mouth reminded me of a largemouth bass. Heavy, afternoon cumulus
clouds were building. Pure white on top, heavy, dark and hanging on the
bottom. Rufus called them big boomers.

What's the most exciting saltwater fish to catch? I asked.

Blue marlin, no question about it. You see a marlin coming up on
your bait, and it's got its pec fins up, and it starts changing colors
and it goes to neon blue and its bill comes out of the water and
grabs your bait, and then it turns. Maybe it's a two-hundred-pound
big boy, and it jumps—the first ten jumps can happen within a single minute. Then it's a dog fight. You watch it take off across the
surface, with that tail propeller turning—it's cruising at thirty, forty,
fifty miles an hour. Man, that's something. You know how when

you take a saw and you start to shake it, and you get it into a certain frequency of oscillation when the saw just wants to take over and run itself? That's the way a blue marlin swims. It can get its body going in an almost effortless oscillation and cover thousands of miles in six weeks.

A great blue heron slid by along the shore, and six pelicans followed, making a sudden, collective dive, splashing hard. They were fishing, too. The tide was picking up and gaining strength, and the boat was moving fast. Rufus and I each hooked a fish at the same time.

"Outstanding," he said. "Your first snook, huh? Five pounds, I'd guess. Congratulations, now we have to throw him back. Let's get going, gentlemen. We ended on a good note."

   IN THE EARLY EVENING, after the big boomers had rolled over, I drove through steaming Jensen Beach. The strip had once been a commercial fishing community and looked it. High-rise condos have not yet touched its shores. Karl Wickstrom, who lives in Stuart on an inlet of the St. Lucie River, had invited me over for a couple hours of fishing and dinner. With a paid circulation of 115,000, his magazine *Florida Sportsman* is the largest sporting journal in the state and bigger than most of the national saltwater fishing magazines. Wickstrom, sixty-four, is married to a self-described forty-nine-year-old former flower child. His kids—three sons and a daughter—are grown, and his sons all work for his business.

I sat in his family room, sweating from the intolerable heat and humidity, and wondered why anyone would live in this state. Then, of course, I recalled the hard tug of that snook on the line. On Wickstrom's coffee table was a copy of *Big Woods,* stories by William Faulkner, and a stack of *Florida Sportsman.* He's a happy man, and a brave one, too. During the 1960s, when Wickstrom worked for the *Miami Herald* as an investigative reporter, he took on organized crime and corrupt law enforcement. He wrote scores of stories that eventually resulted in the indictment of two sheriffs and the election of a reform governor and attorney general.

His inquiries were not appreciated. But Wickstrom knew that criminals seldom take the lives of reporters, at least not in the United States. "They're generally too sophisticated for that. They know they can usually weather the storm. That's the problem with newspapers; they expose something but they don't have tenacity over the long haul. So you'll have an excellent series of articles exposing some scandal and then the coverage just fades away. And nothing changes."

In 1967, Wickstrom left the *Herald* and went to work for a state senator—and helped draft law-enforcement reform legislation. "That didn't accomplish much either," he said. "So I took a vacation. I bought a rod at the drug store and went fishing. Right away caught a couple of fish. And I got the bug." One bug led to another, and in 1969, he launched *Florida Sportsman*—an immediate success, partly because of the state's fast-growing population.

Here is how Karl Wickstrom saved the fish in the Florida seas. Or at least some of them.

"I got intrigued with the politics of fishing," he said. "The decline of our fisheries is a monumental scandal. Swordfish and marlin and some sharks are down 80 percent worldwide since 1975; in the western Atlantic, spawning bluefin tuna have decreased by nearly 90 percent. Sea trout and redfish were decimated." The damage began after World War II. Commercial netters came with new boats made out of fiberglass, the engines became lighter and more powerful, and the nets were made of monofilament. "You put 1,000 yards of limp mono nets out there and you're going to take everything in a school." It's a sloppy business; each year, almost a fourth of the world's commercial catch is thrown out—killed and dumped back in the sea. Factory trawlers in the Gulf of Alaska and the Bering Sea annually discard enough fish to provide 50 million meals. Even so, since 1970, the world's commercial fishing fleets have doubled.

> In Tallahassee, our state capital up in the rural panhandle, commercial fishermen were treated by the good old boy network as wonderful farmers of the sea, the salt of the earth. This is the way it's been; granddaddy netted—why shouldn't I net? The thing they didn't say, of course, was that granddaddy didn't use these monofilament gill nets and big power boats, nor did he have an insatiable market. In recent decades, Asians developed a taste for mullet roe—some of them think it's an aphrodisiac—so roe sold for as much as three hundred dollars a pound. It was a gold mine. We had sheriffs' deputies out netting at night. On a good night you could make fifteen thousand dollars. Oh, you could have a dandy night—but then the mullet dropped down, down, down. And the mullet, a plant eater, is a most basic part of our food chain. Eagles and ospreys and turtle and bottle-nosed dolphins—all of these animals depend on mullet.

Years ago, such large schools of mullet would come through the bays, jumping and thrashing, that they made a tremendous noise. It was called mullet thunder. The thunder was silenced.

Challenge the commercial fishing industry, though, and you confront an ancient, entrenched belief system. In 1609, the Dutch father of international law, Hugo Grotius, wrote, "Everyone admits that if a great many persons hunt on the land or fish in a river, the forest is easily exhausted of wild animals and the river of fish. But such a contingency is impossible in the case of the sea." In reality, most of the expanse of sea is a deep desert; the great majority of the fish live in the waters that hug the shorelines, in only about 10 percent of the oceans' water—a fragile ribbon of sustainability.

Since 1810, the world's human population has risen from 1 billion to 6 billion. As the new century turns, nearly 60 percent of the world's human population lives in the coastal areas. Because of the length and richness of Florida's shoreline, and the fast rise of its population, the state serves as a warning to the rest of the world. Oil spills, industrial and agricultural chemicals and pesticides, wetland drainage, mangrove clearance, coastal development, the massive draining and grading of huge sections of Florida—it all adds up.

Wickstrom believed it was time to shift to less intrusive harvesting methods as well as more inshore fish-farming. "The first half of the twentieth century in America was devoted to learning that we have to decommercialize sensitive animals. Bass and deer and turkey and squirrels and ducks and geese were all gradually removed from the market and their kill was regulated by bag limits and sizes. Now we know that saltwater fish were erroneously considered unlimited. It's time to do the same for many of those fish."

In 1991, *Florida Sportsman* proposed a constitutional amendment to ban gill-netting. A handful of other states, notably Texas, South Carolina, Georgia, and California, had already passed gill-netting bans, but Florida's commercial fishing industry was ten times the size of the industries in any of those states. Wickstrom first suggested the ban in his column. "I placed a coupon in the magazine and asked the readers to send it in if they wanted to support the effort. They had to get their own envelope, their own stamp; it wasn't just a card they could check and send in. Hundreds of these coupons were sent in, covered with supportive comments."

The proposed amendment would ban all gill nets and other entanglement nets from Florida waters and prohibit the use of large seines in the state's inshore waters—rivers and bays—as well as near-shore waters within a mile of land in the Atlantic Ocean or within three miles in the Gulf of Mexico. Shrimp trawlers also would be excluded from these areas.

The commercial fishing industry considered the proposal Draconian and wild. "But we didn't call for a ban on commercial hook and line fishing or traditional cast nets. Using a cast net requires hard, individual work; you throw it out into a five-hundred-foot circle the size of a two-car garage. We didn't want to end that, just the industrial gill nets—those walls of nylon that entangled every living thing."

The Save Our Sealife Committee, formed by Wickstrom and his allies—the Florida Conservation Association, the Florida Wildlife Federation, the Florida League of Anglers, and the Florida Coalition of Fishing Clubs—recruited an army of volunteers to collect signatures to get the proposed amendment on the ballot. The campaign needed 429,438 validated signatures; it collected 540,000. "The campaign coincided with the fiftieth anniversary of World War II, so the commercial fishing lobby called it 'the mother of all fish wars.' Ironically, World War II lasted from '41 to '45; and our 'war' lasted from '91 to '95. We had to go directly to the people because the politicians simply didn't have the guts. Some people in that industry even threatened supporters of the ban."

"Did they threaten you?" I asked.

"Yeah. Mostly verbally, fortunately. They'd tell me they were going to knock my teeth down my throat."

In fact, he received more threats in this fight than he had when, as a *Miami Herald* reporter, he battled organized crime and crooked law enforcers. In some counties, commercial fishermen found out who had signed petitions, approached them in their homes or on the street, and verbally assaulted them. "There were a couple places burned, and there was a drive-by shooting on the Gulf Coast that was attributed to petition opponents, although I don't think it was proven. The head of our marine fisheries commission came back from a boating trip and the wheel of his trailer almost fell off; the lug nuts had been loosened all the way to the end. There were notes and phone calls to me along the line of, 'I'm going to take your eyes out one at a time and squish them on the floor under my feet.'"

He also received a note written with excrement—probably human—that said, "If this thing passes, you better learn to sleep with one eye open." He laughed at this. "Of course, that's how I sleep anyway."

On November 8, 1994, the pro-ban campaign won with 72 percent of the vote. "We drew close to three million votes—a million more than the governor received. On election day, two wives of commercial netters said they voted for us. They wanted their husbands to get better jobs." On July 1, 1995, the net ban took effect. "I was in Port Clinton, Ohio, that day. Port Clinton was a little town outside of Cleveland. At one point, it was in such bad shape that the town was just about giving real estate away. But then the state banned nets in Lake Erie, and the walleyes came back. So did Port Clinton. Now it's being redeveloped and acreage is selling for millions. And that was because of their net ban. So, even as people in Florida were voting, I could see what the fruits of this effort would be."

Wickstrom believes the Florida net ban is the most significant reform in the history of modern fisheries.

Other states are now studying the Florida ban, and plan to adopt its language. "Suddenly fishermen feel like they can fight city hall, that they can win." Significantly, Wickstrom and his allies united in a common cause were two very different cultural groups: those who call themselves conservationists—a term generally used by the more politically conservative—and those who call themselves environmentalists.

Redfish, trout, and mullet are back. The estuaries are healthier, and even sea turtles and porpoises have increased in numbers since the ban. "The inshore fisheries returned faster than we thought they would. Many of these fish are more resilient than we realized—if they're given a chance." As for the commercial netters? Many were hurt economically. Some never recovered. But others moved on to new jobs and industries. Commercial fishing villages like Jensen Beach and Port Salerno are now experiencing an economic revival, because investors like Rufus Wakeman have arrived. "Rufus has invested probably a half million dollars in Jensen, and he says he wouldn't have done that if it weren't for the net ban. Multiply that all over Florida, and you can imagine what's happening. It's clear now that sportfishing brings far more dollars into Florida than commercial fishing ever did."

Karl wanted to go fishing right now, so we grabbed a couple rods from the rod holder in his den and headed for the sliding glass door. Sheila handed us some soft drinks. Karl said we'd be back for dinner. "We'll only be gone for an hour."

She laughed and said, "*Nobody* ever goes fishing for just an hour."

⤸ SHE WAS RIGHT, of course. Karl and I fished for two or three hours, had a fine dinner at his house, and then I drove back to River Palms in the dark heat, hoping to get a good rest before driving through the Everglades to Florida's west coast. The next morning, sapped by the heat, I was sleeping in. *Wham wham wham.* No such luck. The captains of Florida aren't a shy breed.

Pulling on my pants, I opened the door and blinked in the sharp light. Captain Marcia Foosaner grinned at me. "I heard you were looking for me," she said. She was blonde and darkly tanned and seemed formidable. She had already been out saltwater fly-fishing by herself for four hours. She does that nearly every day of the year—with or without clients.

"I hear you want to learn about flats fishing—about wading on the flats and fly-fishing."

That's right, I said. I've never done that.

"Well, today's your lucky day."

A few minutes later, we were sitting at Mary's Gourmet Kitchen. "I can eat there with no shoes on," Marcia said. She's a native; her grandfather arrived in the state in the late nineteenth century, built the first house on a major street in North Miami Beach, and served as its first mayor. Her uncle used to ferry people from the mainland to the beach, via canal, in a rowboat. At fifty-one, she's old enough to have lived on the cusp of the great change. As the pancakes flipped and the heat rose, she told me about old Florida.

> I grew up in North Miami Beach. There was a big freshwater lake across the street from my house and I used to go there every day, beginning when I was eight years old. My mother would call the police and send them looking for me. The police always knew where to find me. When I was growing up, nobody really wanted to be here. Florida was hot and buggy and muggy. We didn't have air-conditioning when I grew up. You dealt with it. You'd come in and lie down on the terrazzo tile floor and cool off. There were wooden bridges in the park—I don't know if they're still there or not. We used to lie across those little wooden bridges and use a hand line to catch fish under the bridge. Where I live today, out in Palm City, developers are tearing up the wetlands across from my house. All these people from New Jersey want to make Florida look like New Jersey, but what they don't understand is Florida's still a swamp, still hot and buggy and muggy, and if they don't like it, they should go back to New Jersey.

After breakfast, she whisked me out on the lagoon in her seventeen-foot Action Craft flats boat, with an extra gizmo that Rufus didn't have: a rear-end, double trolling motor that can be raised or lowered electronically with a hand-held remote control.

"This is one of the most beautiful places on earth," she said as we headed for one of the underwater islands, the flats. "In the wintertime, especially now that the net ban is in effect, the spotted sea trout fishing is terrific; we get pompano now in the winter. Sometimes they literally jump in your boat. Pompanos skip when you motor the boat through a school and they jump right into the boat."

She pulled up in the middle of the lagoon, a mile to shore on each side of us, and stepped out of the boat into warm, gray, incoming tide. I followed her into the water. Here's a short course, she said, in saltwater fly-fishing on the flats.

"The basic technique is silence: You wade with a low profile and the fish will sometimes come within inches of you. If I'm standing on the bow of my boat and a fish is following my bait, even if he goes after it, he'll see the boat and turn. But when I'm down in the water, that fish can't see me and he can't hear me, if I'm quiet and there's no water slapping on me." Usually when she fishes with someone, she walks in one direction and the other person wades in the opposite direction. "No talking. We use hand signals."

Mullet exploded in front of us as we waded. They jumped like comical projectiles, like salmon attempting to walk up a falls.

"They jump when they're happy. That's what I call them, happy mullets. We have little baits here called glass minnows. When you stand next to them in the water they sound like rain falling, just from them shimmering. We'll walk over there and they will shimmer in the water and they will sound just like rain. This morning I was out here in the dark by myself. I come out some evenings on the river; I'll stay overnight. I have a little flashlight I wear around my neck and sometimes when I look down in the water and shine it in the grass, there are thousands of little orange eyes looking back at me. Grass shrimp."

Something large crashed through the shallow water just in front of us, chasing the mullet. Marcia said it was a jack, the fish that gives "the greatest fight in the lagoon." Again, it exploded from a wave, just a few yards from us. Marcia said the jack was probably a twenty-pounder. I pushed forward in the water, heart pounding, gripped the flyrod, raised it, and cast a popper toward it. Nothing.

She warned me not to step high when I walked, to shuffle, so I wouldn't get stabbed by a stingray. That gave me pause. I asked her if there were any alligators out here. Sometimes they come into brackish water, she said, but generally they prefer fresher water.

Given a choice between an encounter with a shark and an alligator, which would she prefer?

"I'll take a shark."

Because?

"Because I can hit him on the nose with my rod. Sometimes I carry a stick when I wade, and I use that. If something's coming at me and it looks too big to be a game fish, I'm gonna assume it's a shark. If it's shallow enough you can see the fin, and I just bump him on the nose and he turns around and runs away."

With a jerk, she pulled her rod up high and it bent over.

Briefly, she fought something large, a sea trout, she thought. And then her line fell limp.

Now pelicans were plummeting into the water on one side of us; more mullet shot up; an osprey materialized in the air and grabbed one of the mullet, which was presumably no longer happy, and flew low across the water toward the horizon, in silhouette.

Marcia jumped. She had stepped on a stingray, but was unharmed.

Hey, what about that shuffling? I said.

"I was shuffling but I picked up my foot because I had a cramp in it. You usually just kick them out of the way." There are other little critters in the water you should avoid stepping on, she said. There's something here called a mantis shrimp: It looks just like a praying mantis. It burrows in the sand. "I've never stepped on one of those either. I've had them grab my bait. If you pull your bait over the sand and there's one there, he'll grab it down in the hole and you can't get it out. They're very strong, unless they decide to let go."

Sometimes she'll even encounter one of the great hulking manatees.

"They feed on bottom vegetation. They like it out on the grass flats. When I'm wading, I'll realize there's one right next to me, holding perfectly still. They must be sleeping—it's the only explanation I can give you for why they're so still, and you wouldn't know they were there unless you walk into them. Or if they breathe. They just stick their nostril out of the water, take a snort, and then sink back down." Manatee speed-zone signs are posted here and there in the lagoon. Boat drivers are required to creep through these zones, lest their propeller slice one of those sea cows. Not long ago, Marcia hit one with her boat—or rather, it hit her.

"When we ran over it the kick of its tail literally threw the front of the boat up in the air. We were covered with mud, and we had a very unhappy manatee who just didn't know what hit him." She tied on a new fly. "A friend of mine has a boat with a black bottom. He says the manatees rub and nuzzle the bottom of the boat. My friend thinks they were trying to breed with him."

We fell silent and spread out on the flats, moving away from each other and the slowly drifting boat. It was eerie wading so far from shore, on an invisible island with so much life, visible and invisible. I was beginning to understand how Florida could grow on you.

Now, suddenly, the flats seemed dead, as if someone had flicked off a switch. The vibration of life was gone.

Marcia shuffled slowly toward me. She stopped. She smiled.

"Listen," she whispered.

"What?"

"Listen."

I heard the sound of rain. I looked up. No big boomers in sight. I looked down. A gossamer cloud of tiny glass minnows cut through the chop around us. The sweet rain passed.

Bring Me the Head of Osceola

～⌒～⌒

Driving south later that afternoon, I headed for the Everglades on Route 1. Old Florida faded fast; now came the strip developments, Wendy's, and all the rest. Then came a stretch of piney woods that seemed intact except for a grid of new suburban roads, not a house in sight—arteries prepared for sclerosis, I thought. A couple hours later, I crossed through the headache of Fort Lauderdale—all freeway entrances, orange traffic markers, sickly palms, steaming heat, and surface streets so crammed with traffic that people seemed to be camping more than driving. But who was I to judge, living as I do in South Florida's counterpart across the continent? Both places, it seemed to me, qualified for Lyle Lovett's description of Southern California: There's too many ants on that candy bar.

Everyone wants a piece of paradise, even invading species. The exotic walking catfish, brought here from Southeast Asia as an aquarium fish, now breeds in south Florida. One to two feet long as adults, they use a portion of their pectoral spine to crawl from one body of water to another on rainy days. They're able to breathe plain air. Only a decade after their introduction, they had slithered from the state's east coast to Naples and Tampa.

I turned west on fast, straight Interstate 75, a highway with the intriguing name of Alligator Alley. That land of childhood dreams was ahead. I passed into great green flatness under a now heavy, clouded sky, with startling seas of blue light up there between the white and gray boomers. All along the way were canals and ponds and lakes, reflecting pools with white egrets in the grass between the lanes of the highway. Now, on my right, there it was, the beginning of the vast swamp—sloughs, marshes, and raised hammocks—and on the left side of the highway, a different kind of prairie: shoulder to shoulder townhouse developments stretching to the horizon. Soon the housing tracts, like the fingers of a grasping hand, receded. And now on both sides of the straight line of pavement was the sea of perfectly flat water/trees/stumps, the saw grass prairie that the Indians here called *pa-hay-okee*—"grassy water." A wide canal ran parallel to the road; two men cast from a lone bass boat. Now came the billboards: airboat rides! swamp buggy tours! More billboards: roasted chicken! motels! factory outlets! I stopped for gas at a bustling truck stop owned and operated by Miccosukee Indians, a branch of the Creeks and part of the Seminole group.

These folks can trace their history hundreds of years before the writing of the U.S. Constitution, but the federal government didn't recognize the tribe. Back when the United States rounded up the other Florida tribes and forced them west, the remnants of Seminole and Miccosukee hid deep in the Everglades, evading the unpleasantness. Today, they're truck stop and casino operators—and probably the salvation of *pa-hay-okee.*

The Everglades, 130 miles long and fifty miles wide, is composed of a chain of freshwater lakes, the Kissimmee River, and other streams that run into Lake Okeechobee, 120 miles south of Orlando. This great river of grass is at the epicenter of one of the nation's most dramatic environmental challenges—in which anglers play a role. In the 1860s, Florida created the Internal Improvement Fund to sell off swampland for pennies an acre to companies that promised to help drain the swamps; in 1909, the first dredging machines arrived. They looked like giant spiders made of steel, bolts, and rivets. These machines dug canals and created the dirt foundations of roads, including the Tamiami Trail, linking the west coast to Miami. This is the road that first gave so many settlers, hunters, loggers, real estate speculators—and anglers—easy passage to the heart of the Everglades, as well as the Big Cypress Swamp, where the Seminoles lived until the creation of the Everglades National Park in 1947, which forced out most of the Seminoles and original settlers. Alligator Alley was built later. By the 1970s, when environmentalists finally began to speak up, the Everglades ecosystem had shrunk to half its original size and, as one writer put it, was "dying of thirst and pollution." Ninety percent of South Florida's wading bird population had disappeared. Some of the vanishing took place virtually overnight. The Cape Sable sparrow, once common in the Everglades' drier prairie lands, fell from an approximate population of sixty-four hundred in 1992 to twenty-six hundred by 1995—and this in a national park of 1.5 million acres, a region set aside to protect nature.

Other species diminished as well. The greatest number of endangered mammals in the United States are found in peninsular Florida—and in Southern California. Florida's major recreational and commercial fishing hole, Lake Okeechobee, was poisoned by agricultural runoff. Florida Bay, which begins at the southern tip of the Everglades and reaches down to the Keys, because of its perfect blend of salt and fresh water, was once one of the world's most productive wombs of life. But in the early '80s, algae growth, caused by water diversion programs in the north, swept over its surface and the fish population dropped precipitously.

Then in the late '90s, scientists found that alligators' testicles were shrinking. They also discovered that the same thing was probably happening to the state's largemouth bass. Scientists at the University of Florida pointed to water pollution and warned: Today alligators and bass, tomorrow human beings. Fred Wright, Jr., writing for the Earth Action Network in 1996, described the source of the problem:

> The focus of this alarm is Florida's third-largest freshwater lake, Lake Apopka, covering 30,000 acres near Orlando and once an internationally recognized mecca for bass fishermen. Now only splintered remnants of once-numerous fishing camps remain because of the lake's shrinking bass and bluegill populations.
>
> Scientists decided to examine bass as well as alligators because both are at the top of the food chain and both are long-lived, giving them a chance to accumulate contaminants in their bodies over time—like humans. "Theoretically, we have data that suggest this could be a fundamental problem elsewhere in Florida and the U.S. It's definitely a canary in a coal mine," suggests Louis Guillette, a UF zoology professor.
>
> Lake Apopka has suffered from what may be called "battered lake syndrome" for decades. Because of relentless development, its alligator, turtle and bass populations have been on the decline at least since the 1980s. UF scientists, who recently received funding for a five-year study of the lake and its environs, have documented a near–90 percent drop in Apopka alligators over 20 years.

Reptile rustling hasn't helped either. That five-foot Indigo snake I bought as a kid, mail-order from Florida, is now a protected species, but still can be bought for two hundred dollars a foot. At today's prices, my fifteen-dollar Indigo snake would cost a thousand dollars.

The Everglades remains the state's great water pump, a filter, and essential to the state's ecological health. And government has at last begun to replumb it. The effort may be too little, too late, but progress is being made. In 1984, Governor Bob Graham signed the Save Our Everglades bill; the first step would be to rechannel the Kissimmee River—to return it to its original meandering course. Then came the landmark Growth Management Act, which was supposed to help halt the encroachment of housing tracts into the Everglades, but became entangled in intercounty political battles. Land speculators, farmers, and developers pressured the legislature, and the act—like the alligators—lost potency. Then came a series of lawsuits, and a remarkable piece of state legislation called the Everglades Forever Act, and the Corps of Engineers was assigned the task of redesigning the plumbing. A buffer would be created to hold back development and farming around Lake Okeechobee and the Everglades park and to expand the water's main natural channel, known as Shark River Slough.

Indians played an important part in the negotiations. Only about five hundred Miccosukees still make their living in and from the Everglades, but the Miccosukees' $50 million casino near Miami helps fund political pressure for Everglades restoration. "The Miccosukees have proved to be some of the quickest draws on the peninsula," *Time* magazine enthused in 1999. The tiny tribe has outmaneuvered "some of Florida's and Washington's strongest lobbies in a legal campaign to help set tougher water-quality standards and break bureaucratic logjams." With all that gambling money, the Miccosukees are doing what, for hundreds of years, they've done best: survive.

Right now, as I drove through cypress swamps—and over the great sheet of water that moves across Florida at the speed of a half mile a day—I was looking forward to meeting a different kind of survivor.

⌐ CAPTAIN BOB MARVIN'S Ford pickup, with a sixteen-foot, olive green johnboat and trailer hooked to it, were parked in front of a Quality Inn outside the coastal town of Naples, where we were to meet. Doug Swisher, the fly-fishing instructor I had met in Montana, had suggested I spend some time with Captain Bob, who is Swisher's fishing partner in Florida. "What's a shame is that this man is going to go to his grave and not have written a book to share the knowledge he has," Swisher had told me. I met Captain Bob in the hotel café, and we headed north.

A monsoon was moving through, but Bob just shrugged. "We're goin' fishing!" He drove through the flat, piney woods. He wore an old ball cap, a light blue and well-worn work shirt. His sleeves were rolled up strong forearms, and he wore khaki shorts and dark socks and black leather shoes. His skin was shiny, tanned like soft leather; his hair gray. He looked more like a midwestern farmer than a captain.

He started talking when I hopped in the cab, and I don't think he stopped until I left the next day.

"My captain's license is forty-five years old," he said, pushing his cap back. His father and his father's father fished for a living. "I can trace my family back to when they came to Florida in 1799. Some English, some Dutch, that's about as much as I know. One of my relatives was the governor of Florida in 1865, right after the war of Northern aggression. Remember that war? Well, we do."

He figures he'll be the last person in his family to fish for a living. "I have three grandsons and a granddaughter and I want them to go on and do something that benefits them monetarily. I have no retirement other than Social Security, that's it. I do live in my own house that I built with my own hands. I chose my way of life because I'm an independent sucker. The only thing is it's hard to eat independence. Either you catch fish or you bring home the bait and boil it." One year he made twenty-five hundred dollars, and it didn't occur to him to ask the government for relief. "As a matter of fact, when I joined the Navy in the mid-'50s and operated a Navy fishing boat out of Key West, one of my fellow sailors said, 'You know, Bob, you're a very poor guy.' I said, 'Gee, I don't know. I eat three squares a day, I fish when I want, come as I go.' I didn't think I was so poor! It was a tough time back then—but I think it's coming up on tougher times."

What do you mean? I said.

"You can't cram so many people on the very tip of one state and expect it to survive." He looked at me in the fading light as we hurtled down the two-lane road.

Some folks would call Bob a cracker, an imprecise term at best. In Florida, "It is not necessarily true that a cracker is a cracker," writes Al Burt, who spent twenty-two years as roving Florida columnist for the *Miami Herald*. A Floridian "might speak one version of cracker and listeners might hear one quite different." By most accounts the word originated with the state's first cowboys, who cracked long cowhide whips. Other theories of origin connect the word to the act of cracking corn to make meal or grits, a staple of the pioneers, or that it came from the Spanish word *Cuacaros* (Quakers), or that it's connected to a Scottish term for braggarts. At some point, the word took on racial shadings, but there are grounds for interpreting cracker simply to mean a Floridian of native birth. Burt insists on using it that way. ("We have enough hate words. We do not need to mess up any of the remaining kind ones.") A cracker might refer to state legislators as sounding like "a bunch of mockingbirds that were raised in an outhouse." A cracker, "noting that conventional progress has resulted in declining quality of air and water,

and in risks to certain foods, would find kinship in the message that author Herman Melville wove into the great novel *Moby-Dick,* that busi-
nesslike madness sometimes passes in the world as reason." If that's true,
Captain Bob's a cracker.

"All these people moving down here, if they're not careful they're going to lose our drinking water, especially on the west coast here. They're
building faster than the environment can handle," he said. "The developer rules here. But while everyone complains about development, nobody votes! The wells are being ruined by salt intrusion because of too
many houses and golf courses that suck up too much water, drawing in
the salt. People are coming down here to live and they're going to pay
dearly for it; they just don't know it's coming."

I mentioned that I had spent an evening with Karl Wickstrom.

Bob lit up with a peculiar mixture of appreciation and exasperation.
The ban on netting had worked well, he said. The saltwater fishery is improving. But the ban hurt his family's shallow-water shrimping business—forced them to sell their forty-ton troller called the *Evening Star.*
Now why, he asked, doesn't government treat fishing as a form of farming? No such luck. No subsidy going in, and no buyout when the government comes up with new rules. "They paid the mullet fishermen for
their nets but they didn't pay the shrimpers. My family had almost a
million dollars wrapped up in our rig. We built it ourselves, we built that
troller with our own hands and then we had to sell it. After she pulled
away from the dock with someone else behind the wheel, it was tough,
it was really tough. It broke our hearts."

Even so, amazingly, Bob was in favor of the proposed law—and spoke
up for its passage.

"I went to a few meetings and I told the mullet netters, some of the
shrimpers too, it's time for us to give it up. Roller trollers, like ours, drag
a square-framed net along the bottom, and it tears everything up,
crushes grass and sponge and crabs and lobsters and sea trout. The fellow
from *Florida Sportsman* was absolutely right, 100 percent. I supported
the netting ban. I went to meetings with 150, 200 mullet fishermen and
said so. They threw me out. I told them. I was even willing to walk out
back to have it out with a few of them."

Luckily, Bob was also in the guiding business, so he had another kind
of fishing to go to.

A half hour later, we arrived at Estero Bay marina. Highly developed,
lined with high-rise condos, pilings and docks and luxury boats, the bay
didn't seem like a likely fishing hole, but Captain Bob guided his johnboat, powered by a fifteen-horsepower engine, to a narrow waterway
lined with thick red mangroves. If you didn't look up at the buildings,

you could imagine that you were deep in the Everglades. He handed me a 7-weight Thomas & Thomas flyrod and rowed us along the shore. He had tied a big, bright yellow fly—a popper—at the end of the line. It was smiling at me. Bob laughed. "I make a lot of silly flies up. Anybody can name a fly the Hair Roach or the Saddle Back, or this or that. But I call mine the Happy Face fly." At the flat tip were two eyes and a pen-drawn smile.

We moved along the mangrove shore, thick and gnarled. The water was stained like tea. I could see fish tailing ahead. Bob wasn't fishing, but he was telling me where to put the fly. "Fade to the right a little bit, that's it. Those are mullets in about an inch of water there. Put some line out there, that's it."

What appeared to be a snook shot out from the mangroves and chased the happy face. My line snapped straight, then went limp. The snook was gone. That's right, he said, put that fly as close to the bank as you can. He was hunkered down, rowing.

Anybody sixty-five or older in the state of Florida doesn't have to buy a fishing license; I think that's wrong. I think they should pay something, even if it's only five dollars a year, and be supportive of the fishery. I mean my goodness, they come down here, they re-tire—God bless them, if they want to come down and quit work-ing, it's just fine. But they all want to go out on a boat and fish and kill whatever they want. . . . Not all of them, there's a lot of old-timers who came down here to retire and think like I do; they throw a few back for a rainy day. But a lot of them come down here and they go crazy when they find out what a fishing hole we've got down here. They should pay something, something! They have to buy a driver's license, a license plate—five dollars or ten dollars isn't going to kill them.

I went to a movie back about two years ago, I was standing out in front of the movie house and the lady asked me if I wanted my senior citizen's discount. I looked at this woman and I said, "How do you know how old I am?" She said, "Well, you've got some gray hair, you must be over fifty." I said, "I am over fifty, but let me tell you something. You see these two kids behind me," a young couple maybe in their twenties. I said, "Give my discount to them. I want them to have my discount." Three or four seniors stepped up, they complained, said, "We earned that right!" And I said, "What right did you earn? You're born, you die. That's the right you have, the same right I have." But I said these kids needed those tickets a lot

more than I did, because a buck doesn't go anywhere today. That's
the way I feel about senior citizen's discounts; give them to the kids.

I volunteer in a grade school. I teach these kids about fishing. I
volunteer and I can't even afford to volunteer. Those keep me on
my toes, I tell you. One time a little girl asked me, "Captain Bob,
how come people are different colors?" I thought about that one. I
said, "I suspect God was bored with just one color."

How old are you? I asked.

"I ain't gonna tell you," he said, laughing. "You wouldn't believe me
anyhow! Let me put it this way here: First captain I worked for, his name
was Chris Columbus. I've been around so long they call me Captain Dirt
because I'm as old as dirt. The good Lord willing I'll die with a fishing
rod in my hands."

We were drifting on dark water below a solid row of high-rise condos.
The lights were on in these condos and I could see the flicker of televi-
sions, but no people were visible. It was an odd thing to be fishing below
this world, down in the dark. I could see glints of these lights reflected
in Bob's wire rim glasses as he looked up at the windows. "Almost all
these condo buildings went up in the last two years," he said.

It's like they get a box of seeds, sprinkle them out and a few
months later you've got yourself a building. The top floors of those
buildings probably go for two and a half, three million. If I had that
much money I wouldn't be living in that place; that's just a gigan-
tic graveyard is all it is. These retired people come down from New
York or Michigan, they don't seem to care about anything anymore:
"I raised my children and I went to my church. I worked at my job,
I paid my taxes," and my, my, my, my, my. You know some of them
have never been in the Everglades? I take people back there and I
can have a person sitting within two feet of an orchid and they can't
even see it. Because they've lived in this little square all their life.
These condos here, these are their *pyramids*. There's so much they
could be doing. I think it's good for a person to retire from their job
after 30 years, but then get a job doing something else for God's
sake. Anything! I'm thinking of a friend of mine, Italian man, came
down from New Jersey. By the third year he was an alcoholic. I tried
to get him interested in fishing but I think he was too far gone when
I got him. Finally what happened was I went over to see him one
night, and his wife said he hadn't been home all day. I went out
looking for him. I had a funny feeling, and there he was. I found him

in a golf course lake. He was drunk and he fell in. He had a red and white shirt on and a pair of shorts, and he was facing down in the water and that was it. He was gone.

Ah, but the exceptions are glorious, said Bob. Especially, well, the ladies.

My oldest gal who I got into fly-fishing is eighty-four years old. She had a very dominating husband who was a professor at some university for years and years. She got up in the bow of my skiff, got the fly to go out maybe thirty feet, and she hooks a snook. She's fighting the snook with all kinds of screeches and whoops. The husband reaches over and starts telling her what to do and she says, "Listen, you old goat, shut up! I've dealt with your crap for fifty goddamn years. This is my sport, now shut up!" I was so happy over that, she had the spring of independence in her body somewhere and she brought it forth. And she wrote me some lovely letters and one day she called me on the phone about ten o'clock at night and I said, "Rosie, we're dating on the phone, people are going to talk!" She said, "Good. I want to get their blood moving." I said, "How's your husband?" and she said, "Who cares? When are we going fishing again?" "Anytime you want, darling. You get on that plane and leave him home, I'll take you anyplace you want."

Now he rowed down a narrow channel, lined with docks, and the walls of the condo canyon grew higher. On a concrete wall along the water, a sign said, "No netting beyond this point." The gill-netters used to come in this far, right here among the condos. "We're going to go up here and do something nasty in a minute," he said, grinning. A few minutes later, in the dark, he eased the boat toward a circle of lighted water at the corner of a dock, where long dark shapes moved. I cast the happy face into the light, once, twice, and then a nice big snook, maybe five pounds, gulped it in and shot to the right. On the flyrod the fish felt twice that size. I got it to the boat and it snapped from the hook and was gone.

⌐ THE NEXT MORNING, Captain Bob picked me up at the motel early and we drove east into the Everglades. On the way, he asked me who else I'd interviewed. I named some names, including Joan Wulff.

"You met Joannie? Oh, my lord. Joannie. I knew her years ago, before she married Wulff. My god, she was a looker. Still is, I bet." Still is, I said. "Oh, I did love Joannie," he said in a faraway voice.

A couple hours later, he pulled up next to a narrow tidal river of slate-green water that led into a maze of mangrove and palms. Right away I noticed the alligators, two of them. Big ones. One of them at least ten feet long. Cruising along with us, watching us through horned, oblique eyes. After we launched the boat from a sandbar, I watched them as I stood casting to the shadows. The unstable boat seemed smaller, and I sat down.

"This is the world people don't see when they come here to live," said Bob. "They don't see Florida. They see a place like Naples and Naples is not Florida. Naples is Ohio, Michigan, New York. This is Florida, now you're gonna see it. I'm gonna take you where some orchids are."

The tail of something large and graceful cut up and over in the water a few feet ahead of us. It was a tarpon, maybe twenty pounds, said Bob. I stood back up in the boat, a bit shaky, and cocked my wrist for the cast.

"I don't want to wear you out catching those big fish. Could be dangerous."

"Really?"

"Oh, sure, you have a long way to drive later, and you'll be exhausted."

"I'll be fine."

He smiled and said, "There's a little offshoot of a creek. We're at the top of the tide now."

Far off, we could hear the sound of an airboat, and Bob shook his head and muttered something. He doesn't like airboats. Sees them as a needless, noisy intrusion.

Another big gator surfaced near us. Or rather, just appeared. I was noticing that you don't actually see an alligator surface. You blink, and he's there.

"When I take the women in here, and they get squeamish, I tell 'em, 'Don't you worry about them gators, little lady, them's man eaters.'" He laughed hard at his own joke. "I'm a chauvinist pig but I'm lovable."

He moved the boat deeper into the swamp. No more tarpon; no more bites. "I didn't bring my harmonica along. That's my second shot. Plan B. Entertainment without fish. I always play my harmonica in the swamp." He looked itchy. He couldn't remember the last time he forgot his harmonica.

"I see some big gators back here."

How big?

"Well, about three weeks ago I was in a place pretty far back in and I smelled a strong smell and I went in there and there were two large gators, I would say eight to twelve feet long. Their tails were cut off. Poachers."

These were dead gators? I asked.
He resisted laughing.

Oh, yeah. It's hard to run off with their tails without killing them. Anyhow as I was going through—I was lying down in the boat to get through the trees—all of a sudden I saw this carcass, about a six- or eight-foot carcass, another dead gator, and it's moving like hell! It's really moving. So as I got over there, a very, very large gator—I would say it weighed half a ton—had the bottom foot of the dead gator and he was dragging it along to get it back underneath the trees. The guy with me says, "What do you think we ought to do?" I said, "What do you mean *we?* We get the hell out of here!" I've had irate females rush the boat, come up underneath the boat and almost turn it over. I usually tell people, "Don't get out of shape." Can we outrun him? they'll ask. Absolutely not because we're in his backyard, he knows what to do and where to go. Generally gators are pretty harmless. They love dogs, and they love little kids. They don't know they're killing the kid, they just know it's a meal, that's all. When people come down here to retire and they bring their grandchildren down to walk Poochie around the dock, and the next thing you know Poochie's gone, the kid's gone. A nice, fat, chubby little kid for dinner. That happened two or three times in the last four or five years. Here's the thing to remember: You don't fool around with an animal that's got a brain the size of a pea.

Now we moved through a narrow passage and suddenly, startlingly, entered what appeared to be a perfectly round hole in the swamp, perhaps three hundred feet across. It was an eerie containment. The edge of this hole was a wall of mangrove and sable palms and gumbo-limbo trees. Except for the wake of the boat, the water was without movement. The sky was clear, reflected in the mirror of the hole. Down was up and up was down. The senses were confused. I felt mild claustrophobia and vertigo. I cast my fly, but the water seemed dead, a black hole—and unresponsive.

Back here in the swamp it's easy to imagine how the Seminoles were the only Indians in the country to remain undefeated by the United States in warfare and never submissive to its authority in peacetime. Some historians have compared the second Seminole War, in which 50,000 U.S. soldiers served, to the Vietnam War—the Seminoles fought a brilliant guerrilla campaign, striking and then fading into the swamps of South Florida. The great Seminole leader Osceola died in captivity from complications of malaria; his head was cut off by his physician and kept as a trophy.

"Look, there," said Bob. He had pulled very near the shore, and he was pointing upward. Barely visible back under the leaves and branches was a faint little clearing, with two low, crooked tables made with what appeared to be hand-hewn planks.

"They used to fish from there, and those were their sleeping tables, many, many years ago," he said.

Whose?

"Seminoles."

A few minutes later, he eased up to the opposite bank of the hole, and pointed up into the branches. "That's what I wanted to show you." Clinging to a branch up there was a rare orchid. Its throat was purple, with a yellow fringe around it. The flower was the size of a coin. "In the market that'd bring a smuggler two hundred dollars. But the best place for orchids is where God put them, on a particular island on a particular branch. I find islands covered with thousands of them and I don't tell anybody about it because I don't want them to take them. I keep my mouth shut."

↬ ON THE WAY to the Keys, driving along the Tamiami Trail, I passed the Miccosukee casino, looming up out of the swamp, and all lit up. Bingo!

I pulled to the side of the road to meet cane-pole fishers.

They were African-American, and they fished along the canals with plain cane poles that appeared to be fifteen feet long. Two sisters sat on folding chairs, wearing bright flowered dresses and holding umbrellas to protect them from the sun. They were large women and taciturn. They studied their conical floats and kept their eyes on a seven-foot alligator floating a few feet from their bait. The alligator seemed to appreciate the fact that the women chummed the water.

"You throw food out there to feed the mullets," said one of the sisters. "Bread and oatmeal, mix it all up together, dog food, and you just throw it out there and the mullet come. I don't think they out there this morning."

Suddenly she whipped the cane pole up and flung a fish high over her head to the grass behind. It wasn't a mullet, but an oscar, one of the tropical aquarium cyclids that, according to Captain Bob, were imported to eat the walking catfish.

She pulled it flopping to her, dropped it off the hook into a plastic bucket.

Why do you use a cane pole? I asked.

She looked at me for the first time, her face impassive.

"Fiberglass poles are expensive. Real expensive."

Right.

We watched the water for a while.

"So is fishing much different from when you were girls?"

"Seems like to me there's not as many fish," said the other sister, grumpily.

The alligator moved a little closer. Another one had arrived. "I caught some bass at the dump. You know a place called the dump down the road? They used to take the trash there from Everglades City," said the first sister.

Now a wind was up, clouds were moving fast over the river of grass, and the air was cooling. I noticed that the alligators had disappeared. I thanked the women for their time and moved on myself.

I drove on. For the first time during the fishing travels, I was feeling quite bleak as I thought about the housing developments and dredging and filling of the Everglades. People do resist, I told myself. The Seminoles and Miccosukee, and others all resist the Machine, in their ways. The beauty of Florida is in the subtle, surviving details: orchids and glass minnows and the echo of distant mullet thunder. Those are the things to focus on, not all the rest. I repeated to myself something that Captain Bob had said: You think about how many hurts you've got too long, it just gets boring.

A FEW HOURS LATER, I entered the Florida Keys. The narrow entrance road was crowded with garish billboards. There was an antique store called Flea Largo. A yellow cab with the name Cheapo Taxi on its side. A house decorated with hub caps. A Hog's Breath Saloon billboard with the slogan, "Hog's Breath is better than no breath at all." The road passes through Key Largo and then, for 133 miles, crosses and hops a string of islands made of sandstone sediments or fossil coral. A few miles outward is a living reef of coral polyps that secrete lime and are fueled by plant cells within their tissues. The Keys, wrote Rachel Carson, are where "living things . . . are able to turn the substance of the sea into rock." To the north are the remains of a fleet of twenty-one treasure-laden galleons driven onto the reefs by a hurricane while attempting to sail from Havana to Spain. The string of islands and reefs curves slowly in a southwesterly direction. The Keys are the southernmost point in the United States outside of Hawaii.

Florida Bay and then the Gulf of Mexico spread to the north, the Atlantic to the south. Here the world is aquamarine and turquoise, land-scaped with mangroves and palms and populated by egrets, herons, pel-icans, American crocodiles, miniature deer, and anglers like Jake Jordan—whom I was to meet in the Middle Keys town of Marathon, sandwiched between Seven Mile Bridge and Long Key Bridge.

Jordan is one of the more famous captains in the Keys—guide to Jimmy Carter, Frank Sinatra, Ted Turner and others of renown. He is a relatively wealthy man himself, but he lives modestly in a clean, well-lighted, and extremely air-conditioned (he keeps the temperature around sixty-five degrees) mobile home. In it, every lamp is decorated with saltwater flies. Fish replicas and photos of fish cover the walls. Spread across the ceiling of one room, his office, is a rack of expensive flyrods.

Jake, fifty-eight, is not a large man, but he fills a room. His hair was perfectly combed. He was wearing khaki shorts and a tee shirt. He was barefoot and opinionated.

"My mom said when I was a kid I used to say that if I ever got a lot of money I was going to buy an aircraft carrier and live in the middle of the ocean, and just fish all the time," he said.

That's pretty much the way his life turned out.

His father was a machinist who helped build the turbines that run the generators and pumps of the Grand Coulee Dam. Jake followed in his father's footsteps; just out of high school, he joined a surveying team, and spent three years working in 39 states. In 1961, he wound up in Cape Canaveral surveying the missile range for the radar tracking station that would be used for the moon shots.

"Then they shot John Kennedy," he said, leaning back in his desk chair, hands on his belly. "And Lyndon Johnson did away with the job. I went back to Jersey and went into the bar business." The bar scene was a rough arena, but he made a bundle of money, and came back to Florida in 1966. There, he bought a house and a used, 103-foot boat. He hired a retired woodworker and a mechanic—not to do the work themselves, but to teach him how to refurbish the boat. A year later, Jake's boat restoration business employed sixty people. He started another business, a fly shop called World Class Angler. To create a clientele and a reputa-tion, he and his wife moved into a lighthouse, and bought a 25-foot custom-built sportfishing boat, which he chartered, and a flats skiff. He hired a publicist and created a fly-fishing school in the Bahamas. He was on his way to making another fortune, and then suddenly his life just went sour.

He recited the facts. Whatever sadness remained was covered by a layer of pragmatism.

In '91, my wife came to me and said, "I don't want to do this any-more," so I sold the World Class Angler. That was in August, I was at a fly tackle dealer show in September and I came home and walked into the house and my wife said, "I don't want to be married any-more, I want a divorce," and she divorced me. I gave her most of my money and sold our big house and bought this little place here. I went from 165 pounds to 240 pounds, sitting, staring at the televi-sion and eating, staying in the house. Just working, fishing, and eat-ing. In about six months I realized I had a problem. I went to an old doctor friend of mine and he said that he wanted to give me Prozac and I told him I didn't want any narcotics, no drugs. He said, "You work seven days a week or you just sit around; everything you do is related to fishing. Here's what I want you to do: I want you to come home from work at five o'clock in the afternoon, take a shower, clean up, and go to a restaurant and eat all your meals in restaurants with people around. I want you to have a drink every night before dinner or after dinner. I want you to take off two days a week from work, and get a hobby outside of fishing. I don't care what it is, but find something you like to do outside fishing."

I lost the weight. I got in shape. In 1994, I sold my fly reel com-pany. I became a traveling angler. I've built a fortune. I can afford to go fishing until I die and not go broke. I live very simply, I've still got one of my Corvettes and I buy a new pick-up truck every year. I have a place in Montana, an apartment in Alaska, and thirteen cus-tomers—I'll accept no more—who have been with me for years. Every one of them is an over-achiever.

Jake also works as a consultant to half a dozen different companies in the boating and fishing industries. He nodded, leaned back farther in his chair. He says he's been hired by people that run Fortune 500 compa-nies. "I come into their companies and look at it from the fisherman's point of view."

I said, hey, that could make a good book. I suggested a title. *The Angler's Guide to Business.*
"Pretty good," he said and launched into a set of angling principles that can be used in business:

Ten percent of people catch 90 percent of the fish . . . To be a fisherman or a businessman you have to be a realist and a preda-tor . . . How many fish you catch is determined more by what's un-der the water than anything you can see . . . In order to catch a sailfish, you have to think like a mullet . . . When you're fishing and there are no fish for ten minutes, stop, finish, end it, try something new . . . If you're under-capitalized, you either run out of bait or you run out of chum, and you're not going to catch any more fish . . . Don't fall in love—with a fishing reel or a particular business—or you'll lose every time. . . .

I mentioned that he was certainly passionate about fishing. Sure he said, but not about the gear, not about the particular approach. He continually alters his methods, material, and attachments. Jake Jordan's secret to business and life is: Don't get trapped.

> You know, I had a guy that was the chairman of a major company fishing in my boat, probably six years ago. He had just caught a tarpon on a fly. He's lying on the front deck, he had fought this fish for an hour and a half. You have to understand, these are 100-pound fish that are swimming in water that's five feet deep. This guy caught the fish; this is the most challenging thing he ever did in his life. He was captain of the football team in high school and in college; he was successful, the valedictorian in his class. He's married to a very wealthy, beautiful woman who's a bitch. He's got Ferraris and Porsches in his garage, a collection of cars, a collection of airplanes. He's got a house in Atlanta, he's got a house in Cincinnati, he's got a house on a lake, a house out in the Hamptons. Investments and bank accounts and real estate and he runs this giant corporation. He's sitting on the bow of my boat with a pair of shorts on, no shirt, no shoes, and he's lying back, and saying, "Oh man, that is so spectacular!" And I'm up on the tower and I say, "You did a really good job and I'm very proud of you. Here's what you did wrong, here's what you did right, and all together you did a spectacular job."
> He says, "This is wonderful. You know, Jake, you've just really got it made!" I say, "What are you talking about? I've got it made? I'm the one poling the boat, you're down there catching the fish. You're the one that's got it made!" He says, "No, no, you don't understand the stress I'm under every day—the wife, the girlfriend, all the bullshit that goes on. I'd trade with you in a minute." I say, "Get out of here! What are you talking about, trade with me?" He says, "I'd trade places in a minute." I say, "OK, let's do it! I'll tell you what we'll do—we'll switch. We'll just change places. You can have all my money, you can have all my real estate, you can have my Corvettes, you can have my truck, you can have my girlfriend, my bank accounts, my boats, my business, all my customers and everything. I'll take what you got and we'll just switch." He says,

"You'd do it, wouldn't you?" I say, "In a *New York minute* I'd do it."
He says, "What would you do then?" I say, "Well, I'd get on an airplane, go to Atlanta. I'd sell all the stocks and all the bonds, turn
them into cash. I would quit the job, I would sell everything—all
the houses, all the cars, all the airplanes, the house up on the lake.
I'd get rid of the girlfriend, I'd get rid of the wife, then I'd get on an
airplane and I'd fly down here and I'd hire you to pole me around
for the rest of my life."

I laughed. I'll bet that wasn't a particularly satisfactory answer for the
executive, I said.

We went outside into the heat and climbed into his new Ford truck
and drove across the Seven Mile Bridge, the largest of sixty-six bridges
that connect the islands. From this bridge, you can see the great expanse
of the Atlantic and the Gulf of Mexico. Painted across these waters are
the islands in the stream. Water from the two seas moves back and forth
in a neverending tidal exchange. "Because of the food attracted by the
movement of water, schools of migratory fish come here—tarpon especially, and bone fish and snappers and permit (a pompano). All around
the bridge, whirlpools attract and hold bait. Parts of the crumbling old
bridge that runs adjacent to the new one have been removed, so the road
and rails crossing it begin and end hundreds of feet in the air, and then
begin again. At one end of that bridge, clusters of anglers—mainly families—huddle under plastic sheeting to protect themselves from the rain
moving over now, and the drilling sun later.

As we cross this high bridge, Jake seems to be the master of this universe, but this is a slippery, fragile place, very vulnerable to acts of God
or man.

"There's been a moratorium on building for about six years now, and
they can't do any major development until the year 2004. By then, there
won't be any water left," he said, echoing what Captain Bob had told me
about Florida. "All of the drinking water in the Florida Keys comes in a
pipeline from Lake Okeechobee. There is no fresh water here. Florida
has overbuilt for years. After the water is gone or ruined, Florida will become a ghost country."

That's a pretty extreme vision, I said. He shrugged. Take it or leave it,
that's what he thinks.

The government isn't going to stop developers from "wrecking the
world," as he puts it. Government is useless, in his view. "Over the past
twenty years, government has confiscated large amounts of land from
the people. The federal government annexed part of the Keys a couple

years ago for a marine sanctuary. The people of the Keys, true environmentalists who catch-and-release and started managing water and picking up the trash before government cared, we were just steamrolled. The
feds came in and said, 'We're going to confiscate this and make it into
federal property' even though the plan was voted down by 82 percent
of the residents." Government, he points out, encouraged the dredging
and filtering of the Everglades, "which until then was the biggest, best
water filtering system in the world." Government continues to allow big
agriculture, especially sugar-cane farmers, to spray more poisons and
pesticides. "So why should we trust government?"

In the early '80s, Keys residents launched what was called the Conch
Rebellion (conch is the local term for descendants of the first settlers
here). "We had a flag made up and named ourselves the Conch Republic. We got all the TV networks to come down and we seceded from the
Union, fired one shot, surrendered, and asked for foreign aid."

Soon Jake and Jake's young friend Captain Bruce Chard and I were
skimming across a glassy sea in search of tarpon, and the conspiracies of
the world were left at the dock.

Jake was explaining the strange power of the tarpon.

> The tarpon is a prehistoric fish. The tarpon have been around far
> longer than humans and they'll likely be around when we're gone.
> A tarpon has a swim bladder that functions as an accessory bladder.
> Its scales are like mirrors. They change colors.
>
> There are good days and there are great days when you're tarpon
> fishing. The only difference between a good day tarpon fishing and
> a great day tarpon fishing is the fly in the mouth of the tarpon. Pe-
> riod. On that day, you think like a mullet, its prey. You strip the fly
> in; you make it swim so that the tarpon thinks his prey is getting away,
> and that makes him come for you. You have made the ultimate pre-
> sentation and convinced that fish to eat that fly, and that is the best
> you can do. You watch him think about it. You watch him make up
> his mind. You watch him open and close his mouth. And you set the
> hook when he comes out of the water. And then he begins his run.
>
> Take a pair of flippers and get in the swimming pool, and from a
> dead stop try to jump out of the water and see how high you can
> jump. Or just stand on the bottom and try it. Better yet, stand on
> the ground and see how high you can jump. From a dead stop, a
> 150-pound tarpon can go fifteen feet in the air, boom, straight up,
> and then come down and hit the water, and then jump and fall
> again and again and again. The force of that tail is beyond physics.

You can know everything about tarpon and still know nothing. I have tracked their migration routes. I've followed fish with tags for 150 miles over ten days and watched the same school of fish day after day, going from one end of the Keys all the way to the other end. I know where that school of fish will be every day. I have released over five thousand tarpon in my life. And they're still a mystery to me.

There is something about a tarpon. I've seen grown men, powerful men, get buck fever—freeze up at the very moment they could make a perfect cast to a 150-pound tarpon. The fish will be coming and I'll be saying, "It's twenty feet from the boat. Can you see it?" "Yeah, but I can't do it." The next thing you know this guy is looking back at me and saying, "Are you laughing at me? I'll kick your ass!" I say, "You're gonna kick my ass? Wait a minute, slow down!" I come off the bow and I say, "My friend, sit down, relax." He says, "I don't want you laughing at me." I say, "You're a customer and you're paying me a lot of money to be here. Don't tell me you're going to kick my ass. Relax a minute, you're having a problem here and it's your problem and I'll help you deal with it. But you have to deal with it."

And he finally overcomes his fear, but it takes him five years to catch a tarpon.

A half hour out, we saw several schools of tarpon rolling along the edge of a reef, arcing over the water, moving at their own unflappable but relentless pace. Bruce, in charge of the boat, chased these fish like a cowboy, positioned the boat so that Jake could make a cast from the side. When no fish would strike, or Jake missed a strike, Bruce immediately charged forward to get in front of the fast-moving fish.

"Get ready, buddy, here he comes," said Bruce.

I moved to one side of the boat so I could see better.

"Don't walk around a lot," Jake told me sternly.

Barefoot so that he could feel the line looping at his feet, Jake watched the tarpon roll. He cast perfectly a few feet in front of its path and stripped the line slowly. On the surface, the fish turned and moved slowly for the fly. Jake strip-set the hook—pointed the rod at the fish and yanked the line back. The fish burst from the water and twisted high into the air and seemed to hang there, as if in freefall.

And the world stopped dead, froze up, became brighter than the sun.

Now it was gone. Jake had deliberately slackened the line so that the hook would drop from the fish's mouth. The moment was enough.

Afterward, we moved on to the shallower flats and fished for permit for a while. We watched a five-foot lemon shark swim lazily around the boat. And Jake began to talk about sharks.

The global travelers—the marlin and tuna and tarpon—all come through here. When the tarpon pass through on their migration, schools of giant sharks follow them. Bull sharks, tiger sharks, but mainly hammerhead sharks. We have a hammerhead shark that lives under the bridge that we call Big Mo. It's now over twenty feet long and weighs more than a ton. I've had him come from under the boat and eat the hundred-pound tarpon at the end of my line— in one bite. His eyes are more than seven feet from side to side. And no one that's ever been eaten by him has ever complained.

In the last few years, I've seen more and more tarpon being followed by sharks. The sharks are taking the stragglers, the weak ones, and the ones that are wounded. If the tarpon are one hundred pounds, the sharks are three hundred to two thousand pounds. You can see this when you're up on the platform. Here's what can happen. You're up there leaning as far back as you can to get leverage on the pole. And then the end of the pole gets caught in the coral or in the rocks, and the boat's moving forward, the pole sticks and pulls you backward. You have to make a decision right then when and how you're going to fall. You've got to push away with your feet so the boat shoots away from you—that way, you won't fall on the propeller. You do a back flip and go into the water. You swim back to the boat and pull yourself up and in.

But recently, every time I go through that thing, and I fall, the first thing that enters my mind is whether the sharks are following. When I hit the water, I'm like a big two-hundred-pound dinner bell going off. It's pretty damn frightening. You're flapping around, you're in a hurry, you want to swim as fast as you can to get away from that shark, if it's there, and into the boat. But the reality is that shark could eat you any time he wants to. A hammerhead is faster than a JetSki, and if he just hits you he's going to kill you. When a shark is eating a tarpon, a straggler, the shark will bite its tail off and let it float there and flap around bleeding, and the shark will go get another tarpon. It will wound two or three tarpon and then go back and slowly eat them.

So if you fall in, it's possible that the shark will bite your feet off and then just leave you there for later. That's what you're thinking about when you're falling backward. And you're thinking that there's absolutely nothing you can do. Everything is up to the shark, if it's there.

No one in the boat said anything for a while. That, I thought, could be a chapter in *The Angler's Guide to Business.*

Renewing Waters

~~~~~~~~~~~~~

Knight, whosoever thou art who beholdest this dread lake, if thou wouldst win the prize that lies hidden beneath these dusky waves, prove the valour of thy stout heart and cast thyself into the midst of its dark burning waters, else thou shalt not be worthy to see the mighty wonders contained . . . beneath this black expanse.

—Don Quixote

Murky Waters: The Morality of Fishing

ᔪᑫᔪ

WHEN I WAS A BOY of eight or ten, I would fish for little perch and chubs and sunfish and crayfish in a creek near my house. I would ride my bike to this creek which ran high sometimes with Missouri muck and leeches and matted oak leaves under a bridge that would shake when the Oldsmobiles and milk trucks clattered overhead. I carried no rod, only a line and bait. I would toss my line with hook and worm or grasshopper impaled through its thorax, or a minnow caught by hand, or simply a piece of raw calf's liver, into the brown water, let it drift until it was caught in a particular eddy, and it sank. Sometimes, after a few moments, the line would tug down and hold.

This became a recurring daymare.

I would pull on the line, hand over hand, pull with all my strength, until a face appeared—slowly, slowly—in the brown current. The size of a football, it would come close to the surface. Eyes would appear, lock onto mine, as a long thin crease of a mouth that dipped down in the middle gripped the line. I would hold the head there for a few seconds, hold it with all my might. The thing and I would stare at each other. Then, every time, the line would break, and the face would sink and fade into the muddy current. As a boy, I was convinced that I had found a troll below the bridge, my own monster. Now I realize it was a large snapping turtle, perhaps an alligator snapper, the kind that lures fish to its open mouth by curling its tongue like a worm—in that way, fishing. Known or unknown, it surely was a monster.

While it is true that we fish because we eat or because fish are jewels of found beauty, we also drop our line in the water and wait for this other thing to appear—the monster. The unknown.

As a child and as an adult, you believe that anything could be down there. You just never know.

↫ SOONER OR LATER, however, good anglers must face the untidy question that my son Jason had asked in Baja: Is it right to hurt or kill an animal for pleasure or curiosity or to face fear or even for spiritual connection? This question—the one forced upon me as I watched the San Juan trout with the trailing jaw—is neither casual nor academic.

This much is surely true: If fishing is cruel, we are not alone in our cruelty. Consider the following description, by writer Bob Cary, of how eagles fish:

> Four miles from my home, where the clear, cool outlet of Splash Lake curls past the ninety-year-old remains of an ancient log sluice and dances through the rapids into Newfound Lake, there is an annual fall spawning migration of pound-size, herring-like tullibees. One November, I was stalking the ridges above the riffle . . . Every few steps, in the thick balsam fir, I paused to watch and listen; I began to hear what sounded like faint cries for help. Concerned that some late fall canoeist might have capsized by the log sluice, I hurried ahead, came over the steep ridge above the rapids to freeze in my tracks. The shrieks and cries came from a dozen huge bald eagles engaged in a fishing frenzy. The great raptors wheeled on five-foot pinions, plunged into the current and came out with talons locked on thrashing, dripping tullibees. Each catch was promptly transferred to shore where the eagles ripped at the heads repeatedly with their sharp, hooked beaks. No more than a few seconds were spent on each fish, then they flew back to the current for more prey. It was a drama of flailing wings, shrieking carnage; the blood-spattered snow littered with fish remnants.

These animals—eagles—have rights in the sense that they do what nature insists that all predators do: kill and eat other animals. We're also part of nature, and in our predation no different from eagles—except on three counts. First, when we do eat our prey, we waste much of what we kill or injure. Second, we plant and nurture animals we hunt and fish—in ways that sometimes defy logic. Every year, the federal government spends some $400 million in tax dollars to manage the fisheries of the Columbia River, and sees tens of thousands of federally protected cormorants, terns, and gulls kill from 10 to 40 percent of the entire spring Chinook salmon smolt population as it attempts to make its way from

Bonneville Dam to the Pacific. Man is a predator who protects predators so that they can kill mutual prey. And third, we consider the moral implications of being predators; unlike eagles or lions, we can choose our food sources. We are the only species with a developed ethical code for catching our prey and then releasing it—in effect, rules for playing rough with another animal.

The rules, and our relationship with nature, may be changing.

In the 1990s, People for the Ethical Treatment of Animals (PETA) declared war on angling. Fishing is "the final frontier of animal rights," announced one PETA leader. Another PETA official told *Bassin'* magazine that the organization's members plan to disrupt fishing around the country by throwing rocks in the water where people are fishing in order to scare fish away. Activists also proposed sending scuba divers into the same waters to spook the fish. And PETA intends to take its antifishing message to public schools—probably a more effective tactic than stone throwing.

Some anglers might laugh off such a threat, but allies and precedent exist. The Royal Society for the Prevention of Cruelty to Animals, the largest British animal-welfare organization, states in its policy guidelines that it is opposed to angling due to the cruelty involved: "The RSPCA is opposed to the infliction of pain and suffering on any animal in the name of sport." In recent years, another British-based organization called Pisces (otherwise known as the Campaign for the Abolition of Angling) has led a successful effort to ban fishing in several localities in England and Germany.

Confrontations with gentleman anglers on English streams may be effective, but the reaction of American anglers will probably be less polite.

Central to PETA's cause is the belief that fish feel pain. The organization frequently quotes a 1980 British study called *The Medway Report*, which states: "The evidence suggests that all vertebrates (including fish) . . . experience similar sensation to a greater or less degree in response to noxious stimuli." PETA literature also quotes Tom Hopkins, a professor of marine science at the University of Alabama: "It's ghastly to conceive, but put yourself in the fish's place. It's like dentistry without Novocaine, drilling into exposed nerves . . . They experience agony parallel to our own."

The problem here is the assumption that we can put ourselves in the fish's place.

Michael La Chat is a professor of Christian Ethics at the Methodist Geological School of Delaware. La Chat has examined the arguments put forth by the antifishing movement, especially those of Peter Singer, whose book *Animal Liberation* is an organizing tract of the animal-rights movement. Singer's ethical theory, as La Chat interprets it, is based on a form of hedonism called "preference" utilitarianism. This theory holds that a morally correct action maximizes the interests of sentient—aware and thinking—creatures, and that sentient creatures are interested in pursuing pleasure and avoiding pain.

In Singer's view, all sentient animals—including humans—are entitled to such ethical treatment. While Singer apparently accepts some killing, if it is done for nontrivial reasons, he considers the killing or wounding of fish to be unnecessary—because humans have the option of being non–fish-eating vegetarians. Other animal-rights leaders do not require that animals be sentient; they believe that every form of life has some form of consciousness and even beliefs.

In fact, one of the basic premises of Amerindian and Inuit cultures is that animal life forms "are as sentient and evolved as human," as one anthropologist puts it. Some tribes, such as the Northwest's Kwakiutl people, believe that human twins are salmon returned and will become salmon again after their death. Anthropologists cite such examples as a woman with a birthmark that was said to correspond to the wound where she, in her former life as a salmon, was speared. Another man recalled having been caught at the same place during his previous life. He said he even remembered being "cooked, canned, and shipped far away." These tribes believe in the existence and power of transformation, of human to animal, animal to human, and the salmon is the perfect symbol of this—with its lifecycle of transformation in color and body shape.

Indians don't play with their food, Billy Frank had said. Or with sentient spirits.

If the only reason that fishers fish is that it's fun (self-interested hedonism), then the antianglers have a strong ethical position, argues La Chat. Having fun is a fine rationale for bowling, but not for taking or injuring life. Nonetheless, the antiangling argument is flawed. La Chat points out that antianglers tend to use the words "pain" and "suffering" interchangeably, exaggerate the similarity of other animals to humans, and by analogy attribute human feelings to fish. (But then, so do many anglers, when they describe, say, the deviousness of certain lunkers, or when they kiss a bass and call it a "sweet thang.") La Chat argues that similarities of fish and humans "cannot be proven legitimate by observation of fish behaviors." An analysis of La Chat's views by *Salmon-Trout-Steelheader* recaps the science well:

> Fish have escape reflexes, but so do some narcotized humans who feel no pain. This distinction between unconscious reception

of stimuli (nerve system responses) and the perception of pain and suffering by humans is the central issue.

Neurobiological studies indicate that pain is first perceived by the thalamus, a source of automatic unconscious reactions to stimuli. In humans, the cerebral cortex is the source of cognitive awareness of pain. Humans can react to pain via the thalamus without awareness, but we become aware of pain and suffer by involving our neocortex. We might even say that pain and suffering in a human sense doesn't exist without a similar neocortex.

The "neurological evidence suggests that fish brains do not have structures comparable with the human neocortex," writes La Chat. "Therefore it is unlikely that fish consciously experience so-called pain stimuli at all." This fact is all that is necessary to refute the postulate argued by Singer. As for more radical convictions that fish somehow have beliefs of their own, that position is unprovable.

One of the finest books written about this conundrum is an old one by Brian Curtis, in 1949: *The Life Story of the Fish: His Manners and Morals*—a funny subtitle, given the context. Curtis is a former supervising fisheries biologist for the California State Division of Fish and Game.*

So, asks Curtis, do fish feel pain? "How the answer can be any other than an unqualified yes is hard to see, and yet many people, of whom I am one, shrink from killing a deer, but have no scruples about the often more lingering death which they inflict on a trout," he writes. "They like to tell themselves that it is because the fish cannot feel pain, while the real reason is that the fish, regardless of what it feels, cannot express pain." However, if "the question is changed to 'Do fish suffer?' Better still, 'Do fish suffer as human beings do?'—then there is room for argument."

In defense of the angler, Curtis offers two arguments for believing that the fish's suffering is comparatively slight. One: Sensation of pain is probably not so keen in fish as in some of the higher animals. Two: The brain of the fish, lacking the cerebral cortex, "fails to provide a home for the conscious association of ideas, and therefore robs pain of an imagination to work on." To illustrate both points, he offers the "well-known and authentic tale of the fish, which was caught with its own eye."

This poor fish was foul-hooked, and the only way to remove the hook was to remove one of the eyes. The fisherman decided he did

---

* The principal exception to this is the shark. "In spite of being a primitive fish the shark's brain is more like that of the higher animals than is the brain of the bony fish, containing a more advanced stage of the rudiments of the cerebral hemispheres."

not want his catch, and replaced it in the water. It then occurred to this man, who must have been of an experimental turn of mind, to see how good a bait the eye might be, so he placed it on the hook and dropped it in the water, to pull out a few minutes later the very fish from which the eye had been taken. Now, disregarding its failure to recognize its own eye, which is hardly surprising in view of the fact that it had never seen it before, the points to bear in mind are these: first, that a very short time after the removal of the eye, its pain from that operation was so unimportant that it was out and about prospecting for food; and second, that the pain which had resulted from taking into its mouth a bait on a hook on a line made so little impression on its mind that it did the same thing again a very few moments afterward. Number one, physical sensation of pain not very keen; number two, mental impression of pain not very keen or else very quickly forgotten. And pain that is forgotten is no longer pain.

He adds a disclaimer: Fish vary in their reactions and learning capacities, individually and between species. But do even the "smarter" fish learn in the way that higher animals do?

Obviously fish do have a capacity for learning—that has been proved by laboratory experiment as well as by field observation—but just as obviously, all the fish that are hard to catch have not had personal experience with the hook which has taught them to avoid it. Do we mean, then, that fish learn from each other? Or are we perhaps trying to put our explanations on too high a plane?

I am inclined to think that this is the case, and that hereditary, or environmentally produced caution plays a larger part than learning . . . (Big fish) are harder to catch than the little ones because they are wary, and they are big because they are wary, and they are wary partly because of what they have learned, but largely because they were born that way . . . . The fish that are easy to catch all get caught when they are small, for life is a struggle, and the rash little fish which goes around poking its nose into everything which arouses its curiosity soon becomes a victim of one enemy or another, beast or human. But the fish which at birth is constitutionally supplied with more than the usual share of caution lives to grow old and large, and to become the anguish and the delight of the angler.

⏤ THE DEBATE IS not only between animal-rights activists and anglers. Within each fishing culture and across them, too, anglers conduct their own raging debates about ethics and ecology. Consider the issue of catch-and-release, which by some accounts began on Michigan trout streams in the 1950s, and was first espoused nationally by Trout Unlimited and bass tournament organizations in the early '70s.

No one knows how many anglers practice catch-and-release, but releasing fish has clearly become an accepted practice—and the only practical solution yet found for overfished waters. The pressure on one fairly typical Connecticut river has grown from eleven thousand anglers a season in the late 1980s to more than forty thousand—all vying for fewer than two thousand trout living in that stretch. Catch-and-release is now so popular that the traditional creel is becoming an endangered piece of equipment; L.L. Bean and Orvis still sell creels in their catalogs, but mainly as nostalgia items. The practice is even catching on in saltwater fisheries. Winter anglers fishing for giant tuna off Cape Hatteras may keep only one fish per boat per day, though they've paid a thousand dollars for the pleasure. An increasing number of river stretches are being reserved for catch-and-release anglers, but those using only barbless hooks.

This would seem to work for everyone, right? Well, not exactly.

The debate over catch-and-release has divided anglers into several camps, says Denis Hancock, a Senior Scientific Programmer/Analyst at the University of Missouri's Department of Agronomy, in an essay titled, "Why I Release—And Why I Don't."

"One might see catch-and-release as a religious system, another sees it as a management tool, and another might use catch-and-release simply as a way to avoid cleaning and eating fish." Catch-and-release, as a management tool, along with minimum-length limits and slot limits (restrictions on vulnerable sizes, not only smaller fish) can restore stressed fisheries and improve good ones. Anglers argue ideology and science; some believe the only well-caught fish is a cooked fish.

"In every catch-and-release fisherman's past there is an old black frying pan," fishing writer John Gierach reminds us.

On some waters, catch-and-release has become a way of life, not only for the anglers, but for the fish as well. In a stretch of the Yellowstone where release is required, cutthroat are caught and released as many as twelve times in a season—and on New Mexico's San Juan River, where Nick Raven and I fished, many trout are caught three or four times in a day, especially from the Texas Hole. According to the state's manager of the San Juan fishery, San Juan anglers catch an average one and a quarter fish per hour, and more if they're with a guide. One survey found hooking scars on 80 percent of the fish in the four miles of most productive water—only two with fungus, which can be caused by human handling. The fishery manager reports that fish in the San Juan's catch-and-release section are larger, healthier, and older—many are seven years old and older—than the fish in catch-and-keep water.

Some of these studies are contradictory or suspect, but it's relatively safe to say at this point that typical mortality rates in catch-and-release waters for trout are in the neighborhood of five percent, according to some studies, but on some waters, such as the Madison's catch-and-release stretches, trout fish-handling mortality can reach as high as twenty percent annually. Survivability varies widely, depending on the type of fish, quality of the water, and the water temperature. Colder is better. Some anglers choose not to fish for trout when surface temperatures exceed seventy-two degrees Fahrenheit. Few trout survive after being caught at that temperature, even if the fight is short. Of course, bass and other warm-water fish survive at a higher rate at those temperatures.

Patrick Trotter, a Seattle-based fishery science consultant specializing in the conservation biology of rare, threatened, and endangered salmonids (he also is the author of *Cutthroat, Native Trout of the West*), conducted an extensive review of the literature and came to the following conclusions.

Fish caught with bait suffer a much higher rate of hooking mortality than those caught with either lures or flies. A major exception: large anadromous fish such as adult steelhead, which usually take baited hooks lightly. The rate of hooking mortality suffered by trout depends on species and on rearing history. Fish caught on barbless hooks suffer lower hooking mortality than fish caught on barbed hooks. Barbless hooks are better than barbed hooks. Trotter dismisses talk of the so-called "stiletto effect"—the theory that barbless hooks are just as lethal as barbed ones, because they drive deeper and are more likely to pierce vital organs. Finding no evidence in the data, he considers that theory to be a myth.

What about the stress factor—the buildup of toxins during the battle? Larger fish do take longer than small fish to recover from being caught and handled, and this is compounded by a longer struggle when larger fish are hooked. Thus, long battles on light line should be avoided, and the time the fish is out of water should be short—seconds for trout, slightly longer for bass, pike, and walleyes, and still longer for catfish.

However the numbers ultimately add up, it's clear that anything short of great care is unsporting and morally questionable.

⌒ NORMAN MACLEAN WAS onto something when he said that in his family, there was no clear line between religion and fly-fishing. We can argue about studies and statistics all we want, but our relationship with other animals is ultimately shaped by our ethical or spiritual or religious views, organized or not.

This is tricky territory, and probably beyond logic.

Consider the example of the Buddhist monks who, in 1997, freed twenty-five hundred goldfish in a New Jersey reservoir. Their purpose was honorable. To them, setting an animal free is an act of compassion that will be rewarded with good karma. Good karma for them, maybe, but not good times for the resident fish—especially the native species. Goldfish are so prolific and so tough that they'll likely overpopulate the water and kill off the other fish. This tale oversimplifies Buddhist beliefs about nature, but many Christians oversimplify the biblical concept of "dominion" as well. Some consider nature secondary, disposable, put here for human domination. Other Christians interpret dominion as stewardship: We are nature's caretaker, not its masters or exploiters.

La Chat lists some of the "far from trivial" benefits of angling. For example, fishing engages us in a spiritual conversation or connection, one that we have difficulty describing. Thousands of books have been written about this connection, none of them considered the final word—evidence that what we do is beyond human description, and therefore not trivial. Anglers, he says, receive psychological, spiritual, and physical nourishment, and in some cases economic gain. As a result, we have a symbiotic relationship with fish—we have incentives to be their stewards, to make sure their populations are healthy, to protect their watersheds and prevent pollution.

Some animal-rights activists oppose the management of fisheries, husbandry, and other human manipulations of the animal world. Considering some of the unintended and damaging consequences of over-reliance on hatchery fish, the activists may have a point. But they ignore their own complicity. "A persistent error of many of my [anti-angling] students is to claim that they do not 'intervene' in nature. But their shoes, cars, houses, pets, children, and even their vegetarian preferences directly and indirectly cause the death of animals," La Chat writes. "Life negates life, and if we have an obligation to future generations for ensuring biodiversity and ecological well-being, then surely we ought to be active managers of fisheries, too. Humans are part of the natural order. By omission or commission, we are predators as well as conservers."

To fish or not to fish? That question and ancillary issues (if we fish, *how* do we fish?) are not answerable with absolutes. Nature, by definition, changes. Organic, consistent in its chaos, it adjusts—it seeks balance. As flawed stewards and evolving fishers, that's about the best we can do: seek balance. Or, stop fishing.

The central issue is not only whether we release the fish we catch, rather it's the context in which the release takes place. Organizations such as B.A.S.S., Trout Unlimited and the Atlantic Salmon Federation rightly promote catch-and-release, but Pete Rafle, a TU official, notes that to some anglers catch-and-release "has become a religion unto itself." His organization regards it as just one of the tools necessary to protect fisheries, along with the guarding and enhancing of fish habitat. The survival of a fish population is determined by how we fish, yes, but more importantly by pollution, watershed destruction, the development of the hills and fields along the waters.

We fish in murky ethical waters, where irony is the current, but this is surely true: In any appreciable numbers, no one cares more about the health of the streams and lakes and oceans than do anglers. *No one*. In practical terms, it's important to remember that most of the fish we catch or release are planted hatchery fish—they would not be alive without human intervention. The challenge will be to widen that care beyond the current and the eddy, to the watershed itself—to the damage caused by logging, massive development and sprawl and the pollution that accompany them. No single interest group owns the morality franchise. A long time before PETA arrived on the stream, anglers were questioning their own ethics—including Harold Ensley, who made his living from fishing and now champions his no-treble-hook cause; Sugar Ferris, whose example forced the bass tournament world to adopt gentler tactics toward fish; Allen Greenwood, the primitive-trout aficionado in San Diego County who now spends more time protecting wild trout than he does fishing—and when he does fish, he ties a hookless clump of feathers onto his line just to watch the beauty of the rise.

Even now, a new angling miniculture is being spawned, the non-catching anglers. One company plans to manufacture a hook called TAG (for "touch and go") with a hook eye at both ends, making setting the hook virtually impossible. The thrill will be in the strike.

The other day, I called my friend Nick Raven and recalled our time together and that moment on the San Juan—the trout with the trailing jaw, that slice of hell on the river of heaven. He told me where he stood.

> My favorite fishing was when Isabel and I would camp for a couple weeks at a time on the streams in northern New Mexico. We'd fish for an hour, catch supper and no more. The truth is I don't fish as much as I used to. Maybe it's a stage in life; fishing has given me so much that I don't think I need it as much as I used to. The prob-

lem I have with catch-and-release is the people who go out and fish all summer long and catch thousands of fish, and may kill and damage more than someone who goes out and catches his six and quits and goes home and eats them. It's nice to be out on a trout stream, but how many fish can you catch like that? It's kind of odd to me. A lot of times now, I'll go fishing, not so much to catch any particular number of fish, but to fish a hard spot. I end up spending a lot of time trying to catch the fish that might be there, because in all the years I've been fishing I didn't have the skill to catch them there. Really just practicing some esoteric technique. But I like to fish and like to eat fish, and what I still prefer is hiking in, catching just enough for a meal, cooking it on a skillet—but not catching all day. Those times with Isabel were the most I ever enjoyed fishing. I'm not trying to take any kind of moral high ground, but other people try to take it, and I wonder.

The fact that many anglers talk about a natural evolution of consciousness—a not necessarily linear transition from the primal to the civilized, from kill-counters to meat-fishers to noncompetitors to mentors to rod-carrying, nonfishing observers of the wild—suggests that many anglers give more credence to animal rights than they let on.

One thing is certain, joy and meaning and mystery are found in the water and the journey. Maybe someday I'll stand in a cold current and cast hookless flies to golden trout just to watch them rise. But not yet.

Fishing with Bobby

~~~~~

My TRAVELS WERE OVER, but of course I could not stop fishing or keep from thinking about what I had seen.

I was still adding it all up when I got an invitation from the local Riverkeeper group to go fishing with Bobby Kennedy, Jr., the organization's guiding light. I took both my boys, Jason and Matthew. As we headed out of San Diego Bay and onto the Pacific in a former tugboat, I couldn't decide whether to focus on today's fish or on the past. That's the way it is when you're at the end of a journey, and that's the way it is, I suppose, when you go fishing with a Kennedy.

A few miles offshore, Bobby (as everyone seems to call him) was focused on the fish and not much else. He was frantically tying on a trolling lure as the boat bucked and heaved.

He wore Patagonia shorts and a faded polo shirt. He looked a lot like his father—taller, but with that same nose and prominent teeth and light-blue eyes that seem to look right through you. Bobby's eyes are a bit haunted, though. Two of his brothers have died tragically, one the previous year. Prone early on to unhealthy addictions, Bobby was one of the wild RFK sons. But who would wish the fame of such a father on any son, or the pain from that father's death?

To his credit, Bobby, then forty-four, has turned all that around. He's one of the country's leading environmental lawyers. He represents two groups, the Natural Resources Defense Council and Hudson Riverkeeper, the latter a coalition of commercial and recreational fishermen that, with a little help from other organizations and the 1972 Clean Water Act, has resuscitated the Hudson River. Bobby's current dream is to create a Riverkeeper group on every major river and bay in the nation. He also envisions a national environmental movement led by fishers, including bass-tournament anglers.

In recent years, Bobby has helped establish several West Coast Riverkeeper and Baykeeper organizations, which sue the pants off polluters. Ken Moser, a former merchant marine (and the boat's skipper), serves as director of San Diego's Baykeeper. He tells how the organization successfully took on the Port District, "which at one point was discharging four hundred thousand gallons of carcinogenic water daily into the bay."

Bobby, by the way, packs a fishing rod and a single lure everywhere he travels. Once he fished from the Puget Sound window of Seattle's Hotel Edgewater (home of the Mudshark Bar). Frank Zappa liked to fish from one of the Edgewater's windows, too. With boyish enthusiasm, he describes his friend and fellow river-conservationist, Bob Nixon, who fishes in the Atlantic with author Peter Matthiessen, and with Peter Benchley, author of *Jaws*. They go monster fishing. That's what they call it. They troll with luminescent globes in the deepest troughs they can find; they hook something huge down there, and they've never been able to raise it to the surface. Most likely, says Bobby, it's a giant squid.

Did your father fish? I asked.

"Yes, but he wasn't a fanatic, not like my brother and me. My father wasn't particularly good at it. I have a picture of myself when I was just a little boy on one of those trips, holding a fish that my father caught in one hand and a string of fifteen or twenty fish I caught in the other hand." He remembers exactly the way it was on that day. "We were up on the Olympic Peninsula hiking at Whiskey Bend."

As we trolled, Bobby handled several rods at once. When we stopped to haul in the lines, he used one of my rods to cast with. It was a garage rod, rusty and pitiful. He cast it anyway, hooked a fish, and ground the reel to a pulp. He lost the fish and waved my rod at me. "This thing *sucks*," he said.

He watched the horizon. He's a freshwater man, he said. "This is my brother Joe's kind of fishing. He never comes back without a fish. It's a contact sport with him. Gales come in and he doesn't care. He whacks the water for fifteen minutes and if there's no fish there, he'll go twenty miles in another direction and stop and say, 'This is it.' And you'll look around and it doesn't look any different from where you were. But he's found the fish. He's famous for that."

The boat groaned as it headed out over the swells. At one point, I snagged my line on the keel, or perhaps on the engine. I was yanking at it and heard a splash. I turned around and Bobby was gone. I looked into the water as the boat heaved up again. I could see a dim shape down

there, disappearing under the hull. Not the kind of thing I'd do to retrieve a lure. But then, I'm not a Kennedy.

Matthew and Jason peered over the side of the boat. Jason held tight
to Matthew's life preserver.

Later, as he was drying off, Bobby asked me about my travels around
the country. Had I learned anything . . . political?

⌐ WELL, YES, I guess I had. I'd discovered fishermen could be a powerful environmental force if only their cultures would just quit fighting
and join hands. I'd wondered about the prospect of a cross-cultural
coalition at the beginning of the journey and I was still wondering about
it. I'd asked that question of many anglers, and most of them were
ambivalent about the idea. Randy Carleson, Orvis's president of dealer
sales, figures the idea's a nonstarter, based on the commercial world.
Hell, the bass guys and the fly gals won't even read the same magazines.
"There's now a publication—*Warm Water Fly Fishing*—just come out
and I'll be honest with you, the company wanted us to advertise in that
new magazine," he said when I met him briefly in Vermont. "I don't
think it's going to work for them, we'll wait and see."

But a few of the folks I met said that anglers have to do that—join
across their cultures—if they're going to save the watersheds from dams,
pollution, and urban sprawl.

Orvis's own conservation coordinator, Andy Good, said he saw the
germ of a new movement happening already. "As far as some of these
different cultures pooling their resources and sort of acting as one voice,
I see that happening in some of the saltwater fisheries," he said.

"There's a group called the Coastal Conservation Association, started
down in Texas, and they're now in fourteen states, including Maine and
Massachusetts. They're really the only sort of voice for marine anglers.
They were started as a result of the redfish being practically wiped out
by the commercial fishery down there." Their membership is growing
and includes saltwater fly-fishermen, bait fishermen, and spin casters.

"What they need to do is expand their membership and their power
base to bring in all these other fishermen. You'd think that's a tough task
but it's happened, they've done it in these Southern states. And they realize that up here [in Maine]. They're trying to reach out now," Good
said.

Sugar Ferris had echoed that sentiment. "The Gulf Coast Conservation people are tough, but if it wasn't for them, we wouldn't have the
coastal fisheries we've got."

Faith Roland, the steelheader and watershed conservationist in Washington, had mixed feelings. "Sportsmen's groups have never been well organized due, in part, to the independent nature of the sport," she said. "None of us want to tell anybody where we caught the fish. Until we get past that, I'm not sure it's going to be effective."

On the other hand, she has witnessed the fly-fishers and the gear-fishers sitting down at the same table, with the Steelhead Cutthroat Advisory Committee, to talk about how to save their favorite fish—and about changes in fishing regulations, licensing fees, and tribal agreements.

So a wider movement is possible. Not probable, Roland said, but possible.

Bobby got agitated when I told him this.

"We've got to target the fishermen," he said. "Fishing today is the biggest sport in this country. More money is spent on fishing than on golf and auto-racing combined, and I think they're ready to mobilize. That's why I'm excited about the Bass Anglers Sportsman Society."

The whole bass-tournament culture was founded by none other than Ray Scott, the conservative, cowboy-hatted founder of the entire bass-tournament culture—who, politically, is the polar opposite of Kennedy.

"Ray Scott is a radical environmentalist, and a born-again Christian. Radical, radical, radical. [Yet] they brought us a case two months ago, where some Alabama fishermen had found that the Coast Guard was throwing batteries in the water routinely when they changed the batteries on the lighted navigational buoys. They had gotten a friend who was a diver to go down and look under one of these buoys, and they found over two hundred batteries down there."

Batteries are toxic polluters because they corrode and leak. River-keepers researched the case and discovered that the Coast Guard had dumped hundreds of thousands of batteries under navigational buoys all over the country. "The Coast Guard's routine practice was to go out, change the battery—they change them every three to six months—and just dump the old ones in the water. They did a partial cleanup beginning a couple of years ago, but it was utterly inadequate, and Ray Scott brought us the case and we signed up all the Riverkeepers and Baykeepers across the country. We filed a lawsuit two weeks ago. *The New York Times* did an editorial on it. *Ray Scott* started that."

Ted Turner, raised on fishing and still an avid angler, "has emerged as the biggest and most important environmentalist in this country," continued Bobby. "He's given a billion dollars—*one billion*—to environmental foundations, environmental issues. He's now the largest private landowner in North America, and all of his land is being preserved. He buys the best trout streams in the country—so he can preserve the trout fisheries. A lot of the funders of the environmental movement these days are fishermen."

The Riverkeepers, he said, succeeded on the Hudson for one reason: The recreational anglers and the commercial fishers joined forces. So it's all possible, he said. Not possible—*probable.*

He was worked up now.

> We're part of nature, and ultimately we're predatory animals and we have a role in nature—and if we separate ourselves from that, we're separating ourselves from our history, from the things that tie us together. We don't want to live in a world where there are no recreational fishermen, where we've lost touch with the seasons, the tides, the things that connect us—to ten thousand generations of human beings that were here before there were laptops, and ultimately connect us to God. We shouldn't be worshiping nature *as* God but as the way that God communicates to us most forcefully. God communicates to human beings through many vectors—through each other and through organized religion, through wise people and the great books, music, and art. But nowhere with such texture and forcefulness in detail and grace and joy as through creation. And when we destroy large resources, or when we cut off our access by putting railroads along riverbanks, by polluting so that people can't fish, or by making so many rules that people can't get out on the water, it's the moral equivalent of tearing the last pages out of the last Bible on Earth. It's a cost that's imprudent for us to impose upon ourselves, and we don't have the right to impose it upon our children. Our children ought to be out there on the water. This is what connects us, this is what connects humanity, this is what we have in common. It's not the Internet, it's the oceans.

Some time ago, *The New York Times* ran a front-page photograph of some African-American kids using cane poles in the R. H. Macy's Fishing Contest (a catch-and-release event) in a lake in Brooklyn's Prospect Park. Animal-rights protesters (middle-aged white people, I noted) were moving in a paddleboat right over the kids' lines. They were holding placards that read: ANIMAL CRUELTY IS *NOT* A SPORT and PLEASE BE KIND TO ANIMALS.

Even without such protests, fishing seems to be losing favor among children.

"Every kid grows up with a mountain bike; it used to be a fishing pole," said *Sports Afield* editor John Atwood. Yes, more Americans are fishing, but the expansion isn't keeping up with population growth.

BOBBY KENNEDY, JR. (LEFT), AND MATTHEW (RIGHT)

Steve Schneider, vice president of marketing for Lowrance Electronics, Inc., a company that makes electronic sportfishing gear, said, "We are challenged by environmental issues, other sports, and the decline in the number of traditional families." In other words, the rise of single parents. There's evidence that he's wrong about single moms; women happen to be the fastest-growing demographic group in fishing, and a lot of them are single moms. Still, hunting and fishing skills used to be passed down from generation to generation, and that may well be fading both because parents are too busy and because the parents themselves have become disconnected from nature.

That special personal freedom, as well as access to nature, that so many of us enjoyed when we were children seems a quaint artifact in an era of kid pagers, mall rats, and Nintendo bass-fishing games.

The very polarity of the relationship between children and nature seems to have reversed. As a boy, I was not aware that my woods were ecologically connected with any other forests. Nobody talked about acid rain or holes in the ozone or global warming. But I knew my woods and my fields. During the past fifteen or twenty years, however, this relationship has reversed for children. Today's kids express extraordinary awareness of the global threats to the environment, but at the same time, their physical contact, their intimacy with nature is fading.

The change is startling: In past decades, summer camp was a place where you camped out and hiked in the woods, learned about plants and animals, or told spooky stories about ghosts or mountain lions. As likely as not today, summer camp is a computer camp. In the early '80s, an advertisement began to appear in national magazines that showed a little boy silhouetted in front of a cabin window, tapping at a computer terminal. Beyond the glass, trees could be seen, and a sailboat moved lazily across a pond. In Southern California, Girl Scouts can attend a "High-Tech Computer Whiz" camp—with fifty thousand dollars' worth of terminals and software. Increasingly, nature—for children and adults—is becoming something to wear, to watch, to consume.

Why the apparent separation of children from nature?

One reason is that parents are rightly worried about what could happen to their children in the canyons or woods or fields. But we're probably too worried. And there is suburban sprawl—the great stretches of auto-dependent residential housing tracts. They have gradually reduced the natural habitat for children and animals. When parks are offered, the designers often create them to satisfy lawyers, not children. Children tend to avoid sterile, flat, safe patches of grass.

A third reason is demographic. Americans born from the '40s to the

'60s may be the last ones to share an intimate, familial attachment to the land and water. Many of us now in our forties or older knew forest or farmland at the suburban rim. We had grandparents or other older relatives who farmed. In 1993, the U.S. Bureau of the Census released its annual report on the U.S. farm population—accompanied by an announcement that it would be the last report of its kind because farm population had dwindled so. Not surprisingly, the cultural references for today's young Americans are almost entirely urban or video-based and seldom connected to nature or the agricultural past. A gifted fourth-grader explained to me one day, when I was interviewing a class about this, "I like to play indoors better 'cause that's where all the electrical outlets are."

If children's direct experience of nature is vanishing, where are future environmentalists going to come from? In 1978, Thomas Tanner, professor of environmental studies at Iowa State University, conducted a study of environmentalists' formative influences—what it was in their lives that had steered them to environmental activism. He polled staff members and chapter officers of major environmental organizations.

"Far and away the most frequently cited influence was childhood experience of natural, rural, or other relatively pristine habitats," according to Tanner. For most of these people, the natural habitats were accessible nearly every day when they were kids, for unstructured play and discovery. "Several studies since mine have supported my findings," he says. "But for some reason, you don't hear many environmentalists expressing much concern about the intimacy factor between kids and nature."

That may be. But let's not forget about Joan Stoliar and her classroom trout, or the many other examples of kids in the classrooms learning about nature through fish—and the many fishing programs for kids sponsored by angling clubs and tournament organizations, and by social services that view fishing as a valuable form of therapy for children with emotional or physical challenges. As Bobby Kennedy said, environmental progress is not just possible, it's probable.

⇜ THE GARDEN SPIDER, the ant highway, the bluegill taking a worm—these are doorways into that other world, the one outside the Nintendo universe. As parents, we can help open those doors. Kennedy told me how he does it. He takes his children fishing. And he takes them scuba diving in the Hudson. He "buddy dives" with them, which is a method to teach correct underwater breathing.

With a single oxygen tank, he and a child descend to the bottom of the river and sit next to a large rock, sheltered from the current. He holds the child around the shoulders or waist (protectively, but also to feel the child's breathing) and the two of them pass the mouthpiece back and forth. They sit down there, next to that rock, among the dancing plants, and watch the fish go by: the aggressive bass and whiskered catfish, and even an occasional sturgeon, monstrous, prehistoric, and graceful.

Most of us, as parents, have experienced such moments of escape and immersion. They're among the finest moments we have.

Kennedy said he was the family's "nature child."

"I spent every afternoon in the woods when I was growing up in Virginia. I loved finding salamanders, crayfish, frogs. From the time I was six years old, my room was filled with aquariums. And it still is today. I have a 350-gallon tank and I have aquariums all over my house." Catfish, eel, bullheads, striped bass, largemouth bass, bluefish, perch, sturgeon, and trout. He and his kids catch them in the Hudson, bring them home alive, and keep them in the aquariums.

Environmental purists might find fault with Kennedy for teaching his children to interact with nature through capture and captivity, but that's the way most of us first experienced it. Today, it's not a given that kids will know nature by any method.

I mention to Bobby that as a boy, I pulled out hundreds of survey stakes that I knew had something to do with the bulldozers that would soon take down *my* woods.

"I did that, too," said Kennedy, excitedly.

He told how, when a highway was scheduled to go through his woods, he and his brother Joe (the former congressman) pulled from the trees the ribbons that marked them for cutting. One day, the boys discovered a stack of concrete culvert pipes that were going to divert their stream, "so we rolled them down a hill and they broke, and we got caught." The authorities hauled the boys home. "My father wasn't really mad." His voice softened. "But he made us work all summer to pay for them. I think he understood how we felt."

Today, Kennedy says, McLean, Virginia, looks "like any other strip mall and tract house development. When I was a boy, I knew every rock in the stream, all the hillocks and the groves, and I knew where to catch any kind of animal, and it's all gone now."

He's not suggesting that kids destroy property; more constructive avenues of resistance are available. Is there, I asked, such a thing as a Jr. Riverkeeper organization?

"No," he said, "but there should be."

↬ MATTHEW AND JASON caught a good number of fish that day. Both boys—even Jason, who asks those uncomfortable questions about fishing and cruelty—hauled in tuna and barracuda, and they forgot all about the fact that they were fishing with the accomplished son of one of the most famous Americans of the twentieth century. But that was our century; the new one is theirs.

Moving On

～～

THE OTHER DAY I stopped by Stroud's and bought some flies I didn't need. I said hello to the Strouds, and John Bowman and I made arrangements. We drove across the mountains east of San Diego to Lake Morena the next morning.

With his white beard and stocky, hard-muscled build, John, seventy-one, could enter a Papa Hemingway look-alike contest and win. It was a cold day and John had forgotten his coat, so I loaned him mine. We wore light waders. The lake reflected the darkness of the low, flat clouds. Sleet and icy wind cut across the water.

We waded out onto the mud flats. When the sun came out and the wind stilled, the trout rose, but the rising stopped when the clouds returned. John picked up a fourteen-inch rainbow that fought hard. Each of us caught a couple smaller trout, and then the water died. We retreated to my van to wait for the weather to change. We poured coffee, watched the slate waters, and talked. John, a retired high-school and college English instructor, told me he was orphaned at four and a half.

I asked him how that happened.

"Well, I don't make most people privy to it, but my stepfather . . . first of all, I was born out of wedlock, OK? My mother remarried and my stepfather was a drunk and a very jealous man," he said. "One night my sister and I came home with my mother, and my stepfather proceeded to shoot my mother and shoot himself, right in front of us kids.

"So that was an experience."

His face seemed blank.

"I can remember as if it happened yesterday and it was in 1931. I can remember every detail. One of my aunts said that I had nightmares

JOHN BOWMAN

about it for years. She said I'd wake up screaming, but I don't recall. Our maternal grandparents took in my sister and me. My grandfather was a very stern disciplinarian. Unfortunately, he died when I was ten so I was left without a male role model."

Suddenly, the blankness was replaced by creased pleasure.

"My grandmother was Spanish, born in the old country and she couldn't speak English worth a damn. Probably loved us too much and pampered us. I used to pull the wool over her eyes just by saying, 'I'm going to be a priest.' And she'd melt like butter because she felt that was going to be her ticket to heaven. When I became an altar boy she called her own mother, who lived in Mexico City, and said they were both going to heaven because I was going to be a priest." He smiled. "What a disappointment I must have been!"

As we sat there watching the dark lake grow darker, I told him I had always been struck by the fact that so many men with the most traumatic experiences with their own fathers became such good parents. He warmed his hands with his coffee cup, and said he had never thought that.

And then he offered a fisherman's view of fathering.

"Raising my kids was not a conscious thing. I think a lot of it was like fishing with nymphs." Nymphs are flies that imitate the larval stage of insects that live on lake or stream bottoms. "You let the nymph drift under the water. You watch the line. You don't usually see the strike, but you do anticipate it. It's very subtle. Of course, you must have a tackle box full of all kinds of lures and equipment, but the most important thing is time. When my wife, Marion, and I were raising our children, I had to really make myself be a father—not as an obligation, but because I was privileged to have them. I always felt like my kids were sent for a purpose. And I always looked at them as being my conscience."

Like fish, he added, children are unpredictable, individualistic. "I have four kids and none of them's the same. Each needs a different approach—or presentation, a term that fly-fishermen use.

"My wife will tell you I paddled the kids and I did, but they never went to sleep without my going in and giving them a big hug and kiss and saying goodnight. When my sister was quite young, I heard her getting a whipping from my grandfather right before bed. I never wanted that to happen to my kids."

A few months before fishing with John, I had gone fly-fishing for sharks with his son, Conway. At thirty, he's the kind of man any father would be proud to call a son.

I asked John what he thought of his son fly-fishing for sharks, out there alone on the ocean.

"That kind of fishing scares me. I don't like it. We don't fish together as much as we used to. He's pulling away. But he's probably, without thinking about it directly, declaring his independence: 'Pop, you served me well, but now it's time for me to step out.' All young men and women must do that, cut the cord sooner or later."

"But not all the way," I said.

"Oh, no, not all the way. Conway says if he has kids of his own, he'll raise them just like I raised him, and that pleases me no end. And I'll tell you, when we're out at a fishing cabin, Conway still kisses me at night before he goes to bed. In fact, just the other day in Stroud's fly shop I was standing behind the counter [where he volunteers], and there were about four people there, and Conway said, 'Well, Pop, I gotta go,' and he came over and he gave me a kiss on the top of the head. Somebody said, 'You must be awfully proud of those kids.' And I said, 'The main thing is they're proud of themselves. That's more important than my being proud of them.'"

John's strong hands rolled his coffee cup back and forth. I thought of how the act of fishing can be the stuff of healing, a glue that binds the generations.

I looked through the van's fogged windows at the choppy lake.
"What do you think of this weather?" I said.
"I don't like it."
We headed out again, wading into water the color of steel.

fin

Notes

෨ඏ෭

PAGE   *Introduction:* Shop Talk

16   *In 1959, according to U.S. Fish & Wildlife Service:* These totals do not include saltwater anglers or anglers under the age of sixteen, which would make the numbers substantially larger. John Merwin and Ken Schultz, "A Century of Piscatorial Progress: Fishing," 100th anniversary issue of *Field & Stream*, October 1995, Vol. 100; No. 6, p. 38.

Headwaters

The Lost World

38   *A visit "provides a window":* Thomas A. Oberbauer, "Sierra de San Pedro Martir," *Fremontia: The Journal of the California Native Plant Society*, Vol. 24:4 (October 1996): pp. 21, 22, 24.

Fish Eyes and Lizard Legs

50   *This fish would be the genetic Adam:* Terry Rodgers, "Steelhead Trout Set to Get Endangered Species Protection," *San Diego Union-Tribune*, August 10, 1997, p. A-23.

55   *"The first Europeans":* Tre Tryckare and E. Cagner, American consultant Frank T. Moss, *The Lore of Fishing*, (Avenel, NJ: Crescent Books, 1994), p. 10.

Flyover Waters

You See That?

64   *There must be something:* Russell Chatham, ed., *Silent Seasons: Twenty-one Fishing Stories* (Livingston: Clark City Press, 1988), p. 127.

72   *"Who says fishing isn't a spectator sport?":* Brent Frazee, "Winters when Fish are Caught on Tape Instead of on Lakes," *Kansas City Star,* March 2, 1997, p. C1.

72   *Like angling in general, Fish-TV:* James R. Babb, "Tube Fishing," *Gray's Sporting Journal,* February 1997, p. 58.

73   *"Actually, no one should have time":* John Husar, "It Will Be Different, He Promises, in 1997," *Chicago Tribune,* January 1, 1997, Sports, p. 10.

Mall Fishing

86   *Anne Moore, a reporter for:* Anne Moore, "Stores Where Rubber Meets the Road: Reality Sells: Retailers Adopt New Sales Mantra: Do Ask, Do Tell—and Touch, Listen, Feel," *Crain's Chicago Business,* February 23, 1998, p. 15.

94   *In a wonderful description of this peculiar way of fishing:* Burkhard Bilger, "In the Monster's Maw," *The Atlantic Monthly,* Vol. 279, No. 2, (1997), p. 92.

The Contender

99   *As the* Florida Times-Union *reports:* Joe Julavits, "Hourly 'Pay' Good for Allen," *Florida Times-Union,* May 26, 1996, p. C-10.

101   *"In five years you can expect":* Steve Bowman, "Casting for Dollars: Fishing Hits Big-Time on FLW Tour," *Arkansas Democrat-Gazette,* June 25, 1997, p. C-1.

104   *Unlike "the urban":* Norman Geoffrey, "The Bass That Ate the South; Bass Fishing; Includes Related Information on Lakes, Records, Personalities and Equipment," *Sports Afield,* April 1997.

105   *"He provided the forum":* Gary Laden, "OUTDOORS BASS: Big Changes, Big Money and Ray Scott Give Quiet Hobby a 25th Anniversary Tournament of World Series Caliber," *Atlanta Journal and Constitution,* July 30, 1992, p. E-1.

105   *"The bass is the most revered":* Charles Satter, "Bass 'Confederacy' Cover Draws Mixed Reaction," *Atlanta Journal-Constitution,* March 23, 1997, p. 18E.

The Contest

117   *Cheating on the circuits:* Ray Sasser, "Anglers Accused of Stashing Bass in Lake Before Tournament," *Dallas Morning News*, June 11, 1997, p. B-7.

133   *Some sponsors, such as PRADCO:* Charles Salter, "Snagging a Sponsor, Echols of Athens Hopes to Introduce Fishing," *Atlanta Journal-Constitution*, October 19, 1997, p. E-16.

Sex and the Bass'n Gals

136   *Lyla Foggia, in* Reel Women: Lyla Foggia, *Reel Women* (Hillsboro: Beyond Words Publishing, 1995), pp. viii, ix, x.

137   *"Sugar Ferris kicked open":* Ray Sasser, "Bass'n Gal Is Gone, but Founder Put Up a Good Fight," *Dallas Morning News*, January 22, 1998, p. B-13.

142   *"Ferris should have seen":* Ibid.

149   *As the* Houston Chronicle *pointed out:* Richard Stewart, "Lady of the Lakes; Although Sugar Ferris' Group Bass'n Gal Has Sunk, It Helped Part the Waters for Serious Women Anglers," *Houston Chronicle*, June 21, 1998, p. 1.

Hidden Waters

Whitefish Willy and the Northern Lights

175   Outdoor Life *reports the rapid evolution:* Dick Sternberg, "Hardwater Breakthroughs: Monster Panfish Are Getting Hard to Find, but New Techniques and Technology Can Put You on Top; Ice Fishing; Includes Directory of Equipment Manufacturers," *Outdoor Life*, Vol. 199, No. 2 (1997): p. 58.

175   *Klinkenborg describes one:* Verlyn Klinkenborg, "It's 10 Below, and the Ice Is 3 Feet Thick, So Let's Go Fishing," *Smithsonian* magazine, December 1996, p. 54–63.

178   *"Ice-fishing struck me":* Juliet Clough, "Missing the Lights Fantastic," *The Herald* (Glasgow), February 15, 1997, p. 29.

179   *Perhaps its greatest single source:* A. J. McClane, *McClane's New Standard Fishing Encyclopedia* (New York: Henry Holt and Company, 1974), p. 473.

Ice Flying

190   *Water is a "'scientific freak'":* Charles Farber, *On Water* (Hopewell: The Ecco Press), pp. 14–15.

Poaching the King's Fish

198   *In 1997, authorities busted:* John Lang, "Poachers Take Aim at Black Bears; Asians Value Bear Parts for Use in Soup and as Medicines," *Pittsburgh Post-Gazette*, February 28, 1999, p. A-3.

198   *In 1994, FBI agents:* Kit Boss, "Caught Fishing—The Trials of a Sturgeon Pirate on the Columbia," *Seattle Times*, March 13, 1994, p. 12.

Flywaters

True Story

209   *Paul Schullery, in* Royal Coachman: Paul Schullery, *Royal Coachman: The Lore and Legends of Fly-Fishing* (New York: Simon & Schuster, 1999), p. 80.

The Fishermom

231   *"A fishermom is a mother who":* Margot Page, *Little Rivers: Tales of a Woman Angler* (New York: Avon Books, 1995), p. 43.

233   *"Private-water" clubs offer":* Joan Wulff, *Joan Wulff's Fly Fishing: Expert Advice from a Woman's Perspective* (Harrisburg: Stackpole Books, 1991), p. 10.

238   *Phenology is the science of appearances:* Bob Scammell, *The Phenological Fly* (Red Deer, Alberta: Johnson Gorman Publishers, 1996).

Industrial Strength Fly-Fishing

252   *Sure, bamboo is back in:* Anita Leclerc, "The Stealthy Angler," *Esquire*, July 1997, p. 78.

259   *"This," Ball tells:* Tom Meade, "Anglers Have Nothing to Carp About," *Providence Journal-Bulletin*, July 9, 1998, p. 3-C.

Lodge Life

269   *"He would look out the window":* Bruce Bigelow, "Posthumous Prominence; Maclean's 'River' Will Hit Screen, Second Book Will Hit Stores Soon," *San Diego Union-Tribune*, August 18, 1992, p. E-1.

281   *The Big Hole really is:* John Holt, *Knee-Deep in Montana's Trout Streams* (Boulder: Pruett Publishing Co., 1996), pp. 70–73.

289   *The wealthy are buying up ranches:* Jim Robbins, "Montana Landowners Right Public on Trout Streams," *The Plain Dealer*, June 1, 1997, p. 21-A.

290   *Jim Short, the owner:* John Randolph, "The Ruby: Public or Private Rights," *Fly Fisherman*, vol. 28:6, September 1997, pp. 4, 20.

290   *Interestingly, two years later:* Paul Drohan, "Anglers Angry at Lost Access," *Calgary Herald,* March 28, 1999, p. A-1.

291   *The Great Land Grab:* John Holt, "Land Grabs in Big Sky Country," *Fly Fisherman,* vol. 26:1, December 1994, p. 10.

Ghostwaters

Nick Raven and the River of Heaven

315   *Huge growth of wealth:* Ben Neary, "Another Paradise Lost? Baca Ranch, New Mexico," *Field & Stream,* Vol. 103, No. 6 (October 1998).

316   *One organization, the Forest Guardians:* David Holmstrom, "Confrontation as Conservation," *Christian Science Monitor,* September 16, 1998, p. B-3.

317   *Stressed ecosystems are:* David J. Rapport and Walter G. Whitford, "How Ecosystems Respond to Stress," *BioScience,* March 1, 1999, p. 193.

The Giveaway

345   *Though many Northwesterners:* Alex Tizon, "25 Years After the Boldt Decision: The Fish Tale That Changed History," *Seattle Times,* February 7, 1999, p. A-1.

City Waters

Down the Potomac

401   Nation's Cities Weekly: "As Urban Fishing Catches On, People Care More About Pollution," *Nation's Cities Weekly,* May 25, 1998, p. 10.

Saltwaters

Bring Me the Head of Osceola

429   *Ninety percent of South Florida's wading bird:* Virginia Morell, "The Sixth Extinction; Biodiversity; Mass Extinction of Animals," *National Geographic,* February 1, 1999, p. 42.

429   *Other species diminished:* Curtis H. Flather, Michael S. Knowles, and Iris A. Kendall, "Threatened and Endangered Species Geography: Characteristics of Hot Spots in the Conterminous United States," *BioScience,* May 1998, p. 365.

430   *Reptile rustling hasn't helped:* Todd Wilkinson, "Reptile Rustlers; Stealing of Reptiles for Illegal Sale from National Parks and Preserves," *Information Access Company,* November 21, 1996, p. 36.

Renewing Waters

Murky Waters

452   *Four miles from my home:* Bob Cary, "Nature's Fishermen," *Shimano Fishing*, Vol. 3 (1995), p. 40.

453   *Central to PETA's cause:* Dave Shiflett, "Take a Fish to Lunch: But You Better Not Eat It, says PETA," *The American Spectator*, December 1997, p. 6.

455   *Curtis is a former supervising fisheries:* Brian Curtis, *Do Fish Feel Pain—Life Story of the Fish: His Manners and Morals* (New York: Dover Publications, 1949), pp. 118–22.

457   *"One might see catch-and-release":* Denis Hancock, "Why I Release— And Why I Don't," *The Missouri Flyfishing Page* (www.agron. missouri.edu/flyfishing), January 1995, p. 1.

458   *Patrick Trotter, a Seattle-based:* Patrick Trotter, Ph.D., "Hooking Mortality of Trout," *Fly Fisherman*, vol. 26:3, March 1995, pp. 22–27.

Fishing with Bobby

468   *There's evidence that:* Patrick Reilly, "Venerable Hunting Magazine Disarms, Tries Kayaking," *Wall Street Journal*, July 6, 1999, p. A-17.

Index

࿐

Page numbers in *italics* refer to illustrations.

continued from page 4

ABOUT THE AUTHOR

RICHARD LOUV is the author of several previous books, including *Childhood's Future* and *The Web of Life*. A columnist for *The San Diego Union-Tribune* and a member of the editorial advisory board of *Parents* magazine, he has spoken on family and community matters at the White House, and his writing on fatherhood has been commissioned and distributed by the United Nations. He lives in San Diego, California, with his wife, Kathy Frederick Louv, and their two sons, Jason, class of 2000, and Matthew, class of 2006.